>> THERE IS A CHINESE CURSE WHICH SAYS, "MAY
HE LIVE IN INTERESTING TIMES." LIKE IT OR NOT,
WE LIVE IN INTERESTING TIMES. THEY ARE TIMES
OF DANGER AND UNCERTAINTY.

>> SENATOR ROBERT F. KENNEDY
>> JUNE 6, 1966

JOEL C. ROSENBERG

EPICENTER

2.0 VERSION: UPDATED & EXPANDED

TYNDALE HOUSE PUBLISHERS, INC., CAROL STREAM, ILLINOIS

Visit Tyndale's exciting Web site at www.tyndale.com

TYNDALE and Tyndale's quill logo are registered trademarks of Tyndale House Publishers, Inc.

Epicenter: Why the Current Rumblings in the Middle East Will Change Your Future

Designed by Dean H. Renninger

Library of Congress Cataloging-in-Publication Data

Rosenberg, Joel C., date.
    Epicenter : why the current rumblings in the Middle East will change your future / Joel C. Rosenberg.
      p. cm.
    Includes bibliographical references and index.
    ISBN-13: 978-1-4143-1135-7 (hc : alk. paper)
    ISBN-10: 1-4143-1135-4 (hc : alk. paper)
    ISBN-13: 978-1-4143-1136-4 (sc : alk. paper)
    ISBN-10: 1-4143-1136-2 (sc : alk. paper)
    1. Bible—Prophecies—Middle East. 2. Bible—Prophecies—End of the world. 3. End of the World. 4. Eschatology.
5. Eschatology, Islamic. I. Title.
    BS649.N49R67 2006
    220.1'5—dc22   2006019939

---

*To our dear friends
Dr. T. E. Koshy and Dr. Indira Koshy,
thank you so much for your love,
your friendship, and your example.*

TABLE OF CONTENTS

EPICENTER 2.0:
INTRODUCTION TO THE SOFTCOVER EDITION

The attack came hard, fast, and without warning.

At 8:07 a.m. on July 12, 2006, in broad daylight, forces of the Iranian- and Syrian-backed terrorist organization known as Hezbollah ("the party of God") launched a brazen, unprovoked raid against an Israeli patrol on the Israeli side of the border with Lebanon. Within minutes, Islamic guerrillas had killed three Jewish soldiers and captured two more: First Sergeant Eldad Regev, twenty-seven, and Master Sergeant Ehud "Udi" Goldwasser, thirty-one, who had just gotten married ten months earlier.

The attack caught 7 million Israelis just starting the new day completely off guard. What's more, it came on the heels of an unprovoked Hamas terror raid on the Israeli side of Israel's southern border with the Gaza Strip just weeks before.

At precisely 5:40 a.m. local time on June 25, "eight armed Palestinians infiltrated Israel through a tunnel leading from the Strip into Israel's territory, and split into three teams once they came out," reported *Yediot Aharonot*, a leading Israeli daily newspaper. "One team approached an armored personnel carrier stationed at the place and fired at it. The APC was empty and no injuries were reported in that attack. Another group simultaneously fired a missile and hurled grenades at a tank standing nearby. The missile hit the tank's rear, hurting the four soldiers that were inside. Two were immediately killed, a third soldier sustained injuries and the fourth was initially reported missing. As the incident developed, security officials came to believe that the soldier has been kidnapped. During the attack, a third terrorist team moved in the direction of a desert patrol army post and engaged in a shooting battle with the soldiers."[1]

The abducted Israeli soldier, Corporal Gilad Schalit, was only nineteen.

Israeli prime minister Ehud Olmert was suddenly faced with a two-front war. He quickly and defiantly rejected negotiations with the radical jihadist groups to get back Schalit, Goldwasser, and Regev. Instead, he ordered the Israeli Defense Forces (IDF) to launch massive military operations on both fronts aimed at recovering Israel's men and crippling the Hezbollah and Hamas organizations. Israeli fighter jets bombed runways at Beirut International Airport. Israeli tanks and troops stormed into Gaza and southern Lebanon. But just as the initial attacks by the terror groups had caught Israel and the world by surprise, so, too, did their response.

Rather than finding quick and easy success, the most powerful military in the history of the Middle East found itself strangely outfoxed and outmaneuvered. Over the course of thirty-three days, Hezbollah launched more than four thousand missiles at civilian Israeli targets as far south as Tiberias on the Sea of Galilee, terrifying the Jewish population and causing tens of millions of dollars worth of property damage. More than one million Israelis living along the northern border with Lebanon were forced to flee their homes or live underground in bomb shelters. Meanwhile, the half-million Israelis living near the southern border with Gaza found themselves subjected to thousands more missiles, rockets, and mortars. Many of the weapons fired by the jihadists were launched from inside private homes, local schools and hospitals, and even mosques, making it extremely difficult for the Israeli air force to retaliate without risking enormous civilian casualties and collateral damage.

I had completed the manuscript for the original hardcover edition of *Epicenter* just a month earlier, making the case that Israel was destined to become the center of global events and interest in the last days of human history. Now a new and devastating geopolitical earthquake was traumatizing the people of the Middle East. Once again, the eyes of the world were riveted on Israel and her neighbors, the epicenter of the momentous events shaking our world and shaping our future. What would the future hold?

The war dominated headlines for weeks. Newspapers, magazines, Web sites, and cable news networks provided almost nonstop coverage of the conflict, even asking whether the war had prophetic implications. In a *USA Today* article entitled **"In the Headlines, Glimpses of the Apocalypse,"** columnist Chuck Raasch raised a question on the minds of many around the world: "Are these the end of times? . . . You can't look at the headlines these days and not conjure up apocalyptic visions. . . . With the war in Iraq persisting, with fresh fighting in Afghanistan, with missiles raining down on even Nazareth, the hometown of Jesus Christ, the world's most powerful governments and the United Nations appear unable or unwilling to stop a chain of events that may be spinning out of earthly control."

Raasch was not alone in his analysis. CNN, FOX, and MSNBC devoted numerous segments of their Middle East coverage to asking whether current events suggest we are living in the last days before the return of Christ, as did other networks. A headline in the *Waco Tribune-Herald* at the time asked, **"Are We Living in the Final Days?"** A *Columbus Dispatch* headline asked, **"Is the Mideast Rupture a Sign of the Rapture?"** Salon.com declared, **"The Apocalypse Is Drawing Closer!"** Newt Gingrich, the former Speaker of the House, merely added fuel to the fire when he said he believes we are living in "the early stages of World War III."[2]

When the shooting stopped and the smoke cleared, attention shifted quickly from prophecy to realpolitik. In just a month, it had become painfully clear to most observers that unlike previous Arab-Israeli wars, this one had not ended with a decisive Israeli victory. To the contrary, Prime Minister Olmert's military and political strategy had failed badly. Israel's three soldiers had not been recovered (and still have not been as of this writing). The military machines of Hezbollah and Hamas had not been crushed. Indeed, they were celebrating their "success" against the "Zionist enemy." Their allies in Tehran and Damascus were suddenly emboldened. Israel no longer looked invincible. Allah, the clerics argued, was preparing to annihilate the Jewish state once and for all.

"The occupying regime of Palestine has actually pushed the button of its own destruction by launching a new round of invasion and barbaric onslaught on Lebanon," declared Iranian president Mahmoud Ahmadinejad, triumphantly, echoing the mood of the moment.[3]

Olmert's approval ratings plunged into the single digits as Israelis blamed the prime minister for effectively losing the war and severely damaging Israel's deterrence against other possible aggressors in the region. A government commission would later describe this "Second Lebanon War" (the first being Israel's war against the Palestine Liberation Organization in the early 1980s) as a "serious missed opportunity" and conclude that the IDF "did not provide an effective response" to the Hezbollah missiles. The commission blasted Olmert and his advisors for "serious failings and shortcomings in the decision-making processes and staff-work in the political and the military echelons and their interface" and found "serious failings and flaws in the lack of strategic thinking and planning, in both the political and the military echelons."[4]

It was clear that the cease-fire between Israel, Hezbollah, and Hamas was temporary at best. No one knew when the next major round of hostilities would break out. Nor did anyone know whether the next war would be prophetic in nature or merely another devastating regional conflict. But there was no question that all sides were rearming, recruiting, refueling, and readjusting to the new realities on the ground. Nor was there any question that the leaders of Iran, in particular, were more determined than ever to wipe the Jewish state off the map and more convinced than ever that such a feat was truly possible. They had been probing for Israeli weaknesses and found many. They were preparing to strike again, and much harder the next time. They had a set of deeply held religious beliefs compelling them. They had a military plan guiding them. They had a sense of destiny driving them. And the clock was ticking.

Into that environment, we launched the *Epicenter* book tour on Tuesday, September 18, 2006. Not surprisingly, perhaps, there was a great deal of interest in a new nonfiction book that examined current events in the Middle East, ancient Bible prophecies, and the possible convergence of the two. C-SPAN covered our first event—an address to some 2,500 people at a Bible prophecy conference near Los Angeles—just hours after covering Iranian president Ahmadinejad's address to the United Nations General Assembly in New York. Interest just seemed to grow from there, from interview and speaking requests, to thousands of e-mailed questions from all over the world, to invitations to meet privately with Jewish leaders, Islamic leaders, foreign ambassadors, military and intelligence officials, high-ranking current and former administration officials, and members of Congress. To be sure, not all of them agreed with my conclusions, but their interest in the subject—and at times even intense curiosity—was, I thought, noteworthy.

But let's be clear: much of the interest at high levels of the U.S. government and within numerous foreign governments has been generated not by the quality of my prose, but by key events that have played out around the world over the past several years. The significance of such events will become clearer as you read further.

That said, there are several points I should like to make up front.

First, nothing in the following original chapters or appendices has been added to, deleted, or changed in any way. If there are any errors of fact or judgment from the first edition of *Epicenter*, they remain so that you will have a baseline of my original thoughts and conclusions to compare to your own thoughts and conclusions with the benefit of more time and consideration. This softcover edition merely adds this new introduction; a new afterword, examining some of the events and trends since the hardcover publication; a new appendix revealing the results of an exclusive new national survey we commissioned on the attitude of American Christians toward Israel, Iran, and the Middle East; and a new appendix with transcripts of interviews I conducted for the *Epicenter* documentary film released in June of 2007 for the fortieth anniversary of the Six Days' War.

Second, as with the original edition, my intent with *Epicenter* is not to persuade anyone of what is coming or what these events mean. Rather it is to explain how I came to write novels that seem to have come at least partially true; to explain various Bible prophecies that have not been given enough attention in the past; to answer many questions that have flowed from the novels and the prophecies upon which they were based; to update readers on new events that are relevant to the prophecies described herein; and to update readers on the work of the Joshua Fund (www.joshuafund.net), our humanitarian relief work in the Middle East. Clearly I have strong beliefs or I would not have written this book. But I do not seek to impose my beliefs. To the contrary, I deeply respect the reader's right to draw his or her own informed conclusions.

Third, even an updated and expanded edition such as this cannot possibly do justice to the fast-moving developments in Russia and the Middle East. I would encourage readers who would like to know more to visit my weblog (www.joelrosenberg.com). There I track and analyze such events on a daily and weekly basis. Those readers so inclined may also sign up for "Flash Traffic," weekly and biweekly e-mail updates (free of charge) in which I discuss the most important events and trends from the epicenter.

Thank you so much for your interest in this new edition of *Epicenter*. It is my sincerest hope that you find it helpful and thought-provoking, come what may.

Joel C. Rosenberg
WASHINGTON, DC
APRIL 2008

INTRODUCTION
ALL EYES ON THE EPICENTER

When Saddam Hussein ordered the invasion of Kuwait in 1990 and threatened to use chemical weapons to destroy half of Israel, the *Washington Post* described the event as a "political earthquake" whose aftershocks "will be apocalyptic for the Arab world."[1]

When U.S. and coalition forces invaded Afghanistan in 2001 and Iraq in 2003 and vowed to build the first democracies in the region aside from Israel, the Associated Press called such developments a "political earthquake" that "shook the political foundations of the Middle East," an assessment echoed around the globe.[2]

When in the summer of 2005 Iranians elected a new president who vowed to accelerate Tehran's nuclear program and provoke a direct confrontation with the United States (the "Great Satan") and Israel (the "Little Satan"), Agence France-Presse characterized the election as a "political earthquake."[3]

These were not isolated examples. Yasser Arafat's death was described by the media as a "political earthquake." So was Ariel Sharon's stroke and sudden fall from power, together with the rapid rise of Hamas to power in the West Bank and Gaza shortly thereafter. Indeed, a search of a leading news database found 729 news stories published or broadcast over the past decade that described tumultuous events in the Middle East as "political earthquakes."[4] And these do not even begin to include coverage of the first Palestinian uprising (*intifada*) in 1987–88, the Iran-Iraq War in the 1980s, the overthrow of the shah of Iran and the Soviet invasion of Afghanistan in 1979, the Arab oil embargoes of the 1970s, the Yom Kippur War in 1973, the Six Days' War in 1967, the rebirth of the State of Israel in 1948, or any of the terrorist attacks or peace talks that have occurred over the past several decades.

To be sure, much about the politics of the region is murky and confusing to Western minds. But one thing is increasingly certain: the eyes of the nations are riveted upon Israel and the Middle East, the epicenter of the momentous events shaking our world and shaping our future. And now a new crisis is brewing.

IRAN GOES NUCLEAR

The man Iranians elected to be their president in the summer of 2005 was Mahmoud Ahmadinejad, who until then had been the mayor of Tehran. Few outside the capital city knew much about him at the time. Even those inside may not have fully appreciated what they were getting themselves into. But with each passing day, the picture became clearer—and more troubling.

Upon taking office, Ahmadinejad undertook a series of moves that sent shock waves through world capitals, rattled global markets, and drove up the international price of oil. He told associates that he believed the end of the world was just two or three years away. He said he believed he had been chosen by Allah to become Iran's leader at this critical hour to hasten the coming of the Islamic messiah known as the Twelfth Imam or the Mahdi by launching a final holy war against Christians and Jews. He publicly vowed to annihilate the United States. He vowed to wipe Israel "off the map." He also dramatically accelerated Iran's effort to build, buy, or steal the nuclear weapons necessary to bring about the end of days, in accordance with his Shiite Muslim theology.

The first public hint of just how central Islamic eschatology would be to Ahmadinejad's foreign policy came during his first address to the

United Nations General Assembly in New York in September 2005. Ahmadinejad stunned the audience of world leaders and diplomats by ending his speech with this prayer: "O mighty Lord, I pray to you to hasten the emergence of your last repository, the Promised One, that perfect and pure human being, the One that will fill this world with justice and peace."[5]

Back in Iran, Ahmadinejad then stunned a group of Islamic clerics by claiming that during his UN speech he was "surrounded by a light until the end" and that "all of a sudden the atmosphere changed there, and for 27 or 28 minutes all the leaders [in the audience] did not blink. . . . I am not exaggerating when I say they did not blink; it's not an exaggeration, because I was looking. They were astonished, as if a hand held them there and made them sit. It had opened their eyes and ears for the message of the Islamic Republic."[6]

The following month, Ahmadinejad gave a speech in Tehran in which he further clarified his objectives. "Is it possible for us to witness a world without America and Zionism?" he asked a gathering of terrorist leaders from such groups as Hamas and Islamic Jihad. "You had best know that this slogan and this goal are attainable, and surely can be achieved." He then urged Muslims around the world to prepare for the day when "our holy hatred expands" and "strikes like a wave."[7]

Six months later, Ahmadinejad upped the ante yet again, declaring in a nationally televised address that Iran had successfully enriched uranium and joined the "nuclear club," leading a number of Western intelligence agencies and experts to predict that Iran could have operational nuclear weapons in the next two or three years—just in time for the Bush administration to leave office and, presumably, for the end of the world to begin.[8]

"TIME IS NOT ON OUR SIDE"

With Iran's countdown to the apocalypse running, the stakes could not be higher.

Were Iran to smuggle nuclear bombs into the United States (across the Mexican border, for instance), entire American cities would be vulnerable to cataclysmic terrorist attacks with little or no warning. Experts say the blast from a single ten-kiloton nuclear bomb in Washington, DC, for example, would destroy everything within a half mile of ground zero, contaminate 3,000 to 5,000 square miles with toxic levels of radiation, and kill 300,000 people within a matter of minutes.[9]

Were a similar bomb detonated in the heart of Times Square in New York City, a leading expert on nuclear terrorism says, "The blast would generate temperatures reaching into the tens of millions of degrees Fahrenheit. The resulting fireball and blast wave would instantaneously destroy the theater district, the *New York Times* building, Grand Central Terminal, and every other structure within a third of a mile of the point of detonation. . . . On a normal workday, more than half a million people crowd the area within a half-mile radius of Times Square. A noon detonation in midtown Manhattan could kill them all. Hundreds of thousands of others would die from collapsing buildings, fire, and fallout in the ensuing hours. The electromagnetic pulse generated by the blast would fry cell phones, radios, and other electronic communications. Hospitals, doctors, and emergency services would be overwhelmed by the wounded. Firefighters would be battling an uncontrolled ring of fires for many days thereafter."[10]

Israel is even more vulnerable, given its small size and closer proximity to Iran. Were Iran, for example, able to equip high-speed ballistic missiles with nuclear warheads, Mahmoud Ahmadinejad would suddenly be in position to accomplish in about six minutes what it took Adolf Hitler nearly six years to do—kill more than 6 million Jews. This appears to be just what Ahmadinejad has in mind when he says that Israel is "heading toward annihilation" and "one day will vanish."[11]

President Bush has warned that Iran is part of an "axis of evil" whose weapons of mass destruction pose "a grave and growing danger" to world peace and security. He cautions that the mullahs, or religious leaders, "could provide these arms to terrorists, giving them the means to match their hatred. They could attack our allies or attempt to blackmail the United States. In any of these cases, the price of indifference would be catastrophic. . . . Time is not on our side."[12] The president insists that the U.S. will defend Israel militarily should an Iranian attack come.[13] What's more, he has pointedly refused to rule out preemptive nuclear strikes, insisting that in a worst-case scenario, "all options are on the table."[14]

Nor is President Bush alone in his concern over this gathering storm. Leading Democrats have also expressed grave concerns about the emerging Iranian nuclear threat, despite their misgivings about the administration's handling of the Iraq war.[15] New York Democratic senator Hillary Rodham Clinton has warned that "a nuclear-armed Iran would shake the foundation of global security to its very core."[16]

Americans increasingly agree. Two out of three American adults view Iran as a security threat to the United States. Nearly nine out of ten Americans view Iran as a threat to Israel, while six in ten see the regime in Tehran as a threat to Europe. Moreover, nearly six in ten Americans believe it is inevitable that "Iran will use nuclear weapons against its enemies if it acquires the technology."[17]

"I THINK WE COULD HAVE ARMAGEDDON"

Stopping Iran from fulfilling its cataclysmic plans will not be easy.

Americans are deeply divided over whether the U.S. should take preemptive military action against Iran. What's more, even if the American president was to do so, Iranian leaders say "any invader will find Iran to be a burning Hell for them."[18]

If attacked, Iran has vowed to retaliate by unleashing a wave of 40,000 suicide bombers against American, Israeli, and European targets and into Iraq. The plan, which includes activating some fifty terrorist sleeper cells allegedly pre-positioned in the U.S., Canada, and Europe to use chemical and biological warfare against civilian and industrial targets, is ominously code-named Judgment Day.[19]

Also increasingly worrisome is the fact that Iran is steadily building an alliance with another nuclear power: Russia. Despite Ahmadinejad's incendiary rhetoric and provocative actions, Russian president Vladimir Putin has done little to stop Iran from going nuclear. To the contrary, Moscow has aggressively pursued ever-closer political, economic, and military ties to Tehran, in defiance of U.S. and European protests. Putin and his team have systematically stymied international efforts to sanction the radical Islamic regime. They have also authorized the sale of nuclear technology to Iran, permitted the training of more than 1,000 Iranian nuclear scientists, and approved a billion-dollar arms deal to provide Ahmadinejad and the mullahs with the latest high-tech weaponry and air-defense systems, making the prospects for a preemptive attack by the West far more difficult.[20]

In light of such developments, a number of world leaders are talking about the Iranian nuclear crisis in increasingly apocalyptic language.

British prime minister Tony Blair says he has been both stunned and sickened by the unprecedented nature of the threats emanating from Tehran. He has also strongly hinted that the West may eventually have to resort to the use of military force against Iran if diplomacy fails. Blair told leaders of a European summit that he felt a "real sense of revulsion" from Ahmadinejad's rhetoric and said, "I have never come across a situation of the president of a country saying they want to wipe out—not that they've got a problem with, or an issue with, but want to wipe out another country. . . . Can you imagine a state like that with an attitude like that having nuclear weapons?"[21]

Israeli prime minister Ehud Olmert has been more specific, saying Ahmadinejad "talks like Hitler" and is "a psychopath of the worst kind." Olmert and his advisors are believed to be drawing up plans for a possible preemptive strike against Iran, saying, "God forbid that this man ever gets his hands on nuclear weapons."[22]

Israeli vice premier Shimon Peres, winner of the 1994 Nobel Peace Prize, has ratcheted up the rhetoric even further, saying that not only does Iran represent "the greatest danger" to world peace and security since the Nazis, but that "Ahmadinejad represents Satan" himself.[23]

Still, it was Senator John McCain, the Arizona Republican widely touted as a possible future president of the United States, who may have been the most blunt about the implications of the developing crisis in the Middle East. Appearing on NBC's *Meet the Press* in April of 2006, McCain warned that "there's only one thing worse than using the option of military action, and that is the Iranians acquiring nuclear weapons." If Iran gets the bomb, he says, "I think we could have Armageddon."[24]

WHAT DOES THE FUTURE HOLD?

Senator McCain is well-known for straight talk and is highly respected for his experience on national-security and foreign-policy issues. He is not, however, known for alluding to the book of Revelation on national television, much less linking Middle East crises to biblical end-times prophecies. So when he did, heads naturally began to turn, and questions began to mount.

Soon after McCain's comments, I happened to have dinner with a high-ranking Arab government official visiting Washington. He knew I had worked for a number of U.S. and Israeli political leaders over the years. He also knew that I had written a series of political thrillers about the Middle East whose plotlines have had an eerie way of coming true. Someone had recently given him a copy of my book *The Ezekiel Option*, in which a dictator rises to power in Russia, Iran builds nuclear weapons, and then Russia and Iran form a military alliance—a nuclear alliance—vowing that Israel will be "wiped off the face of the map forever."

"You wrote this all before Ahmadinejad came to power?" he asked me.

"Yes, sir."

"And you based all this on a Bible prophecy?" he pressed, knowing, too, that I am an evangelical Christian from an Orthodox Jewish heritage.

"Yes, sir."

"Which one?" he asked.

"It comes from the Jewish Scriptures, the book of Ezekiel, chapters 38 and 39," I replied. "It's what many refer to as the War of Gog and Magog."

"And this prophecy says that in the end times, Russia and Iran will attack Israel?"

"Among other things, yes, it does," I confirmed.

The leader, a Sunni Muslim, sat back and sighed. "Our world is threatening to destroy itself," he said, openly worrying about the apocalyptic language of the Shiites coming out of Tehran. "Perhaps God has given you the key to understanding what the future holds." And then, to my surprise, he asked me to explain the story behind my novels, the prophecies that informed them, and the biblical view of what will happen in the Middle East in the last days.

I must confess I was hesitant at first. I certainly did not want to offend my new Muslim friend or the regime he so ably serves. But when he persisted, I proceeded to give him an executive summary of the book you now hold in your hands. He was not, after all, the only one who has raised questions about current events in the Middle East and how, if at all, they may relate to biblical prophecy. Indeed, in recent years, I have been invited to speak about such matters at the White House, on Capitol Hill, with U.S. and foreign ambassadors, and with high-ranking military and intelligence officials in the U.S. government and in a number of Middle Eastern governments, in addition to numerous media interviews.

My intent with *Epicenter* is not to persuade anyone of what is coming. Rather it is to explain how I came to write *The Last Jihad*, *The Last Days*, *The Ezekiel Option*, and *The Copper Scroll* and to answer the questions that have flowed from the novels and the prophecies upon which they were based.

Among them:

- Just how serious is the current nuclear crisis with Iran? Is there any way to avoid a direct military confrontation? Or is another cataclysmic Middle East war just around the corner? And if so, how will such a war change our world?
- Why is Russia selling arms and nuclear technology to Iran, given the seriousness of the present situation? Is there any way to encourage Moscow to use its influence to move Iran back from the brink? Have Russian leaders in the post-Soviet era given up their dreams of dominating the world, thus ensuring that the twenty-first century will be a time of global stability and security? Or is the Kremlin destined to lurch back to totalitarianism, rebuild its military, and once

again set its eye on the oil-rich nations of the Middle East, as it has so many times in the past?

- What is the future of the Arab-Israeli conflict in the post-Arafat world? What should we make of recent Israeli efforts to withdraw from Gaza and the West Bank? What effect will the rise of Hamas have on the peace process? Is there any hope for real peace and reconciliation between Israel and her neighbors in our lifetime?

- What is the future of Iraq in the post-Saddam world? Will the violence there simply go from bad to worse? Will our troops be bogged down there forever? Will Americans continue to sacrifice their lives there? Will regional instabilities continue to drive up the price of oil, threatening both the health and vitality of our own economy as well as the global economy? Or is there any real hope for peace and prosperity in Iraq, where the West has invested so much blood, sweat, and financial resources?

- Will a resurgent and increasingly radicalized Islamic movement establish the worldwide caliphate, or global empire, of which its leaders dream and for which they pray and fight? Is Islam really the world's fastest-growing religion, and will it soon overcome Christianity as the world's largest religion? Or can Christianity make a comeback, particularly in the Middle East—the land of its birth?

In the pages ahead, you will find answers to these and similar questions. Indeed, it is the premise of this book that the earthshaking events that lie ahead can actually be forecast with a surprising degree of accuracy.

In writing *Epicenter*, I have pored over previously classified intelligence documents, internal White House and State Department memos, thousands of U.S. and foreign news articles, scores of books and research studies by a wide array of government officials and private citizens, and the sacred writings of Christians, Jews, and Muslims in the ancient Middle East. I have traveled to Israel, Egypt, Jordan,

Turkey, Morocco, and Russia. I have also interviewed political, military, intelligence, business, and religious leaders who live and work in the epicenter and are helping shape its future, including

- **Benjamin Netanyahu,** former Israeli prime minister
- **Shimon Peres,** former Israeli prime minister
- **Natan Sharansky,** former Israeli deputy prime minister
- **Ali Abdul Ameer Alawi,** Iraqi minister of finance
- **Sinan Al-Shabibi,** governor of Iraq's Central Bank
- **General Georges Sada,** senior advisor to Iraqi president Jalal Talabani and former senior military advisor to Saddam Hussein
- **Saeb Erekat,** chief Palestinian negotiator and senior advisor to Palestinian Authority chairman Mahmoud Abbas
- **General Nasser Youssef,** national security advisor to Palestinian Authority chairman Mahmoud Abbas
- **Abdul Salam al-Majali,** former Jordanian prime minister
- **Ahmed Abaddi,** advisor to Morocco's King Mohammed VI
- **Serge Berdugo,** advisor to Morocco's King Mohammed VI
- **Alexei Mitrofanov,** member of the Russian State Duma and chief political strategist for Russian ultranationalist leader Vladimir Zhirinovsky
- **Caspar Weinberger,** former secretary of defense under President Reagan
- Western and Middle Eastern intelligence officials, active and retired
- Western and Middle Eastern diplomats, active and retired
- Western oil executives working in the Middle East
- Russian government officials and political analysts
- Arab and Iranian political dissidents
- Arab and Iranian Christian leaders
- Messianic Jewish leaders in the U.S. and Israel.

Some of these spoke to me specifically for this book. Others spoke to me for other books and articles I have written over the years. Such sources will not all agree with the analysis found in these pages, but I am exceedingly grateful for their valuable time and helpful insights. I have no doubt this book is richer for the assistance they provided.

Robert Kennedy was right. Like it or not, we live in interesting times. May you find this book as interesting to read as I have found to research and write.

Joel C. Rosenberg
WASHINGTON, DC
JUNE 2006

GREENLAND
GREENLAND SEA
Denmark Strait
Reykjavik
ICELAND
NORWEGIAN SEA
ATLANTIC OCEAN
NORWAY
Oslo
SCOTLAND
NORTH SEA
Skagerrak
Edinburgh
Belfast
IRELAND
Dublin
DENMARK
Copenhagen
ENGLAND
WALES
Cardiff
NETHERLANDS
The Hague
London
Berlin
BELGIUM
Brussels
GERMANY
Paris
Luxembourg
LUXEMBOURG
CZECH
FRANCE
Vienna
Bay of Biscay
Bern
SWITZERLAND
AUSTRIA
Ljubljana
SLOVENIA
Bilbao
Porto
Andorra la Vella
Monaco
San Marino
PORTUGAL
Madrid
ANDORRA
ITALY
Lisbon
Barcelona
Rome
SPAIN
Sevilla
Malaga
Strait of Gibraltar
Gibraltar
MEDITERRANEAN
Algiers
Casablanca
Rabat
Tunis
MOROCCO
Marrakech
MALTA
Las Palmas
TUNISIA
El Aaiun
Tripoli
WESTERN SAHARA
ALGERIA
MAURITANIA

Tarabulus
Qornet es Saouda
LEBANON
Jebal Halimah
JEBEL LIBAN
JEBEL ESH SHARQI
Beirut
MEDITERRANEAN
SEA
Sayda
Damascus
Al Kiswah
Tyre
Qiryat Shemona
SYRIA
El Qunaytirah
Nahariyya
'Akko
Haifa
Lake Tiberias
(Sea of Galilee)
Shaykh Miskin
Tiberias
Nazareth
Afula
Dar'a
Irbid
GILEAD
Hadera
Jenin
Netanya
Tulkarm
Ajlun
Mafraq
Jebel Um ed Daraj
Nablus
Herzliyya
Tel Aviv
WEST
BANK
Zarqa
Salt
Rishon le Zion
Amman
Ba'al Hazor
Rehovot
Ramallah
Jericho
Jerusalem
Ashdod
Madaba
Ashqelon
Bethlehem
DEAD SEA
Qiryat Gat
GAZA
STRIP
Gaza
Hebron
Dhiban
Khan Yunis
Mazra
Quatrana
Beersheba
Karak
ISRAEL
JORDAN
Dimona
EGYPT
JEBEL ITHRIYAT
Tafila
Ardh es Suwwan

CHAPTER ONE:
PREDICTING
THE FUTURE

Few Americans will ever forget what they were doing on September 11, 2001, when they first heard the news that the United States was under attack by radical Islamic jihadists using jet planes on kamikaze missions. I certainly never will.

On that beautiful, sunny, crystal clear Tuesday morning, I was putting the finishing touches on my first novel, a political thriller called *The Last Jihad,* which opens with radical Islamic terrorists hijacking a jet plane and flying an attack mission into an American city. What's more, I was doing so in a town house barely fifteen minutes away from Washington Dulles International Airport, where American Airlines Flight 77 had just taken off. At that very moment, the plane was being seized and flown right over our home toward the Pentagon.

At the time, I had no idea anything unusual was under way. A literary agent in Manhattan had read the first three chapters of *Jihad* six months earlier. He was convinced that he could get it published and urged me to finish it as quickly as possible. Given that he worked for the agent who had discovered Tom Clancy back in the early 1980s, I took the advice seriously, working feverishly to get the book done before my savings account ran dry.

As had become my morning ritual, I had breakfast with my wife, Lynn, and our kids, threw on jeans and a T-shirt, and settled down to work on the novel's second-to-last chapter. I didn't have radio or television on. I was simply typing away on my laptop when, about an hour later, Lynn burst into the house and turned on the news. She quickly explained that after dropping off two of our kids at school, she had turned on the radio and heard that the World Trade Center had been hit by two planes. We turned on FOX News and saw the horror begin to unfold for ourselves.

We saw the smoke pouring out of the North Tower. We saw the constant replays of United Airlines Flight 175 plowing into the South Tower and erupting into a massive ball of fire. And then, before we could fully process it all, we saw the World Trade Center towers collapse.

People ask me what my first reaction was, but I don't recall thinking that my novel was coming true. I simply remember the feeling of shock. I had been to the top of the World Trade Center as a kid with my father, an architect who had grown up in Brooklyn and loved to show me the architectural landmarks of the city he loved. I had been at the top of the North Tower just a few weeks earlier for lunch at the Windows on the World restaurant. Now, before my eyes, these two testaments to man's engineering genius were gone, as were the lives of those trapped inside.

Then came the news that the Pentagon had been hit and word that the White House and the Capitol were being evacuated and rumors that *Air Force One* might be a target. Washington, the city that had become home for Lynn and me since our marriage in June of 1990, was suddenly under siege. Not a single commercial jet was in the air. Instead, fighter jets flew combat air patrols over the city. Troops were being deployed on the streets, along with armored personnel carriers, Avenger antiaircraft missiles, and all kinds of military assets.

I remember calling friends at the White House and on Capitol Hill and my agent in New York, hoping for word that they were safe but unable to get through with so many phone lines jammed. I remember calling Steve Forbes at his office in Greenwich Village to see if he was okay. Steve and I had worked together from 1996 through the 2000 Republican primaries and had traveled together to nearly forty states on almost every kind of plane imaginable, from a twin-engine prop over rural Georgia to a gleaming Gulfstream IV en route from Dallas to Newark to a series of jam-packed Southwest flights to who knows where. Was he on a commercial flight that morning? After repeated attempts to get through, I finally got his executive assistant on the line. Steve was safe, she said. He had been coming over one of the bridges into Manhattan when he actually saw the second plane hit. At that moment, his driver slammed on the brakes, spun the car around, and headed back to Steve's home.

Lynn and I got our boys back from school. Several friends came over to spend the day. We tracked events on television, e-mailed friends around the country and around the world with updates from Washington, and prayed for those directly affected by the crisis. We prayed for our president to have the wisdom to know what to do next. Were more attacks coming? Would there be a 9/12, a 9/13, a 9/14? Would there be a series of terrorist attacks, one after another, as Israel experienced for so many years?

It was not until sometime in late November or early December, I believe, that events began to settle enough for my thoughts to turn back to *The Last Jihad*. What was I supposed to do with it? My agent, Scott Miller at Trident Media Group in Manhattan, agreed that we could not very well send it to a New York–based publisher. We couldn't send it to *any* publisher. No one wanted a novel that opened with a kamikaze attack against an American city. It was no longer entertainment. It was too raw, too real. I stuck it in a drawer and tried to forget about it while I sought out new clients and tried to rebuild the communications-strategy company I had largely neglected for most of 2001.

And then something curious happened. My wife and I were watching the State of the Union address in January of 2002 when President Bush delivered his now-famous "axis of evil" line and warned Americans that the next war we might have to face could be with Saddam Hussein over terrorism and weapons of mass destruction:

Our second goal [after shutting down terrorist camps and bringing terrorists to justice] is to prevent regimes that sponsor terror from threatening America or our friends and allies with weapons of mass destruction. Some of these regimes have been pretty quiet since September the eleventh. But we know their true nature. . . . Iraq continues to flaunt its hostility toward America and to support terror. The Iraqi regime has plotted to develop anthrax, and nerve gas, and nuclear weapons for over a decade. This is a regime that has already used poison gas to murder thousands of its own citizens—leaving the bodies of mothers huddled over their dead children. . . . States like these [including Iran and North Korea], and their terrorist allies, constitute an axis of evil, arming to threaten the peace of the world. By seeking weapons of mass destruction, these regimes pose a grave and growing danger. They could provide these arms to terrorists, giving them the means to match their hatred. They could attack our allies or attempt to blackmail the United States. In any of these cases, the price of indifference would be catastrophic. . . . We'll be deliberate, yet time is not on our side. I will not wait on events, while dangers gather.[1]

Lynn and I looked at each other as if we were living in an episode of *The Twilight Zone*. It was one thing to write a novel that opened with a kamikaze attack against America that essentially comes to pass. But until that moment, few people had been talking publicly about the possible necessity of going to war with Iraq. Except me. You see, as the plot of *The Last Jihad* unfolds, the FBI and CIA trace the trail of terror back to Baghdad, and suddenly the president of the United States and his senior advisors find themselves in a showdown with Saddam Hussein over terrorism and weapons of mass destruction.

Scott Miller called me the next day. "Do you work for the CIA?" he asked.

"No, of course not," I assured him.

"Sure, sure," he replied. "That's what you'd have to say if you *did* work for the CIA and just couldn't tell me."

Scott was convinced that the dynamic had just changed dramatically. He believed publishers would now be very interested in *The Last Jihad*. The country had largely recovered from the initial shock of the 9/11 attacks. We were now on offense in Afghanistan against the Taliban, Osama bin Laden, and the forces of Al-Qaeda. People were reading everything they could get their hands on regarding the threat of radical Islam. Audiences were responding positively to the new movie *Black Hawk Down*, which took them inside the incredibly brave lives of U.S. special forces units operating in radical Islamic environments. And there were no other novels in print or on the horizon that could take readers inside the Oval Office and White House Situation Room as an American president and his war council wrestled over the morality of going to war against the regime of Saddam Hussein. As such, Scott wanted to move quickly.

I have to admit I was surprised at first. By then I had largely written off any hope of ever publishing *Jihad*. But Scott had a point. Even the most established and successful thriller writers were wrestling through what this new War on Terror might look like and how their fiction should reflect the new geopolitical realities in which radical Islam—not Communism—had suddenly become the new enemy. And even if they had begun writing entirely new novels based on post–9/11 scenarios on September 12, Scott noted that it would still take well over eighteen months before their novels would hit the market. Mine was already done. Almost, anyway.

Jihad needed a few tweaks. For one thing, I needed to acknowledge that 9/11 had already happened. Why? Well, imagine yourself as an aspiring young writer in the spring of 1941 who wakes up one day thinking, *What if I write my first novel about a Japanese surprise attack on the United States that leads to a nuclear war between Washington and Tokyo?* Then imagine that on the very day you are finishing your novel, you hear the horrifying news about the Japanese surprise attack on Pearl Harbor, followed by the president of the United States describing December 7 as "a day that will live in infamy." No matter how prescient your book might seem, it would be a little odd to publish your novel without at least letting your readers know that you were not sleepwalking through history, that you understood that real life had suddenly become stranger than fiction.

This was essentially the scenario I found myself facing. I added a few lines into the first chapter explaining that the 9/11 attacks had happened during President Bush's tenure in office and the Taliban had been obliterated, but Iraq had not been dealt with directly (which at the time, of course, was true). I gave President Bush two terms in office and noted that Vice President Dick Cheney had no interest in running, thus positioning my fictional President James MacPherson to succeed Mr. Bush in 2009, just as America was beginning to catch its collective breath from the War on Terror. That, I hoped, would give readers a bit of real-world context as I invited them to slip into my fictional world— a world, as it turned out, that was about to be overtaken by actual events.

By February, Scott had a deal in place with Tor/Forge Books, a thriller imprint connected to St. Martin's Press, which scheduled *Jihad* for an April 2003 release. *2003?* I should have been elated. After all, I had been dreaming about writing novels and screenplays since I was eight years old, and now I had my first book deal. But to be honest, I was more than a little concerned about getting the novel out before more of its story actually came to pass in the real world. A year is a lifetime in domestic politics and an eternity in geopolitics. A war with Iraq could be over by then. What interest would there be in a novel like mine *after* Saddam had been toppled from power?

Even after signing the contract, I continually had to remind myself that the New York publishing industry was a vastly different animal from the Washington political world I was so immersed in, that my editors were smart and capable people who knew what they were doing, that everything was going to be fine, and that patience was a virtue. It was all true, but irrelevant. By August of 2002, every molecule in my body was shaking with the conviction that regime change in Iraq would be complete before *Jihad* ever saw the light of day.

Reading between the lines of speeches and comments made by President Bush and senior administration officials and listening carefully to the nuanced comments made by my friends in the White

House and on Capitol Hill, I became convinced that President Bush was going to use his September 12 speech to the fall session of the United Nations General Assembly to lay down the gauntlet vis-à-vis Iraq. Nothing had been made public yet, and the sources I was using for my weekly column in *World* magazine steadfastly refused to confirm my instincts. But if I was right, I knew that a vote authorizing the use of force against Iraq could well come before Christmas.

The timing would be eerily similar to the chain of events in the fall of 1990 that had led President Bush 41 to begin major combat operations in Iraq and Kuwait on January 16, 1991. Could Bush 43 be looking at a January or February strike date? If he was, a ferocious national and international debate was imminent. The entire world would soon be wrestling with the morality of going to war with Iraq. The debate would likely reach a fever pitch by November and December, and fighting could break out soon thereafter.

On vacation with my family in Colorado, I called Scott back in New York and explained my sense of the geopolitical landscape. I asked if there was any way he could persuade our publisher to move up the release date. He was sympathetic and said he would take a run at it, but warned me not to get my hopes up. After all, the novel hadn't been printed yet. It hadn't even been edited. Or put in the publisher's catalog. The sales team wasn't yet aware it existed. No bookstores had committed to stocking it, nor had they even been approached. And that was just the beginning of hurdles that lay ahead.

A few days later Scott called me back. To his surprise, the publisher's top executives were intrigued with my analysis of the Iraq situation. They understood the stakes and were willing to do whatever was necessary to get the book to market, but it was not their decision alone to make. Even if they could physically produce books by November at the earliest, if they could not persuade at least one major book chain to stock it, the issue was moot.

What happened next could be a book in itself. But three quick points are important for our story: First, President Bush did, in fact, use his September 12 speech to lay down the gauntlet for Saddam and the international community. Second, my friend Sean Hannity graciously agreed to have me on his radio and television show on the day of *The Last Jihad*'s release. And third, Barnes & Noble quickly agreed to stock the book for the Thanksgiving, Christmas, and Hanukkah seasons.

They were taking a risk, to be sure. No one had ever heard of me or my book. And though I had helped a number of business, media, and political leaders with their books over the years, I had no sales record of my own. Still, with its "ripped from the headlines" feel and the promise of Sean Hannity's massive audience (some 10 million people) hearing about the book, *The Last Jihad* at least had a chance of finding an audience. Once B&N placed an order, other major stores and chains did too.

The publisher's decision to get the book out before the U.S. went to war with Iraq paid off. When *The Last Jihad* was released on November 23, 2002, the book caught fire. It sold out in most stores in less than twenty-four hours and prompted nine reprintings before Christmas. In less than sixty days, I was interviewed on more than 160 radio and TV talk shows, including Rush Limbaugh's. The questions were less about the novel itself than the story behind the novel. How could I possibly have written a novel that seemed to foreshadow coming events? Did I work for the CIA? Did I have friends at the Pentagon slipping me inside information? And far more important, what did my mysterious crystal ball say would happen next?

As media coverage surged, so did sales. *Jihad* quickly hit #1 on Amazon.com, #4 on the *Wall Street Journal* hardcover fiction bestseller list, and #7 on the *New York Times* list. It stayed on the *Times* list for eleven weeks. Was it a fluke? Did I get lucky? Or was there something else going on?

"MODERN NOSTRADAMUS"

In January 2003, my publisher asked if I would like to write another book.

Sure, I thought, *it beats working.* But I felt compelled to caution them that I could not guarantee a second novel would have the same "ripped from the headlines" feel as *Jihad.* After all, I would most likely be writing about events set *after* a U.S.-led war in Iraq, *after* the collapse of Saddam Hussein's regime, and *after* the emergence of a democratic and pro-Western provisional government in Iraq. None of this had actually happened yet, nor was there any guarantee that any of it would ever happen. There were numerous diplomatic initiatives under way in Europe and the Arab world trying desperately to prevent a war, and President Bush himself was saying he hoped hostilities could be avoided.

Apparently unconcerned, the publisher gave me a green light to move forward with my second book.

On March 19, 2003, the U.S. did, in fact, launch a war against Iraq.

I turned in the manuscript of *The Last Days* in late July. When it was released on October 21, 2003, it quickly became a national best seller. But what intrigued people most was not the prose or the characters. It was the sense that *The Last Days*, like *The Last Jihad* before it, was somehow telegraphing future events.

The novel opens with the death of Yasser Arafat and an American president pushing for peace and democracy in the Middle East in the messy aftermath of a brutal war in Iraq. The first pages put readers inside a U.S. convoy filled with diplomats and CIA officials heading into Gaza as part of the peace process when it is suddenly attacked in a massive explosion.

On October 15, 2003, fiction seemed to morph into reality.

"U.S. Convoy in Gaza Bombed" read the *Haaretz* headline.

"Explosion Targets CIA Convoy in Gaza" read the *Jerusalem Post* headline.

"A massive explosion ripped apart a U.S. diplomatic vehicle Wednesday, killing three Americans and wounding one in the first attack on a U.S. target in three years of Israel-Palestinian fighting," reported the Associated Press. "The attack was condemned by Palestinian officials who said those killed were members of a U.S. monitoring team sent to the region to supervise implementation of a U.S.-backed peace plan."[2]

There was no way the terrorists could have used my book as a blueprint for their murderous plans. It did not hit bookstores for another six days. But the event triggered an avalanche of media interest.

Over the next few weeks, I did hundreds of radio, TV, and print interviews, including *CNN Headline News*, MSNBC, CBN, and the *New York Times*. *U.S. News & World Report* published a story describing me as a "modern Nostradamus." Paul Bedard, the magazine's political columnist, wrote:

> It's getting a little weird being Joel Rosenberg, the *New York Times* bestseller of terrorism thrillers and speechwriter in Steve Forbes's 2000 presidential campaign. First, he wrote *The Last Jihad* about a terrorist's kamikaze attack on a U.S. city and the subsequent hunt for Iraqi weapons of mass destruction. That was well before 9/11. Now he has written *The Last Days,* which opens with a Palestinian attack on a U.S. convoy, just like what happened a few weeks back. And look out, Yasser Arafat: Rosenberg offs you on Page 28.[3]

A year later, Arafat was dead.

It happened November 11, 2004. I remember it distinctly, as I was in Turkey doing research for my next novel when I got a call from my publicist back in Washington. No sooner had news of Arafat's death hit the wires than he had a stack of interview requests from radio talk-show hosts who had interviewed me when *The Last Days* was published. They were convinced the book was coming true and were curious to know what I thought would happen next.

What would the post-Arafat world look like? Could a moderate, pro-democratic, pro-Western leader now emerge, someone able and willing to make peace with Israel? Or would radical Islamic jihadists seize control of the West Bank and Gaza? Or were the Palestinians doomed to suffer a bloody civil war as various factions battled it out for supremacy?

I spent the rest of the day doing U.S. radio interviews from the phone in my hotel room, noting that any one of those scenarios was possible, but that the first thing to watch for was the outbreak of internecine violence and the emergence of an atmosphere of chaos.

In *The Last Days*, a fictional CIA expert sends a top-secret e-mail entitled "Possible Palestinian civil war erupting" to the president. He warns that the "battle to succeed Arafat could be brutal" and urges top administration officials to "watch for PLO factions to mobilize" against one another. As the novel unfolds, the warnings come to pass, top Palestinian officials are assassinated, and the West Bank and Gaza sink into anarchy.

Once again, fiction soon became fact. On November 14, the Associated Press reported that "militants firing assault rifles burst into a mourning tent for Yasser Arafat . . . just moments after the arrival of the Palestinian leader's temporary successor, Mahmoud Abbas, forcing security guards to whisk him away to safety. The shooting, which killed two security guards and wounded six other people, raised grave concerns about a violent power struggle in the post-Arafat era."[4]

The next day an Asian news service ran this headline: **"Civil War Looms over Palestine after Arafat's Death."** An Israeli news service ran a headline that read **"Rival Gangs Violently Vie for Control in PA"** [Palestinian Authority].[5]

By the end of the week, Palestinian prime minister Ahmed Qorei was demanding that "armed chaos must cease. Armed demonstrations must cease. Everybody must respect law and order."[6] But few were listening.

In the end, several years of chaos played into the hands of Hamas, which took over the Palestinian Authority in January 2006, not long after President Bush decided to make democracy in the Middle East the centerpiece of his second-term agenda.[7]

"A LITTLE EERIE"

My third political thriller was *The Ezekiel Option.*

Picking up where *The Last Days* left off, it centered on a dictator rising to power in post-Soviet Russia. Iran is feverishly trying to acquire nuclear weapons. Then Russia and Iran begin to form a military alliance—a nuclear alliance—with a coalition of Islamic countries who unleash an apocalyptic attack against Israel, bringing the world to the brink of nuclear war.

The Ezekiel Option was set for release on June 27, 2005, this time from Tyndale House Publishers. But Sean Hannity, who had asked me to be on his radio program the day it launched, as he had for both of my other novels, was leaving for vacation that week. He asked if I could reschedule the interview for Friday, June 24. Grateful for his continuing support, I readily agreed and we set the interview for 5:30 p.m. eastern. My public-relations team quickly booked additional radio interviews for me following Hannity, and Tyndale made June 24 the new official launch date. What caught everyone off guard, however, was the series of events that would unfold that particular day.

"It's a little eerie, Joel," Sean said as the interview began, noting that my past two novels had "run parallel with modern events" and that I was scaring him with the plotline of this new one. "So Saddam's gone. Arafat's dead. An American president and his advisors are pushing hard for an Israeli-Palestinian peace deal. All hell is breaking loose around the world, and a dictatorship begins rising out of Russia. Well, what's the news about Vladimir Putin today?"[8]

Sure enough, just before we went on the air, Matt Drudge posted a link to a breaking Associated Press story out of Moscow: **"Putin Amendment May Allow Third Term."**

According to the story, legislative allies of the Russian president were "considering an electoral amendment next week that could open the way for [Putin] to run for a third term, prompting the opposition to accuse his supporters of trying to cling to power." The article went on to say that "speculation has been rife that Putin would seek to stay in power beyond 2008" and noted that "during his time in power, Putin has placed national television under effective state control, abolished the direct election of regional governors to make them virtual Kremlin appointees, and eliminated the right of independent lawmakers to run for parliament."[9]

I summarized the AP story for the listening audience, then said, "You know, Sean, I was in Moscow last fall doing research for this novel, and I met with top Russian officials, U.S. Embassy officials, and Russian political analysts, and I asked them, 'Do you believe that Putin is going to leave office in 2008?' Every single one of them said yes—yet each of them had just spent the last hour convincing me of all the different things Putin was doing to consolidate power. Now, my character [in *Option*] is not Putin. But he feels like Putin, and I think there's an interesting question whether Putin is really a friend of the United States. I know that President Bush has looked into his soul [and found him trustworthy]. I think, though, the president—to be fair—is reevaluating that right now because Putin has been allowing nuclear technology to be sold to Iran, the worst terror state on the planet."

"Well, that's part of your book, too," Sean pointed out. "You write about a dictatorship rising in Russia and Iran feverishly pursuing nuclear weapons. . . . I don't know where you get all this from. You've got, like, a blessing over your head because every time you write a book it just seems to fit in with modern events, and that happened with your last two novels and now it's happening here."

He was referring to the fact that on the exact same day, a radical Islamic hard-liner named Mahmoud Ahmadinejad had just won a landslide victory to become president of Iran, vowing to build a "powerful Islamic society," defy Israel and the United States, and accelerate Iran's bid to become a nuclear power.[10] Western government officials and political analysts were both stunned and alarmed by Ahmadinejad's rapid rise to power and the implications of his victory for regional security.[11]

But not the Kremlin. Putin immediately congratulated the new Iranian president-elect and said Moscow was eager to continue selling nuclear technology and research facilities to Tehran. "The construction of the Bushehr nuclear plant [in Iran] is near an end, and we are ready to continue cooperation with Iran in the nuclear energy sphere," Putin said in a letter to Ahmadinejad released by the Kremlin, adding that the development of Russian-Iranian nuclear ties "contributes to global peace and stability."[12]

SADDAM'S NOVEL, AND MINE

If all this were not "coincidence" enough for one day, a new story out of Amman, Jordan, suddenly popped up on the Associated Press wires with a headline that read **"Novel Written by Saddam to Be Published."**[13] Curious, I scanned the article and was stunned to learn that

Saddam had actually finished writing a political thriller on March 18, 2003, just one day before coalition forces invaded Iraq.

To be sure, Saddam's title was punchier than mine—*Get Out, Damned One.* But the parallels between our two novels were curious, to say the least. Not only had Saddam written about an apocalyptic war in the Middle East in which a coalition of Arab Muslims square off against the Jews and the Christians, but the central character of his novel was a Jew named Ezekiel, and the novel was coming out the same week as my own. "The story is apparently a metaphor about a Zionist-Christian plot against Arabs and Muslims," noted the AP. "Ezekiel is meant to symbolize the Jews."

Michael Reagan asked me about the story when I appeared on his nationally syndicated radio show later that night. He had previously praised *The Last Days,* calling it "a gutsy new breed of political thriller— almost prophetically forecasting what you'll read in tomorrow's head-lines." But this was surreal. It was one thing to release a novel about the rise of a Russian dictator forming a nuclear alliance with Iran on the very day the world was discussing Vladimir Putin's latest power grab and the election of an Iranian hard-liner vowing to go nuclear with Russian technology. But it was quite another thing to be publishing mirror-opposite novels with the likes of the Butcher of Baghdad.

FICTION OR REALITY?

I should note here that my novels do not precisely match the events that have actually unfolded in real life. While *The Last Jihad,* for example, does open with a kamikaze attack on an American city, my fictional ter-rorists use a private business jet rather than commercial jumbo jets, and they fly their murderous mission into Denver, not the World Trade Center or the Pentagon. Likewise, while *The Last Days* does open with the death of Yasser Arafat, in the novel he is assassinated, while in real life it is believed he died of natural causes. Moreover, in the novel, Mahmoud Abbas is assassinated as well, rather than succeeding Arafat as the head of the Palestinian Authority, as he did in real life.

That said, however, these and other differences between fact and fiction have not seemed to dampen people's interest in my novels. To the contrary, each new political earthquake in the Middle East and Russia has spurred even more interest. By the end of 2005, I had given hundreds of media interviews. I had addressed audiences of CEOs, university students, church groups, and foreign diplomats in more than two dozen cities across the U.S., Canada, and the Middle East. I'd even delivered a talk on politics, prophecy, and the last days at the White House. And book sales soared.

When you write your first novel, you just hope your parents can find a copy at a bookstore within a hundred miles of their house. But suddenly there were more than one million copies of these novels in print. Thousands more were being printed in Holland, Poland, Portugal, Spain, and Turkey, with Hebrew, Russian, and Romanian editions in development. The books had spent month after month on the *New York Times* and *USA Today* best-seller lists.

"How are you doing this?" people wanted to know. "Is there a secret formula? Do you have a crystal ball? And what do you think is going to happen next?"

The *Dallas Morning News* called me "eerily prophetic." A *Washington Times* profile said my novels felt "ripped from the headlines—tomorrow's headlines." A radio talk-show host in Las Vegas said, "Your books are amazing. They're uncanny. It's like you can predict the future. Could you come out to Vegas to do a book signing and then help people with the blackjack tables?" (I politely declined.) And nearly every radio host would begin the interview by citing the *U.S. News & World Report* story calling me a "modern Nostradamus."

The truth, of course, is that I am neither a psychic nor a clairvoyant. I do not call Miss Cleo in the middle of the night to get my plot ideas. But it isn't luck—dumb, blind, or otherwise. There is a reason these books seem to have predicted the future. There is a way to connect the dots, to anticipate future headlines, and in the chapters ahead, I will explain what is coming, how I know, and why it matters.

But first I want to share with you some background on how I was originally introduced to a 2,500-year-old prophecy that seems to be coming to fulfillment before our eyes.

CHAPTER TWO

THE GENESIS OF JIHAD

I met Natan Sharansky for the first time in New York City on the morning of September 11, 2000, one year to the day—indeed, almost to the hour—before America was attacked by the forces of radical Islam. Neither of us had any specific idea of what horrors lay ahead, but it was that meeting and what he would share with me over the next few days that set the Last Jihad series into motion.

Two months earlier, Sharansky had been one of the top officials in the Israeli government. But on July 9—the eve of the Middle East Peace Summit that President Clinton had convened at Camp David—Sharansky resigned as Israel's interior minister, a move that threatened to bring down the government of then–prime minister Ehud Barak. At the time, the world was beginning to wonder if a final settlement between Israel and the Palestinians might actually be at hand. Top Clinton aides certainly hoped so and were doing everything they could to make it possible. But Sharansky had serious reservations.

For one thing, Barak was keeping the full details of his own peace plan secret even from members of his own cabinet, raising serious questions about what the prime minister's ideas for achieving peace actually were. For another thing, what tidbits were known were disturbing, to say the least.

Rumors (which later proved to be true) were flying that Barak was poised to give away all of Gaza, 90 percent or more of the West Bank, and half the Old City of Jerusalem—including the Temple Mount—to the terrorist leader Yasser Arafat for the creation of a Palestinian state. Yet Sharansky saw no indications that Barak would insist upon enforceable security guarantees to protect the Israeli people from terrorist attacks, much less insist that the Palestinians embark upon true democratic reforms or start protecting the human rights of its own people, including moderate Muslims or evangelical Palestinian Christians, long the brunt of severe persecution under the Arafat regime.

Sharansky was certainly on record as being in favor of making painful choices if a serious peace deal could be struck with the Palestinians. But he now argued that Barak's plan (as much of it as was known) gave away too much, too fast, to the wrong partner, and under the wrong conditions, and he had asked me over the phone to help him make his case to the American people.

Sharing his convictions and impressed with his courage, I immediately agreed and began helping him and his team place op-eds in the *New York Times,* the *Wall Street Journal,* and the *Washington Post*; issue press releases; book English-language TV and radio interviews for him and his surrogates to do from Jerusalem; and answer questions for American print journalists covering the day-to-day machinations of the Camp David summit.[1]

Whatever momentum Clinton and Barak had going into the summit, Sharansky's resignation brought it screeching to a halt, as did the resignation of two other Israeli political parties that had been part of Barak's coalition. On top of that, Israeli foreign minister David Levy made the stunning announcement that he would not be traveling with the prime minister to Camp David, as a protest against Barak's expected sweeping and ill-considered concessions.

"Barak's Coalition Crumbles on Eve of Summit Talks" read the front-page *New York Times* headline on the morning of July 10. Once again, the Holy Land and the Holy City were at the epicenter of an international media storm, and a *Newsweek* cover story perfectly captured the drama of the moment: **"The Fate of Jerusalem: Inside the Fight over a Sacred City's Future."**[2]

For the next fifteen days, I helped Sharansky and his colleagues respond to a torrent of media requests and explain to the American people and particularly to evangelicals and the Jewish community why Barak's plan to divide Jerusalem and create a new terror base camp for the likes of Yasser Arafat was a grave mistake.

The summit collapsed on July 25 without a deal, and Sharansky asked me to issue the following statement to all American reporters, producers, and editorial writers covering the peace talks: "I will be very happy to see a peace agreement signed between Israel and the Palestinians. However, under today's conditions, the agreement that would have been reached at Camp David would have torn Israeli society apart from the inside and would have been disastrous for Israel's national interests."[3]

Our work had only just begun. The summit itself was over, but the feverish Clinton-Barak bid to get a deal with Arafat—seemingly at all costs—before President Clinton left office was far from over. Sharansky asked me to set up a three-day media tour through New York and Washington so he could press his case in person, as well as announce the formation of a new organization—OneJerusalem.org—dedicated to rallying international support for keeping Jerusalem the undivided capital of the Jewish state. Again, I readily agreed. After all, I not only shared his objectives, I was also looking forward to finally meeting this political maverick, for despite all the work we had been doing together over the past ten weeks or so, we had still spoken only by phone.

Thus, at just before 9 a.m. on September 11, 2000, I was picked up from my hotel in Manhattan and driven to the Harvard Club, where Sharansky and several of his colleagues were having breakfast.

My excitement grew during the drive. After more than a decade working in Washington, I had yet to meet anyone with a more remarkable personal story than Natan Sharansky. Born into a secular Jewish family in Soviet Russia during the coldest years of the Cold War, Sharansky had been trained as a computer scientist but quickly shifted gears and became internationally known as a human-rights activist after being denied an exit visa to Israel. Arrested by the KGB and falsely accused of high treason and collaborating with the CIA, he was sentenced to thirteen years of solitary confinement and hard labor in the Soviet concentration camps known as the Gulag.

Miraculously released in February 1986 after nine years—the first political prisoner *ever* released by Mikhail Gorbachev (under intense pressure from Ronald Reagan)—Sharansky immediately emigrated to Israel, where he wrote his memoir, *Fear No Evil*. He became an internationally recognized champion of democracy and freedom and was awarded the U.S. Congressional Gold Medal. Not content to fritter away his own freedom, however, he went on to launch the first Israeli political party for Soviet Jews, and by 1996—ten years after he was released by the KGB—Sharansky was elected to the Israeli parliament, where he would eventually rise to become deputy prime minister, the second-highest-ranking official in the Israeli government.

Inside the Harvard Club, I found Sharansky and several aides waiting in the lobby. He immediately and graciously shook my hand and greeted me with a thick Russian accent, and we headed off to begin the day's whirlwind schedule of media events.

SHARANSKY MEETS PUTIN

Over the next several days, we met with reporters and editors from the *Wall Street Journal*, the *Washington Post*, *Newsweek*, the *New York Post*, and *National Review*, and Sharansky was interviewed by Charlie Rose and C-SPAN. Sharansky explained his views of the Israeli-Palestinian conflict and his critique of Barak's approach, and he offered alternative ways of making peace and promoting democracy.

During our time in Washington, Sharansky asked me questions about my family's history and about my career. He asked whether he'd heard correctly that my family was from Russia.

"Yes," I told him. "My father's parents and grandparents were Orthodox Jews in Minsk."

He asked when they had left.

"Around 1907, during the pogroms, when the czar was wiping out thousands upon thousands of Jews."

How had they gotten out?

"They hid in a hay wagon that was about to cross the border. Czarist soldiers actually plunged their swords into the hay to see if anyone was in there. By God's grace, no one was injured. By God's grace, none of the children—of which there were several—sneezed or coughed or asked, 'Are we there yet' or said, 'I need to go to the bathroom!' And by the grace of God, my family didn't get out of czarist, anti-Semitic Russia only to say, 'Phew! Let's settle in Germany or Poland or Austria.' Instead they made their way across the continent of Europe, caught a steamship to the New World, were processed at Ellis Island, and like any good Jewish family, they set up shop in Brooklyn, which is where my father grew up."

Sharansky laughed and commended my family for getting out just in time.

"I've been blessed to grow up in freedom," I replied.

"You have indeed," he said. "So you were raised Orthodox?"

Not exactly, I explained. By the time my parents met and got married in 1965, my father was fairly agnostic, as was my mother, though she was raised in the Methodist Church and came from a Protestant background, not a Jewish one. By the time I was born in April of 1967, they were on a real spiritual journey, reading the Koran, the Bhagavad Gita, and the New Testament in search of the truth. In 1973, both of them came to believe that Jesus was the Jewish Messiah—and both became evangelical Christians. It took me a few years to wrestle it through for myself, I explained, but I was now a follower of Jesus as well.

Sharansky seemed surprised, but curious.

He went on to ask me about my various jobs in Washington and about my four and a half years working for Steve Forbes, during his 1996 presidential campaign and right through the 2000 Republican primaries.

"It was great," I said, "right up to the point where we got mowed down by Governor Bush."

He laughed.

On Wednesday, September 13, we headed to Reagan National Airport, where we boarded a US Airways Shuttle back to New York. As we settled in for the forty-five minute flight, I pulled out my dog-eared, paperback copy of *Fear No Evil*, and asked him to sign it. A bit nostalgically, he flipped through the pages and noticed all of my underlining, notes, and other markings.

He turned to the title page, pulled out a pen, and wrote, "To Joel—you do the same what I did in Moscow with American press—but much better—so be careful. With appreciation and friendship, Natan Sharansky." [*sic*]

This time it was I who laughed, hoping nine years in the Gulag wouldn't be the price for helping this remarkable man make his case to the world.

"I'm curious," I asked him as we approached cruising altitude. "When you were sitting in your cell all those years, did you ever imagine yourself serving in the Israeli cabinet as a senior advisor to the prime minister himself?"

Not at all, he said. But stranger still, he confided, was in 1997 when he was serving as minister of industry and trade and then–prime minister Benjamin Netanyahu actually sent him back to Moscow to strengthen economic ties between Israel and Russia.

In February of 1999, Netanyahu sent Sharansky to Moscow a second time. Officially, the trip was billed as another high-level trade delegation. But privately, Netanyahu wanted Sharansky to hold a series of secret talks with Vladimir Putin, then head of the Russian intelligence services known as the FSB—the successor to the KGB—to discuss Israel's growing fears that Russian nuclear scientists and/or Russian nuclear warheads could fall into the hands of radical Arab and Islamic regimes in the Middle East, namely the mullahs of Iran or Saddam Hussein's Republic of Iraq.[4]

Putin knew what was on the agenda, but as Sharansky explained it to me, Putin used their first meeting to launch a charm offensive, offering to show Sharansky the files the KGB had kept on him when they had tracked his human-rights activities in the 1970s and then charged him with working with the CIA. Sharansky had requested to see the files during his 1997 trip but had been denied. Now Putin seemed to be saying that Russia was a different kind of country and that he was a different kind of spy chief.

At once grateful and caught somewhat off guard, Sharansky spent hours poring over the so-called dirt the KGB had amassed (i.e., made up) over the years. But eventually the two men got down to business. Why was Russia selling nuclear technology to Iran, the worst terror state on the face of the planet? Why was Russia building an $800 million nuclear reactor for the Iranians in Bushehr, near the Persian Gulf? Didn't Moscow understand the dangers of a state like Iran developing nuclear weapons, especially given Russia's bloody battle with radical Islamic jihadists in Chechnya? Did Russia appreciate how seriously the government of Israel viewed the possibility of an enemy like Iran going nuclear?

Putin dismissed Netanyahu's concerns and sent word back through Sharansky that Israel had nothing to worry about.

A chill ran down my spine, and three thoughts flashed across my mind.

First, God forbid that either Iran or Iraq should be able to acquire nuclear warheads. It was a nightmare scenario. The damage either country could do to U.S. national security either directly or through surrogate terrorist networks—to say nothing of the damage that could be done to Israel—with nuclear weapons would be catastrophic.

Second, I was struck by how remarkable it was that God had given me the opportunity to sit here with this amazing man and get a rare inside look into the minds of Vladimir Putin and Benjamin Netanyahu, two leaders at the epicenter of world events.

Third, I found myself thinking what a fascinating novel all this would make. I had always dreamed of writing novels and screenplays. Perhaps now was as good a time as any to write my first political thriller.

And then as I stared out the window of the US Air shuttle, mulling over what Sharansky had just told me, I suddenly thought back to a book I'd read years before, and I began to wonder if a much larger scenario was beginning to unfold.

THE FUTURE ALLIANCE OF RUSSIA AND IRAN

Sometime around 1992, my wife gave me a nonfiction book called *The Coming Peace in the Middle East* that unexpectedly captured my imagination.

At the time, I was serving as an assistant to the senior vice president and director of research at the Heritage Foundation, a think tank based in Washington, DC. It was my first job in DC—low-level and low-paying—but it did give me a front-row seat to witness the dramatic changes under way at home and around the globe. My third day on the job, for example, Henry Kissinger came for lunch to discuss the fall of the Berlin wall and what it meant for the future of the Western alliance.

My job was mostly to type memos, serve coffee, and keep quiet. But soon my boss, Burt Pines, let me carve out a niche of my own, researching the prospects for free-market economic reform and a new era of peace and prosperity in the Middle East now that Kuwait had been liberated and Saddam's Republican Guard had been defeated by coalition forces. As such, I was soon talking to every Arab and Israeli expert I could find and reading everything I could that might give me insight into helping the people of that troubled region find new hope. [5]

Coming Peace, however, was unlike any other book I had found. It was not written by a current or former secretary of state or national security advisor or director of Central Intelligence. Nor was it written by a president, prime minister, or king of any Middle Eastern country, past or present. It was, instead, written by a theologian, offering a 189-page analysis of a biblical prophecy from chapters 38 and 39 of the book of Ezekiel. Specifically, it described a coming period of security and prosperity in Israel, followed by the rise of a military alliance between Russia, Iran, and a group of other Islamic countries that would target Israel and drive the world to the brink of the apocalypse in what Ezekiel described as the "last days."

The book offered no policy prescriptions for preventing such a Russian-led threat against Israel and U.S. interests in the region. Instead, its author, Dr. Tim LaHaye (who would go on to cowrite *Left Behind*, the first novel in what became the biggest-selling fiction series in

American publishing history, with more than 63 million copies sold) simply stated that such matters were foreordained.

In his introduction, LaHaye wrote:

> The eyes of the world are fixed on the Middle East. Every day, the headlines of all major countries carry lead stories about Lebanon, Syria, Iran, Israel, Egypt, Jordan, Saudi Arabia, other Middle Eastern nations, the PLO, and Beirut. Most of the world looks for war. . . . Yet the Bible assures us that peace will reign in the Middle East someday—perhaps before the Lord returns. . . . The Jews will enjoy rest, safety, and prosperity unmatched since the days of Solomon. Unfortunately, it will be short-lived, for Russia will "think an evil thought," mount up its forces, stir up Arab hatreds, and attack Israel with the greatest army in the history of the world. The threat of this attack will terrify Israel into turning to God for help. And their cries will not be in vain, for the Almighty will put on a demonstration of power unequaled since the plagues of Egypt and the parting of the Red Sea. The result? Israel will continue in peace, and the world will know there is a God in heaven.

LaHaye then went on to suggest that this scenario "could well occur during our lifetime."[6]

At first glance, the theory seemed ludicrous. In the early 1990s, Russia was hardly a threat to the U.S. anymore, much less to Israel; nor was it likely to be for some time to come. The Evil Empire had just collapsed like a house of cards. Its military machine was being withdrawn from Eastern Europe. Its missiles were being dismantled. More than a million Jews were pouring out of the former Soviet republics and heading to Israel. The Kremlin barely had important economic ties to Iran, much less a military alliance, and its relations with the rest of the Arab and Islamic world were, at best, on hold as it dealt with its own serious internal turmoil. Moreover, the United States was now effectively the world's only superpower, and Washington's military and economic ties to Jerusalem were stronger than ever.

Still, I found myself intrigued with the book's premise on several levels. First, given my family background, I had always been fascinated with both the history and the future of Russia. I could not help but be curious about the notion that the Scriptures spoke of Russia at all, to say nothing of the idea that Russia would attack Israel, perhaps in my lifetime.

Second, as an evangelical Christian, I believed what the Bible said about God giving the land of Israel to the Jewish people as an everlasting covenant, one that could not be broken, no matter what mistakes we Jews made throughout the centuries. I had also had the opportunity to study for a semester at Tel Aviv University during my junior year and found those six months one of the most fascinating periods of my life. Thus, any prophecy that dealt with Israel's future was one that piqued my curiosity as well.

Finally, I had met Dr. LaHaye on a number of occasions. My wife worked for his wife, Beverly, at the time. I had always found him to be a strong friend of Israel and the Jewish people, as well as one of the most insightful and counterintuitive thinkers in the evangelical world. True, he was controversial in some circles, but if he saw such a scenario within the pages of Scripture, I decided I should not be so quick to dismiss it.

As I sat with Natan Sharansky on that flight to New York in the fall of 2000, I tried to connect the dots. Never before in human history had Russia and Iran been allies. But according to LaHaye, Scripture said they would be in the last days. Was it possible that such an alliance was now beginning to form?

ISRAEL, THE MODERN MIRACLE

When Sharansky's media tour was complete and I got back home to Washington, I dug out LaHaye's book from a box in my garage and re-read it. I also reread the book of Ezekiel. What struck me first was that much of Ezekiel 36 and 37 had already come true.

In Ezekiel 36:10, for example, God vows to bring the Jewish people back to the land of Israel. "I will greatly increase the population of Israel, and the ruined cities will be rebuilt and filled with people." Verse 24 picks up that theme. In it, the Lord promises to "gather you [Israel] up from all the nations and bring you [the Jewish people] home again to your land." In verse 30, God promises to "give you great harvests from your fruit trees and fields, and never again will the surrounding nations be able to scoff at your land for its famines," echoing his promise in Isaiah 27:6, which reads, "The time is coming when Jacob's descendants will take root. Israel will bud and blossom and fill the whole earth with fruit!"

As I read through Ezekiel 37, I found the prophet's vision of the "valley of dry bones." Ezekiel looks out over mountains of dead, dry, brittle bones—bereft of life and hope—stretching out as far as his eyes can see. He hears the Lord describe these bones as "the people of Israel," but he also sees the Lord do a miracle. For as Ezekiel looks on in stunned amazement, the bones suddenly come back together. They take the shape of skeletons. They are wrapped in muscles and tendons and flesh, and then God breathes life into them and Israel once again becomes a fully living, breathing modern nation, with "a great army" and one leader at its helm.

This has already happened, I thought to myself. *My parents and grandparents and I have seen these exact things come true right before our very eyes.*

Indeed, out of the trauma of the pogroms and the ashes of the Holocaust, and despite the violent resistance of the Muslim world, Israel had been reborn as a modern state, and Jews were returning to the Holy Land just as Ezekiel said they would.

Consider the numbers. When Israel declared her independence on May 14, 1948, the country's population stood at only 806,000. Yet by the end of 2005, nearly 7 million people lived in Israel, 5.6 million of whom were Jewish. Thousands more arrive every year. In 2005 alone, some 19,000 Jews immigrated to Israel. In fact, today more Jews live in the greater Tel Aviv area than in New York City, as many Jews live in Israel as in the United States, and it will not be long before more Jews live in Israel than Jews who do not.[7]

At the same time, the ancient ruins of Israelite cities and towns like Jerusalem, Bethlehem, Nazareth, Jericho, Hebron, Caesarea, and

Tiberias have been rebuilt to house the massive influx of Jewish immigrants. Hundreds of new office buildings, hotels, shopping centers, restaurants, movie theaters, gas stations, and government ministry buildings were built during this period, and every time I visit Israel I see more construction under way.

If this were not enough, the deserts of Israel are blooming again after centuries of neglect, filling the Holy Land and the world with fruit, vegetables, and flowers, just as the Bible said would happen. Take citrus exports as one example. Before 1948, Israel had no international citrus market to speak of. Yet by the 1960s, Jaffa oranges were world famous and actually made up 30 percent of Israel's rapidly growing export market. By 1980, Israeli citrus exports had hit nearly one billion dollars, an extraordinary figure for such a small and newly developed country.[8]

In the first three decades of the new Jewish state's existence, total Israeli agricultural exports increased a whopping 4,000 percent.[9] What's more, a remarkable 40 percent of Israel's vegetables and field crops were grown in sparsely populated desert regions, and by the year 2000 some 90 percent of Israeli melon exports were coming from the desert regions known as the Arava.[10]

Agriculture is now a $3.3 billion annual business in Israel, 20 percent of which is exported.[11] Cotton exports rose from virtually nothing to $25 million a year by 2004. Exports of fresh flowers, particularly to Europe, have soared from less than $100,000 in foreign sales in 1949 to a stunning $238 million in 2004.[12] Israeli potato exports have also exploded over the same period from virtually nothing to more than a quarter of a billion in annual export sales today.[13]

And one hardly needs to recount the size, strength, or feats of the Israeli Defense Forces. Suffice it to say that Israel has been an island of a few million immigrants in a sea of 300 million enemies yet has proven victorious in the 1948 War of Independence, the 1956 Suez Crisis, the 1967 war, the War of Attrition (1968–1970), the Yom Kippur War of 1973, and the Lebanon war of 1982, while also saving the world from an Iraqi nuclear bomb when Israeli pilots took out the Osirik reactor in June of 1981.

Maybe LaHaye's theory wasn't so ludicrous, I thought. He had, after all, published *The Coming Peace in the Middle East* in 1984, at a time when very few people believed the Soviet empire would ever allow a million Jews to flee for the Promised Land. But that is precisely what happened, and for me it raised an intriguing question: If the rebirth and repopulation of Israel described in Ezekiel 36 and 37 were coming true in my lifetime, was it not at least remotely possible that the peace and prosperity—and future war and divine rescue—described in chapters 38 and 39 could soon come true as well?

I was not about to speculate about such things in public, of course—not if I ever wanted to work as an advisor to U.S. and Israeli political leaders and not be perceived as a lunatic. But I admit, I was intrigued. In what little spare time I had, I began studying these ancient prophecies, the latest developments in the Arab-Israeli peace process, and the emerging relationship between Russia and Iran. What's more, I began to consider the possibility that someday I might write a novel about how the Ezekiel scenario could unfold. What I didn't know then was how soon that day would be.

CHAPTER THREE:
CONNECTING
THE DOTS

About a week after Sharansky returned to Israel, I received a phone call from a top strategist for Benjamin Netanyahu. Could I meet the former Israeli prime minister the following week when he came to the U.S.?

With Barak's government on the verge of collapse, the strategist explained, Netanyahu was being urged to run for prime minister again when new elections were called, perhaps as early as the spring of 2001. He was, therefore, quietly forming a new inner circle of Americans to complement his Israeli team. Netanyahu wanted to map out a possible comeback, and he wanted to talk to me about serving as one of his communications advisors.

If the interview went well, I would be invited to join the half dozen or so other advisors already on board and stay for the six-hour strategy meeting to follow. I accepted without hesitation.

Just before 8:00 a.m. on Monday, September 25, 2000, I entered the lobby of Netanyahu's hotel in Manhattan and was taken by a security guard directly to the former prime minister's suite, where I was greeted by the strategist who had talked to me over the phone. We chatted about the latest developments in the Bush-Cheney campaign against Vice President Gore and Senator Joe Lieberman and about the morning's headlines from Israel.

A few minutes later, Netanyahu entered the room. He looked tanned, fit, and very relaxed, sporting a black polo shirt and dress slacks. His hair was a bit grayer than when he had been in office, but he seemed rejuvenated and ready to get back into the arena. He gave me a firm handshake and asked me to sit.

"So, Joel, tell me a little about yourself," Netanyahu began.

I tried to compose my thoughts. There was something remarkable about meeting the ninth prime minister of the modern State of Israel, a man who'd literally had his finger on the button while facing down enemies like Saddam Hussein and the ayatollahs of Iran.

"Well, sir, my first job was at the Heritage Foundation. . . ."

I had barely gotten the words out of my mouth when Netanyahu broke out in a smile and told me how much he loved the work Heritage did for the cause of freedom and how long he had been friends with the organization's founder, Ed Feulner.

"What did you do after Heritage?" he asked.

I explained that my next job had been working for Bill Bennett and Jack Kemp. This, too, elicited a strong reaction. Netanyahu was friends with both men. As I recall, he referred to Jack as "Yitzhak Kemp," a nickname the famed quarterback turned congressman turned secretary of housing and urban development had earned through years of supporting Israel through thick and thin.

Netanyahu also turned out to be a big fan of Rush Limbaugh, for whom I'd worked as director of research from 1994 until I joined Steve Forbes's presidential campaign in 1996. And when I mentioned working for Steve as his communications director and later as deputy campaign manager during the 2000 primaries, that was apparently all Netanyahu had to hear. He couldn't say enough good about the flat tax, Steve's passion for free-market reform, and the Jubilee Business Summit they had cochaired together in October 1998. The interview had been under way for barely five minutes, and already it was over.

"Why exactly are we having this meeting?" Netanyahu asked,

standing. "If you were good enough for them, you're good enough for me. Let's get started."

Startled, I stood as well and shook his hand. I was in.

"ALL HELL IS BREAKING LOOSE"

By the end of November, less than three months after that initial strategy meeting in New York, Netanyahu led Barak by a stunning seventeen points, forty-six to twenty-nine. We had run no ads. There was no official political campaign in operation, yet the numbers were exploding, and Barak's camp was in full panic mode. So what had happened?

Yasser Arafat had happened.

Rather than pocket the most generous deal ever offered by any Israeli prime minister in history (too generous, in our judgment) and declare victory, Arafat chose instead to launch a bloody campaign against Israel, hoping to force Israel to make even more concessions. Using the pretext that Ariel Sharon's visit to the Temple Mount on September 28 (a visit I have made several times and which is and should be perfectly legal) had somehow violated a Muslim holy site (though Sharon never entered the Dome of the Rock or the Al-Aksa Mosque), Palestinians began rioting on the Temple Mount, throughout East Jerusalem, and all over the West Bank and Gaza.[1]

Day after day they torched cars, threw firebombs, and fired automatic weapons at Israeli soldiers and civilians alike. Then, on October 6, Arafat's Fatah Party, along with the Islamic resistance movement known as Hamas, ratcheted up the crisis even further, calling for a Palestinian "day of rage," thus intensifying the clashes.

Six days later, on the morning of October 12, 2000, I woke up to an urgent call from one of Netanyahu's advisors. "Turn on your television," he told me. "All hell is breaking loose." He was actually understating it.

In Ramallah, Arafat's capital on the West Bank, Palestinian mobs had lynched and butchered two Israeli reserve soldiers—a thirty-eight-year-old father of three and a thirty-three-year-old newlywed—on worldwide television. One of the teenage murderers had actually slathered his own hands in the men's still-warm blood and held them out a window for the media and a cheering Palestinian crowd to see.

In Lebanon, meanwhile, Hezbollah guerrillas had seized three Israeli hostages and declared their own day of rage, vowing to set the border with Israel on fire. In Yemen, Al-Qaeda terrorists operating at the direction of Osama bin Laden had just launched a suicide-bombing mission against the USS *Cole*, an American warship in port for refueling. The attack killed seventeen American sailors and wounded thirty-nine others. And in Iraq, Saddam Hussein not only issued a chilling new threat to destroy Israel if he was given access through Jordan; he also began moving an armored division of 15,000 Republican Guard troops westward out of Baghdad toward the border of Jordan and Israel, a highly provocative move in such a volatile climate.[2]

Once again, the Middle East was the epicenter of a massive political earthquake. Saddam, Arafat, and bin Laden were all moving on the same day, and the world was looking on in horror. My phones were soon ringing off the hook as American journalists, radio talk-show hosts, and network news producers sought Netanyahu's reaction.

On November 2, a car bombing in Jerusalem killed two Israelis and wounded ten more. On November 20, an Israeli school bus filled with children was ripped to shreds by a roadside bomb, leaving two dead and nine seriously injured. Two days later, Palestinian terrorists blew up a bus in Hadera, killing two Israelis and injuring sixty more. On and on the violence went, and Barak appeared powerless to stop it.[3]

During the Camp David summit, Netanyahu had warned that Barak's concessions were putting Israel's security at risk because the Palestinian leadership would view them as being offered not out of strength but out of weakness.[4] Now such warnings were playing out before the eyes of the world.

Netanyahu was no prophet. Rather, he was a man who understood the nature of evil. He had coldly and correctly assessed the character and intentions of Yasser Arafat and Saddam Hussein and the leaders of jihadist movements such as Hamas, Hezbollah, and Al-Qaeda. He knew how they thought, how they operated, how they collaborated, what they wanted, and how far they were willing to go to get it. And the Israeli people began to see that he was right.

Netanyahu now had a commanding fifteen- to twenty-point lead over Barak in nearly every public poll. He certainly seemed poised to become Israel's next prime minister. The strategist who had introduced me to Netanyahu now asked me to consider working full-time as his English-language press secretary when the campaign officially launched early in 2001. It would mean moving my family to Jerusalem for several months, but it was the chance of a lifetime.

Still, I had one question: "You know that I'm an evangelical Christian, right?"

It was a sensitive subject in Israel, especially coming from an Orthodox Jewish heritage as I did. But it would be better to deal with the issue up front, I thought, than risk causing Netanyahu or his team problems later on, particularly in the white-hot battle of a political campaign.

The strategist looked at me for a moment as if to say, *Do you think you would have gotten within a hundred miles of the former prime minister of Israel if we didn't already know everything about you?* But what he actually said was, "It's not an issue for us if you don't make it one."

I appreciated the confidence of Netanyahu and his team and their willingness to build strategic ties with evangelical Christians, who are among Israel's most loyal and steadfast friends. In the end, however, neither my family nor I moved to Jerusalem to serve on the campaign. There was no campaign. For as quickly as Netanyahu's political fortunes had soared, they just as suddenly came to an abrupt end.

CHECKMATE

On Saturday, December 9, I received an unexpected call at home from Jerusalem. "Barak's resigning," said one of Netanyahu's top aides. "He's expected to hold a press conference in the next few hours."

That was good news, wasn't it?

Not exactly, the aide explained.

Rumor had it Barak was going to call for special elections under the pretext of a national-security emergency. That meant voters would go to the polls to choose the nation's prime minister in just sixty days. But such a move would also trigger a provision within Israeli law that allowed only a sitting member of Israel's parliament to run.

Barak's gambit suddenly became clear. Netanyahu was no longer a Knesset member. After his defeat to Barak in 1999, he had stepped down to spend more time with his family, travel a bit, write a book, give some speeches, and get some rest. If Barak had waited for the normal election cycle to roll around or for his government to officially collapse via a parliamentary vote of no confidence, Netanyahu could have legally reentered the political arena and soundly defeated him. By resigning the way he did, however, Barak had put his strongest opponent in checkmate and positioned himself for a run against Ariel Sharon, who appeared far easier to beat.

In the end, however, Barak's gambit failed disastrously. Arafat's war on Israel grew bloodier. One Palestinian suicide bomber after another wreaked havoc on the psyche of the Israeli people. Netanyahu threw all his political support behind Sharon. And lo and behold, Israel's "most notorious hawk" wound up beating Barak in the biggest landslide in modern Israeli history, sixty-two to thirty-seven.[5]

From Beirut to Baghdad and from Moscow to Washington, Sharon's almost-overnight rise to power shook long-held assumptions about the future of the Middle East to their core. No one knew what to expect. Not Arafat. Not Saddam. Not the newly elected President Bush, who had actually toured Israel with Sharon back in 1999 when neither man could have known they would soon simultaneously lead their respective nations.

On a more personal level, I had to accept the fact that a new political era was being born in the Holy Land, and I was not going to be a part of it. Thus, as December unfolded and I recovered from the initial shock of Netanyahu not running, I began to assess my options. I was still running November Communications, the consulting company I had formed after the Forbes campaign to help business and political leaders "discover, develop, and drive their message." But the more my wife, Lynn, and I thought and prayed about our next move, the more I thought about putting myself through political detox.

Maybe it's time to get out of politics altogether, I told myself. *The last ten years have been an exciting ride, but you're exhausted. You're hardly ever home. You barely see your kids. Maybe it's time to stop being so dependent on the ups and downs of political polls and personalities. Maybe it's time to stop ghostwriting for others and start writing your own novels.*

That, of course, was easier said than done. I had never written a novel in my life (no surprise to my critics). I had not taken a single fiction-writing class in college (though when I was writing for Rush Limbaugh's political newsletter back in the early 1990s, my liberal friends insisted I *was* writing fiction). I had barely even had time to read any fiction over the previous decade, except for an occasional Clancy or Grisham thriller my sister-in-law might give me for Christmas. What's more, I had no story, no characters, and little idea of how to construct a Clancy-like thriller, no matter how much I wanted to.

Yet sometime around New Year's, as life slowed down and the phones stopped ringing and the snow fell gently over the Virginia countryside, I found myself thinking back over all that had happened in the past few months: The Camp David summit and Arafat's new war for Jerusalem. Sharansky's meetings with Putin and the emerging alliance between Russia and Iran. Saddam's threat to wipe out Israel and his recent troop movements toward Jordan. Ezekiel's prophecies and *The Coming Peace in the Middle East.* Was there a novel in any of that? Would anyone publish it if there was? And even if someone did, would anyone buy it?

A PLAUSIBLE SCENARIO

Most Americans at the time were not paying attention to the Middle East, as tumultuous as events there were. They were still reeling from the photo-finish presidential election between George W. Bush and Vice President Al Gore, and understandably so. The air was filled with talk of hanging chads, voter intent, and the Supreme Court, not the future of Russia, radical Islam, or weapons of mass destruction. If I was going to write a novel that had any hope of seeing the light of day—much less breaking out and truly capturing people's imagination—it would have to be unique, to say the least.

I decided that any political-thriller writer worth his or her salt had to begin with a what-if scenario that was as plausible as it was provocative, and it struck me that the scenario arising out of Ezekiel 38 and 39 actually wasn't bad: *What if a dictator rose to power in Russia, formed a military alliance—a nuclear alliance—with Iran, and tried to attack Israel and seize control of the oil-rich Middle East? How might such a crisis play out if it were to happen in my lifetime? How would NATO respond? How might Bush respond? How might an Israeli prime minister like Netanyahu or Sharon respond?*

A reader of such a novel would not necessarily need to buy into Bible prophecy to accept both the plausibility and the chilling implications of such a high-stakes plot and the vexing moral questions it would trigger for any world leader. After all, from the days of Peter the Great, Russian leaders had been scheming of ways to gain control of central and near-east Asia. It was why the Soviets had armed the Arab world to the teeth during the Cold War and backed them in the 1956, 1967, and 1973 wars against Israel. It was why Moscow had invaded Afghanistan in 1979, amid the chaos engulfing revolutionary Iran at the time. It certainly was not out of the realm of possibility that a future leader of Russia might recklessly play the same game again.

Pentagon planners have been preparing for the possibility of a Moscow-led invasion of the Middle East for years. In their 1996 book *The Next War*, former Reagan defense secretary Caspar Weinberger and coauthor Peter Schweizer, a scholar at Stanford's Hoover Institution, laid out five scenarios for current and future war planners and policy makers to consider in the post-Soviet world. Among them: an ultranationalist radical seizes control of Russia to reconquer the former Soviet empire, and a nuclear-armed Iran launches a new war in the Persian Gulf and initiates a wave of radical Islamic terrorism across Europe and the U.S.[6]

By the time Lynn and I returned home from one of the Bush inaugural balls a few weeks later, I had made my decision. I was going to take a shot at turning this Ezekiel-driven, what-if scenario into a full-blown political thriller. I had no guarantee of success, of course, but I had a little time, a little money in the bank, and a dream long unfulfilled. If I didn't try my hand now, I knew I might never try at all.

But no sooner had I begun than I ran into a problem. On the one hand, I wanted this novel to be both as riveting *and* as plausible as I could possibly make it, and I hoped to draw upon my time in Washington and my experiences with Netanyahu and Sharansky and their advisors in the process. On the other hand, as a Christian I also wanted to be as true to the scenario presented by the prophet Ezekiel as I possibly could. I could not be certain exactly when or precisely how the prophesies would come to complete fulfillment, but I had no doubt they would someday and thus felt compelled to handle the biblical text with care. This immediately created a tension I was not sure how to overcome.

Let me give you an example to illustrate my dilemma. In the first few verses of Ezekiel 38, the prophet lays out a list of countries that will join Russia and Iran in a coalition against Israel in the last days. It is a list I will describe in more detail in later chapters, but suffice it to say here that two countries struck me as conspicuously absent.

The first was Egypt. Nowhere in Ezekiel 38 or 39 is Egypt mentioned directly. Yet Egypt has been a leading enemy of the children of Israel going back to the times of the pharaohs and the slavery of the Jews, which lasted four hundred years. More recently, Egypt was a driving force in all of the major wars against Israel, including 1948, 1956, 1967, and 1973. Was it really possible, then, that Egypt would *not* participate in what could be the next great war against Israel?

As I pondered that question, however, I immediately thought of the 1979 Camp David Accords and the peace treaty that had been historically signed by Egyptian president Anwar Sadat and Israeli prime minister Menachem Begin. It has been a cold peace, to be sure, but it has held for nearly three decades. As I realized that, it suddenly struck me that for the first time since Ezekiel had written this prophecy 2,500 years earlier, it actually *was* plausible that Egypt could sit out the next war. In my novel, therefore, I could credibly exclude Egypt from the

Russian-Iranian coalition against Israel in a way that would never have seemed realistic prior to 1979.

The second country conspicuously absent from Ezekiel's list was Iraq, and that made absolutely no sense to me. The rulers of the lands known throughout Scripture as Babylon and Mesopotamia had been enemies of the Jewish people nearly as long as the rulers of Egypt. It was the Babylonians who had conquered Jerusalem in 586 BC, destroyed its Holy Temple, and carried off its people and Temple treasures back to Babylon, where the Jews remained in captivity for seventy years. More recently, Iraq had also been heavily involved in the 1948, 1967, and 1973 wars against Israel, and unlike Egypt, Saddam Hussein had never signed a peace treaty with the Jewish state. To the contrary, during the Gulf War of 1991, Saddam had fired thirty-nine Scud missiles at Israel. He had vowed to destroy Israel with chemical weapons, and he had repeated his murderous threats just a few weeks earlier. How, then, could I possibly write a political thriller in 2001 that didn't include Saddam Hussein as part of the coalition attacking Israel?

This conundrum left me with only two alternatives, as I saw it. I could ignore Ezekiel's list and add Iraq into the coalition on the premise that I was, after all, simply writing fiction, so what did it really matter? Or I could treat Ezekiel's list as an intercept from the mind of an all-knowing God, just as a CIA analyst might treat an intercept from the cell phone of a world leader—as a piece of credible, actionable intelligence that I might not initially understand but that was true nonetheless.

As an aspiring thriller writer, I was naturally tempted by the former approach. But as a Bible-believing Christian, I felt compelled to adopt the latter. In other words, I had to rule Iraq out as a coalition partner. Which could only mean that Saddam Hussein was no longer ruling Iraq. Which meant that I was going to have to back up my story by several years and start with a novel about how Saddam might disappear from the world stage before I could write *The Ezekiel Option*.

How might Saddam go? I wondered. There were a number of possibilities. He could die of natural causes, be assassinated, be overthrown in a coup, or be toppled by the invasion of a foreign power. Death by natural causes was not exactly the stuff of a riveting best seller, so I ruled that out. Assassination and coups had been attempted numerous times during Saddam's reign of terror, yet none of them had been successful, and I doubted they would be successful in the future given Saddam's renowned paranoia, multiple layers of security, and many body doubles.

In the end I concluded that the most likely way the Butcher of Baghdad would be taken down was by foreign invasion. Of course, in January 2001, the only country truly capable of launching such an invasion was the United States, but why would we? President George Herbert Walker Bush ("Bush 41") had not invaded Iraq in 1991 when there was the clear provocation of Iraq's invasion of Kuwait. What would move his son, or *any* future U.S. president, to take such a risk?

I thought about the warnings Netanyahu had given over the past several months—and over the past several decades—that state-sponsored Middle Eastern terrorists were not content to simply target Israel but would target the West as well, and particularly the United States, known throughout the Muslim world as the Great Satan. In his 1995 book *Fighting Terrorism,* for example, Netanyahu wrote, "It can only be a matter of time before this terror is turned inward against the United States, the leader of the hated West and the country responsible in the eyes of militant Muslims for having created Israel and for maintaining the supposedly heretical Arab regimes."[7]

Netanyahu noted that "the rapidly increasing use of suicide bombings by Islamic terrorists . . . suggests that at least some of the people involved have no qualms about blowing themselves up at the service of their ideology (a phenomenon Americans will remember from the Japanese kamikazes of World War II)."[8] But he also warned that conventionally armed suicide bombers and kamikazes were not the most serious threat facing the West. "In the worst of such scenarios, the consequences could be not a car bomb but a *nuclear* bomb in the basement of the World Trade Center."[9]

In his 1993 book *A Place among the Nations,*[10] Netanyahu warned against the West's "tendency to see the end of the Cold War as the 'end of history.'" He argued that Middle Eastern bloodshed is a "perpetual-motion machine that requires no outside assistance to maintain itself or to threaten the peace and stability of other nations."[11] Remarkably, he also described Saddam's Iraq as "a menace of the sort that has previously been the stuff only of suspense novels: a terrorist state with a leader seeking to graduate from car bombs to nuclear bombs."[12]

As I chewed over such things, the dots began to connect.

- What if radical Islamic terrorists pulled off a major attack inside the U.S., such as hijacking a plane and flying it into an American city?
- Wouldn't an American president have to declare a war on terror that would target both the terrorists themselves and the states that sponsored them?
- Wouldn't that lead the president's attention to Baghdad, where Saddam Hussein not only harbored notorious international terrorists and paid Palestinian families more than $25,000 to send their sons and daughters to become homicide bombers against innocent Israeli women and children, but where Saddam also had a long and sordid record of developing chemical, biological, and nuclear weapons?[13]
- Wouldn't the president have to conclude that he could no longer in good conscience leave Saddam Hussein in power with the motive, means, and opportunity to equip anti-American terrorists with weapons of mass destruction?
- And couldn't that lead to an American war to topple Saddam, thus bringing ancient biblical prophecies that much closer to fulfillment?

It was this analysis from which the Last Jihad series was conceived in January 2001, and, tragically, it was this scenario that was born nine months later.

CHAPTER FOUR

THE THIRD LENS

When *The Last Jihad* was published, I was constantly asked how I could have anticipated radical Islamic terrorists flying a kamikaze mission into an American city when so many in Washington had not. I replied that the September 11 attacks, in my view, were not so much a failure of intelligence as they were a failure of imagination. It was a line the 9/11 Commission would later echo in their final report.

BLINDSIDED

The FBI and CIA, the nation would later learn, actually had a remarkable amount of information at their fingertips prior to 9/11 that suggested both the nature and even the specific targets of the coming attacks. But in the end, none of it mattered. Too few in our law enforcement and intelligence communities actually believed that such evil was possible. The nature of the attacks that would be carried out against the United States was beyond their ability to imagine. They had the dots. They simply could not connect them, at least not in time.

As President Bush put it, "Nobody in our government . . . and I don't think the prior government, could envision flying airplanes into buildings on such a massive scale."[1]

Condoleezza Rice, then the national security advisor, concurred. "No one could have imagined them . . . using planes as a missile," she told the 9/11 Commission. "I could not have imagined [it]."[2]

Richard Armitage, who was serving as deputy secretary of state under Colin Powell on 9/11, testified, "I know that the director of Central Intelligence had, on at least one occasion to my knowledge, talked about hijacking of aircraft. I just don't think we had the imagination required to consider a tragedy of this magnitude."[3]

Major General Paul Weaver, head of the Air National Guard on 9/11, admitted, "We never considered this threat. Who could have ever imagined that our own airlines would be used against us?"[4]

In its final report, the 9/11 Commission concluded, "The most important failure was one of imagination. We do not believe leaders understood the gravity of the threat."[5]

Unfortunately, it was not the first time.

A similar failure of imagination at the highest levels of government took place in 1990.

When I first moved to Washington in January 1990 to work for the Heritage Foundation, it seemed increasingly clear to me that Saddam Hussein was going to invade Kuwait, attack Israel, and draw the world into a bloody new Middle East war. I had no access to classified intelligence and knew no one in the CIA or Mossad at the time. I simply listened to Saddam Hussein's threats and took him at his word. Amazingly, however, many so-called Middle East experts did not.

In April of 1990, for example, the *Los Angeles Times* ran a page-one story on Saddam's new threat to destroy "half of Israel" with chemical weapons. Yet the *Times* cited an expert from London's International Institute for Strategic Studies who dismissed the threat as "good propaganda, saber-rattling stuff."[6]

The June 11 issue of *Time* magazine also dismissed the prospects of an Iraq-led war, chalking up Saddam's increasingly hostile rhetoric to "saber rattling," a term that practically became a mantra of the "experts" who told us we had nothing to worry about.[7]

On July 2—precisely one month to the day before Iraq invaded Kuwait—a front-page headline in the *Washington Post* read **"New Middle**

East War Seen Unlikely: Threats, Saber-Rattling Abound, But Deterrents Curb Both Sides."

On July 26, just days before the actual invasion, a headline in the influential *Times* of London read **"Experts Believe Iraq Will Stop Short of Invasion."** The article twice used the term *saber rattling* and reported that "the consensus among Middle East experts yesterday was that Iraq would not invade Kuwait, but could succeed in forcing it to cut oil production."[8]

As the summer progressed, I kept asking experts throughout Washington, "Doesn't all the evidence add up to invasion, not just bluster?" Most of them said no. And it was not only what they said, it was how they said it, as if the only sophisticated, intellectually defensible answer was "Of course not, you uneducated moron."

I was certainly new to Washington and as green as they came. I had no master's or PhD in the history or politics of the Middle East. I had lived but a semester in the Middle East, and Israel at that, not in an Arab or Islamic country. And my job at the time was essentially to serve up coffee, not political analysis. But I could not shake the overwhelming feeling that the experts were about to be blindsided.

On August 2, 1990, Iraqi forces began moving across the Kuwaiti border. Official Washington was stunned. The *New York Times* reported that President Bush (41) and his administration were "surprised by the invasion this week and largely unprepared to respond quickly."[9] The U.S. ambassador to Iraq had actually left the country for a vacation.[10] The *Washington Times* reported that "the attack surprised most Defense Department officials."[11]

Recently declassified documents from the U.S. Defense Intelligence Agency (DIA) paint an even more detailed and troubling portrait of how badly our government was blindsided by the Iraqi invasion.[12]

- In November 1989, a DIA assessment concluded, "Iraq is *unlikely to launch military operations* against any of its Arab neighbors over the next three years. . . . To protect its image of moderation, *Iraq is unlikely to take military action against Kuwait.*" (emphasis added)

- On July 20, 1990, the DIA advised top Pentagon officials that *"Iraq is unlikely to use significant force against Kuwait,"* though it conceded that "small-scale incursions are possible." (emphasis added)
- On July 25, a Defense Special Assessment stated, "Iraq is using rhetoric, diplomatic pressure, and significant military posturing to force Kuwait to comply with recent oil and economic demands. *Although unlikely to use military pressure*, Iraq is marshaling forces sufficient to invade Kuwait." (emphasis added)
- On July 27—just days away from the actual invasion— the DIA actually reported to top Pentagon and Bush administration officials that "tensions between Baghdad and Kuwait are *subsiding.* . . . Kuwait will give Saddam most of what he wants to avoid military confrontation." (emphasis added)

A miscalculation of such magnitude simply boggles the mind. This was not a secret conspiracy plotted in the shadowy caves of Afghanistan. To the contrary, Saddam had broadcast his ambitions and his intentions to the whole world. He amassed tens of thousands of men and hundreds of millions of dollars' worth of military equipment on Kuwait's border in full view of U.S. spy satellites and Western news reporters. Yet so few believed him. Why? How could people so smart, so well versed in ancient and modern history, and so well informed by the best classified intelligence money can buy have so badly misread the situation?

Again, the answer lies not in the failure of intelligence gathering per se but in the failure of imagination. The experts simply refused to believe that Saddam was so evil that he would order the rape and pillaging of an Arab neighbor. They refused to believe that he was so evil that he would launch thirty-nine Scud missiles against Israel, and more Scuds against Saudi Arabia. What's more, they refused to believe Saddam when he described himself as a "modern Nebuchadnezzar," one of the most evil tyrants ever described in the Bible. And therein lies the problem.

Too many in Washington today have a modern, Western, secular mind-set that either discounts—or outright dismisses—the fact that evil is a real and active force in history. They insist on interpreting events *only* through the lenses of politics and economics. Yet to misunderstand the nature and threat of evil is to risk being blindsided by it, and that is precisely what happened on August 2, 1990, and September 11, 2001. Washington was blindsided by an evil it did not understand, just as it had been blindsided by Auschwitz, Dachau, and Pearl Harbor, and much as I believe it will be blindsided by future events.

As an evangelical Christian whose family escaped the persecution of the Jews in czarist Russia, I have no doubt there is real evil in our world. Nor do I have any doubt that it is a powerful and pernicious force in history. I am not threatened by it, for I know there is a God and Savior who promises to defeat evil in due time. But until then, I fully expect evil to gather its forces and strike at the good. Thus, I try to anticipate how and where it might strike, and in doing so I find Scripture a useful guide.

At the very least, the Bible helps me understand the mind-set of tyrants like Saddam Hussein, Yasser Arafat, and Mahmoud Ahmadinejad and the mullahs of Iran, to put them in historic context and anticipate their future moves. At times, it even provides me specific "intelligence" of coming events.

THE THIRD LENS

This brings me to the central premise of this book.

While it is fashionable in our times to analyze world events merely by looking through the lenses of politics and economics, it is also a serious mistake, for it prevents one from being able to see in three dimensions. To truly understand the significance of global events and trends, one must analyze them through a third lens as well: the lens of Scripture. Only then can the full picture become clearer.

The Bible is not shy about describing itself as a supernatural book, written by an all-seeing, all-knowing, all-powerful God who chooses to give his people advance warning of future events he deems of utmost importance. To the Hebrew prophet Jeremiah, God said, "Call to Me and I will answer you, and I will tell you great and mighty things, which you do not know" (Jeremiah 33:3, NASB). To the Hebrew prophet Amos, he explained that "the Lord GOD does nothing unless He reveals His secret counsel to His servants the prophets" (Amos 3:7, NASB).

When King Nebuchadnezzar had dreams of future events so troubling that he could not sleep, he turned to the Hebrew prophet Daniel, who told him that it is the God of heaven who "removes kings and establishes kings" and "it is He who reveals the profound and hidden things" (Daniel 2:21-22, NASB). "As for the mystery about which the king has inquired," Daniel explained, "neither wise men, conjurers, magicians nor diviners are able to declare it to the king. However, there is a God in heaven who reveals mysteries, and He has made known to King Nebuchadnezzar what will take place in the latter days" (Daniel 2:27-28, NASB). Daniel then foretold the coming rise of four great world empires—Babylonian, Media-Persian, Greek, and Roman—with startling accuracy.

In one of the most intriguing passages to me in the New Testament, Jesus sharply criticized his followers for not analyzing current events through the third lens of Scripture. "When you see a cloud rising in the west, immediately you say, 'A shower is coming,' and so it turns out. And when you see a south wind blowing, you say, 'It will be a hot day,' and it turns out that way. You hypocrites! You know how to analyze the appearance of the earth and the sky, but why do you not analyze this present time?" (Luke 12:54-56, NASB).

Why such a strong rebuke? Because while those living in first-century Palestine certainly knew the many ancient Hebrew prophecies describing the coming Messiah (that he would be born in Bethlehem, born of a virgin, live in Galilee, teach in parables, do miracles, care for the poor, be a light to the Gentiles, etc.), they could not—or would not—connect the dots and accept that it was Jesus himself to whom the prophets were pointing.

Yet how many today, living in the twenty-first century, are truly familiar with the many ancient biblical prophecies concerning the second coming of the Messiah and are able—much less willing—to connect the dots and see what is coming?

Not all events are described in advance in the Bible, of course. Nor can the prophecies be used to determine the future of every country. But there are key events and trends that will occur in certain countries—epicenter countries—that the Bible does describe with surprising specificity for anyone willing to look carefully.

AMERICAN ATTITUDES TOWARD BIBLE PROPHECY

Today there is no shortage of people who think that those who believe the Bible offers a reliable guide to coming events are lunatics.

In his 2000 book *The End of Days*, Israeli journalist Gershom Gorenberg called belief in biblical prophecies of the end times a "fantasy" and "dangerous."[13]

Bill Moyers, the longtime PBS journalist, marveled in a 2004 speech that there are actually "people who believe the Bible is literally true," and specifically called the end-times beliefs of Americans "bizarre." Christians, said Moyers, believe that "once Israel has occupied the rest of its 'biblical lands,' legions of the Antichrist will attack it, triggering a final showdown in the valley of Armageddon. . . . True believers will be lifted out of their clothes and transported to heaven where, seated next to the right hand of God, they will watch their political and religious opponents suffer plagues of boils, sores, locusts and frogs during the several years of tribulation that follow. I'm not making this up. . . . I've read it in the literature."[14]

In his best-selling 2006 book, *American Theocracy*, former Republican strategist Kevin Phillips echoed such sentiments. He warned that Americans who believe in biblical prophecy are "overimaginative" at best and "radical" at worst, asserting that "the rapture, end-times, and Armageddon hucksters in the United States rank with any Shiite ayatollahs."[15]

What really stuns and infuriates such skeptics is the enormous number of Americans who believe that world events are unfolding just as the Bible foretold.

In February 2006, curious to see just how many there were, I commissioned a national survey of American adults to better understand contemporary attitudes toward Bible prophecy. The poll was conducted by the respected firm of McLaughlin & Associates, founded by John McLaughlin, who works with some of the world's leading business and political leaders, including Steve Forbes, Benjamin Netanyahu, and Speaker of the House Dennis Hastert.[16]

We asked people if they agreed with the following statement:

> Events such as the rebirth of the State of Israel, wars and instability in the Middle East, recent earthquakes, and the tsunami in Asia are evidence that we are living in what the Bible calls the last days.

Remarkably, more than four out of ten Americans (42 percent) said they agreed. And common stereotypes notwithstanding, it was not just white Anglo-Saxon Protestants or rural, Bible Belt, southern men who said they agreed.

- One in three Jews believe we are living in the last days.
- One in three New Englanders believe we are living in the last days.
- One in three Americans on the "Left Coast" believe we are living in the last days.
- Four in ten Democrats believe we are in the last days.
- Four in ten Catholics believe we are in the last days.
- Half of all Republicans believe we are in the last days.
- Half of all women believe we are in the last days.
- Nearly half of all senior citizens believe we are in the last days.
- Nearly six in ten young people age eighteen to twenty-five believe we are in the last days.
- And a whopping 75 percent of African-Americans believe we are in the last days.

The numbers were even more surprising when we narrowed the question.

The rebirth of the State of Israel in 1948 and the return of millions of Jews to the Holy Land after centuries in exile represent the fulfillment of biblical prophecies.

This time, a remarkable 52 percent of all Americans said they agreed. Only 22 percent said they disagreed, while 26 percent either did not know or chose not to answer the question. And again, belief was not limited to the "usual suspects."

- Seven out of ten self-described evangelical Christians believe Israel is a prophecy that has come true before our very eyes, as would be expected. But so do half of all Catholics (52 percent) and nearly six in ten American Jews (57 percent).
- Two out of three conservative Republicans believe modern Israel is the fulfillment of Bible prophecy, but so do nearly half of self-described liberal Democrats (44 percent).
- Six in ten Southerners agree, but so do nearly half of all New Englanders (47 percent) and half of all Americans from the "Left Coast" (48 percent).
- Half of white Americans agree, but so do nearly half of all Hispanics (46 percent) and fully six in ten African-Americans.

THE ROAD AHEAD

Just because tens of millions of Americans say they believe that Bible prophecy is coming true before their eyes or that they are living in the last days does not, of course, mean they are aware of the specific events the Bible says are right around the corner. In the chapters ahead, therefore, I will lay out ten future headlines we will read, the scriptural basis of such predictions, and the latest events and trends that suggest such headlines may be closer than previously thought.

ISRAEL DISCOVERS MASSIVE RESERVES OF OIL, GAS

When I began writing the Last Jihad series, I based it in large part on prophecies in the book of Ezekiel that indicate two things that must occur before Israel's last-days showdown with Russia and Iran. The first "prerequisite" is that there must be a period of calm and stability in Israel before the War of Gog and Magog. The second is that Israel must build up significant wealth.

In the next chapter, I will discuss the "peace prerequisite." But first I want to take a look at the "prosperity prerequisite" from Ezekiel 38. In this passage, the ancient prophet is conveying a message from God to a future dictator of Russia:

> After many days you [dictator of Russia] will be summoned; in the latter years you will come into the land that is restored from the sword, whose inhabitants have been gathered from many nations to the mountains of Israel which had been a continual waste; but its people were brought out from the nations,

and they are living securely, all of them. . . . And you will say, "I will go up against the land of unwalled villages. I will go against those who are at rest, that live securely, all of them living without walls and having no bars or gates, to capture spoil and to seize plunder, to turn your hand against the waste places which are now inhabited, and against the people who are gathered from the nations, who have acquired cattle and goods, who live at the center of the world." Sheba and Dedan [ancient names for modern-day Saudi Arabia and the Gulf states] and the merchants of Tarshish [historically southern Spain, though it could refer more generally to Europe or the Mediterranean states] with all its villages will say to you [the Russian dictator], "Have you come to capture spoil? Have you assembled your company to seize plunder, to carry away silver and gold, to take away cattle and goods, to capture great spoil?" (Ezekiel 38:8, 11-13, NASB)

It's important to note that this passage comes *after* the rebirth of the modern State of Israel prophesied in chapter 36 yet *before* the Russian-Iranian attack. According to the passage, prior to the attack

- the Jews have poured back into the land of Israel;
- the Jews are settling and in the process rebuilding the ancient ruins and "formerly desolate cities" of Israel— that is, there is a building boom under way;
- the Israelis have become wealthy enough to acquire silver, gold, livestock, and other material goods;
- Israel is so wealthy that even the Saudis and those who live in the Gulf states can see that Russia and her allies covet Israel's treasures.

Ezekiel 36:11 provides yet another clue: "I will increase not only the people [in the land of Israel], but also your animals. O mountains of Israel, I will bring people to live on you once again. *I will make you even more prosperous than you were before.* Then you will know that I am the

LORD" (emphasis added). *That would be quite a development,* I thought when I first read this passage. After all, when Solomon was king of Israel, he was one of the wealthiest men in the world. Yet Ezekiel was saying that modern Israel would be wealthier still.

In *The Coming Peace in the Middle East,* Dr. LaHaye had considered a number of ways that Israel could become so peaceful and prosperous. Among them: "Suppose that a pool of oil, greater than anything in Arabia . . . were discovered by the Jews. . . . This would change the course of history. Before long, Israel would be able independently to solve its economic woes, finance the resettlement of the Palestinians, and supply housing for Jews and Arabs in the West Bank, East Bank, or anywhere else they might choose to live. Even if something besides oil were discovered, it would have the same far-reaching effect if it were able to produce high revenues."[1]

When I first read that, I nearly laughed. *Oil in Israel? Wouldn't that be nice?* Israelis have long complained that if they are really the chosen people, why in the world didn't God resettle them in Saudi Arabia? As the late prime minister Golda Meir once put it, "Moses dragged us for forty years through the desert to bring us to the one place in the Middle East where there was no oil!"[2] But the more I thought about LaHaye's theory, the more it seemed exactly like something God would do—unveil a dramatic plot twist near the end of the story.

Then in the fall of 2000, as I was working for Sharansky and Netanyahu, the *New York Times* published two headlines that captured my attention:

GAS DEPOSITS OFF ISRAEL AND GAZA OPENING VISIONS OF JOINT VENTURES

The New York Times, SEPTEMBER 15, 2000

ARAFAT HAILS BIG GAS FIND OFF THE COAST OF GAZA STRIP

The New York Times, SEPTEMBER 28, 2000

Wrote reporter William Orme: "Drilling deep below the seas off Israel and the Gaza Strip, foreign energy companies are discovering gas reserves that could lift the Palestinian economy and give Israel its first taste of energy independence. Industry experts, including those on this giant platform, say the Palestinians and Israelis will both profit if they can work together in a high-stakes partnership."[3]

What's more, experts had calculated that Israel had "some three to five trillion cubic feet of proven gas reserves," and according to Yehezkel Druckman, Israel's petroleum commissioner, "there may be more." At current prices, Orme reported, "the value of the strike was estimated [at] $2 billion to $6 billion, depending on pressure, quantity, and other variables."[4]

Israel? Proven reserves? Billions? When I read those words, the hair on the back of my neck stood up. True, the stories spoke only of natural gas, not a massive oil strike. But what if Commissioner Druckman was right? What if this was only the beginning? What if there was more where that came from?

By the time I sat down to write *Jihad*, I had decided to add a fictional oil strike—discovered by a fictional American investment company working with a fictional Israeli company called Medexco, run by a fictional Russian Jewish petroleum engineer named Dmitri Galishnikov. I did so not because I believed that the Bible *specifically* predicted it, but because it suddenly seemed plausible, and I wanted this thriller to seem as realistic as humanly possible.

Little did I know.

BLACK GOLD

Just days before *Jihad* was released in November 2002, a curious headline flashed across the newswires: **"Israeli Geologist Drills for Oil Based on Biblical Guidance."** The article told the story of Tovia Luskin, an Orthodox Jew born and raised in Russia who became so convinced by studying the Bible that there was black gold buried under the sands of the Jewish state that he moved to Israel, conducted extensive research, launched a limited partnership called Givot Olam, and came to the conclusion that "there are 65 million barrels of oil" in central Israel alone.[5]

There was just one problem. Tovia Luskin was wrong. A year later, just before *The Last Days* was published, the news broke that Luskin and his colleagues had discovered oil reservoirs at their Meged-4 drilling site in central Israel holding not 65 million barrels but *100 million barrels*.[6] A few months later came even more stunning news: new testing had revealed that the Givot Olam site contained not 100 million barrels but upward of a *billion* barrels, leading the Associated Press to report, "An Israeli oil company has made the largest oil find in the history of the country" and driving Givot Olam shares on the Tel Aviv Stock Exchange up 30 percent.[7]

People e-mailed me from all over the country to see if I had seen the stories and to ask me yet again if my novels were coming true. But the gusher of headlines about oil in Israel had only just begun to flow.

NATURAL GAS, OIL FOUND IN DEAD SEA
Jerusalem Post, APRIL 1, 2004

ISRAEL STRIKES BLACK GOLD
ARUTZ SHEVA, MAY 4, 2004

OIL BARON SEEKS GUSHER FROM GOD IN ISRAEL
REUTERS, APRIL 4, 2005

IN ISRAEL, OIL QUEST IS BASED ON FAITH
Wall Street Journal, MAY 1, 2005

HIS MISSION: SEEK AND YE SHALL FIND OIL
USA Today, MAY 19, 2005

A VISION OF OIL IN THE HOLY LAND
Newsweek, JUNE 13, 2005

MOSES' OILY BLESSING: WILL ISRAEL FIND OIL?
The Economist, JUNE 18, 2005

SEARCHING FOR OIL IN ISRAEL

CBS News, September 20, 2005

IS ISRAEL SITTING ON AN ENORMOUS OIL RESERVE?

WorldNetDaily, September 21, 2005

The story in the respected London-based *Economist* magazine particularly caught my eye. It turned out that Tovia Luskin was not the only businessman who believed the Bible talked specifically about the existence of oil in Israel: "In the 1980s, John Brown, a Catholic Texan cutting-tools executive, and Tovia Luskin, a Russian Jewish geophysicist and career oilman, both had religious epiphanies. Mr. Brown became a born-again Christian, while Mr. Luskin joined the Orthodox Jewish Lubavitch movement. Soon after, each found inspiration in chapter 33 of the book of Deuteronomy, in which Moses, nearing death after guiding the tribes of Israel to the border of the Promised Land, leaves each tribe with a blessing."[8]

The article went on to describe the blessing Moses gave to Ephraim and Manasseh, two tribes descended from Joseph: "Their land, says Moses, will yield the 'precious fruits' of 'the deep lying beneath,' of the 'ancient mountains' and of the 'everlasting hills.'"

Luskin believed Moses was giving "a classic description of an oil trap." The name of his company, Givot Olam, means "everlasting hills." According to the article, John Brown came to a similar conclusion, founding his own company, Zion Oil, in the hope of discovering the treasures Moses had described.

Intrigued, I tracked down Luskin at his office in Jerusalem and chatted with him by phone about all the headlines he was generating.

Luskin, a graduate of Moscow State University with a degree in geology and a love for oil exploration, explained that he left Russia in 1976 and moved to Canada, where he worked for Shell Oil and other petroleum companies. Later he worked for oil companies in Indonesia and Australia before immigrating to Israel with his family in 1990.

"Initially," he told me, "I came to the idea of looking for oil in Israel from reading the *Chumash*, the first five books of Moses. And then I came to Israel and started studying the geology here. . . . When I got the Israeli geological data it was striking in that it was very similar to the Syrian Basin, which seemed to me to extend down to Israel, which turned out to be exactly right. . . . Since 1993, we've drilled three wells and all three wells encountered oil. It's a big oil field."

"So, how close are you to commercial production?" I asked him.

"We are about to start a new well," he said. "Hopefully this well will take us to production stage. Eventually, we will probably need to drill around forty wells."[9]

OIL AT ARMAGEDDON?

In August 2005, while on the *Ezekiel Option* book tour, I had lunch in Dallas with Gene Soltero, the president and CEO of Zion Oil, the company founded by John Brown. I had never heard of the MIT-trained economist and petroleum engineer before, but I took a liking to him immediately. Balding, with short tufts of gray hair over each ear and small, wire-rimmed glasses, Soltero was a soft-spoken man in his sixties who looked more like a professor of management at some college in the American Midwest than a treasure hunter in the Mideast. But he had quite a story to tell, and a lot of questions for me.

On a recent visit to Israel, an investor in his company had picked up a paperback copy of *The Last Jihad* in Ben Gurion International Airport. He'd read it on the plane home and gotten so excited about it that he had e-mailed Soltero and everyone else in the company, urging that they read it too. Why? Because to Soltero and his colleagues, the discovery of oil in the Holy Land described in the novel wasn't fiction. It was their lives.

As Soltero explained it, all the top executives in the company quickly read *Jihad* and *The Last Days*. The more Soltero and his colleagues read, the more intrigued they got. How had I come up with such an oil-and-gas story line? Did I know about all the biblical prophecies that said Israel would, in fact, discover oil in the last days? More to the point, did I know just how close their company and others were to seeing these prophecies come to pass?

I had questions of my own.

What had gotten him involved in such a risky and speculative hunt for oil in the Holy Land? What exactly were these prophecies upon which he and Brown and Luskin were basing their companies? And what did he believe the future held?

As we shared our stories, Soltero, who had worked in the oil-and-gas business for more than four decades, explained that he joined Zion Oil not long after Brown had founded the company in 2000 because Brown had such a compelling way of looking at Israel. Soltero didn't use this terminology, but what he meant was that Brown looked at Israel through the third lens.

In 1981 Brown had visited a church in Clawson, Michigan. There he heard a sermon by the Reverend James Spillman, who wrote a short book called *The Great Treasure Hunt*.

In his book Spillman argued:

Biblical prophecy describes an event in which the armies of the world, led by Gog and Magog, would invade Israel "to take a spoil." What could Israel possibly possess in the last days that would make it such a prize for conquest that the world's armies would meet there to fight for the spoils? . . . Countries don't invade their neighbors for pomegranates and olive oil, but they do go to war over another kind of oil. Petroleum. . . . The problem, however, is that Israel is an oil poor country. Fifty years of oil exploration and production in Israel have produced about 20 million barrels total. That's a little over two days of the oil production coming out of Saudi Arabia. Armies will go to war over oil, but not two days' worth. But what if a significant amount of oil were discovered in Israel?[10]

That night Spillman made a similar case to Brown and the rest of the assembled congregation, then walked them through a series of Old Testament passages describing God's ancient promise to unlock enormous wealth and treasures for the children of Israel in the last days.

- **Genesis 49:1**—And Jacob called unto his sons, and said, "Gather yourselves together, that I may tell you that which shall befall you *in the last days.*" (KJV, emphasis added)
- **Genesis 49:25**—From the God of your father who helps you, and by the Almighty who blesses you with blessings of heaven above, *blessings of the deep that lies beneath,* blessings of the breasts and of the womb. (NASB, emphasis added)
- **Deuteronomy 33:13**—Of Joseph he said, "Blessed of the LORD be his land, with the choice things of heaven, with the dew, and *from the deep lying beneath.*" (NASB, emphasis added)
- **Deuteronomy 33:19**—They will call peoples to the mountain; there they will offer righteous sacrifices; for they will draw out the abundance of the seas, and *the hidden treasures of the sand.* (NASB, emphasis added)
- **Deuteronomy 33:24**—Of Asher he said, *"More blessed than sons is Asher; may he be favored by his brothers, and may he dip his foot in oil."* (NASB, emphasis added)
- **Deuteronomy 32:12-13**—*The LORD alone guided him,* and there was no foreign god with him. He made him ride on the high places of the earth, and he ate the produce of the field; *and He made him suck honey from the rock, and oil from the flinty rock.* (NASB, emphasis added)
- **Isaiah 45:3**—I will give you *the treasures of darkness and hidden wealth of secret places,* so that you may know that it is I, the LORD, the God of Israel, who calls you by your name. (NASB, emphasis added)

As Soltero explained it, John Brown was electrified. He went home and carefully studied these Scriptures and many others Spillman had laid out, asking God to help him understand them and know how, if at all, he could be involved in finding such a treasure. For the next two decades, Brown traveled back and forth to Israel, learning everything about the oil-and-gas business he possibly could, meeting everyone in the industry that he could, studying maps, researching locations, cross-checking with the Scriptures, and praying for wisdom all the while. By April of 2000, he finally felt he knew enough to begin a company. He launched Zion Oil with the help of an Israeli lawyer named Philip Mandelker, using the following mission statement:

> Zion Oil & Gas was ordained by G_d[11] for the express purpose of discovering oil and gas in the land of Israel and to bless the Jewish people and the nation of Israel and the body of Christ (Isaiah 23:18). I believe that G_d has promised in the Bible to bless Israel with one of the world's largest oil and gas fields and this will be discovered in the last days before the Messiah returns.[12]

The company was soon awarded a license by the government of Israel to explore for oil and gas on 28,800 acres in northern Israel, and it was during this time that Gene Soltero joined the company.

"So how is it going?" I asked.

"We were recently awarded an expanded permit to explore some 219,000 acres in northern Israel," Soltero told me. "We've been drilling for the past several months and the initial results are very exciting. For legal reasons, I can't say more right now. But let's just say it's possible that your novels have vastly understated how much oil is out there."

As he described where they were drilling, I realized it was only a few miles from the Jezreel Valley and the ancient city of Megiddo. "Wait a minute," I said. "Are you telling me you think you've found oil under Armageddon?"

Soltero smiled. "I wish I could say more, but right now I can't," he demurred.

In talking to other oil experts in Israel and the U.S. over the next few months, I was able to confirm that there is, in fact, both oil and natural gas under the region known in the Bible as Armageddon, where the Scriptures say the final cataclysmic conflict of history will occur. Just how much is there remains unclear as I write this. There is more testing to do, and many technical challenges abound before any of it will be commercially viable to pump and refine, challenges that Tovia Luskin and his team are encountering as well, despite having already found a billion barrels of oil not far away.

What intrigues me is that Zion Oil and Givot Olam are not alone in their efforts to examine Israel's economy and geology through the third lens of Scripture. Philip Mandelker, Zion Oil's lawyer, told me that their company is one of six whose founders were originally inspired to start drilling because of Old Testament passages.[13] And several of them are beginning to see promising results.

Will one of these companies hit the big one? Will they all? Will someone else? The truth is, we cannot know exactly who will tap into the oil reserves believed to be waiting beneath Israel's soil or exactly when it will happen, because the Bible does not tell us. But the Bible *does* make it clear that Israel will be wealthy before the Russian-Iranian coalition attacks. That much we can take to the bank. And I believe the Bible's hints about the existence of oil in Israel present a viable means for the fulfillment of that prophecy. Thus, expect to read future headlines like this one: "**Israel Discovers Massive Reserves of Oil, Gas**."

ISRAEL, HOME OF MILLIONAIRES

That said, let's be clear: Israel has already become enormously wealthy over the last six decades—far wealthier than her immediate neighbors. Finding oil would simply be icing on an already impressive cake.

Despite a population of only 7 million people, for example, Israel is now home to more than 6,600 millionaires. Of these, seventy possess liquid assets of $30 million or more. Of the 500 wealthiest people in the world, six are now Israeli, and all told, Israel's rich had assets in 2004 of more than $24 billion, up from $20 billion in 2003, according to a report published by Merrill Lynch.[14]

Today Israel has become an economic powerhouse, one of the world's high-tech leaders, and a magnet for foreign investment. "Israel is like part of Silicon Valley," Microsoft founder Bill Gates said on his first trip to the country in October 2005. "The quality of the people

here is fantastic. . . . It's no exaggeration to say that the kind of inno-
vation going on in Israel is critical to the future of the technology
business. So many great companies have been started here."

In May 2006, Warren Buffett, the world's second-richest man,
announced that he was investing $4 billion in a Galilee-based metal-
working company. Given that this was the largest investment Buffet
had ever made outside the United States, it was widely seen as an enormous vote of confidence in the present vitality and the future potential
of the Israeli economy.[15]

No wonder, then, that more Israeli-based companies and companies started by Israelis are listed on NASDAQ than from any other
country. Or that Intel, whose next-generation chip was designed in
Israel, broke ground in February 2006 on a new $3.5 billion microchip
factory and research-and-development facility in the town of Kiryat
Gat and reported that it now has more employees in Israel than in Silicon Valley. Or that Google announced in 2005 that it was opening new
research-and-development facilities in Israel. Or that over the past
decade, more than $8.7 billion has poured into Israeli venture-capital
funds. Or that an Israeli professor, Robert Aumann of Hebrew University in Jerusalem, won the 2005 Nobel Prize for Economics.[16]

And it is not just high-tech successes that Israelis are experiencing
today. Israel now leads the world in exports of industrial oils, fertilizers,
and polished diamonds. In 2005 the tiny Jewish state placed eighth
worldwide in per capita exports. Tourism, too, is surging, climbing 26
percent in 2005 and up 78 percent in the number of first-time visitors.
The list of economic achievements could go on and on.[17]

That is not to say Israel does not still struggle with poverty, unemployment, and underemployment. It certainly does, and these are
challenges its leaders must constantly and compassionately address.
But Israel has made extraordinary—some would say miraculous—
economic gains since 1948 and has become dramatically wealthier than
any of its immediate neighbors.

What's more, Israel is poised for even more explosive economic
growth, quite apart from future oil and gas discoveries. Ben Gurion
International Airport has been expanded and modernized. New high-

MIDDLE EAST COUNTRIES GDP

COUNTRY	GROSS DOMESTIC PRODUCT
Israel	$123 billion
Egypt	$81 billion
Syria	$26 billion
Lebanon	$21 billion
Jordan	$12 billion

SOURCE: CIA WORLD FACT BOOK, 2005

ways and light railways are being built. Inflation, which raged at 100 percent or more a year in the early 1980s, was a mere 1.2 percent in 2004. Interest rates are historically low. The exchange rate has been stable. And after a serious recession in 2001–2002 due to the global economic downturn combined with the Al-Aksa Intifada (aka Arafat's War), growth is surging again, hitting 4.4 percent in 2004 and 5 percent in 2005.

In June 2005, I attended a $1,000-a-plate dinner with Benjamin Netanyahu at the St. Regis Hotel in New York. The evening was part of a fund-raising event for Israel's leading free-market-reform think tank, the Israel Center for Social and Economic Progress, run by Daniel Doron, who has been a friend and mentor of mine on all things Israel since the early 1990s.

That night Netanyahu, who was then serving as Ariel Sharon's finance minister, talked about the sweeping changes enacted during his tenure—deep tax cuts, privatization of state-owned industries, banking deregulation, and so forth—and the remarkable economic growth that had resulted. But he insisted there was much more to come.

"In ten years, Israel could be one of the ten richest countries in the world," Netanyahu explained, noting that nine of the ten wealthiest countries in the world are small countries with fewer than 10 million people each and that many of them were not on the list at all a decade or two ago.

Ireland, for example—a country of only about 4 million citizens, roughly two-thirds of Israel's population—was barely a blip on the global economic radar for most of the twentieth century, Netanyahu observed. By 2005, however, the Emerald Tiger had a roaring, low-tax economy and was ranked the eighth richest country in the world in GDP per capita.

"There is absolutely no reason why Israel can't soon become one of the most successful countries in the world," Netanyahu concluded.[18]

Looking back, I am grateful for the opportunity to attend that night. For whether he meant to or not, Netanyahu had just confirmed that Ezekiel's promise of a dazzling economic future for Israel in the last days was rapidly coming to pass.

TREATIES AND TRUCES LEAVE ISRAELIS MORE SECURE THAN EVER BEFORE

None of this remarkable prosperity in Israel would be possible, of course, without a significant degree of calm and stability. Such security has seemed almost impossible until recent years, yet this is precisely what Ezekiel tells us to anticipate.

Note that the Hebrew prophet does not go so far as to say there will be a comprehensive peace treaty between Israel and all of her neighbors, or that all—or even most—hostilities in the Middle East will have ceased. But he does make it clear that in "the last days" (Ezekiel 38:16, NASB) before the Russian-Iranian attack, the Jewish people are "living securely" in "the land that is restored from the sword" (Ezekiel 38:8, NASB).

Some might say this is a bit of a conundrum. How could Israelis possibly feel secure in the last days if an increasingly hostile Russia, Iran, and other once-and-future enemies are looming over the horizon and preparing for the War of Gog and Magog? Moreover, how could this peace prerequisite possibly square with what Jesus told his disciples in Matthew 24:6, that in the last days before his return "you will be hearing of wars and rumors of wars"(NASB)?

Which is it? some are tempted to ask. War or peace? You can't have both.

Maybe you can. I would argue that we are seeing such a conundrum developing in the Middle East at this very hour.

In February 2005, for example, Israeli prime minister Ariel Sharon said he believed Israel was steadily approaching the point of a "historic breakthrough" with the Palestinians and "a new period of tranquility and hope."[1] Sharon was not a man known for being wildly optimistic about the prospects for peace in the region, so his comments turned a lot of heads. A few days later, I ran into a senior advisor to President Bush at the National Prayer Breakfast in Washington, DC. He told me the White House was surprisingly optimistic about striking a deal between both sides before the end of the president's second term. If so, he said, "we're about to make history."

In the summer of 2005, I had breakfast at the historic King David Hotel in Jerusalem with Major General Yaakov Amidror, former head of assessment for Israeli Military Intelligence. We were discussing Prime Minister Sharon's plan to withdraw unilaterally from Gaza (which would take place two months later) and how it might affect Israel's security down the road. In the course of that conversation, I asked Amidror to sum up Israel's current security situation in light of everything he knew and everything going on in the region. His answer intrigued me.

"Unless or until Iran gets nuclear weapons, Israel today is more strategically secure than at any other point since her birth," Amidror said unequivocally. By way of explanation, he pointed to a number of specific recent developments:

- The Soviet Union has collapsed.
- Saddam Hussein and his regime are gone.
- Yasser Arafat is dead.
- Israel has a formal peace treaty with Egypt.
- Israel has a formal peace treaty with Jordan.
- The Syrians are withdrawing from Lebanon.
- Israel has a strong, well-trained, well-equipped army.

- Israel has the most advanced and effective air force not just in the region but in the world.
- Israel's Arrow missile defense system is steadily improving.
- Through better intelligence, targeted assassinations of Palestinian terrorist leaders and operatives, the security fence around Gaza, and the partially completed security fence in the West Bank, Israel has become increasingly successful at stopping suicide bombings and other attacks. (Terrorist attacks dropped nearly 70 percent between 2001 and 2005.)[2]
- The U.S. is a strong and steady ally and has a forward strategy against terrorists and state sponsors of terrorism in the Middle East.
- Israel's economy is healthy and growing.

"And when I talk to those who worry about Israel's security," Amidror—an observantly religious Jew—told me, "I pull out a copy of the Bible and say, 'Ultimately, we have security in God.'"[3]

He was right on all accounts, of course. Looking at Israel's current security status through geopolitical and economic lenses, the situation is far more favorable than most Westerners realize—until Iran gets the bomb. And looking through the third lens of Scripture, it is clear that the God of Israel is in charge, no matter what happens with Russia, Iran, Hamas, or other current or future enemies.

Anyone who has been to Israel recently can attest to experiencing this conundrum for him- or herself. On one hand, media reports in Israel as well as in the U.S., Europe, and elsewhere are often filled with talk of "wars and rumors of wars." On the other hand, day-to-day life in Israel feels very peaceful. People are not paralyzed by fear of what could be. They are going to work, to the malls, to the movie theaters, to the beaches and the mountains, nearly as anyone in a truly peaceful country would.

What's more, if you read the headlines carefully, you will spot stories not only about Iran and Hamas but also about historic and often counterintuitive new trends toward peace in the region. Among them:

THE INTIFADA IS FINISHED

CHARLES KRAUTHAMMER, NATIONALLY SYNDICATED COLUMN, JUNE 21, 2005

EGYPTIAN LEADER PRAISES SHARON

AGENCE FRANCE-PRESSE, AUGUST 9, 2005

ISRAEL AND PAKISTAN HOLD FIRST HIGH-LEVEL MEETING

The New York Times, SEPTEMBER 1, 2005

PAKISTAN, ISRAEL IN LANDMARK TALKS

BBC NEWS, SEPTEMBER 1, 2005

BAHRAIN, KUWAIT TO MEND ISRAELI TIES

ASSOCIATED PRESS, SEPTEMBER 24, 2005

BREACHING A TABOO, KUWAITIS TALK OF SOFTER STAND ON ISRAEL

International Herald Tribune, OCTOBER 6, 2005

KUWAIT PAPERS PROPOSE NORMAL TIES WITH ISRAEL

REUTERS, OCTOBER 8, 2005

ISRAEL, JORDAN MARK 11 YEARS OF PEACE TWO-WAY TRADE REACHED $185 MILLION LAST YEAR, UP 41% OVER 2003

ASSOCIATED PRESS, OCTOBER 26, 2005

ISRAEL, ARAB WORLD ENGAGE IN HIDDEN TRADE EXPERTS SAY CAMOUFLAGED TRADE BETWEEN ISRAEL, ARAB COUNTRIES HAS BEEN GOING ON FOR YEARS

ASSOCIATED PRESS, DECEMBER 26, 2005

On September 10, 2005—just a day before the fourth anniversary of the Al-Qaeda attacks on New York and Washington—I posted an item on my weblog noting the historic news that Pakistan had begun to move publicly toward diplomatic ties with Israel, a previously unthinkable development.

- First, Pakistan's Foreign Minister recently met with Israel's Foreign Minister, another Muslim country with whom Israel has diplomatic ties.
- Then came the news in the Islamic world media that Pakistan has been having secret diplomatic contacts with Israel for years.
- Then Israel revealed more details about secret diplomatic contact with Pakistan over the years.
- Then Pakistan's President Gen. Pervez Musharraf publicly praised Sharon as "courageous" for withdrawing from Gaza. "I think such actions need courage and boldness," Musharraf said. "What we have seen on the TV, Israelis not wanting to leave, being forced out, is a courageous thing to do. We hope that he shows [an] equal amount of courage finally in the creation of the Palestinian state."
- If that weren't enough, Palestinian Prime Minister Mahmoud Abbas publicly said he welcomed Pakistan's diplomatic contact with Israel.

"The foreign ministers of Israel and Pakistan, a Muslim country that has long taken a hard line against the Jewish state, met publicly for the first time Thursday, a diplomatic breakthrough that follows Israel's withdrawal from the Gaza Strip," reported the *New York Times*. "Israeli Foreign Minister Silvan Shalom hailed the meeting as 'historic' and said that following the Gaza withdrawal it is 'the time for all of the Muslim and Arab countries to reconsider their relations with Israel.'"[4]

As 2005 came to a close, Lt. General Dan Halutz, the chief of general staff for the Israeli Defense Forces, gave an address at Tel Aviv University in which he summed up the apparent conundrum between war and peace.

On one hand, he warned that "economic sanctions won't stop Iran's determined efforts to acquire nuclear weapons" and that "Israel needs to prepare for the worst existential threat in its history."

On the other hand, echoing Major General Amidror, Halutz said that ironically Israel was now enjoying one of the most secure seasons in its modern history. "I believe that our strategic reality at the moment is the best ever for the state. . . . When I look about, I find it difficult to see an Arab coalition rising against Israel. There is no unifying interest today for the Arab nations as there [was] in the past."[5]

THE BEAR HUG

So which is it? Are Israel and her neighbors moving closer to war or to peace?

Nowhere was this conundrum more vividly on display for me than at the "Peace: Dream or Vision?" conference I attended in Israel in the fall of 2005, commemorating the tenth anniversary of the assassination of Yitzhak Rabin, the beloved Israeli prime minister who signed the historic peace treaty with Jordan's King Hussein in 1994.

Outside the conference center at the Strategic Dialogue Center of Netanya Academic College were all the reminders of the "wars and rumors of wars" that Jesus said would plague the world until his return—a phalanx of heavily armed security guards, metal detectors, bomb-sniffing dogs, and so forth. To get in I had to not only show my passport to the security staff but give it to them to hold on to until I left, and my camera, camera bag, tape recorder, and briefcase were all searched carefully—as was I—before I was allowed to proceed.

But inside were all the reminders of Israelis "living securely" in "the land that is restored from the sword," which Ezekiel predicted. One moment I was watching former Mossad chief Danny Yatom chatting like old buds with Dr. Abdel Salam Majali, the former Jordanian prime minister, and Osama El-Baz, the chief political advisor to Egyptian president Hosni Mubarak. The next moment I was watching Saeb Erekat, the Palestinian chief negotiator, give a bear hug to former Israeli prime minister Shimon Peres. Once they were all enemies. Now they were all friends. Once they were plotting each other's demise. Now they were talking about their shared vision for a "new Middle East."

Such warm relationships between Arab and Israeli leaders may seem insignificant, but they most certainly are not. They actually represent enormous progress toward resolving the conflict. Let me give you a little anecdote to provide some context.

In April of 1988, ABC's Ted Koppel took *Nightline* to Israel for a week of broadcasts on the outbreak of the Palestinian uprising known as the intifada and the increasingly desperate need for peace and reconciliation between the two sides. Having recently returned to the States after nearly six months in Israel, where I had studied at Tel Aviv University and witnessed the outbreak of the intifada, I watched Koppel's show with great interest every night in my dorm room at Syracuse University.

On April 25, Koppel held the first-ever town hall meeting between Israelis and Palestinians, broadcast live from the historic Jerusalem Theater. It was bound to be riveting television, for never before had Israeli and Palestinian leaders sat on the same stage together, much less engaged in anything close to a dialogue. But when the show began, I was surprised to see a three-foot-high stone wall running down the middle of the stage. The Israelis sat on one side, the Palestinians on the other. It was a sad symbol of the divide between the two peoples.

Years later, I was interviewed by Koppel on *Nightline*. After the taping was finished, I had the opportunity to ask Koppel about that wall. "It came up at almost the last minute," he explained, remembering the moment vividly. "We were just a few hours from going on live from Jerusalem—at 6:30 in the morning, Israel time, mind you, so that the show would be on at 11:30 p.m. back in the U.S.—and suddenly the Palestinians said they refused to appear onstage with the Israelis without sitting in a booth, so they didn't appear to actually be talking to the Israelis. We said absolutely not. So they asked that we put razor wire down the center of the stage, and again we said no. Finally, they asked that we build a wall—just a small wall, they said—to represent how divided Arabs and Jews are. They threatened not to appear at all if we didn't do it, so we did it. It was an amazing night."[6]

It certainly was. And one of the Palestinians who appeared onstage that night was Saeb Erekat. Then he had refused to shake hands with the Israelis. He had barely made eye contact with them. And he had demanded a wall. Now, at the peace conference in Netanya, he was giving bear hugs. How much the world had changed.[7]

"A NEW AGE" IN THE MIDDLE EAST?

Shimon Peres is a living legend in Israel and is one of the country's founding fathers. I have long disagreed with his Socialist economic views and a foreign policy too dovish, in my opinion. But I have always respected this man who served his country not once but three times as prime minister and in numerous other ministerial positions and who won the Nobel Peace Prize in 1994.

I had never met the former prime minister before that conference in Netanya, but having worked for Benjamin Netanyahu—who defeated Peres in 1996—I was very much looking forward to it.

Now in his eighties, Peres is quieter and slower and more grandfatherly than he once was, but he is still a dreamer. He told the assembled dignitaries that he believes the Middle East is entering "a new age" and that he has never been more optimistic that a final peace agreement with the Palestinians can be reached in the not-too-distant future.

"The Lord is in charge of the beginning and the end, but we are responsible for the middle," he said, insisting that there is no contradiction between fighting terror and negotiating for peace. "When a cat is chasing a mouse, there's no sense for the mouse to ask for a cease-fire. He must deal with the cat and insure his own safety."

After Peres's keynote address, I had a few minutes to interview the former prime minister. "Is it your sense that Israel is more secure today—before we get to the point of the Iran nuclear bomb—than it has been in its history so far?" I asked.

Peres agreed with that assessment. "I would say that Israel's security was globalized," he explained in his distinctive, gravelly voice, suggesting that with the U.S. as a strong ally, the fall of Saddam, and peace treaties in place with Egypt and Jordan, the threat Israel faces today is "the problem of terror, rather than a classical attack" by a conventional Arab army or air force.[8]

Had the passing of Arafat—the Nobel Peace Prize winner who never actually made peace—helped or hurt the prospects for a final deal with the Palestinians? I wondered.

"With him, [the peace process] wouldn't have started," Peres insisted. "With him, it wouldn't be finished."

When Peres's address was complete, attention turned to Saeb Erekat—the bald, tanned, fiery chief diplomatic spokesman for the Palestinian Authority—who delivered remarks on behalf of President Mahmoud Abbas. Erekat was as passionate as ever but not nearly as provocative as I had heard him in the past. To the contrary, he said he believed "it's probable that we would have had peace if Mr. Rabin had not been assassinated" and called Israel's evacuation from Gaza "an historic step." And then he stunned me and much of the audience by saying that he and Abbas believed the end of the conflict with Israel was not only in sight but within reach.

"We are prepared to make a final settlement with Israel," Erekat said, explicitly on behalf of Abbas. "We have the experience. We have the knowledge. We have learned from our mistakes. . . . We need no more than six months to conclude a final peace agreement with the Israelis. . . . What we are going through now are labor pains."

Erekat went on to clarify that neither Abbas nor he was saying that a final deal would be wrapped up six months from *then*, November 2005. But they were saying that once Palestinians and Israelis held elections, put their governments in place, and finally came back to the negotiating table ready to get serious, enough of the diplomatic work had already been done that both sides were now truly within striking distance of a historic deal.

After Erekat stepped down from the podium, I met with him outside the conference center to press him on that point.

"You really think you're within *six months* of a deal?" I asked, still wondering if I had heard him right.

Apparently I had. Erekat not only confirmed what he had told the roomful of Arab and Israeli diplomats, ex-military leaders, professors, political analysts, and students. He went further.

"What people don't know is that me and my [Israeli] colleagues in the last days of [the administration of Israeli prime minister Ehud] Barak drafted three chapters of a permanent status treaty." Most of the work was finished, he told me. "You don't need to reinvent the wheel now. We know what it's going to take."

Still a bit taken aback, I asked him, "Isn't this the most optimistic a Palestinian negotiator has ever been?"

He shook his head. "Look, I don't base anything on optimism or pessimism. But when I say this line on behalf of my president, I know what I'm talking about. . . . We're doing this because we realize it's not a zero-sum game. . . . Two states. This is it. You want it? Okay, then let's do it."[9]

DOES HAMAS NIX PROSPECTS FOR PEACE?

All this talk of a final peace deal was before the radical Islamic movement Hamas was voted into leadership in the Palestinian parliament by a landslide election in January 2006. And before Ariel Sharon's stroke and subsequent coma. And Iran's threat to "wipe Israel off the face of the map." And the Kremlin's invitation for Hamas leaders to wine and dine in Moscow. But despite the assessment by many that the Hamas victory nullified any prospects for a peace deal, several important voices in the region say that is not necessarily the case.

Israeli prime minister Ehud Olmert is one such voice. Convinced that Israel is more secure than at any other time in its modern history, he has vowed to draw Israel's final, permanent borders by 2010, with or without a Palestinian partner. He says that he will wait for a while to see if Hamas will renounce violence and accept Israel's right to exist. But, he adds, "I don't intend to wait forever." If the Palestinians do not or cannot step forward to negotiate a final agreement, Olmert will unilaterally decide upon "Israel's permanent borders, whereby we will completely separate from the majority of the Palestinian population." His plans call for Israel's withdrawing from roughly 80 to 90 percent of Judea and Samaria (commonly known as the West Bank) while annexing major Jewish settlement blocs around Jerusalem and retaining the strategic Jordan Valley as a buffer zone against any future ground-force attacks from the east. Such plans also include dividing Jerusalem and allowing the Palestinians to declare part of Jerusalem as their own capital.

Shaul Mofaz, a top military advisor to the prime minister, confirms that Olmert prefers to negotiate the final agreement with the Palestinians based on the Road Map drafted by the Bush administration, but he says, "If we see that we do not have a partner, then I think we will need to take our fate into our own hands and make a decision where it is right to be and where it is not right to be."[10]

As the Palestinians' chief negotiator, Saeb Erekat is another voice saying the Hamas victory is not a deal killer. "We urge Mr. Olmert to resume permanent status negotiations with us," says Erekat, though he adds that "the road to peace and security in the region is not through unilateralism, the building of walls and settlements."[11]

Erekat's boss, Palestinian president Mahmoud Abbas, agrees. "We are in a historic period, in which we must decide whether we will move toward peace and a better future for our children," Abbas told *Haaretz*, one of Israel's leading daily newspapers. "I can promise that you have a partner for this peace. . . . The leadership of both peoples and also of the international community has a supreme responsibility to exploit this opportunity. It may be the last hope to accord the two peoples their right to live in security and stability. The coming generations will not forgive us if we let it slip by."[12]

Abbas noted that despite the Hamas victory, a majority of Palestinians reject the Hamas platform of liquidating Israel. "If we reach an agreement [with Israel]," he insisted, "I will be the one to sign it. If needed, I will put it to a referendum. I received 62 percent in the elections, in which I condemned violence outspokenly. I am certain that I will also succeed in getting a majority for a peace agreement."

But Abbas warned that time is of the essence and that the opportunity must not be allowed to slip away. "According to [the] Oslo [Accords], we were supposed to reach a final status agreement by May

1999, and we saw what happened," the Palestinian leader told *Haaretz*. "Yitzhak Rabin was assassinated. Shimon Peres lost the elections, and Benjamin Netanyahu destroyed everything. I am proposing to you to sit now and discuss the end of the conflict. I [have] proposed to [Shimon] Peres and the Americans to open a back channel of talks, far from the spotlight. And I am convinced that . . . we will be able to sign an agreement."

In June of 2006, I discussed Abbas's views with General Nasser Youssef and Abdel Salam Majali.

Youssef once served as a senior military advisor to Yasser Arafat but became disillusioned by the rampant corruption in the Palestinian Authority and the lack of real peace and prosperity for the Palestinian people despite years of negotiations with the Israelis. In fact, in September 2003, when Youssef was appointed interior minister, he actually called Arafat "the most incompetent revolutionary leader in history" to Arafat's face.[13] Today he serves as national security advisor to the Palestinian chairman, a position that almost cost him his life when radical Islamic gunmen shot up his house in January 2006 while he was inside.

Majali was the prime minister of Jordan who took the lead in negotiating the peace treaty between Jordan and Israel and actually signed the treaty with Israel in 1994. Today he serves in the Jordanian senate and remains a top advisor to King Abdullah II.

Remarkably, both men share Abbas's optimism about hammering out a final peace deal with Israel in the not-too-distant future. In fact, they believe that such a deal should include some sort of formal federation or confederation between the Palestinian entity and the kingdom of Jordan.

"All sides would benefit from such a relationship" between the Palestinians and Jordan, says Youssef. "I believe Palestinians will achieve their hopes of achieving a state by working closely with Jordan."[14]

Majali, who first floated the idea of such a West Bank–Jordanian alliance in 1988, suggests the new entity be called the "United Arab States" or the "United Hashemite States" and be patterned after the European Union or the "Benelux" countries of Belgium, the Netherlands, and Luxembourg. There would essentially be two distinct states—one Palestinian and one Jordanian—but they would be tied together diplomatically, militarily, and economically. Citizens would choose their nationality, either Jordanian or Palestinian, on their passports and ID cards. Both governments would be democratic. Militants would be arrested or deported. And the leadership of the entity would rotate between a Jordanian and a Palestinian executive every four years.

"This idea could really be the light at the end of the tunnel" of the Arab-Israeli conflict, says Majali. "A Palestinian state alone is not going to be viable. . . . But a confederation with Jordan will give Palestinians the prospect of being part of a truly functioning and successful state. It will give Jordanians assurance that the West Bank won't become a breeding ground for radicals and militants. And it will give the Israelis the assurance that Jordan will help maintain internal security as well as a secure border to the East. . . . You have to give the Israelis the feeling of security, otherwise the Palestinians will never get a state."[15]

Are Olmert, Abbas, and these others only dreaming? Perhaps, and events in the region are far too volatile to make any predictions about when a final agreement between the Israelis and Palestinians will happen or what such an agreement will look like.

What's more, I should note here that while I strongly support giving the Palestinians autonomy to govern themselves without interference from Israel in return for true peace and stability in the lands run by the Palestinians, I personally oppose the notion of the State of Israel giving away the ancient lands of Judea and Samaria in order to create a sovereign Palestinian state that could become a base camp for anti-Israel and anti-Western terrorism and that could form alliances with radical Islamic regimes such as Iran, which would pose a clear and present danger to Israel, Jordan, and American interests in the region. But that is not the point of this chapter.

The point here is that never before in her modern history has Israel been so secure, so prosperous, so eager to give up land for peace, and—with Yasser Arafat off the political stage—seemingly so close to consummating the deal.

Could we see Israel sign a peace treaty with the Palestinians (and even other Arab nations, such as Lebanon or Syria) before the War of Gog and Magog unfolds? Yes, we could. Could the Jewish state discover massive reserves of oil and gas and become phenomenally wealthy before Moscow, Tehran, and their allies make their move against Israel? Yes, it could.

I certainly would not be surprised to see more signs of peace and prosperity, but with so many signs in place already, I am not convinced that more are needed. For the first time since the book of Ezekiel was written more than 2,500 years ago, it is now possible that the two prerequisites of relative peace and rising prosperity in Israel are already checked off God's to-do list, and that the rest of the prophecies will soon come true as well.

Israel has been reborn as a country. Millions of Jews have poured back into the Holy Land. The deserts have bloomed. The economy is booming. The ancient ruins are being rebuilt. Israel has signed peace treaties, truces, cease-fire agreements, and/or other diplomatic and economic accords with all of its immediate neighbors. It has all happened just as Ezekiel told us it would happen, and all of it begs the question: What will happen next?

A CZAR RISES IN RUSSIA, RAISING FEARS OF A NEW COLD WAR

A few months after *The Ezekiel Option* was published, I was invited to the United States Capitol to meet with some of the most powerful political leaders in the country. They had heard about the novel and were curious about my track record for writing fiction that had an eerie way of coming true. They were particularly intrigued by the notion that 2,500 years ago an ancient Hebrew prophet had been able to look down the corridors of time and see nations that were not yet born and alliances that were not yet formed. With all the events unfolding in Moscow, Tehran, and elsewhere, they wanted to know more.

As I began explaining the War of Gog and Magog and how it will profoundly affect U.S. foreign and domestic policy, as well as the entire global economy, one of the leaders asked if we could back up for a moment and go directly to the source. He wanted to read Ezekiel chapter 38 and better understand the prophecy itself before considering its implications. The others readily agreed.

I was a bit taken aback. I had never led a Bible study for such an influential group. But I appreciated the seriousness with which they took the matter. So we all pulled out copies of the Scriptures. I proceeded to read the first five verses of Ezekiel 38. Then each leader read another set of five verses until we had made it through the entire chapter.

The questions began to flow immediately. Who is Gog? What is Magog? Why don't the words *Russia*, *Soviet Union*, or *Moscow* ever appear in the text? Do such words appear elsewhere in the book of Ezekiel? If not, how could I be so certain that one day the world would see headlines announcing that a dictator has risen to power in Russia, is rebuilding the Russian military, and is drafting a plan to conquer the Middle East and destroy Israel?

These were excellent questions and took us right to the heart of the matter. Limited time permitted me to give only brief answers on Capitol Hill. But let me now walk you through the answers in a bit more detail. And let's start where these leaders did, by examining the prophecy itself.

In Ezekiel 38:2-4, God says to Ezekiel, "Son of man, set your face toward Gog of the land of Magog, the prince of Rosh, Meshech and Tubal, and prophesy against him and say, 'Thus says the Lord GOD, "Behold, I am against you, O Gog, prince of Rosh, Meshech and Tubal. I will turn you about and put hooks into your jaws, and I will bring you out, and all your army, horses and horsemen, all of them splendidly attired, a great company with buckler and shield, all of them wielding swords"'" (NASB).

Ezekiel 39:1 then restates the central actors in the prophecy so we do not miss them: "Son of man, prophesy against Gog and say, 'Thus says the Lord GOD, "Behold, I am against you, O Gog, prince of Rosh, Meshech and Tubal"'" (NASB).

As you can see for yourself, the words *Russia, Moscow, Soviet Union*, and *czar* never appear in these passages. Nor do they appear anywhere in the book of Ezekiel. Nor are they ever mentioned anywhere in the Bible. But there is no doubt that the ancient prophet was referring to the nation we now know as Russia.

Like so much intelligence obtained from a foreign source, this text is initially confusing. So let us break it down phrase by phrase.

The first thing we need to understand is that *Gog* is probably not actually a personal name, but more likely a title, like *czar* or *pharaoh*. Thus, we are not looking for the rise of a specific person whose first or last name is Gog so much as a "prince" who will arise in "the land of Magog" (Ezekiel 38:2), a geographic territory in the "remote parts of the north" (Ezekiel 38:15, NASB). In *The Ezekiel Option,* Dr. Eliezer Mordechai (a fictional former head of the Mossad, Israel's foreign intelligence agency) explains to Jon Bennett (a fictional senior White House advisor) that this means Gog is a political leader from a country due north of Israel. A quick check of any world map reveals that there are only five such countries today: Lebanon, Syria, Turkey, Ukraine, and Russia. The one farthest north, of course, is Russia.

As good intelligence analysts, however, let us not stop there. Let us keep digging to see what other clues we can find, particularly about this word *Magog.*

Curiously, one clue comes from Voltaire, the eighteenth-century French philosopher. He was hardly a religious man. Indeed, he was a self-declared enemy of Jesus Christ. Voltaire once wrote a letter to Frederick the Great, king of Germany at the time, arguing that Christianity "is assuredly the most ridiculous, the most absurd, and the most bloody religion which has ever infected this world."[1] Yet, for some reason, he was intrigued with solving the ancient riddle of Gog and Magog, and through his own research he became convinced—nearly 150 years before the rise of Russia as a major world power—that Magog was Russia.

"There is a genealogical tree of the events of the world," he wrote in *The Philosophical Dictionary*, noting that "it is incontestable that the inhabitants of Gaul and Spain are descended from Gomer, and the Russians from Magog, his younger brother."[2]

Interestingly enough, the genealogical tree to which he referred actually finds its origin in the very Bible for which he had so little regard. Magog is first mentioned in Genesis 10—Magog was a son of Japheth, who was a son of Noah (he of Noah's-ark fame). The Bible lays out Noah's entire family tree. It shows how Noah's descendants migrated to Africa, Europe, and Asia, establishing civilizations on those continents. In trying to decode the Gog and Magog prophecy, Voltaire studied Noah's genealogical tree, then compared it to the histories of these different continents in hopes of determining where each of Noah's descendents ended up.

Here the Roman historian Josephus can offer us another clue. In *The Antiquities of the Jews*, his twenty-volume classic written in the first century after Christ, Josephus wrote of the descendants of Noah: "After [attempting to build the tower of Babel—see Genesis 11] they were dispersed abroad, on account of their languages, and went out by colonies everywhere; and each colony took possession of that land which they light upon and unto which God led them. . . . Magog founded those that from him were named Magogites, but who are by the Greeks called Scythians."[3]

The Scythians, we learn from our history books, were absolute barbarians—expert horsemen but fierce, bloodthirsty killers who actually used skulls as mugs to drink the blood of their victims. Genetically, they were Aryans. Geographically, they lived in the areas now known as Russia, the former Soviet republics, and central Asia. One reference work describes a Scythian as a "member of a nomadic people originally of Iranian stock who migrated from Central Asia to southern Russia in the 8th and 7th centuries B.C. . . . Scythians founded a rich, powerful empire that survived for several centuries."[4]

In late August 2004, my father and I traveled to Russia to do research for *The Ezekiel Option*. We were curious about this apparent Scythian heritage of Russia, since this concept is not commonly spoken of in the West. So while we were in Moscow we toured the State Historical Museum. Sure enough, as we spent several hours walking the floors of the enormous redbrick building facing Red Square, we found in glass case after glass case numerous Scythian artifacts, dug up by Russian archeologists and anthropologists and all on display in the Russian equivalent of our Smithsonian. Not only was Russia's Scythian heritage real, we learned, but the Russian government was proud to let the whole world know.

ROSH, MESHECH, AND TUBAL

This brings us to the next big question: where are "Rosh, Meshech and Tubal," of which Gog is "prince"? A study of ancient Hebrew, ancient history, and modern-day geography points us to Russia, Moscow, and Tobolsk (in Siberia), respectively.

The word *Rosh* in Hebrew can mean "head" or "chief," leading some scholars to the conclusion that Gog is the "chief prince" of Meshech and Tubal. But both the Septuagint and the Masoretic Text, two of the oldest and most reliable copies of the Holy Scriptures, translate *Rosh* as the proper name of a geological place. The Septuagint is the oldest Greek translation of the Hebrew Scriptures. It was translated in Alexandria, Egypt, several hundred years before Christ. The Masoretic Text is the full Hebrew text of the Tanakh, or Old Testament, upon which most Jewish Bibles are based. (Ironically, one of the oldest and best-preserved copies we have of the Masoretic Text—one giving us complete versions of Ezekiel's vision of Gog and Magog—is called the

Leningrad Codex and is housed in the Russian National Library in St. Petersburg, Russia.)

In his seminal work *Gesenius' Hebrew-Chaldee Lexicon to the Old Testament*, William Gesenius—the father of modern Hebrew lexicography (the science behind compiling dictionaries)—concluded that the Rosh to which Ezekiel refers is a proper name. He also concluded that Rosh is "undoubtedly the Russians, who are mentioned by the Byzantine writers of the tenth century, under the name of Ros, dwelling to the north of Taurus [in Turkey]."[5] What is interesting to me about this assessment is that it was written in 1846, long before the Communist revolution or the subsequent rise of the Soviet Union as a nuclear superpower. In this case, Gesenius was not using a political or economic lens to reach his conclusions. He was using *only* the third lens of Scripture, and the evidence pointed him to Russia more than 160 years ago.

Dr. Arno C. Gaebelein, the distinguished twentieth-century Bible expositor, came to the same conclusion. In his classic work *The Prophet Ezekiel,* published in 1918—just after the Communist revolution—Gaebelein wrote that "careful research" of biblical and historical sources "has established that . . . Rosh is Russia" and that *"the prince of Rosh* means, therefore, the prince or king of the Russian empire. But he is also in control of Meshech and Tubal, which are reproduced in the modern [words] Moscow and Tobolsk."[6] Tobolsk is the modern Siberian oil city located on the Tubal River.

In 1958 Dr. J. Dwight Pentecost, distinguished professor of Bible exposition at Dallas Theological Seminary, concluded from his own extensive research and review of the work of other Bible scholars that "the identification of Rosh as modern Russia would seem to be well authenticated and generally accepted."[7]

These scholars are not alone in their assessment. There is some disagreement as to the identification of Meshech as Moscow and Tubal as Tobolsk, as some believe these refer to ancient tribes that settled portions of modern-day Turkey. But there is widespread agreement among leading Bible scholars and prophecy experts that Magog and Rosh do, in fact, refer to Russia and the lands and people of the former Soviet Union, and that Gog is the dictator at their helm.[8]

Based on the textual, linguistic, and historical evidence, we can, therefore, conclude with a high degree of confidence that Ezekiel is speaking of Russia and the former Soviet Union in chapters 38 and 39. We can also be confident that the figure known as Gog will be a powerful political leader who commands a vast amount of territory, people, natural resources, and armies. This leader will use his time in office to get his military forces and political alliances prepared for the coming war with Israel.

A careful look at Ezekiel 38 reveals other important intelligence items for our consideration:

- Ezekiel 38:10 tells us that this Russian leader will "devise an evil plan," suggesting a political and military strategist already familiar with evil. (NASB)
- Ezekiel 38:18-19 tells us that God will oppose this Russian leader with "fury" and "anger" and with "blazing wrath." (NASB)
- Ezekiel 38:4 and 38:9 tell us that this Russian leader will head an enormous and fearsome army (a "great horde"), one that, when allied with the armies of Islam, will come "like a storm" against Israel and "like a cloud covering the land" with all of Russia's troops, and "many peoples with you." (NASB)
- Ezekiel 38:7 tells us that in the time leading up to this war, this Russian leader will be thinking, "Be prepared, and prepare yourself, you and all your companies that are assembled about you, and be a guard for them." (NASB)

But knowing what to watch for is not enough. We must now heed the words of Jesus in Luke 12:56 and "analyze this present time" (NASB).

THE RIDDLE THAT IS RUSSIA

The fact is, extraordinary changes are under way in Russia and the former Soviet Union—changes that strongly suggest that the fulfillment of Ezekiel's prophecy is increasingly close at hand. Allow me to explain by mapping out some of the important changes I have witnessed first-hand over the past two decades.

My first trip to Russia was in the summer of 1986, when the Soviet Union still existed. Mikhail Gorbachev had recently come to power. Three college friends and I applied to the Soviet Embassy in Washington for visas, explaining that we wanted to learn more about this "riddle wrapped in a mystery inside an enigma," as Winston Churchill had once called Russia. It was true. We really did want to see the Kremlin and its subjects through the three lenses of politics, economics, and Scripture. But we had another agenda as well. We were participating in a clandestine missions project called Northstar, run by Campus Crusade for Christ, to smuggle Bibles into the Soviet Union and to share our faith in Christ with students we met along the way.

Twenty years later I can still vividly remember the almost overwhelming sense of anxiety and excitement I felt as we took a train from Vienna, Austria, through Czechoslovakia and came to the border of the *Sovietsky Soyuz*, the Union of Soviet Socialist Republics. Just as if I were in the movies, I suddenly found myself staring at guard towers, barbed-wire fences, German shepherds, and severe-looking soldiers—many as young as me, and I was only nineteen—armed with machine guns and sworn to protect their atheistic society from all religion, harshly derided as the "opiate of the people."

As the border officers checked my passport and my luggage, I prayed my version of the Smuggler's Prayer, made famous by Brother Andrew, who helped smuggle millions of Bibles to people trapped behind the Iron Curtain during the coldest days of the Cold War. *"Lord Jesus, while you were on earth, you made the blind eyes to see. I pray now that you would make seeing eyes blind, that I might take your Word to people who have never heard the good news of your salvation."* That day as on so many since, God proved yet again that he is a prayer-hearing and a prayer-answering God.

Remarkably, we made it in without incident, and for the next four weeks we shared our faith and gave away our Bibles in Moscow, in L'vov (a city in Ukraine not far from Chernobyl, which had just melted down), and in three predominantly Islamic cities in central Asia—Tashkent (the capital of Uzbekistan), Alma-Ata (now called Almaty, the capital of Kazakhstan), and Frunze (now called Bishkek, the capital of Kyrgyzstan). What we saw astounded us. We occasionally had the humbling privilege of meeting with secret believers in small but passionate underground churches, memories I have always cherished, for these were, in my eyes, true heroes of the Christian faith. But we also saw firsthand churches that had been turned into museums of atheism. We witnessed the nation's rampant material and spiritual poverty. What's more, we observed the hesitancy in most people's faces to spend any time with Americans for fear of being harassed or incarcerated by the secret police.

If that were not enough, we also got a brief but bitter taste of the religious repression most Russians at that time had known all their lives. Twice my friends and I were detained by the KGB and questioned at length about who we were, why we were there, and why we were breaking Soviet laws, thus putting ourselves at risk of being imprisoned or deported. Both times, by the grace of God, we were released without being charged. Both experiences still rank among the most frightening and exhilarating I have ever had. Yet at the same time, these experiences helped me understand in a small, personal way what President Reagan was talking about when he described the Soviet Union as the focus of evil in the modern world whose last chapters were even then being written and what Jesus Christ was talking about when he promised that "I will build my church; and the gates of hell shall not prevail against it" (Matthew 16:18, KJV).

Such an evil system could not long survive, I began to realize. How could it? The Soviet government had set itself in direct opposition to fundamental truths about human nature and behavior that the free world found self-evident: that we are endowed by our Creator—not by the state, particularly the Communist state—with certain inalienable rights, including the right to life, liberty, and the pursuit of happiness. Even more important, the Kremlin had set itself in direct opposition to God himself, a foolish and shortsighted move if there ever was one. Sooner or later, the government of Russia was doomed to the ash heap of history, while the church of Russia was destined not only to survive but to grow.

"You and your colleagues say you have no god," we once told a KGB officer interrogating us. "But that's not true. You worship at the altar of Marxism-Leninism. You hold up Vladimir Lenin as the savior of Soviet society. We're going to Moscow to see for ourselves the Lenin you worship, still lying in his tomb. But we worship the living God, the true God. Go to Jerusalem. Visit the tomb of Jesus Christ. He's not there. He has risen. He has conquered death and says to all who will listen, 'I am the Way, the Truth, and the Life. No one can come to the Father except through Me.' Someday, we hope you and everyone in your country will know and experience Christ's love and plan for your lives. Until then, we'll be praying for you every day."

And we meant it. For here was a country whose state religion was no religion, a country responsible for the deaths of tens of millions of people during the twentieth century, a country that had subjugated most of its continent to a godless tyranny, a country from which my Orthodox Jewish grandparents and great-grandparents had been fortunate enough to escape, but in doing so had left behind millions of other Jews and Christians who went on to suffer some of the worst religious persecution in the history of mankind. Yet as tempting as it was to curse the Soviets for all the evil they had done, as followers of Christ we could not. For in Matthew 5:43-44, Jesus said plainly, "You have heard that it was said, 'You shall love your neighbor and hate your enemy.' But I say to you, love your enemies and pray for those who persecute you" (NASB).

As best we could, we endeavored to obey those words, praying for that totalitarian system to come crashing down and for the gospel to go pouring in. What we did not realize was just how quickly those prayers would be answered.

By the time I finally returned to Moscow in the late summer of 2004, everything had changed. The Evil Empire had collapsed. The Soviet Union was gone. An entirely new era was under way. But somehow, the riddle that is Russia remained.

There is no doubt that Russians became significantly freer after the

Soviet flag was lowered over the Kremlin for the last time on Christmas Day 1991, and nowhere was this more evident than in the religious life of the country. Where once it had been illegal for me to share my faith in Christ, in 2004 I was able to speak publicly in one of the fastest-growing evangelical churches in Russia. And far from it being illegal to distribute God's Word in Russia, I could now see that Bibles and other Christian literature were pouring in from around the world, as well as being legally printed inside Russia's borders. Indeed, between 1992 and 2002, Josh McDowell—himself an atheist turned evangelist—and his team distributed nearly 20 million Bibles and Christian books inside the former Soviet Union through his ministry with Campus Crusade for Christ.[9]

But the more time I spent in Moscow, the clearer it became that the tide of freedom was going out. The remarkable season of political, economic, and religious freedom that had begun with Boris Yeltsin's courageous insistence on free markets and free elections was systematically coming to an end under the reign of Yeltsin's handpicked successor, Vladimir Putin. And the West seemed unwilling or unable to do anything about it or to see its prophetic implications.

THE GATHERING STORM

On Wednesday, September 1, 2004, my father and I were in Moscow, doing research for *The Ezekiel Option*. At that point I had written roughly two-thirds of the novel. The opening chapter began with Chechen terrorists hijacking a Russian jetliner.

As it turned out, truth ended up being stranger than fiction—a common theme in my life since starting to write these books.

From my hotel room a few blocks from the Kremlin, I posted an item to my weblog detailing some of the events taking place around us:

> Three days before we left Washington for Moscow, Chechen terrorists blew up two Russian jetliners, killing 90 innocent civilians.
>
> Last night—exactly one week to the day after the airplane

attacks—a female Chechen suicide bomber blew herself up at a subway station just blocks from our hotel, killing at least 10 and wounding 50 more.

Today, Chechen terrorists have seized a school in southern Russia and at the time I write this are holding over 400 Russians as hostage, including hundreds of school children. Security has been dramatically heightened here in the country's capital, as well as around the country.

No one knew at that time how long the wave of terror would last. The question on everyone's mind was whether Russian president Vladimir Putin was up to the job of defending his country.

[Putin] won reelection with a Sovietesque 71% of the vote. He has thrown political opponents in jail, driven them into exile or frightened them into silence. He has essentially banned negative stories about him on national television. The latest story in the Moscow Times this morning: a small newspaper with a circulation of 10,000 is being threatened to be shut down by the Kremlin for running stories critical of Putin.

The image Putin has tried to cast is one of stability. Elect me and I will be tough—tough on the terrorists, tough on the billionaire oligarchs, tough on the Russian mafia. Yes, I will take away your freedoms and ignore the democratic reformers. But you need me because I will keep Russia from falling apart. But in talks with leading political analysts here . . . we hear again and again a common theme: was the deal the people made with Putin so wise?

Personal freedoms are evaporating. Putin is centralizing all power to himself. He is becoming a new Czar for a new Russia.[10]

Thirteen days after I posted this item on my weblog, Putin stunned the world by further centralizing power, using the pretext of the terrorist attacks to unveil plans for a "radically restructured" political system in which direct elections of the nation's eighty-nine regional governors would end and he would appoint those governors instead.

"Under current conditions, the system of executive power in the country should not just be adapted to operating in crisis situations, but should be radically restructured in order to strengthen the unity of the country and prevent further crises," Putin said in a nationally televised meeting in the Kremlin. "Those who inspire, organize, and carry out terrorist acts seek to bring about a disintegration of the country, to break up the state, to ruin Russia."[11]

Criticism of the brazen power grab was quick and severe.

"It's the beginning of a constitutional coup d'etat," said Sergei Mitrokhin of Russia's pro-democracy Yabloko Party. "It's a step toward dictatorship. . . . These measures don't have anything to do with the fight against terrorism."[12]

Viktor Pokhmelkin, another pro-democracy member of the State Duma (Russia's lower house of parliament), called Putin's plan evidence of the restoration of "imperial management" and warned, "Today a very serious mistake has been made. The mistake is a threat to the future of the Russian state."[13]

Vladimir Tikhonov, the governor of Russia's Ivanovo region, blasted Putin's plan as "undemocratic and unconstitutional."[14]

Former Soviet leader Mikhail Gorbachev called the plan "a step back from democracy" and warned that "under the motto of war on terror" Putin was "sharply limiting democratic freedoms" and "citizens are [being] stripped of the opportunity to directly express their attitude toward the government."[15]

Even former president Boris Yeltsin—the man who put Putin in office—cautioned, "We should not allow ourselves to step away from the letter or the spirit of a constitution that the country adopted in a national referendum. . . . The strangling of freedoms, the rollback of democratic rights—this can only mean that the terrorists won."[16]

Not that such criticism had any effect. Putin's plan was soon passed by the parliament, two-thirds of whose members were already controlled by the Kremlin.[17]

And Putin was only getting started.

In October the *Washington Post* reported that the ex-Soviet republic of Belarus had "held a referendum on making strongman Alexander Lukashenko, who already has agreed to reunite his country with Russia, the equivalent of president-for-life. An exit poll conducted by the Gallup Organization showed that the proposition failed. But when Belarusan authorities announced it had passed with 77 percent of the vote, Russia pronounced the vote free and fair."[18]

Meanwhile, in the former Soviet republic of Ukraine, Putin aggressively backed Viktor Yanukovych, a close friend of the Kremlin, to be the country's next president and prime minister against pro-democracy candidate Viktor Yushchenko. Putin repeatedly praised Yanukovych. He traveled to Ukraine twice to campaign for him. Russian state television gave Yanukovych glowing coverage, all of which could be seen by neighboring Ukrainians. Russia even "supplied half of the $600 million that Yanukovych is spending on his campaign—including a $200 million payment from the Kremlin-controlled energy giant Gazprom," the *Washington Post* reported.

"In return," the *Post*'s account continued, "Yanukovych promised Putin at their last meeting that he would end Ukraine's policy of seeking membership in NATO, promote an open border and dual citizenship for Russians and Ukrainians, make Russian the country's second official language, and subordinate Ukraine's bid for membership in the World Trade Organization to the requirements of forming the 'single economic space,' the Putin initiative to create a new union with Ukraine, Belarus, and Kazakhstan."[19]

By November the vastly underfunded Yushchenko—who was mysteriously poisoned during the campaign, terribly disfiguring his previously telegenic face—had fought Putin's handpicked man to a draw. But Putin publicly opposed a runoff, summarily declared Yanukovych the winner, and demanded that the West not interfere. The gambit backfired—sparking what became known as the Orange Revolution as hundreds of thousands of Ukrainians took to the streets to demand a free and fair runoff. In the end, the election was settled fairly, with Yushchenko the eventual winner, but Putin's plans to rebuild the Russian empire piece by piece had been exposed.[20]

By year's end, the question of "Where is Russia going?" was becoming clearer—and more disturbing. On Friday, December 3, 2004, as I put the finishing touches on *The Ezekiel Option*, I posted the following item on my weblog:

In September I was in Russia for ten days doing research for my next novel. I met with a senior member of the State Duma (legislature), senior officials at the U.S. Embassy, leading Russian political analysts, and the New York Times' Moscow bureau chief and an economic reporter for the Times.

To each one, I tossed out a possible scenario: a fascist, ultra-nationalist coup in Moscow leads to the assassination of the democratically elected leader of Russia and leaves a nuclear-armed dictator in power itching for a dangerous new confrontation with the West. One by one, each told me there was no need for a coup; the dictator is already in place. And so he is.

Over the past eighteen months or so, Vladimir Putin has steadily turned the clock back on Russian democracy, centralizing power back in the Kremlin and slowly morphing himself into an all-powerful Czar.

He has nationalized Russian television networks; thrown political opponents in prison on suspect charges; all but threatened to seize and nationalize one of Russia's largest petroleum companies; announced Russia's governors will no longer be popularly elected but rather appointed by the Kremlin; and steadfastly supported a presidential candidate in Ukraine even after international observers protested the candidate was trying to steal the election.

Meanwhile, Putin is selling nuclear power plants, fuel, and technology to Iran—the most dangerous state sponsor of terrorism on the planet—has announced a 40% increase in the Russian military budget, and just announced the development of a new class of Russian strategic nuclear missiles.

"We are not only conducting research and successful

testing of the newest nuclear missile systems," Putin told commanders at the Ministry of Defense, according to the New York Times (11/17/04). "I am certain that in the immediate years to come we will be armed with them. These are such developments and such systems that other nuclear states do not have and will not have in the immediate years to come."

The Times added that the Russian military "is widely reported to have been trying to perfect land- and sea-based ballistic missiles with warheads that could elude a missile-defense system like the one being constructed by the Bush administration."

Which brings us to today.

During a speech in India, Putin lashed out at Washington, accusing the Bush administration of seeking a "dictatorship of international affairs.

"Even if dictatorship is wrapped up in a beautiful package of pseuo-democratic phraseology, it will not be in a position to solve systemic problems," Putin said in New Delhi.

Dictatorship?

To be sure, the situation in Russia isn't nearly as bad today as it was during the Cold War. And Putin has done some things right; he has, for example, been supportive of U.S. efforts in the war on terror; has permitted U.S. and NATO planes to fly over Russian territory to support war efforts in Afghanistan; opposed but didn't directly attempt to block the U.S.-led war against Iraq; and his 13% flat tax plan, among other pro-market economic reforms, has, in fact, helped the Russian economy grow significantly in recent years and attract U.S. and Western foreign investment and companies.

That said, however, the trend lines are disturbing. Russia is lurching back in the wrong direction. Putin is a dictator in the making.[21]

I was not alone in these assessments. A growing number of journalists, editorial boards, and Kremlin watchers both inside and outside Russia were connecting the same dots as I was. And they continue to do so, if the following headlines are any guide:

CZAR VLADIMIR

Boston Globe, SEPTEMBER 15, 2004

IS RUSSIA GOING BACKWARD?

Commentary, OCTOBER 2004

IS DEMOCRACY RUSSIA'S FUTURE? PUTIN AGAIN RAISES DOUBTS

USA Today, NOVEMBER 29, 2004

PUTIN SETS RUSSIA ON FASCIST PATH

Omaha Herald, DECEMBER 16, 2004

RUSSIA'S DOWNHILL SLIDE TO DICTATORSHIP: PUTIN'S REGIME PARALLELS WEIMAR GERMANY

Los Angeles Times, JANUARY 9, 2005

THE EMPIRE STRIKES BACK A CONFIDENT KREMLIN IS THROWING ITS WEIGHT AROUND.

Newsweek, JANUARY 30, 2006

RUSSIA'S PUTIN RECLAIMING DOMINANT ROLE IN FORMER SOVIET UNION

ASSOCIATED PRESS, MARCH 20, 2006

PUTIN IN HIS OWN WORDS

Vladimir Putin was trained by the KGB and at one time was Russia's top spy, yet surprisingly he has not been secretive about his long-term objectives or his strategies for achieving them. To the contrary, he has been quite candid, for those who are watching closely and listening carefully.

In 1999, for example, Reuters ran the following headline: **"Russian Premier Vows to Rebuild Military Might."** Putin, then prime minister under Yeltsin, had just delivered a speech declaring that "the government has undertaken to rebuild and strengthen the military might of the state to respond to the new geopolitical realities, both external and internal threats." He focused special attention on "new threats [that] have emerged on our southern frontiers." Putin also announced a 57 percent increase in military spending in the year 2000.[22]

No sooner had Yeltsin stepped down than Putin repeated the vow to rebuild his country's badly withered military machine. "Our country Russia was a great, powerful, strong state," he declared in January 2000, "and it is clear that this is not possible if we do not have strong armed forces, powerful armed forces."[23]

Putin has kept his word. Consider 2004.

In January Putin ordered the largest maneuvers of Russian nuclear forces in two decades, scrambling strategic bombers, launching cruise missiles, test-firing ballistic missiles, and sending new spy satellites into orbit, in what analysts described as "an imitation of a nuclear attack on the United States."[24]

In February Putin insisted that Russia "does not have and cannot have aggressive objectives of imperial ambitions." Yet he ordered dramatic improvements in the Russian military to achieve a more "combat-capable army and navy," causing one of China's leading dailies to worry about "the resurrection of the Russian military."[25]

In August Putin ordered a 40 percent increase in Russia's defense budget, including new fighter aircraft, new rockets, and two new army divisions.[26]

In December, as the election crisis in Ukraine was still unfolding, Putin ordered the test launch of a Cold War–era Russian intercontinental ballistic missile known as the SS-18 Satan, the first time the Russians had fired such a missile since the Soviet Union collapsed.[27]

With the rebuilding of Russia's conventional military and strategic nuclear-missile forces under way, Vladimir Putin then delivered a speech on April 25, 2005, that I believe ranks as the most dangerous presidential address of our times.

"First and foremost," he declared, "it is worth acknowledging that the demise of the Soviet Union was the greatest geopolitical catastrophe of the century. As for the Russian people, it became a genuine tragedy. Tens of millions of our fellow citizens and countrymen found themselves beyond the fringes of Russian territory."

Putin went on to argue that since the threat to Russia from terrorism was "still very strong," the Kremlin must be strong to eradicate such terror. "The moment we display weakness or spinelessness, our losses will be immeasurably greater." Then he insisted that Russia should remain "connected" to "the former republics of the USSR." He argued that Russia and her neighbors have "a single historical destiny" together and said he wants to "synchronize the pace and parameters of [the] reform processes" in Russia and those former Soviet republics.[28]

Consider for a moment what such a speech says about the lenses through which the leader of Russia views his country and the world. When Vladimir Putin looks out over the vast expanse of the twentieth century, he is not primarily concerned with the 20 million people who perished under Stalin's reign of terror. Or the 6 million Jews who died in the Holocaust under Adolf Hitler. Or the 3 million who died in the killing fields of Cambodia under Pol Pot. Rather, he believes that the disintegration of the Evil Empire ranks as the "greatest political catastrophe of the century" and that its reintegration and synchronization is a matter of "historical destiny."

Such fondness for an empire so murderous and cruel would be chilling if it were voiced by the leader of *any* country possessing 10,000 nuclear warheads. But it is particularly chilling coming from the leader of Russia, a country described in the Scriptures as having expansionist ambitions in the last days.

Yet this was not the first time Putin had discussed such views or ambitions on the record. In 2000 three Russian journalists—Nataliya Gevorkyan, Natalya Timakova, and Andrei Kolesnikov—published *First Person*, in my view the most important book ever written about Putin. It is important not because the journalists offered their own insights or analysis into Putin but because they let Putin speak for himself. They interviewed the Russian leader six separate times. Each interview lasted about four hours. The book is merely a transcript, and when it comes to understanding Putin's ambitions and approach, it is a gold mine of intelligence.[29]

- **Putin on his mission in life**: "My historical mission," he insisted, is to stop "the collapse of the USSR" (p. 139). To do this, he vowed to "consolidate the armed forces, the Interior Ministry, and the FSB [the successor to the KGB, the secret police of the Soviet Union]" (p. 140). "If I can help save Russia from collapse, then I'll have something to be proud of" (p. 204).
- **On his style:** "Everyone says I'm harsh, even brutal," Putin acknowledged, without ever disputing such observations. "A dog senses when somebody is afraid of it, and bites," he observed. "The same applies [to dealing with one's enemies]. If you become jittery, they will think they are stronger. Only one thing works in such circumstances—to go on the offensive. You must hit first, and hit so hard that your opponent will not rise to his feet" (p. 168).
- **On the czars**: "From the very beginning, Russia was created as a supercentralized state. That's practically laid down in its genetic code, its traditions, and the mentality of its people," said Putin, adding, "In certain periods of time . . . in a certain place . . . under certain conditions . . . monarchy has played and continues to this day to play a positive role. . . . The monarch doesn't have to worry about whether or not he will be elected, or about petty political interests, or about how to influence the electorate. He can think about the destiny of the people and not become distracted with trivialities" (p. 186).
- **On his choice of history's most interesting political leader**: "Napoleon Bonaparte" (p. 194).
- **On his rise from spy to president:** "In the Kremlin, I have

a different position. Nobody controls me here. I control everybody else" (p. 131).
- **On his critics:** "To hell with them" (p. 140).

Putin has repeatedly promised that he will not attempt to extend his time in office when his second term ends in 2008, and every person I interviewed in Russia in 2004—including every political officer and diplomat I spoke with at the U.S. Embassy in Moscow—told me they believed he would leave peacefully when the time came. Should he really do so, Putin will pass on to his successor executive power unparalleled since pre-Gorbachev times and a dynamic that suggests a future of more, rather than less, centralization of power.

But how seriously should Putin's many pledges be taken? On at least six separate occasions after becoming president, he vowed not to end direct elections of Russia's regional governors and appoint them himself. Yet in 2004, when it suited his purposes, he did just that.[30] Why should his promise to leave office in 2008 be any different?

Now in his fifties, Putin is still a young man, at the top of his game, with no professional experience of any kind other than being a KGB-trained suppressor of dissidents and a rising political leader.[31] What if he wants to change the constitution to allow himself to stay? Belarus did it in 2004 (and President Alexander Lukashenko was "reelected" in 2006 with 83 percent of the vote).[32] Other ex-Soviet republics have done it as well, including Kazakhstan, Turkmenistan, and Tajikistan.[33]

What if Putin is looking for a pretext to become a new Russian monarch? Would a terrible new series of terrorist attacks—perhaps similar to the Beslan school hostage crisis—be enough? What about an assassination attempt or attempts at a coup or new revolutions in the former Soviet republics? What about polls showing that in the absence of Putin, the leading two contenders for Russia's presidency are ultranationalist Fascist Vladimir Zhirinovsky and Communist hardliner Gennady Zyuganov?[34]

Might "the will of the Russian people" suffice? In 2004 only 27 percent of Russians supported a third Putin term. (Perhaps this is why every expert I spoke with dismissed the possibility.) By June 2006, however, the number had shot up to 59 percent.[35]

Then again, support for Stalin is growing too. Asked if they would vote for the Soviet dictator if he were alive and running for president, a remarkable one in four Russians now say they would. In large measure this is because some two-thirds of the Russian people feel there is less order in their country today than in the past. As such, they are looking for a strong hand to rule, and Putin is providing just that.[36]

THE BIG QUESTION

The more one learns about the Russian leader, the more one can understand why nearly everywhere I speak these days, people ask me, "Is Vladimir Putin Gog? Is he the Russian leader Ezekiel predicted would attack Israel?"

It is an interesting question, given recent trends. Putin is certainly perceived as a rising czar. He speaks fondly of Russia's historic monarchy. He is centralizing political power and control to himself. He is rebuilding Russia's military for offensive purposes. He speaks of the collapse of the Soviet Evil Empire as a catastrophe and talks of restoring the historical glory of Mother Russia. He is operating in a social and political climate that increasingly desires a leader along the lines of Joseph Stalin. What's more, he is steadily building political, economic, and military ties with the very countries Ezekiel described in his vision of the future, as I will describe in detail in the next two chapters.

All that said, however, one can neither definitively conclude that Putin is the one of whom Ezekiel spoke nor conclusively rule him out. Not yet, at least. More needs to happen in Russia and the Middle East before we can know for sure, one way or the other. Putin may, after all, simply be setting the stage for someone else to rise.

CHAPTER EIGHT

FUTURE HEADLINE
KREMLIN JOINS "AXIS OF EVIL," FORMS MILITARY ALLIANCE WITH IRAN

On May 4, 2006, Vice President Dick Cheney delivered a speech at a conference in Vilnius, Lithuania, that infuriated the Kremlin.

He warned that while America wants to see Russia truly emerge as a healthy and vibrant democracy and a trusted partner in the global economy, under Vladimir Putin's leadership, the country was in the process of reversing the gains of the last decade.

"In many areas of civil society—from religion and the news media, to advocacy groups and political parties—the [Russian] government has unfairly and improperly restricted the rights of her people," Cheney said. He also warned that "no legitimate interest is served when oil and gas become tools of intimidation or blackmail, either by supply manipulation or attempts to monopolize transportation. And no one can justify actions that undermine the territorial integrity of a neighbor, or interfere with democratic movements."

Russia's leaders have a choice to make, Cheney explained. They can choose the path of freedom and democracy or the path of tyranny and aggression. He noted that the future of peace and security in the twenty-first century will be profoundly affected by the decisions Moscow makes in the coming years, and he insisted that Western leaders are optimistic.

"None of us believes that Russia is fated to become an enemy," he said.[1]

It was a thoughtful, well-reasoned, and much-needed speech, and I was glad the White House chose to send such a strong message to President Putin and his top advisors. But that last line troubled me, for when one looks at Russia through not only the political and economic lenses but also through the third lens of Scripture, one sees that Russia is, in fact, destined to become an enemy of the West, and particularly of Israel, in part because of its alliance with Iran.

Let me explain.

WHAT TO WATCH FOR

A careful study of Ezekiel 38 makes it clear that a Russian leader will one day mount an attack against Israel. What's more, we learn that Russia's czar will not attack Israel alone. Rather, he will build a military coalition—much as the United States did when it sought to bring down Saddam Hussein's regime in 2003. Here Ezekiel provides us extraordinarily precise intelligence. Though he wrote more than 2,500 years ago, the Hebrew prophet was able to tell us what to watch for. In fact, he gave us a detailed list of countries that will join Russia's anti-Israel coalition in the last days.

The first specific country he named as part of the Russian alliance was Persia (Ezekiel 38:5). Until March 21, 1935, Persia was the official name of the country we now call Iran. But never in the last 2,500 years have Russia and Iran had a military alliance. This caused many a skeptic to think, *See, the Bible has no idea what it's talking about. The Russians have always hated the Iranians. The Iranians have always hated the Russians. There's no way they are ever going to form an alliance against Israel or anybody else. This just proves the Bible is full of errors.*

Such a conclusion may have seemed reasonable to many until recently. The Russians, after all, briefly occupied portions of northern Iran several times: in the nineteenth century, in 1912, during World War I, and from 1941 to 1946. But Moscow has never had an alliance with Iran. To the contrary, repeated occupations by the Soviets drove Iran into a military alliance of sorts with the U.S. for several decades.

After the Red Army left Iran in 1946, Tehran established close relations with the United States as Mohammed Reza Shah Pahlavi (commonly known as "the Shah") accepted large amounts of American military aid and arms to build a counterweight to Soviet ambitions to take over Iran's oil fields and the rest of the Middle East.

In 1979, the U.S. lost Iran during the Islamic revolution as the Shah was overthrown and forced into exile and American embassy personnel were taken hostage for 444 days. But as serious a blow as this was to U.S. interests, the rise of the Ayatollah Khomeini hardly created the opening Moscow would have hoped for—or the one the Bible predicted. The fervently religious Khomeini had no intention of creating any semblance of an alliance with the atheists to the north. What's more, after the Soviets invaded neighboring Afghanistan in December 1979, Khomeini feared the Kremlin was coming to take over Iran next.

It was Saddam Hussein, ironically, who forced Khomeini to begin forming ties to the Communists. By the late 1980s, Iran was suffering economically and militarily from year after year of a brutal and seemingly never-ending Iran-Iraq war (1980–1988). Tehran needed help from one of the superpowers, and they certainly were not going to turn to Washington. So Khomeini and the mullahs turned to Moscow instead, figuring that if Mikhail Gorbachev was pulling troops out of Afghanistan, he was not about to send them into Iran.

A MILITARY ALLIANCE EMERGING

Today, even the biggest skeptic of Ezekiel's intelligence would have to admit that a military alliance between Russia and Iran is emerging for the first time in history.

Economic and political ties between Russia and Iran began to develop steadily in the 1990s. Military ties grew even more rapidly. Tehran was desperate to rebuild its forces after its long war with Iraq. Moscow was desperate for hard cash after the collapse of the Soviet Union and for a beachhead into the oil-rich Middle East.

It was a match made in hell.

The Clinton administration became concerned enough that in 1995 it pressured the Russians to sign an agreement whereby Moscow would stop selling arms to Iran and would promise to complete the delivery of all weapons systems previously sold to Tehran by the end of 1999. But the deal signed by Vice President Al Gore and Russian prime minister Viktor Chernomyrdin may go down as one of the least effective accords ever. Russian arms sales to Iran between 1992 and 2000 topped $4 billion.[2]

When Vladimir Putin took office as president, he quickly abandoned the 1995 agreement with the Americans. In December 2000, he sent Russian defense minister Igor Sergeyev to Iran to meet with Iranian defense minister Ali Shamkhani to begin discussing a dramatic new military relationship between the two countries. In March 2001, Putin welcomed Iranian president Mohammed Khatami to Moscow. Khatami was the first Iranian leader to visit the Russian capital in the twenty-seven years since the Shah's visit.[3] The visit made big headlines around the world and raised serious concerns in Washington and Jerusalem.

During his three-day visit, Khatami toured Russian nuclear facilities, missile factories, and Russia's space command. Putin and Khatami and their advisors also accelerated negotiations for a ten-year, multibillion-dollar arms deal between their two countries, despite U.S. warnings to the Kremlin not to assist the radical Islamic regime.[4]

Over time, the nature of the relationship hammered out between the two countries has become even clearer, as evidenced by world media headlines:

RUSSIA PLANS 5 MORE NUCLEAR POWER PLANTS IN IRAN

Washington Post, JULY 27, 2002

KREMLIN JOINS "AXIS OF EVIL," FORMS MILITARY ALLIANCE WITH IRAN

NEW RAILWAY TO LINK RUSSIA AND IRAN VIA AZERBAIJAN

AGENCE FRANCE-PRESSE, MAY 22, 2004

RUSSIA FAVORS IRAN ROUTE FOR CRUDE EXPORTS

Tehran Times, JUNE 14, 2004

PUTIN: IRAN DOESN'T PLAN TO BUILD ATOMIC ARMS

ALJAZEERA, FEBRUARY 18, 2005

PUTIN DEFENDS ARMS SALES TO SYRIA, IRAN

ASSOCIATED PRESS, APRIL 28, 2005

IRAN REGARDS RUSSIA AS POSSIBLE PARTNER TO BUILD 20 NUCLEAR POWER PLANTS

MOSNEWS.COM, SEPTEMBER 7, 2005

KREMLIN READY TO DEFEND IRAN

MOSNEWS.COM, SEPTEMBER 13, 2005

RUSSIA AGREES TO $1 BILLION ARMS DEAL WITH IRAN

ASSOCIATED PRESS, DECEMBER 2, 2005

IRAN'S NUCLEAR AMBITIONS

What makes all this so troubling, of course, is that the Kremlin is selling these conventional arms and providing such nuclear fuel, technology, and assistance to the most dangerous radical Islamic terrorist regime on the face of the planet, a country President Bush specifically cited as a member of the Axis of Evil.

Putin has tried repeatedly to assure world leaders that Iran does not intend to build nuclear weapons. After a February 2005 meeting in the Kremlin with Hassan Rowhani, Iran's top nuclear negotiator, Putin insisted that "the latest steps on Iran's behalf persuade us that Iran has no intention of building an atomic weapon. Consequently, we will continue to cooperate with Iran in all fields, including nuclear energy."[5]

Two months later, during a news conference in Jerusalem on his historic trip to Israel—the first ever for a Russian leader—Putin explained that "we are working with Iran in order to develop the atom for peaceful ends and we are against any program seeking to endow Iran with an atomic weapon."[6]

Yet the intentions of Iran to obtain nuclear weapons go back many years. During a January 1987 speech to Iran's nuclear scientific community in Tehran, Iran's then-president Ali Khamenei (who later became Iran's Supreme Leader, the Ayatollah Khamenei, after the death of the Ayatollah Khomeini) made a direct link between Iran's nuclear program and Iran's national security and stressed the urgency of going nuclear as rapidly as possible.

"Regarding atomic energy, we need it now," Khamenei said. "Our nation has always been threatened from outside. The least we can do to face this danger is let our enemies know that we can defend ourselves. Therefore, every step you take here is in defense of your country and your evolution. With this in mind, you should work hard and at great speed."[7]

In an October 6, 1988, address to the Islamic Revolutionary Guards, Ali Akbar Hashemi-Rafsanjani made the country's nuclear intentions even more clear. "We should fully equip ourselves both in the offensive and defensive use of chemical, bacteriological, and radiological weapons. From now on, you should make use of the opportunity and perform this task."[8] In 1989, Rafsanjani was elected president of Iran, where he served until 1997.

Lest there be any doubt, Rafsanjani was even more provocative in the wake of the terrorist attacks on New York and Washington. On December 14, 2001, the Iran Press Service ran a story entitled **"Rafsanjani Says Muslims Should Use Nuclear Weapon against Israel."**[9]

According to the story, Rafsanjani asserted that a nuclear attack would "annihilate Israel," while costing Iran "damages only." He said, "If a day comes when the world of Islam is duly equipped with the arms Israel has in possession, the strategy of colonialism would face a stalemate because application of an atomic bomb would not leave anything in Israel but the same thing would just produce damages in the Muslim world." The article pointed out that "not only [was] Mr. Hashemi-Rafsanjani's speech the strongest against Israel, but also the first time that a prominent leader of the Islamic Republic openly suggest[ed] the use of a nuclear weapon against the Jewish State."

To fulfill such a mission, Rafsanjani again ran for president in 2005. He was defeated by the even more hard-line and anti-Semitic Mahmoud Ahmadinejad—who vowed to accelerate Iran's nuclear program—on the very day *The Ezekiel Option* was released.

The timing of Ahmadinejad's victory and the book's release was eerie enough, but eerier still were the similarities between the novel and what was happening in Iran in real life.

On page 333 of *Option*'s hardcover edition, my fictional Iranian leader calls for the annihilation of Israel, saying, "The world must understand—the Zionists must be humbled. Death to Israel. . . . This cancerous Jewish tumor is the most dangerous threat on the face of the earth. But the Night of the Jews is almost over. Allah, we beseech thee, annihilate them with your wrath." On page 358, a fictional Islamic scholar who supports Iran in its battle against Israel warns that "Allah is not on the side of the Jews. He will not be mocked by claims that he is. The world will know who the One True God really is when Israel is wiped off the face of the map forever."

In the fall of 2005, fiction once again became reality:

AHMADINEJAD: WIPE ISRAEL OFF MAP
ALJAZEERA.NET, OCTOBER 26, 2005

WIPE ISRAEL "OFF THE MAP" SAYS IRANIAN
New York Times, OCTOBER 27, 2005

ISRAEL SHOULD BE WIPED OFF MAP, SAYS IRAN'S PRESIDENT
The (U.K.) Guardian, OCTOBER 27, 2005

Ahmadinejad, speaking at the "World without Zionism" conference in Tehran, not only told his fellow Islamic radicals that "Israel must be wiped off the map" because Israel is trying "satanically and deceitfully to gain control" of all of Palestine. He also warned that "anybody who recognizes Israel will burn in the fire of the Islamic nation's fury" and any Islamic leader "who recognizes the Zionist regime means he is acknowledging the surrender and defeat of the Islamic world." And he threatened the United States as well. "Is it possible for us to witness a world without America and Zionism? . . . [Y]ou had best know that this slogan and this goal are attainable, and surely can be achieved."[10]

The remarks triggered widespread international condemnation, but Ahmadinejad did not back off. On December 9, he gave a speech in Mecca to the Organization of the Islamic Conference in which he called Israel a "tumor," questioned whether the Holocaust had ever really happened, and suggested that if Europeans were so concerned about the fate of the Jews, they should move Israel to Europe.[11]

"THE POINT OF NO RETURN"

Ahmadinejad's incendiary rhetoric against Israel and the U.S. should not be mistaken for empty threats, any more than Saddam Hussein's threats to invade Kuwait were empty in the years leading up to August 2, 1990. Rather, Ahmadinejad's words suggest a countdown to a new and terrible war in the Middle East.

In late 2005, during a trip to Israel, I met with one of the top Iran experts in the Mossad, Israel's primary foreign-intelligence agency (the Israeli version of the CIA). "Please listen to what this regime is telling us, and please believe them," the agent, an operative who himself spent years undercover inside Iran, told me. "The regime in Iran first and foremost is against the U.S., not Israel. Israel is just a tool to get to the U.S. Israel is the Little Satan. You are the Great Satan.

"Remember," the Mossad agent continued, "the Iranians invented the chess board. They are playing three or four moves ahead of us. . . . We should remember Hitler and other Fascist regimes throughout history. They always signaled their ultimate intentions ahead of time. . . . A top advisor to Mahmoud Ahmadinejad recently said, 'A clash between Islam and the West is inevitable, and we must be prepared.' We ignore such warning at our peril. We must be prepared, too."[12]

The Iranian leadership has certainly been preparing for a clash between Islam and the West as they feverishly try to build, buy, or steal nuclear weapons, as well as the missiles to deliver such weapons to their intended targets. In July of 1998, the Commission to Assess the Ballistic Missile Threat to the United States—headed by Donald Rumsfeld—issued a sobering report in which its members (top U.S. military and intelligence officials) unanimously concluded that "the only issue as to whether or not Iran may soon have or already has a nuclear weapon is the amount of fissile material available to it. Because of significant gaps in our knowledge, the U.S. is unlikely to know whether Iran possesses nuclear weapons until after the fact."[13]

The commission found that Iran—whose missiles can already reach Tel Aviv, Paris, and London—could build an intercontinental ballistic missile capable of hitting the U.S. "within five years of a decision to proceed," though again the members stressed that officials in Washington might not know when such a decision was made. They pointed out that "a 10,000 km-range Iranian missile could hold the U.S. at risk in an arc extending northeast of a line from Philadelphia, Pennsylvania, to St. Paul, Minnesota."

Even more disturbing, the commission warned that countries such as Iran were seeking ways to launch Scud missiles off the back of a tramp steamer or other commercial container ship, putting Iranian nuclear, chemical, biological, or simply conventional warheads within range of major American, European, or Israeli cities with effectively no warning whatsoever.

And that was in 1998. Today the threat to the American homeland from an Iranian ship-launched missile has increased dramatically. "Some 75 percent of the total U.S. population of 290 million people and 75 percent of its military bases are within 200 miles of the coast," reported a United Press International story in 2005. "The number of potential launch platforms is immense, with 130,000 registered merchant ships in 195 countries. . . . Thousands of SCUDs and other inexpensive short-range ballistic missiles have been dispersed, sold worldwide with some in countries where terrorist groups operate openly. Iran test-launched a tactical ballistic missile from a ship last year and the threat has become much worse with the rapid proliferation of cruise missiles. China has already supplied many to Iran."[14]

Since the publication of the Rumsfeld commission's report, we have learned much more, including the fact that for nearly two decades, Iran had successfully hidden expensive and sophisticated nuclear research facilities from U.S., Israeli, and other Western intelligence agencies. Only when a group of Iranian dissidents known as the National Council of Resistance held a press conference on August 14, 2002, revealing the existence and location of such facilities did the world have any idea just how aggressively Tehran was pursuing nuclear weapons.

In their Natanz facility, it turns out, the Iranians were planning to enrich uranium to weapons-grade standards. In their Arāk facility, the Iranians were planning to extract plutonium for military purposes.

"We knew back in 2000–2001 that Iran had secret nuclear sites, and we were actually trying to find out where they were," said David Albright, a former nuclear inspector for the International Atomic Energy Agency (IAEA). But when he finally found out, he admitted he was stunned by the magnitude of Iran's efforts. "Within a few days [of finishing the Natanz and Arāk facilities], they could make enough [nuclear fuel] for a bomb. Not just one bomb. The two massive underground facilities—each the size of a football field—are designed to hold 50,000 or more centrifuges. That could produce uranium for 25 to 50 nuclear bombs a year."[15]

Kenneth Pollack, a high-ranking U.S. National Security Council official who was in charge of Iran and Persian Gulf affairs during the 1990s, admitted, "Despite the promises the Clinton administration had heard from Khatami's informal interlocutors that the reformists [in the Iranian government] understood the United States' concerns about Iran's nuclear program and would work to accommodate us, Iran's nuclear program had never slowed down. In fact, it had made tremendous progress."[16]

During the writing of this book, I spoke to at least a half dozen senior Israeli military and intelligence officials who, on the condition of anonymity, told me that Iran either is at or is rapidly approaching what they call the "point of no return." This is the point at which Iran will have all the technical know-how, trained scientists, bomb-making blueprints, enriched uranium, and other critical components to build a nuclear device.

Once the mullahs have all the chefs and ingredients they need to cook up their thermonuclear poison, these sources say that perfecting an actual bomb could happen very quickly. Some estimate Iran could have the "Islamic Bomb" called for by Rafsanjani as early as 2007. Others say sometime between 2008 and 2011 is more likely. But the truth is no one knows for sure, and that is what is so dangerous.

What we do know for sure is that Russia is helping speed the process, not slow it down. "I am sometimes asked if Iran wants to create such [nuclear] weapons or is thinking about the possibility, and I always reply that it does and is," says Viktor Mikhailov, director of the Institute of Strategic Stability of Russia's Ministry of Atomic Energy and widely considered one of the fathers of the Iranian nuclear industry. "It is impossible to retain national independence and sovereignty now without nuclear weapons. . . . I think that the nuclear sector of the Iranian economy is maintained at a very high research and technical level. . . . Iran will create—can create—its nuclear bomb in five to ten years. It will not be as sophisticated as the nuclear weapons of Russia or the U.S., but it will do. The Americans are afraid of this . . . because nuclear death can come not from the air but in many other ways. They fear a single nuclear explosion in their territory."[17]

Over 1,000 Iranian nuclear scientists have been trained in Russia or by senior Russian scientists. Russia has vowed to finish building Iran's first nuclear power plant in Bushehr (perhaps by 2007), despite intense international pressure to stop helping Iran go nuclear. Russia is also negotiating with Iran to build as many as twenty more nuclear power plants, despite the fact that Iran is sitting on an ocean of oil and natural gas and hardly suffering from a lack of energy supplies. Russian diplomats have repeatedly stalled efforts by the U.S. and the European Union (EU) to place sanctions on Iran for its illegal nuclear activities. And Vladimir Putin has put his personal stamp of approval on Russian nuclear assistance to Iran, despite Mahmoud Ahmadinejad's vow to annihilate the Jewish state.

The question is why.

WHAT RUSSIA WANTS

"Russia has two interests in Iran," Dr. Dore Gold told me when I saw him in Tel Aviv in the fall of 2005. "First, they want to resurrect the supposed glory of the Soviet Union. And second, they want to make money."

I first met Gold, the former Israeli ambassador to the United Nations, during the summer of 2000 when Ehud Barak was trying to give away the store to Yasser Arafat. Gold, one of the first Israeli diplomats to ever meet personally with Arafat, had taken me inside Arafat's thinking and helped me understand who he was and what he wanted. He was enormously helpful to me as I was doing research for *The Last Days*, and I later helped him promote the release of his *New York Times* best seller *Hatred's Kingdom: How Saudi Arabia Supports the New Global Terrorism*.

But Gold was not only an expert on Arafat and the Saudis. He had also been closely monitoring Russian activities and ambitions in the Middle East for years and served as a senior advisor to Israeli prime minister Sharon.

"The Russians want an empire, and to get one they need to establish 'special relationships' with Arab and Islamic regimes in the Middle East whom they can use as their agents of influence," he told me one morning over coffee. "From 1948 to the collapse of the Soviet Union, the Soviets were the main backers of the Arab threat to Israel. But they were never able to secure Iran as an ally until now. . . . Iran is pivotal in Russian thinking. It is a major regional power in its own right, and it is a gateway into the rest of the Middle East."

What's more, he noted, Moscow figures that a strong relationship with Iran lessens the likelihood that the mullahs will aggressively support the rebels in Chechnya or any other effort to foment a coup in the Russian capital.[18]

Gold, an American who emigrated to Israel, went on to argue that while Russia's economy is much stronger today than it was in the early 1990s, that is largely due to the oil-and-gas industry. The military-industrial complex, on the other hand—the engine that for years provided millions of jobs for Russian workers—has been dramatically downsized since the end of the Cold War. Thus, Russia needs to sell billions of dollars' worth of arms to countries like Iran or their military production facilities will have to scale down even more or shut down entirely. Unemployment would surge, as would poverty, thus increasing the possibility of domestic instability of the kind the Kremlin fears most.[19]

Dr. Yuri Shtern shares a similar assessment as Dore Gold but adds some color commentary from a unique vantage point. Born in Moscow in 1949, Shtern graduated from Moscow University with a PhD in economics. He agitated—as Natan Sharansky did—for Soviet Jewish rights until he was finally allowed to emigrate to Israel in 1981. There he managed a Jewish settlement in Judea and worked for a time for the Federation of Israeli Chambers of Commerce, trying to drum up business between Israel and the former USSR after years of pushing for boycotts of Soviet products due to Soviet persecution of Jews. In 1996 he was elected to serve as a member of the Knesset (the Israeli parliament) and is now the number-two official in Yisrael Beitenu, one of Israel's fastest-growing political parties.

Shtern and I first met in February 2004 at the National Prayer Breakfast in Washington, DC, where he was part of a seven-person Israeli delegation. We met again at the Dan Panorama Hotel in Tel Aviv the following year, and I asked him why the country of his birth was arming his worst enemies.

"Russia—after Israel—is the second strangest place in the world," Shtern told me one night after dinner. "It has a history of Christianity and education but also a deep tradition of tyranny. The danger now is that Russia may lurch back to tyranny."

Part of the reason is that "Russia is in great danger of Islamicization," and "it's unbelievable how many Russian officials are being bought by Islamists" from Iran, Saudi Arabia, and elsewhere in the Middle East. That, Shtern said, is a big reason why Russia is helping Iran go nuclear. Russian workers need the jobs. Russian companies need the cash. Russian politicians are getting paid off. And he warned that more trouble lies ahead. While the world's attention has been focused on the troubles in Iraq for the last several years, Shtern insists that "the future of the world is being shaped by Russia."[20]

A few months before these meetings with Gold and Shtern, I sat down with Natan Sharansky at the Madison Hotel in Washington, DC, to talk to him about Putin, Iran, and the growing nuclear threat. At the time, he was still a member of Prime Minister Sharon's cabinet, serving as Israel's minister for Jerusalem and Diaspora Affairs. I was writing a story for *World* magazine about President Bush's summit with President Putin in the Slovak capital of Bratislava.

I started by asking him about the big picture. "A growing number of observers in the West are concerned that Vladimir Putin is becoming a new Russian dictator. They point to the Kremlin's takeover of television stations, jailing of political opponents, and ending democratic elections for the governors of Russia's provinces. As someone who grew up in Russia and spent nine years in a KGB Gulag as a dissident, what is your sense about the future of democracy in Russia?"[21]

"We hear two types of statements these days," Sharansky told me. "The first is that Russia went back to the past because Russians like their old totalitarian regimes, and that is proof that Russians can't be democrats or don't want democracy. This is nonsense. The other sentiment is that the Russian government is engaged in some serious retreats from democracy and the world should be concerned. That is absolutely true. Look, for a thousand years Russia never was a democracy. But I believe the Russian people want freedom and democracy. There have been tremendous changes there in the past ten or fifteen years. Millions of people are not enslaved in Gulags. Millions are not working for the KGB. Millions do not live in fear that one mistaken word and they'll be thrown in prison. This is real, historic progress. That said, there have been some serious retreats. But look, twelve years after the French revolution there was Napoleon. There are ups and downs in the development of democracy in any country. Now Putin is restricting many areas of Russian life. The free world should not be hesitant to raise these issues and encourage the Russian government to expand freedom, not restrict it."

I asked him why he thought Russia was selling nuclear technology to Iran when Iran was widely recognized as a terrorist state and, in President Bush's famous phrase, part of the Axis of Evil.

"Well, you know that I was involved for a long time in the negotiations to persuade the Russians to stop selling these technologies to Iran," Sharansky explained, noting his meetings with Putin and "many other meetings with Russian leaders over the years" on this issue. "And it is important to point out that it wasn't the Russian government that was directly selling the technologies. It was various Russian companies, and the Kremlin wasn't fighting it enough. . . . Putin told me personally—and he happened to be absolutely right about this—that the day will come when it is clear that it is Western sales of technologies to Iran which will be just as critical to helping Iran develop weapons of mass destruction, maybe more so, not just Russian technologies. And sure enough, a year ago when the scope of Iranian activities were discovered, everyone could see that the technologies that flowed through Pakistan, England, and Holland have created a big danger that within one or two more years Iran will develop nuclear weapons."

"Nevertheless, does your government believe this emerging Russian-Iranian alliance is a direct threat to Israel's national security?" I asked.

"The free world is blind to taking effective measures to stopping this impending disaster," he replied. "Now it must be clear that the free world cannot afford to permit the regime of the Ayatollahs to have nuclear weapons and the missiles to deliver them. The Iranians have made themselves perfectly clear. They intend to destroy Israel and the other 'Satans' in this world."

"What should be done to stop Iran from acquiring the bomb?" I wondered.

"As I point out in my book [*The Case for Democracy*], Iran is a unique example of a country where in one generation a society of true believers in radical Islam has become a society of double-thinkers," said Sharansky. "That is, in their hearts and minds they are disgusted with their government and disillusioned with radical Islam, even though with their lips they must avoid being critical because they fear government reprisals. There are many Iranians eager to change their government.

With some encouragement from the free world I think we can help the people of Iran to bring democratic change. I was glad to see President Bush speak directly to the Iranian people in his State of the Union address. But it is not enough. The United States and Europe—the entire free world—must do much more to encourage the forces of freedom and reform within Iran, before it is too late."

"What if it is already too late?" I asked. "Can you picture a scenario in which Israel is forced to take military action against Iran?"

"If it is too late and democratic change will not happen in Iran, and so much time was wasted, and the free world was too cautious to support the dissidents in Iran, then there is a very real danger that Iran will get nuclear weapons. And the free world will have no choice but to act. But I don't want to discuss specific scenarios. Let us hope it does not go that far."

Actually, it may have already gone that far.

WORST-CASE SCENARIOS

In February 2006, I asked Steve Forbes if he would arrange an interview for me with Caspar Weinberger, who served as U.S. defense secretary from 1981 to 1987 and was now publisher of *Forbes* and a foreign-affairs columnist for the world's foremost business magazine. Steve graciously agreed and set up a time for me to call Weinberger at his home in Connecticut. It turned out to be just weeks before Weinberger passed away.

As one of the key architects of Ronald Reagan's strategy to bring down the Evil Empire, a man who literally had his finger on the button during some of the tensest years of the American showdown with the Soviet military, few knew the Russians better than "Cap" Weinberger.[22] Moreover, few had as much experience at the highest levels of the U.S. government going head-to-head against the mullahs in Iran. Weinberger, after all, had access to all U.S. intelligence about the ayatollah and the revolutionary regime in Tehran. He was there when the U.S. hostages were freed by Iran in 1981. He was there when the Reagan administration built ties to Iraq as a counterweight to Iranian aggression. He was even targeted by a grossly unfair prosecutor in the Iran-Contra arms-for-hostages affair that engulfed the second term of the Reagan administration, though he was later pardoned by President George H. W. Bush, who rightly called him a "true patriot" who gave "extraordinary service to our country."

Weinberger, who was eighty-eight when he died, could not have been more generous with his time or more insightful with his answers. When we spoke, his memory was still sharp and his analysis still bore the distinct evidence of his decades of experience on the front lines. I asked him about a wide range of issues related to Russia and Iran, particularly if he thought Iran would go nuclear over the next few years. His answer floored me.

"I think they probably already have gone nuclear," he told me. "I think they have probably equipped themselves to construct some types of nuclear weapons and . . . I think they could probably do quite a lot of damage right now."[23]

That, Weinberger believed, was very likely why Ahmadinejad was being so provocative toward Israel—because he already possessed nuclear weapons and was preparing for a direct military confrontation.

It was a chilling theory. "If Iran has already gone nuclear," I asked, "then why have the Russians been helping Iran build nuclear plants and providing nuclear training and technology to a country most of the world agrees is so dangerous?"

"The answer is your first clause—it's the Russians," Weinberger replied. "It's the way they operate. . . . The Soviets [during the Cold War] were trying to increase their influence in the whole Mideast. They were using one of the traditional routes to the oil fields, coming through Afghanistan, and trying to seal not only their bases but their supply routes. We were taking actions and preparing ourselves to prevent that domination from succeeding. . . . [But] they have never accepted the idea that they were destined to be a second- or third-class power. They want to get their superpower status back, and that's a lot of what Putin is doing now. . . . They [Putin and his advisors] have not really accepted the idea of democracy or a transparent form of government in which the people are able to run things. . . .

They are not going to accept the fact that they were utterly and completely defeated."

"That said, how dangerous is Vladimir Putin?" I asked.

"I think he has a suitable background for why people are worried," Weinberger said. "He was a Soviet spy. His whole background and training was in the interest of the old Soviet policies, and I don't think he's changed very much. I don't think you get far and advance as rapidly as he did unless you're doing pretty well what you're wanted to do [by the KGB leadership]."

Weinberger's concerns didn't stop with the current leader of Russia. He raised other worst-case scenarios, including someone more dangerous than Putin emerging in Moscow through election, assassination, or coup.[24]

In his 1996 book *The Next War,* Weinberger and coauthor Peter Schweizer envisioned a Russian ultranationalist seizing power in a coup in 2006 and then threatening the world with a nuclear war. I asked if he still thought this was a possibility.

"It is a possibility," Weinberger told me, noting that while recent revolutions in ex-Soviet republics such as Ukraine, Georgia, and Kyrgyzstan have been pro-Western and pro-democracy in nature, they have only heightened fears among Russian nationalists and ultranationalists that Russia could be next if the Kremlin doesn't crack down on dissent and rule with a heavy hand. "[Our scenario] was presented not just as a possibility but as a suitable scenario for war college and advanced strategic thinking and studying, and I think it's still a possibility. I think you have in Russia an angry loser [and] I think it's wrong and immature for anybody to believe that Russia has joined the Western camp. . . . We would be dangerously naive if we thought that winning the Cold War was all we had to do."

WHAT AHMADINEJAD WANTS

The problem is that the Kremlin is playing with fire.

As I mentioned in the introduction, Iranian president Mahmoud Ahmadinejad has told friends he believes the end of the world is only a few years away. He has also said that he believes the way to hasten the arrival of the Islamic messiah is to unleash an apocalyptic holy war against Christians and Jews. Thus, he has vowed to annihilate the U.S. and Israel and is feverishly preparing his military to accomplish just that.[25]

The best way to understand Ahmadinejad's brand of Shiite eschatology (end-times theology) is to listen to Iranians describe it themselves.

Amir Taheri is a European-based columnist who used to serve as the executive editor of *Kayhan*, Iran's largest daily newspaper. In an April 2006 essay entitled "The Frightening Truth of Why Iran Wants a Bomb," Taheri wrote that just before announcing to the world that Iran had "gatecrashed 'the nuclear club,'" President Ahmadinejad "disappeared for several hours" to have a secret meeting with the Islamic messiah, a figure known as the Twelfth Imam or Mahdi. Taheri wrote, "According to Shia lore, the Imam is a messianic figure who, although in hiding, remains the true Sovereign of the World."

The article described Ahmadinejad's claim to be one of a select group of men specifically chosen by the Twelfth Imam to be his representatives and helpers in the world prior to his return. Ahmadinejad "boasts that the Imam gave him the presidency for a single task: provoking a 'clash of civilizations' in which the Muslim world, led by Iran, takes on the 'infidel' West, led by the United States, and defeats it."

The article continued:

From childhood, Shia boys are told to cultivate two qualities. The first is entezar, the capacity patiently to wait for the Imam to return. The second is taajil, the actions needed to hasten the return. For the Imam's return will coincide with an apocalyptic battle between the forces of evil and righteousness, with evil ultimately routed.[26]

Hossein Bastani is an Iranian journalist living in exile. He has written numerous accounts of Shiite leaders in Iran claiming to have witnessed physical sightings of the Twelfth Imam and saying that he will reveal himself to the world soon. "But despite these sightings," Bastani noted in one column, "it is the President [Ahmadinejad] himself who presents the strongest claims of being in touch with and thus supported by the twelfth Imam." He added that in 2005, "at a meeting with the Foreign Ministers of Islamic countries and in response to a question that Iran displayed signs of a crisis, President Ahmadinejad said that these were the signs of the return of the twelfth Imam, who will definitely return in two years."[27]

Ayatollah Ibrahim Amini is a professor at the Religious Learning Center in Qom, Iran, and one of his country's most respected Shiite scholars. In his book *Al-Imam al-Mahdi: The Just Leader of Humanity*, Amini described the signs of the coming of the Mahdi in great detail. Chief among them: a massive earthquake and the launching of a global war to kill and/or subjugate Jews, Christians, and other "infidels."

In one passage Amini quoted the prophet Mohammed (though not from the Koran), who is believed to have said, "Listen to the good news about the Mahdi! He will rise at the time when people will be faced with severe conflict and the earth will be hit by a violent quake. He will fill the earth with justice and equity as it is filled with injustice and tyranny. He will fill the hearts of his followers with devotion and will spread justice everywhere."[28]

Other key passages:

When the world has become psychologically ready to accept the government of God and when general conditions have become favorable to the idea of the rulership of the truth, God will permit the Mahdi to launch his final revolution. . . . A few selected individuals . . . will be the first ones to respond to his call, and will be drawn to him like iron to a magnet in that first hour of his appearance. . . .

On seeing the fulfillment of many of the signs promised in the traditions, a large number of unbelievers will turn towards Islam. Those who persist in their disbelief and wickedness shall be killed by the soldiers of the Mahdi. The only victorious government in the entire world will be that of Islam and people will devotedly endeavor to protect it. Islam will be the religion of everyone, and will enter all the nations of the world. . . .

The Mahdi will offer the religion of Islam to the Jews and the Christians; if they accept it they will be spared, otherwise they will be killed. . . .

It seems unlikely that this catastrophe can be avoided. . . . Warfare and bloodshed [are] inevitable. [29]

The coming of the Twelfth Imam is never mentioned in the Koran. Rather it stems from supposed sayings of Mohammed and his followers soon after the Koran was complete. Thus, not all Muslims share the brand of theology I have just outlined, nor do all Shiites.[30] But Ahmadinejad and his close aides and advisors leave no doubt that they are driven by the belief that the Islamic messiah will appear in the next two or three years and that by launching a war to annihilate Israel, in particular, they can hasten that day.

MOSCOW EXTENDS MILITARY ALLIANCE TO INCLUDE ARAB, ISLAMIC WORLD

In his classic treatise *The Art of War*, the ancient Chinese strategist Sun Tzu wrote, "What enables the wise sovereign and the good general to strike and conquer, and achieve things beyond the reach of ordinary men, is foreknowledge. [T]his foreknowledge cannot be elicited from spirits; it cannot be obtained inductively from experience, nor by any deductive calculation. Knowledge of the enemy's dispositions can only be obtained from other men. Hence the use of spies."[1]

It should not be surprising, then, that a man like Saddam Hussein was determined to know as much as he possibly could about the enemies arrayed against him in the days leading up to the commencement of Operation Iraqi Freedom on March 19, 2003. What may be surprising to some is the role that Vladimir Putin and Russian intelligence played in tipping off Saddam to the precise composition and location of American fighter aircraft, helicopters, naval ships, cruise missiles, tanks, armored vehicles, artillery, and even the location and number of special-forces units.

Top secret Iraqi documents captured by the U.S. military during the invasion of Baghdad and recently released to the public by the Pentagon reveal an intriguing look inside Saddam's war room and the startling degree of cooperation between Putin and Hussein, despite Putin's well-publicized friendship with President Bush and their supposed partnership in the War on Terror. One handwritten document is a memo written to Saddam and his top advisors, describing a meeting with Russia's ambassador to Iraq about two weeks before the outbreak of hostilities.

Captured Iraqi Document CMPC-2003-001950
[Handwritten, undated, but written before March 5, 2003][2]

To: Office of the President, Mr. Secretary
Re: Meeting with the Russian Ambassador
Our warmest greetings!

We would like to inform you that the Russian ambassador met this evening with [Iraqi officials] and he informed us of . . . the departure of Russian specialists working on projects belonging to our ministry without delay for the period March 5-8, with the last plane departing on March 9, as he conveyed. He explained that the request for the evacuation of Russian citizens came at the order of the Russian president. . . . During this meeting the ambassador presented the following information about the American military presence in the Gulf and the region as of March 2:

- Number of forces: 206,500, including 98,000 marines and 36,500 infantry. Ninety percent of these forces are in Kuwait and on American military vessels.
- American forces have also reached Bubiyan Island.
- Number of tanks: 480
- Number of armored vehicles: 1,132
- Number of artillery pieces: 296

- *Helicopters (Apache): 735*
- *Fighter planes: 871*
- *Units of the American fleet: 106, including 68 in the Gulf and the remainder in Oman, Aden, the Red Sea, and the Mediterranean*
- *Number of aircraft carriers: 5, including one nuclear-powered [carrier]; three of them are in the Gulf, one in the Mediterranean, and the other in [unclear, ed.]*
- *Number of cruise missiles: 583, belonging to the American navy, distributed among 22 naval vessels*
- *Number of aircraft-borne cruise missiles: 64*
- *Number of heavy planes (B-52H) in the Indian Ocean: 10*
- *Number of B-1B at the American base in Oman (Thumrait): 8*

The ambassador indicated that what concerns us is the increase in the number of planes in Jordan. He explained that the number of these planes at Al-Salt Base is now as follows:

- *24 F-16s*
- *10 Tornadoes*
- *11 Carriers [F-18s]*

He also indicated that there are five A-10 tank killers at the King Faisal Base in Jordan. The ambassador also indicated that a number of individuals from the 82nd [Airborne] Division have begun arriving [in] Kuwait. This division was located in Afghanistan, and the number of individuals who have arrived is 750.

Captured Iraqi documents reveal that even after the war began, Russian intelligence continued to provide Saddam Hussein and his top advisors updated information on U.S. and coalition forces and plans, as well as the highly sensitive movements of the U.S. 4th Mechanized Infantry Division and elite Delta Force.[3]

Fortunately, Saddam was not able to use such intelligence to defeat the U.S. or coalition forces. What's more, some of the Russian intelligence turned out to be flat-out wrong.

Still, such documents are valuable for several reasons. They give us a sense of the extent to which Moscow will go to support one of its client states in the Middle East, no matter how evil that client state's regime is. They give us a sense of how determined the Kremlin is to be a player in the Middle East and to counter U.S. and Western involvement there. What's more, they underscore the insight of Sun Tzu that foreknowledge of the enemy's plans, allies, and dispositions is critical in all warfare, both ancient and modern.

EZEKIEL'S FOREKNOWLEDGE

This brings us back to Ezekiel and the foreknowledge he reveals.

While Iran is the first country identified as a future ally of Russia, there are others, and it is important that we identify them before we look to see if Russia is building military partnerships with such countries today.

In Ezekiel 38:2-6 we find such cryptic-sounding countries as Cush, Put, Gomer, and Beth-togarmah. Let's decode these names one by one.

Cush

The first biblical mention of the people of Cush is in Genesis 10:6, which reads, "The sons of Ham were Cush and Mizraim and Put and Canaan" (NASB). Sons of Cush settled in Arabia, Mesopotamia, and Assyria (Genesis 10:6-11). But the Scriptures identify the Cushites themselves as geographically centered in Africa. Several major English translations of the Bible, for example, translate Cush as "Ethiopia."[4] The ancient historian Josephus also traced the Cushites (he called them Chusites) to the land of Ethiopia.[5] But the land once known as ancient Ethiopia encompassed far more territory than does the country we know today by that name. It included the modern-day country of Sudan and possibly modern-day Eritrea as well.[6]

Put

Josephus wrote that "Phut . . . was the founder of Libya, and called the inhabitants Phutites."[7] But, again, ancient Libya actually encompassed more territory than does the country we know by that name today. Thus, it is reasonable to believe that Ezekiel's Put also included the modern-day countries of Algeria and Tunisia, though it may not have extended as far as Morocco.[8]

Gomer

There is no clear historical consensus on the present-day location of Gomer "and all its troops" or "all its bands" or "all its hordes," though the dominant theories are modern-day Turkey and/or modern-day Germany. We do know from Genesis 10 that Gomer—like Magog, Meshech, and Tubal—was a son of Japheth, which puts them all into one big, violent clan. From there it gets a bit murky.

Josephus, for example, wrote that "Gomer founded those whom the Greeks now call Galatians, but were then called Gomerites."[9] The Galatians of the New Testament lived in the region of Turkey to which the apostle Paul wrote the book of Galatians and from which the Ottoman Empire emerged to take over much of the Middle East.

The question is whether the Gomerites drifted from what we now call Turkey to other countries over the centuries. Voltaire wrote that "it is incontestable that the inhabitants of Gaul [France] and Spain are descended from Gomer."[10] Other sources say the Gomerites and their relatives migrated northward to Germany. Genesis 10:3 identifies one of Gomer's relatives as Ashkenaz. Today, Israelis describe Jews from Germany, Austria, and Poland as "Ashkenazim."

Dr. Arno Gaebelein argued in his 1918 book *The Prophet Ezekiel* that "valuable information is given in the Talmud; Gomer is there stated to be the Germani, the Germans. That the descendents of Gomer moved northward and established themselves in parts of Germany seems to be an established fact." Bible scholars today seem to agree that Gomer probably refers either to Turkey or to Germany.[11]

Beth-togarmah

The word in Hebrew means "the House of Togarmah." Josephus identified the people of Togarmah as "the Thrugrammeans, who, as the Greeks resolved, were named Phrygians."[12] Phrygia was a western kingdom in Asia Minor—what we now call modern-day Turkey—from around 1200 to 600 BC. The apostle Paul "traveled through the area of Phyrgia and Galatia" in Turkey on his second missionary journey, according to Acts 16:6. The Greek historian Herodotus wrote that the people of Armenia were originally from Phrygia before they crossed into the territory we now call Armenia—the area of the Caucuses, eastern Anatolia, and southern Russia—around 700 BC.[13] Thus, Bible scholars generally believe that Beth-togarmah refers to the people of Turkey and Armenia and the Turkic-speaking peoples who spread out over time across central Asia, including those in modern-day countries of Georgia, Azerbaijan, Turkmenistan, Uzbekistan, Kazakhstan, Kyrgyzstan, and Tajikistan.[14]

Other Allies

Beyond the countries mentioned specifically, Ezekiel indicates there will be other allies. In Ezekiel 38:2, for example, the prophet cites Magog, which as we discovered earlier is not limited to Russia alone but includes territories where the Scythians spread out over time, namely the former republics of the Soviet Union, particularly those in central Asia.

In Ezekiel 38:6, after explaining that Gomer and Beth-togarmah are part of the Russian-Iranian coalition, the prophet adds that "many others" will be part of the coalition as well. This could simply mean that many troops will amass for the War of Gog and Magog against Israel. It could mean that other specific countries besides the ones already mentioned will join in the attack against Israel. Or it could also mean that the armed forces of the nations that have been mentioned will be comprised of multiple ethnicities (which is currently the case with the former Soviet republics).

In Ezekiel 38:13, the prophet refers to "Sheba" and "Dedan" and the "merchants of Tarshish" with "all its villages" (NASB) or all its "young lions" (KJV). It is widely agreed among Bible scholars that Sheba and Dedan refer to the peoples of the Arabian peninsula, including modern-day Saudi Arabia, Yemen, and Oman, and the Gulf countries of Kuwait and the United Arab Emirates.[15]

Tarshish, meanwhile, was the region encompassing what we now call southern Spain, but the term was also used in ancient times to describe the westernmost part of human civilization. Thus, many Bible scholars believe "the merchants of Tarshish" and its "villages" and "young lions" refer to the market-based economies of western Europe and perhaps even the United States. Clearly, the U.S. and most European nations are not going to attack Israel, and in the passage they are not described as part of the Russian-Iranian coalition but as questioning the motives and objectives of that coalition. Whether the Arab countries of the Gulf will actively participate in the Russian-Iranian alliance or tacitly approve it or remain neutral with the Western powers is simply not clear from the passage.

Finally, Ezekiel 38:8 says this coalition will be gathered from many nations "to the mountains of Israel." Ezekiel 39:2 also says the coalition will drive "toward the mountains of Israel." Ezekiel 39:4 says these forces will "die on the mountains." The mountains of Israel are mainly located on the country's northern borders with modern-day Syria, Lebanon, and northern Jordan (notably the strategically important Golan Heights). Since the Russian-Iranian coalition is described by the prophet as coming primarily from the north, it is reasonable to conclude that Syria and Lebanon are participants in the coalition. Jordan may be as well, though this is not entirely clear.

The Coalition against Israel

In summary, Ezekiel describes a series of specific nations that will form a future anti-Israel coalition. Russia is described as the leader of this newly constituted Axis of Evil. Iran is mentioned first among equals. Nearly all of Russia's and Iran's allies described by Ezekiel are nations that today are either predominantly Islamic or have high percentages of Muslim citizens. It is not clear if all of the former Soviet republics will participate, but it is likely that a significant number of them will, particularly those in central Asia since they are covered by both the Magog and Beth-togarmah citations. Saudi Arabia and the Gulf states are mentioned in the prophecy but, again, it is not clear if

THE COALITION AGAINST ISRAEL

ANCIENT NATIONS	MODERN NATIONS
Magog, Rosh, Meshech, and Tubal	*Russia and the former Soviet republics*
Persia	*Iran*
Cush	*Sudan, Ethiopia, and possibly Eritrea*
Put	*Libya, Algeria, and Tunisia*
Gomer	*Turkey and possibly Germany and Austria*
Beth-togarmah	*Turkey, Armenia, and the Turkic-speaking peoples of Asia Minor and central Asia.*
Countries with mountainous borders with Israel	*Syria, Lebanon, and northern Jordan*
Many peoples with you	*Possible additional Islamic allies*
[Sheba and Dedan]	*[Saudi Arabia, Yemen, Oman, and the Gulf states]*

they are participants or simply observers. Notably missing from the list are any direct references to Egypt or Iraq.

ECHOES OF MODERN ANTI-ISRAEL ALLIANCES

Now that we have examined the intelligence provided by Ezekiel, let us briefly consider recent Arab-Israeli wars as well as the current state of the Middle East conflict to get a better sense of how soon this prophecy could come to fulfillment.

"We Israelis have a history of facing overwhelming odds against us," former Israeli UN ambassador Dore Gold once told me. Indeed they do. For example, on the very day Israel declared independence, May 14, 1948, forces from seven Arab armies—Egypt, Syria, Transjordan, Lebanon, Iraq, Saudi Arabia, and Yemen—attacked the fledgling Jewish state from the north, south, and east.

The 1948 war thus offered echoes of the coming War of Gog and Magog. But it could not have been the war Ezekiel foretold. Neither Russia nor Iran participated in that war, nor did other coalition members specifically cited by Ezekiel. To the contrary, Moscow formally recognized the State of Israel in its earliest days. Also, Egypt and Iraq fought against Israel in 1948, while Ezekiel never said they would be involved.

The Six Days' War of June 1967 provided another prototype of the War of Gog and Magog. Israel was again surrounded by hostile Arab and Islamic forces and once again won a tremendous victory, in this case winning back the biblical lands of Judea and Samaria (the West Bank), the ancient Philistine territory of the Gaza Strip, and the strategically critical "mountains of Israel" to the north (the Golan Heights). Israel also reunified the holy city of Jerusalem.

But the Six Days' War could not have been the War of Gog and Magog, for while the Soviets that time provided arms, training, intelligence, and other support to their Arab clients, they did not directly participate in the war against Israel. Nor did Iran or other coalition members specifically mentioned by Ezekiel. Egypt and Iraq, meanwhile, took leading roles, contrary to the scenario laid out in the prophecy.

In many ways, the Yom Kippur War of October 1973 was even closer to Ezekiel's prophecy, though it, too, bears crucial differences. Israel again found herself surrounded by an enemy coalition, led by Egypt, Syria, Jordan, and Iraq. Other nations played important roles as well. Saudi Arabia, Kuwait, Libya, Algeria, Tunisia, Morocco, Sudan, and Pakistan assisted with varying degrees of financial aid, ground forces, combat pilots, and military equipment. Even Cuba and Uganda sent forces to help defeat the Israelis. Israel won a surprising, against-the-odds victory. But again, while the Soviets were major sponsors of the anti-Israel coalition, they did not send forces. Nor did other Ezekiel-specific countries such as Iran and Turkey. Egypt and Iraq, however, again played key roles.

What is most significant about the Yom Kippur War vis-à-vis Ezekiel's prophecy is that it set into motion a peace process that has neutralized Egypt as a direct combatant against Israel. Convinced that the Soviets were not a reliable ally and that Egypt could never win the Sinai Peninsula back through military means, Egyptian president Anwar Sadat finally decided to bring the conflict to an end through negotiations. He made a historic visit to Jerusalem, spoke directly to the Israeli people and before the Israeli parliament, and ultimately signed a peace treaty with Israel known as the Camp David Accords.

As I've pointed out, Egypt's involvement in these previous conflicts is one of the main reasons none of them could have been the war predicted by Ezekiel. But the 1979 peace treaty between Egypt and Israel actually brings the War of Gog and Magog scenario an important step closer to being fulfilled.

However, no such peace process ensued with Syria, Israel's prime enemy to the north. Thus, "the mountains of Israel" known as the Golan Heights remain hotly disputed land and will eventually become ground zero in the War of Gog and Magog.

PUTIN'S ISLAMIC INITIATIVE

Based on Ezekiel's intelligence, we should expect Russian influence throughout the Islamic world to increase dramatically as the time of the War of Gog and Magog approaches. And that is precisely what is happening.

As Vladimir Putin got himself settled into office in 2000, rebuilding Russia's tattered alliances in the Middle East became an increasingly top priority. In August of that year, Putin welcomed Yasser Arafat to Moscow, fresh from Arafat's visit to Tehran. Arafat pointedly asked Putin to get Russia more actively and aggressively involved in the Middle East than either Gorbachev or Yeltsin had. Putin, noting that he had been following the regional peace talks "very closely," agreed.[16]

By the spring of the following year, Putin had welcomed Iranian president Mohammed Khatami to Moscow—the first visit by an Iranian leader since the Islamic Revolution of 1979—to discuss increasing arms sales, nuclear cooperation, and other trade deals.[17]

And then, as if he were working his way down Ezekiel's list, Putin expanded what I call his Islamic Initiative well beyond Iran.

In December 2001, the Russian leader welcomed Ethiopian prime minister Meles Zenawi to the Kremlin and signed the first major treaty between Moscow and Addis Ababa. Putin agreed to sell Ethiopia more Russian arms, including fighter jets and other combat aircraft as well as transport helicopters. Putin also agreed that year to write off $5 billion in debt that Ethiopia owed the Soviet Union in return for new trade deals and the opportunity for Russian petroleum companies to develop oil and gas fields in the African country.[18]

In September 2003, Putin welcomed Saudi Arabia's crown prince Abdullah Ibn Abdul Aziz to Moscow. It was the first visit of such a high-ranking Saudi leader since 1932, and given that the Saudis had channeled billions of dollars to the *mujahedin* of Afghanistan to defeat the Soviets after their 1979 invasion—and that the U.S. still had military bases in the Saudi kingdom at the time—the meetings were historic. The two countries signed new trade deals and discussed regional security and future arms deals. "Russia occupies a special position in our interests and hearts as it was the first country to recognize the new Saudi state [in 1926]," the crown prince said.

Putin responded, "We view the Arab and Islamic world through the greater part of modern history in their being our closest partners and associates."[19]

In October 2003, Putin traveled to Malaysia to address the Organization of the Islamic Conference and to call on the OIC to accept Russia as a member, given that about one in seven Russian citizens (about 20 million people) are Muslims. "For centuries, Russia as a Eurasian country has been intertwined with the Islamic world," Putin told the gathering. "The last decade was a time of revival of the spiritual life of Russia's Muslims."

He noted that in 1991, Russia had only 870 mosques while today there are more than 7,000 and added that "Russia is also actively developing contacts with the majority of the states represented in this hall, essentially keeping up the long-standing, mutually beneficial traditions of cooperation and profound respect for each other."

The move was widely praised throughout the Middle East. It did, in fact, open numerous doors for Putin to build new relationships and alliances, and Russia was accepted into the OIC with "observer status."[20]

In October 2004, Putin accepted Iran's invitation to visit Tehran, further signaling the seriousness of the emerging Russian-Iranian alliance. "We do not have a concrete date for a visit by the president to Iran, but there is a firm agreement with the Iranian side that this visit will take place in the foreseeable future," Russian deputy foreign minister Alexander Alekseyev told reporters.[21]

In September 2004, while I was in Moscow, Putin was scheduled to visit Turkey but had to postpone the trip due to the terrorist attack on the elementary school in Beslan. When the trip eventually took place that December, it was understandably big news in both countries. Putin, after all, was the first Russian leader to *ever* visit modern Turkey, a longtime regional rival and still a member of the NATO alliance. In Ankara, Putin discussed ways to build economic and security ties and sell Turkey more Russian oil and gas. "Russia and Turkey are moving toward cooperation and the flourishing it will bring with it," Putin said.[22]

In February 2005, Putin sent Russian troops to Sudan. The expressed purpose was to support "peacekeeping" efforts, but Russia had been arming the radical Islamic regime in Khartoum for years, as had the Iranians.[23]

In April 2005, Putin became the first Russian leader in more than forty years to visit Egypt. He not only met with President Hosni Mubarak but also visited the headquarters of the Arab League. There he held talks with Secretary-General Amr Musa and addressed the permanent representatives of Arab countries in what Aljazeera called "Russia's wider bid to restore its Soviet-era influence in the Middle East."[24]

On that same April 2005 trip, Putin became the first leader of Russia or the Soviet Union ever to visit Israel and the Palestinian Authority. He met in Jerusalem with Prime Minister Ariel Sharon and other top Israeli officials. In the West Bank town of Ramallah, Putin met with Mahmoud Abbas, president of the Palestinian Authority. He defended recent Russian missile sales to Syria and nuclear cooperation with Iran, laid a wreath at the grave of Yasser Arafat, and pledged to sell new arms to the Palestinians.[25]

In January 2006, Putin extended an invitation to the newly elected Hamas leadership to visit Moscow for high-level talks and again offered to sell the Palestinians new arms. What's more, during a trip to Spain, Putin explained that he did not see Hamas as a terrorist organization and said he viewed the Hamas electoral victory as "a big setback, an important setback for American efforts in the Middle East, a very serious setback," using the word *setback* three times and almost appearing to relish the development.[26]

It should be noted that Putin made these moves despite international efforts to isolate Hamas diplomatically and to cut off the group's funding until it renounces violence and accepts Israel's right to exist. Several days after Putin made the invitation, Hamas leader Khaled Mash'al delivered a sermon at a mosque in Damascus, directly threatening the national security of the United States, the European Union, and Israel. Yet Putin did not back off. Instead, the Kremlin welcomed Hamas leaders to Moscow several weeks later.[27]

On and on it goes. Every week, it seems, new headlines appear with fresh evidence of Putin's Islamic Initiative, along with evidence that Iran is simultaneously building alliances with many of these same countries.

PARTNERS IN TRADE, TURKEY AND RUSSIA EYE CLOSER DEFENSE COOPERATION

Turkish Daily News, DECEMBER 8, 2004

ETHIOPIA HAS SAVED UP MONEY FOR RUSSIAN ARMS

Kommersant, JANUARY 13, 2005

RUSSIA SAYS IT'S READY TO ARM SAUDI ARABIA

Moscow Times, FEBRUARY 10, 2005

RUSSIANS TO SELL MISSILES TO SYRIA

London Telegraph, FEBRUARY 17, 2005

LIBYA AND ALGERIA READY TO BUY RUSSIAN ARMS
IF RUSSIA WRITES OFF DEBTS

MosNews.com, February 17, 2005

IRANIAN PRESIDENT CEMENTS SYRIAN ALLIANCE

Associated Press, January 19, 2006

IRAN, TURKEY INK SECURITY AGREEMENT

Islamic Republic News Agency (Iran), February 22, 2006

In March 2006, Putin became the first Russian leader since the collapse of the Soviet Union to visit Algeria. There he signed a $7.5 billion deal to sell arms to the North African nation, a deal that one Russian military analyst called "the biggest military contract signed by post-Soviet Russia."[28]

Putin also addressed a conference in Moscow called "Strategic Outlook: Russia and the Islamic World," where he urged "close cooperation" and said "pooling our efforts" with the Muslims of the Middle East would be a top Russian priority.[29]

WHAT IT MEANS

There is no question at this point that Putin has concluded it is in Russia's vital interests to build a political, military, and economic alliance with the Arab and Islamic world, regardless of the risks such an alliance poses to Moscow's relationship with Washington, London, or Brussels. The main question is how quickly such an alliance will turn against Israel.

Whether he realizes the prophetic implications of his actions or not, Putin has clearly embarked upon an aggressive and systematic effort to build new alliances with countries specifically cited in Ezekiel 38–39, as well as with those countries that could be involved in the War of Gog and Magog but are not clearly defined in the text. And the clock is ticking.

So watch closely, for such efforts will only intensify as the time of Ezekiel's vision comes to fulfillment.

GLOBAL TENSIONS SOAR AS RUSSIA TARGETS ISRAEL

In the spring of 2006, I came across a headline on an Internet news site that read **"Russia Would Never Harm Israel: Olmert."** Curious, I clicked onto the link and found a story from Agence France-Presse, which began, "Israeli leader Ehud Olmert said he had been assured by President Vladimir Putin that Russia would 'never do anything to harm Israel' despite his invitation to Hamas for talks in Moscow.[1]

"'President Putin told me that he had previously given a commitment to Ariel Sharon that Russia would never do anything to harm the state of Israel and that that commitment applies to me as it did to Ariel Sharon,'" Olmert explained. The Israeli prime minister's official Web site later noted that "Russian President Putin emphasized several times [in his call with Olmert] that Russia would not take any step directed against Israeli interests and would not harm Israel's security."[2]

If only we could take such assurances to the bank. Unfortunately, we cannot.

While it may be tempting to believe that the Russian Bear is dead and buried and poses no threat to Israel, the U.S., or anyone else, Ezekiel makes it clear that the Bear is only hibernating and will soon be back with a vengeance.

Ezekiel 38:8 says that in the latter years Russia "will come into the land that is restored from the sword, whose inhabitants have been gathered from many nations to the mountains of Israel" (NASB). Ezekiel 38:12 says Russia will target Israel, the epicenter, the people who live "at the center of the world" (NASB). Ezekiel 38:14 says Russia will target "My people Israel" (NASB). Ezekiel 38:18 says Russia "comes against the land of Israel" (NASB). Ezekiel 39:2 says Russia will come "against the mountains of Israel" (NASB). Ezekiel 38:10 makes crystal clear that the Russian dictator in charge of this operation will be executing "an evil plan" (NASB).

Despite such specificity, however, there will be those who misunderstand the nature and threat of this "evil plan" and thus will be at risk of being blindsided by it.

"THE FINAL THRUST SOUTH"

While Putin has not yet tipped his hand about any specific designs on Israel, there are men around Putin who have. One such leader is the current deputy speaker of the State Duma, one of the highest-ranking political leaders in the Russian government and a strategic ally of Putin.

Consider excerpts from a book written by this Russian leader in 1993, in which he details his plans for expanding the Russian empire to the south—toward and ultimately through Israel:

- The operation should be carried out using the code-name "Final Thrust to the South." Our army will carry out this task. It will be a means for the nation as a whole to survive and a way to restore the Russian army. . . . Russia reaching the shores of the Indian Ocean and the Mediterranean Sea is a task that will be the salvation of the Russian nation. . . . Russia will grow rich.

- The Arabs and Europeans . . . have a vested interest in seeing to it Russia establishes her new borders. . . . Only in this way can they escape the Israeli trap.
- Can't Russia, mustn't Russia, make just one move, one little move southward? . . . The Germans want this. . . . The world will understand that if Russia needs it that means it's good.
- The Russian army needs this. It will let our boys flex their muscles instead of sitting around the barracks, worn out by hazing, in the depths of Russia, not knowing who and where the enemy is and what moral and physical preparations they should make.
- Only America would not be pleased, but she won't interfere. The alternative to this development of this situation is too grave for her if she interferes.
- This is . . . Russia's fate, and without it Russia is doomed to stop growing and die. . . . Russia has been given a great historical mission. Therefore it must act decisively.
- Let Russia make its final "thrust" to the south. I can see the Russian soldiers gathering for the final expedition southward. I can see Russian commanders in Russian division and army headquarters, mapping out the route for the military formations and the endpoints of those routes. I see aircraft gathered in air bases around the southern regions of Russia. I see submarines surfacing . . . and amphibious assault ships near the shore . . . and armored infantry vehicles are on the move and great masses of tanks are rolling through. Russia will finally make her last military expedition. [3]

The author of this book, titled *The Final Thrust South,* is Vladimir Volfovich Zhirinovsky, the bombastic, often ridiculed, but influential ultranationalist founder of the woefully misnamed Liberal Democratic Party of Russia (LDPR). In 1994, when few intelligence analysts in Moscow or Washington took him seriously, Zhirinovsky triggered a political earthquake when his LDPR won a quarter of the seats in the Russian parliament, just a year after laying out this Fascist and imperialist vision of Russia's future.

A 1994 *Time* magazine cover story titled "Rising Czar?" noted:

Zhirinovsky is no ordinary politician. [He] has slugged fellow lawmakers in the halls of parliament, hobnobbed with ex-Nazi storm troopers in Austria and posed, au naturel, for photographers while cavorting in a steam bath in Serbia. He has been kicked out of or denied access to nearly half a dozen European countries. He has threatened to restore Russia's imperial borders, annex Alaska, invade Turkey, repartition Poland, give Germany "another Chernobyl," turn Kazakhstan into a "scorched desert," and employ large fans to blow radioactive waste across the Baltics. To Western eyes, the incendiary rhetoric and exuberant loutishness of this barnstorming Bonaparte have marked him as something of a buffoon. But to many Russians, Zhirinovsky offers a kind of touchstone for their deepest yearnings and frustrations.[4]

Indeed he does, and that is his danger. As Heritage Foundation Russia expert Ariel Cohen wrote in 1994, "It is tempting to dismiss Zhirinovsky's outrageous book as political polemic. But a failed Austrian painter and former army corporal was similarly ignored when he published his own tract: *Mein Kampf*. The tendency to dismiss Zhirinovsky as a buffoon and to assume that his supporters did not know what they were voting for may be a naïve, even dangerous, response to his election and his position as de facto opposition leader gives him influence that cannot be ignored."[5]

THE MAN BEHIND THE MAN

When I last visited Moscow, I sought a meeting with Zhirinovsky. In *The Ezekiel Option*, after all, I was writing about a Fascist, anti-Semitic ultranationalist who rises to power in Moscow, becomes a czar, and leads the Russian army south to the Mediterranean. Why not meet such a person in real life?

Zhirinovsky's personal support among Russians had slipped since he had landed on the cover of *Time*. In the December 2003 elections, the LDPR received only 11.6 percent of the vote and 38 seats in the Duma. But he was still a player. Zhirinovsky and his colleagues represented the third-biggest political force in the country, behind Putin's United Russia Party (222 seats) and the Communist Party (53 seats).[6] What's more, several Russia experts I trust suggested that the LDPR's drop in the polls had nothing to do with Russians becoming less nationalist but with Putin becoming more so. Why vote for "Mad Vlad," they argued, when Putin was the real deal—a tough-as-nails leader, a czar in the making, without any of Zhirinovsky's rhetorical baggage? The more authoritarian Putin has become, they explained, the more votes he has siphoned off of the nationalist and ultranationalist parties into his own camp.

"Actually, the guy you want to see," one of my Russian friends told me, "is not Zhirinovsky himself. I mean, he's fun to talk to. You'd get some great quotes. But the guy you really want to talk to is the man behind the man, Zhirinovsky's brain."

"Who's that?" I asked.

"Alexei Mitrofanov," he said. "He's the number two guy in the LDPR. For years he was the chairman of the Geopolitical Committee of the Duma, roughly the equivalent of the [U.S.] House Foreign Relations Committee. He's Zhirinovsky's chief strategist. But far more importantly, he's a guy who is quietly, carefully helping shape Putin's direction, and thus Russia's."

My father and I met Mitrofanov for coffee at the Hotel National, across the street from Red Square and the Kremlin, on Wednesday, September 1, 2004. We had never met a Fascist before, and certainly not one with real political power. We didn't even know what Mitrofanov looked like and weren't quite sure what to expect. But soon a large, plump man not much older than myself (he was born in 1962, I in 1967) arrived with several bodyguards who took up positions by the doors of the restaurant.

In manner, he was the complete opposite of Zhirinovsky—well educated, soft-spoken, almost shy—and was clearly intent on putting a "kinder, gentler" face on his boss's vicious brand of politics. But it soon became readily apparent that this was indeed "Zhirinovksy's brain." They think exactly alike.

"We are pragmatic people," Mitrofanov began, speaking of himself and his party. "But Russia is in danger of collapsing within ten years. . . . Gorbachev made foolish decisions. He lost the whole empire for nothing. But it just proves that if the leader will be weak, Russia will be ruined. . . . Russians want a strong dictator."[7]

"What about Putin?" I asked. "Is he a czar?"

"Putin is a nationalist, a pragmatic nationalist," Mitrofanov replied. "I had many private conversations with him before he became president and I know that he is close to our party in his heart. . . . But he is not a strong leader. He has too many limitations."

Well, that was a twist, I thought, someone who thinks Putin isn't czarlike enough. "What about your boss? Is he the next czar?"

"Zhirinovsky wants to be like Stalin," he said, "like Lenin. He wants to have power and make Russia number one in the world again."

"Does he have a chance at succeeding Putin?"

"I think yes," Mitrofanov explained. "Not in the next elections, in 2008. But in 2012, I think Zhirinovsky will be the president of Russia. He will be sixty-six. He will have been in politics for twenty years. People will know his name, his brand, like Marlboro, like Coca-Cola. . . . Besides, Zhirinovsky will be very quiet [until then]. He is changing."

"Changing how?" I asked.

"Changing his style and his ideas, gaining experience. . . . He is the man Russia needs."

"What would he do as president, in foreign policy, for example?"

"He would build a coalition," Mitrofanov replied without hesitation. "Russia must control four countries in order to have quiet borders—Afghanistan, Iran, Iraq, and Pakistan." Then, after a moment's pause, he added, "And Turkey."

"Why these?"

"Zhirinovsky wants to rebuild the Byzantine Empire," he said matter-of-factly.

I just stared at him, trying to process what he was saying and why he was being so open about his party's ambitions. *The Byzantine Empire?* I thought. *That would include a lot more land than just those five countries. It would include Syria, Lebanon, Jordan, Egypt . . . and Israel.*

"We need it," Mitrofanov explained, "or we will have instability."

"Doesn't such a position run the risk of having the LDPR be accused of being anti-Semitic and anti-Israel?"

"Russia is very quiet towards the Jews today," he said. "There's no anti-Semitism here. Not like in Europe. . . . I know people in the Russian military—very nationalistic people—who have ideas that Jewish people have ruined Russia, and they have an idea to attack Israel. Colonel [Pavel] Chernov of the FSB, for example. He believes we should say to the Muslim world, 'We have the power, the land, and the nuclear weapons. You have one billion people, living bombs. Let's work together.' He said Russia must be Muslim, not Orthodox Christian. . . . He wanted to push Jews out of all leadership positions in Russia."

"What's Chernov doing now?" I asked.

"He used to be in the LDPR," Mitrofanov freely admitted. "He played an important part in the party for a while. He was number two, in fact, until Zhirinovsky fired him. He drank too much. Fired off a machine gun. But he had lots of supporters."

I looked at my father, and he looked back at me. He didn't say anything then; nor did I. But we were thinking the same thing. We were sitting with a man who believed that an ex-FSB officer's offense was getting drunk and blowing off some steam, not his desire to form a nuclear alliance with Iran and the rest of the Muslim world to blow up Israel. And as evil as that was, this was no crank we'd met at the Moscow circus. Mitrofanov is a respected member of the Russian parliament. He was a senior advisor to the deputy speaker of that parliament. And he had no hesitation to tell two Americans that he and his party want Russia to build an empire and launch the "final thrust south."

We thanked him for his time, paid our bill, and left as quickly as we could.

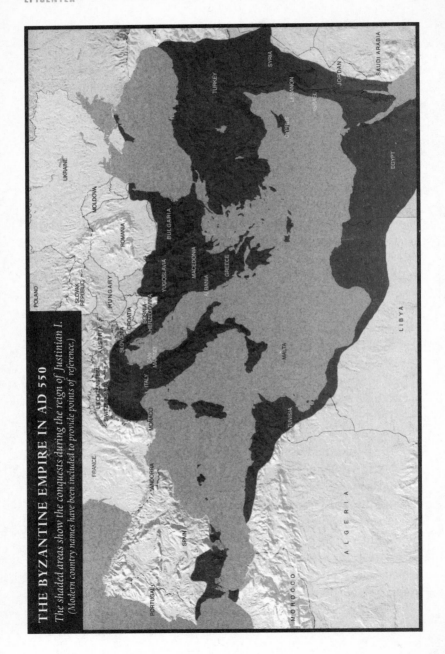

THE BYZANTINE EMPIRE IN AD 550

The shaded areas show the conquests during the reign of Justinian I.
(Modern country names have been included to provide points of reference.)

1982: THE THREAT FROM THE NORTH

Since the times of Czar Peter the Great, Russian leaders have had designs on central Asia and the Near East, and for nearly half of the twentieth century, Moscow armed Israel's enemies and encouraged them to attack and destroy the Jewish state. But now a fuller and more disturbing picture is emerging. Previously classified White House, CIA, and State Department documents, as well as interviews with top U.S. and Israeli leaders and historians, reveal that Moscow has on more than one occasion planned direct Russian invasions of Israel.

In the summer of 1982, for example, then–Israeli prime minister Menachem Begin went public with a story that prior to that time had been known only to the upper echelons of Israeli and U.S. intelligence. The Israeli Defense Forces, he explained, had uncovered a secret but massive cache of Soviet weaponry in deep underground cellars and tunnels in Lebanon that had caught him and his top advisors completely off guard. The weapons appeared to have been pre-positioned by Moscow for the launching of a full-scale invasion of Israel and the oil-rich nations of the Middle East.

Begin said Israel had found "ten times more Russian weapons than were previously reported." The haul, he told reporters, included 4,000 tons of ammunition, 144 armored vehicles and tanks, 12,500 pieces of small arms, 515 heavy weapons, 359 sophisticated communications devices, and 795 "optical instruments" (including night-vision goggles and field glasses). It was enough, Begin believed, to equip at least five Russian combat brigades and required, according to one report, "a fleet of 10-ton trucks, working day and night for six weeks, to haul them back to Israel."[8]

"I can now tell you," the Israeli prime minister continued, "that only yesterday . . . we found other arms depots containing fully ten times as many weapons as we had found before, enough to equip not five brigades, but five or six divisions. We shall need literally hundreds of trucks to evacuate these weapons from Lebanon, where we shall undoubtedly find more arms."

Begin said that Israeli intelligence had badly underestimated the

Russian threat from the north. Israel certainly knew the Soviets were arming Yasser Arafat and the Palestine Liberation Organization for their terrorist attacks against Israel. That was why Israel had invaded Lebanon in the first place. But Begin conceded that neither he nor his colleagues had any idea of the extent to which Moscow was preparing for a massive future ground assault against the Jewish state.

"Something happened which nobody knew," Begin admitted. "In fact, the evidence at hand points to a conspiracy, that pre-positioning by the Soviet Union of such massive quantities of arms—and I mean modern, highly sophisticated weapons—could only be in preparation for some indeterminate future date to overrun Israel, then Jordan, and then Saudi Arabia and other Persian Gulf States. Otherwise, there is no explanation for the quantities of weapons we have found. The [Palestinians] couldn't have used them, having neither the necessary manpower nor the skills."

The *Washington Post* reported the story of the Soviet arms cache on July 7, 1982. But the implications of such an important discovery got lost amid a series of other earthshaking events in the Middle East. Just one month earlier, an Israeli air strike had destroyed the Osirak nuclear reactor and thus Iraq's entire nuclear-weapons development program. And just two months after the discovery of the Soviet arms, members of the Maronite Phalange militia massacred hundreds of Palestinian men, women, and children in Lebanese refugee camps known as Sabra and Shatila.

The Osirak bombing and the Sabra and Shatila massacres, along with the international outcry over whether Israeli defense minister Ariel Sharon was responsible for letting the massacres happen, dominated worldwide headlines for months. Sharon eventually resigned his post as defense minister. Begin found himself and his entire government on defense in the global public-relations wars. And the Soviets' plans and preparations for invading Israel and the rest of the Middle East were lost to a world that either never heard the story, did not remember, or did not care.

When I interviewed Caspar Weinberger, who was the U.S. defense secretary in 1982, he both remembered and confirmed Menachem

Begin's story for me. He also admitted that the discovery of the Soviet arms cache "was perhaps larger than most people [in Washington] would have expected." Weinberger conceded that he and others in the Pentagon were surprised by the "size, scope, and speed"—and se- crecy—of the Soviet pre-positioning in the Middle East, given how carefully the U.S. was watching the Soviet military.

But Weinberger said he was not surprised that the Soviets had been preparing for an invasion of Israel, Saudi Arabia, and the Persian Gulf region. To the contrary, these were precisely the concerns that were driving the Reagan administration's anti-Soviet policy at the time.

"We [in the Reagan White House and the Pentagon] were all con- cerned about growing Soviet influence and growing Soviet attempts to increase their stature in the whole Mideast," Weinberger told me. "And the fact that here was confirmation of this by this discovery of a very large stash of weapons was continually disturbing, but not surpris- ing. . . . The fact that they [the Soviets] were building up their weapons and planning to use various Mideast spots as bases for military action was not a surprise—it was the size, scope, and speed with which it was being carried out that was further reason, we thought, why their mo- tives had to be watched quite carefully."[9]

I asked Weinberger specifically if he and President Reagan had shared Prime Minister Begin's concerns that the Soviets might try to overrun Israel, Jordan, Saudi Arabia, and the other Persian Gulf states.

He confirmed that they had. "The Soviets were trying to increase their influence in the whole Mideast. They were [targeting] the oil fields. . . . We were taking actions and preparing ourselves to prevent that domination from succeeding."

Did he believe the discovery of the Soviet arms justified the Israeli invasion of Lebanon and attempts to destroy the PLO? Weinberger said Israel's move was at first "disturbing" because it was a "unilateral action" and threatened to upset the fragile balance of power in the Mid- dle East, and this was "not good."

That said, however, he suggested that on balance the Israelis were probably right to go in, especially given what they found and the Soviet invasion they may have stopped. It was a total surprise. It unleashed international condemnation of Israel, including pointed criticism from the Reagan administration itself. But the result was that Israel effectively staved off far more cataclysmic evils that were coming from the Russians.

Then Weinberger warned that the discovery of the secret Soviet arms cache was disturbing evidence "that military actions are being planned" or "made increasingly possible" in the Middle East that can elude the detection of even the world's best intelligence services.

1973: THE BRINK OF NUCLEAR WAR

On October 6, 1973, combined Arab forces from Egypt, Syria, and numerous other Arab and Islamic countries attacked Israel on Yom Kippur, the Day of Atonement, the holiest day of the Jewish year.

Tensions had been building for months. Rumors of war were in the air. But both Israeli and U.S. intelligence officials and political leaders were caught almost completely off guard, not believing the war would really come. Israeli prime minister Golda Meir was so sure fighting would not break out that she had refused to order a preemptive strike or even to mobilize the Israeli reserves, not wanting to provoke hostilities if they could be avoided. That hesitation nearly led to the annihilation of the Jewish state.

Over the course of the first week of the war, the Arab coalition made stunning gains. In the north, 1,000 Syrian tanks and 600 pieces of Syrian artillery stormed up the Golan Heights and advanced toward the vulnerable Israeli farmlands of the Galilee region. To the south, some 400 Egyptian tanks crossed the Suez Canal, wiped out Israel's forward defenses, and began working their way across the Sinai Desert. Meanwhile, Arab air forces shot down three dozen Israeli fighter planes in just the first few days.

It was clear to the general public at the time that the Soviet Union was providing the weaponry, ammunition, intelligence, and military training to help the Arab and Islamic coalition destroy Israel, a key ally of the United States. What was not known publicly was the extent to which the Soviets were orchestrating the war from behind the scenes and preparing to enter it directly.

By the second week of the war, the momentum had begun to shift. The Israelis had retaken the Golan Heights and were bombing Damascus. They had also retaken most of the Sinai Peninsula, crossed the Suez Canal, and had ground forces within a hundred kilometers of Cairo. By the third week, Moscow was under tremendous pressure from the entire Arab world not to let the Israelis humiliate Syrian president Hafez al-Assad or Egyptian president Anwar Sadat, so Moscow began to move. The Soviets began a massive airlift of arms and ammunition to their allies. The U.S., in turn, began a massive, round-the-clock airlift of arms and supplies to Israel.

On October 24 at around 10:00 p.m. eastern time, the Soviet ambassador to Washington, Anatoly Dobrynin, telephoned Secretary of State Henry Kissinger and dictated the text of a top secret message from Russian general secretary Leonid Brezhnev to President Richard Nixon. In the message, Brezhnev accused Israel of refusing to abide by a ceasefire called by the UN Security Council and then issued a chilling threat: "I will say it straight: that if you find it impossible to act jointly with us in this matter, we should be faced with the necessity urgently to consider the question of taking appropriate steps unilaterally. We cannot allow arbitrariness on the part of Israel."[10]

It was cloaked in the language of diplomats, but there it was: if the Nixon administration did not stop the Israelis from advancing and agree to send a joint Soviet-American ground force to the region to act as peacekeepers, the Soviets would send ground forces in "unilaterally."

Top U.S. officials in the White House and National Security Council were stunned as Brezhnev threatened to turn an already dangerous regional confrontation into an overt global showdown between East and West. What's more, they knew they would have no choice but to match any move by the Soviets to escalate the situation. Washington had to defend Israel or send a devastating message to her allies that the U.S. could not be counted on in a direct showdown with Russia.

And then the Soviets began to escalate. At least seven Soviet combat-ready airborne divisions in East Germany and elsewhere in

Eastern Europe were put on alert and mobilized for immediate departure for the Middle East. Soviet transport planes were positioned and
prepped to insert these forces into the fight with Israel. Soviet warships
moved into the Mediterranean.

The U.S., in turn, ordered its own military forces on alert. The
Pentagon ordered U.S. nuclear forces to DEFCON 3, the highest
state of peacetime readiness. The Joint Chiefs of Staff also ordered
the 82nd Airborne Division to prepare to head to the Middle East.
Additional U.S. naval forces—including another aircraft carrier—
moved into the Mediterranean, all out of a real and rising concern
that the Soviets were about to make an unprecedented military
move against Israel.[11]

Kissinger drafted for President Nixon (who was deeply embroiled
in the Watergate scandal at the time) a reply that was sent to General
Secretary Brezhnev on October 25. In the letter Nixon bluntly said to
the Soviet leader that the U.S. had "no information which would indicate that the ceasefire is now being violated on any significant scale."
He agreed to "take every effective step to guarantee the implementation of the ceasefire" and said the U.S. was working closely with Israel
to bring about a peaceful resolution to the crisis.

But he also warned that "in these circumstances, we must view
your suggestion of unilateral action as a matter of the gravest concern
involving incalculable consequences. . . . [W]e could in no event accept
unilateral [Soviet] action. This would be in violation of our under-
standings, of the agreed Principles we signed in Moscow in 1972, and of
Article II of the Agreement on Prevention of Nuclear War. . . . Such action would produce incalculable consequences which would be in the
interest of neither of our countries and which would end all we have
striven so hard to achieve."[12]

Nixon's firm letter, combined with the heightened American military posture, soon made it clear to Moscow that any move they made
against Israel would be met with the full force of the United States.
Within days, the Soviets backed off. Tensions began to defuse, and a
full cease-fire was eventually achieved. Not since the Cuban Missile
Crisis of 1962 had the U.S. and Soviet Union come so close to the brink

of nuclear war, and this time the motivating factor was a Russian leader's threat to attack Israel directly.

Yet for all that, Kissinger would remark to his top aides that the Soviet military "did not maneuver as provocatively as they did in 1967."[13]

1967: THE KREMLIN PREPARES FOR WAR

War clouds had been building for months. The Israelis found themselves increasingly surrounded by Soviet-backed forces of the Arab and Islamic world, all of whose leaders were vowing to "throw the Jews into the sea," and the Israelis were considering striking first. The element of surprise might be their only hope of survival, they figured. But President Lyndon Johnson had warned Israeli prime minister Levi Eshkol in no uncertain terms that such a move would be a serious mistake.

As historian Michael B. Oren noted in his highly praised book *Six Days of War: June 1967 and the Making of the Modern Middle East*, Johnson sent a secret message to Eskhol, saying, "It is essential that Israel not take any preemptive military action and thereby make itself responsible for the initiation of hostilities. Preemptive action by Israel would make it impossible for the friends of Israel to stand at your side." Oren noted that Johnson specifically "warned of the possibility of direct Soviet intervention."[14]

Marshal Andrei Antonovich Grechko, the Soviet deputy defense minister, had told his Egyptian counterparts in Cairo that the Kremlin had dispatched "destroyers and submarines to the waters near Egypt, some armed with missiles and secret weapons" to help wipe out the Zionists.[15] One of Israel's top experts on Soviet foreign policy told Israeli Defense Forces intelligence that "the USSR would muster all its influence and power to maintain its Middle East position." When asked if the Soviets would intervene directly, the expert replied, "Of course."[16] Soviet premier Aleksey Kosygin, meanwhile, sent a cable to Prime Minister Eshkol, warning, "If the Israeli Government insists on taking upon itself the responsibility for the outbreak of armed confrontation then it will pay the full price of such an action."[17]

But at 8:44 a.m. on the morning of June 5, 1967, Eshkol sent an urgent message back to President Johnson informing him that it was too late. War had begun.

Explaining his rationale for the preemptive strike Israel had just launched, Eshkol wrote:

> After weeks in which our peril has grown day by day, we are now engaged in repelling the aggression which [Egyptian president] Nasser has been building up against us. Israel's existence and integrity have been endangered. The provocative [Arab] troop concentrations in Sinai, now amounting to five infantry and two armored divisions; the placing of more than 900 tanks against our southern frontier; . . . the illegal blockade of the Straits of Tiran; . . . the imminent introduction of MiG-21 aircraft under Iraqi command [into the theater]; Nasser's announcement of "total war against Israel" and of his basic aim to annihilate Israel. . . . All of this amounts to an extraordinary catalogue of aggression, abhorred and condemned by world opinion and in your great country and amongst all peace-loving nations.[18]

Eshkol also noted that three Israeli towns had been bombed that morning by Arab forces, citing these as the last straws that led to war. He thanked Johnson for America's support and expressed hope that "our small nation can count on the fealty and resolution of its greatest friend." But he also had a request: that the U.S. "prevent the Soviet Union from exploiting and enlarging the conflict" at this, Israel's greatest "hour of danger."

"Eshkol knew and feared the Russians," noted Michael Oren. "War with Syria [and Egypt] was risky enough; with the USSR, it would be suicidal." But Eshkol calculated that without U.S. support, the Soviets would find themselves compelled to get involved directly. Moscow had "invested massively in the Middle East, about $2 billion in military aid alone—1,700 tanks, 2,400 artillery pieces, 500 jets, and 1,400 advisers—since 1956, some 43 percent of it to Egypt."[19]

Sure enough, as the Israelis demolished the forces of the Arab coalition over the next three days and captured the Sinai, the West Bank, the Gaza Strip, and the Golan Heights, reunified the holy city of Jerusalem, and began an offensive against Damascus, Moscow saw itself staring into the face of a geopolitical disaster. Those were, after all, Soviet-trained soldiers being defeated. Those were Soviet-made arms being seized or destroyed. Those were billions of dollars in Soviet funding to their Arab client states being poured down the drain. And— it would later be learned by U.S. and Israeli intelligence—the Egyptian war plan itself (code-named Operation Conqueror) had actually been written in 1966 by the Soviets.[20] As a result, the Soviets feared their prestige was quickly unraveling.

U.S. intelligence was already picking up signs of this fear in the Kremlin. In the "President's Daily Brief" on June 9, for example, the CIA informed President Johnson that "the Soviets are finding it hard to conceal their shock over the rapid Egyptian military collapse. A Soviet official [identity still classified] could not understand 'how our intelligence could have been so wrong.' He asked despairingly, 'How could we have gotten into such a mess?'"[21]

So the Kremlin decided to dramatically up the ante.

On June 10, at 8:48 a.m. Washington time, Soviet premier Aleksey Kosygin used the "hotline" to call President Johnson in the White House Situation Room. His message was as blunt as it was unnerving: "A very crucial moment has now arrived which forces us, if [Israeli] military actions are not stopped in the next few hours, to adopt an independent decision. We are ready to do this. However, these actions may bring us into a clash which will lead to a grave catastrophe. . . . We propose that you demand from Israel that it unconditionally cease military action. . . . We purpose to warn Israel that if this is not fulfilled, necessary actions will be taken, including military."[22]

The Soviets quickly broke off diplomatic relations with Israel, and the Soviet-bloc governments of Czechoslovakia and Bulgaria soon followed.[23]

CIA Director Richard Helms would later recall that the conversations in the Situation Room for the next several hours were in "the lowest voices he had ever heard in a meeting of that kind" and that "the atmosphere was tense" as the president and his most senior military, diplomatic, and intelligence advisors contemplated the possibility of a direct Soviet strike at Israel.[24]

Johnson, a devoted friend of Israel and an ardent anti-Communist, was not prepared to kowtow to Moscow or let Israel be destroyed. He immediately ordered the U.S. 6th Fleet in the Mediterranean to turn around—it was then heading west toward the Strait of Gibraltar—and steam toward Israel as a show of solidarity and to warn the Soviets not to get directly involved.[25]

He did the right thing, for according to Isabella Ginor, a Russian-born correspondent for the BBC World Service and other international news services, "new evidence now reveals that the Soviets were indeed poised to attack Israel . . . and had been preparing for such a mission all along."[26]

On June 10, 2000—the thirty-third anniversary of Kosygin's ominous hotline threat to Johnson—Ginor published an article in *The Guardian* (London) entitled "How the Six Day War Almost Led to Armageddon: New Evidence of 1967 Soviet Plan to Invade Israel Shows How Close the World Came to Nuclear Conflict." In December of that year, she published a longer and more detailed article in the *Middle East Review of International Affairs* entitled "The Russians Were Coming: The Soviet Military Threat in the 1967 Six-Day War." In these and other articles, she quoted Soviet military officials who paint a fragmentary but still disturbing picture of the attack that was being prepared.

Ginor noted that "in his recently published memoirs, Nikita S. Khruschev asserts that the USSR's military command first encouraged high-ranking Egyptian and Syrian delegations, in a series of 'hush-hush' mutual visits, to go to war, then persuaded the Soviet political leadership to support these steps, in the full knowledge they were aimed at starting a war to destroy Israel."[27]

Soviet acting defense minister Andrei A. Grechko and KGB Chairman Yuri V. Andropov, meanwhile, "were pressing for the immediate dispatch of Soviet forces to the Middle East." Retired Soviet air force lieutenant Yuri V. Nastenko confirmed in 1998 that bomber and fighter jets, such as the MiG-21s that were under his command, were put on full operational alert on the evening of June 5, 1967, and that he was convinced this was in preparation for "real combat."[28]

Yuri N. Khripunkov, a former Soviet naval officer who was serving on one of thirty Soviet warships that had been moved from the Black Sea southward to the Mediterranean in June 1967, told Ginor that he and his colleagues were preparing to unleash Soviet forces onto the Israeli mainland. His own platoon, he said, was "ordered to penetrate Haifa—Israel's main commercial harbor and naval base."[29] Russian professor Alexsandr K. Kislov, who was stationed in the Middle East in 1967, told Ginor that the strike force the Soviets had prepared for insertion into Israel included "desant [landing] ships with well-prepared marines."[30]

Some respected historians and diplomats have disputed the notion that the Soviets were planning to attack Israel in 1967.[31] But while the evidence available from declassified documents and interviews with direct participants may not yet be conclusive, it is compelling. What's more, Soviet premier Kosygin's threat of direct military intervention into the 1967 war with Israel alone stands as chilling evidence of Moscow's historic and recent animus toward the Jewish state—and as a warning of things to come.

NEW WAR ERUPTS IN MIDDLE EAST AS EARTHQUAKES, PANDEMICS HIT EUROPE, AFRICA, ASIA

In a moment, we will walk through the intelligence Ezekiel provides us describing the magnitude of the coming War of Gog and Magog. We will also consider how such events will directly affect every person on the face of the earth. But first we must ask a more fundamental question: Why is the war coming at all?

The simplest answer can be found in Genesis 12:1-3, where God promises to bless Abraham and the Jewish people, build Israel into a great and influential nation, and defend them against their enemies. "I will bless those who bless you," God says, "and the one who curses you I will curse" (NASB).

One cannot read the Hebrew Scriptures or the New Testament without realizing how much God loves the Jewish people and the nation of Israel and that he has a plan and purpose for them both. Yet throughout the ages, many world leaders have refused to humble themselves before the living God. They have also refused to view Israel through the third lens of Scripture. In turn, they have not only set their hearts against God, they have also set their hearts against his chosen people and the land he promised to them. As a direct result of this profoundly spiritual conflict, such leaders have chosen to curse the Jewish people. Some have even sought to enslave the children of Israel or to annihilate them altogether. It is a phenomenon that began with the pharaohs of Egypt, but clearly this pathology of evil has existed throughout history and continues right up to today.

Consider the case of Adolf Hitler.

The Nazi leader thought of himself as a secular messiah, "uninhibited by any religious sanctions whatever and with an unappeasable appetite for controlling mankind," observed the renowned historian Paul Johnson. Hitler explicitly rejected the idea of God as an authority figure over himself. He rejected biblical principles and authority, and he bitterly opposed all who claimed to live their lives according to the Holy Scriptures.

"Hitler hated Christianity with a passion which rivaled [Vladimir] Lenin's," Johnson once wrote. "Shortly after assuming power in 1933, he told Hermann Rauschning that he intended 'to stamp out Christianity root and branch. . . . One is either a Christian or a German—you cannot be both.'"[1]

This hatred of Christianity and the Bible upon which it is based led to an even more virulent hatred of the Jewish people who wrote the Bible and were the first true followers of God. Adolf Hitler wrote in *Mein Kampf*:

Wherever I went, I began to see Jews, and the more I saw, the more sharply they became distinguished in my eyes from the rest of humanity. . . . Later I often grew sick to the stomach from the smell of these [Jews]. . . . Was there any form of filth or profligacy, particularly in cultural life, without at least one Jew involved in it? If you cut even cautiously into such an abscess, you found, like a maggot in a rotting body, often dazzled by the sudden light—a [Jewish person]. . . . Gradually, I began to hate them. . . . For me this was the time of the greatest spiritual upheaval I have ever had to go through. I had ceased to be a weak-kneed cosmopolitan and become an anti-Semite.[2]

Driven by this hatred of God and his chosen people, Hitler went on to murder 6 million Jews in a campaign known as The Final Solution that was designed to wipe out all Jews. Such a campaign might very well have succeeded if the U.S. and allied forces had not been able to destroy Hitler's regime.

Joseph Stalin, leader of the Soviet Union in the 1930s and 1940s, likewise hated all who looked to the Bible as a source of inspiration and authority, and he reserved particular cruelty for the Jewish people. He had a favorite saying by which he lived and by which multitudes of Jewish people died, notes Soviet expert Arnold Beichman: *"Est chelovek, est problema, net cheloveka—net problemy."* It meant, "A person, a problem; no person—no problem." As Beichman put it: "Millions of people in the Soviet Union became un-persons during [Stalin's] quarter-century rule . . . and he had a particular hatred for Soviet Jews. Stalin's own daughter, Svetlana, attested to that psychosis: 'What was originally political hate gradually became a feeling of racial hatred against all Jews, without exception.'" During Stalin's reign of terror, tens of millions of Russians died from purges, wars, and famines. Many of these were Jews, at least a million of whom were deported from Moscow in 1953 and sent to slave-labor camps in Siberia, never to be heard from again.[3]

Today the murderous anti-Semitic and anti-Christian spirit of Adolf Hitler and Joseph Stalin is being carried on by Iranian president Mahmoud Ahmadinejad. As we have seen, he has called for the complete destruction of the Jewish state, echoing the words of the Ayatollah Khomeini: "Israel must be wiped off the map."[4] He is feverishly seeking nuclear weapons to accomplish the complete annihilation of Israel and the United States. He believes that the Islamic messiah's return "will be preceded by cosmic chaos, war, bloodshed, and pestilence." And he believes it is his job to bring about such apocalyptic events by launching a global jihad against Jews and Christians.[5]

Osama bin Laden also made it his mission in life to curse the Jews, destroy their state, and destroy anyone—first and foremost the United States—who seeks to bless Israel and stand by her during a time of jihad. "We are sure of Allah's victory and our victory against the Americans and the Jews, as promised by the Prophet, peace be upon him," bin Laden told a reporter in 1998. "Judgment Day shall not come until the Muslims fight the Jews, where the Jews will hide behind trees and stones, and the tree and stone will speak and say, 'Muslim, behind me is a Jew. Come and kill him.'"[6]

A careful examination of Scripture reveals a number of different ways that God has dealt with tyrants who curse the Jewish people throughout history. But Ezekiel warns us that certain leaders of certain nations will face an unprecedented and cataclysmic judgment in the last days. That is what the War of Gog and Magog is all about, and it may be here sooner than most people think.

THE WAR AHEAD

Let us now turn our attention to understanding just what will transpire during this War of Gog and Magog and how the nations of the world will be affected by this unprecedented event.

In Ezekiel 38:9, we learn that Israel will face overwhelming odds. The Russian-Islamic alliance will come "like a storm," and its troops will "be like a cloud covering the land" (NASB). The military forces commanded by the Russian dictator will come "out of the remote parts of the north" and appear as "a great assembly and a mighty army" (Ezekiel 38:15, NASB).

Nowhere in the text, however, does Ezekiel indicate that any nation will come to Israel's side to defend her against such a massive onslaught. Ezekiel 38:13 suggests that an international discussion is under way over Russia's motives and objectives. Perhaps this will occur in the UN General Assembly or in the Security Council itself. It will certainly happen on radio and television as the storm clouds build. But in the end, Israel will stand alone, on the brink of extinction, facing what many will openly predict at the time as another holocaust.

It will, therefore, be a lonely and frightful time for Israelis in particular and for the Jewish people around the world as their enemies advance ever closer to Israel's borders, day by day, until she is completely surrounded, cut off, and alone. One can reasonably surmise from the context, from biblical history, and from recent history that Israel's enemies will be taunting her, boasting of their strength, of her weakness, and of the imminent and glorious triumph of Islam.

One can also reasonably expect Israeli leaders to be making preparations for war and considering a preemptive strike. They will likely be considering what some have called the Samson Option, wherein Israel—convinced she is about to be destroyed—chooses to take all of her enemies with her to the grave.

The Samson Option is named for the ancient Hebrew judge who prayed in Judges 16:28-30, "Sovereign LORD, remember me again. O God, please strengthen me just one more time. . . . Let me die with the Philistines." In Samson's case, he pushed over the pillars holding up the roof of the temple that he and his captors were standing in, and the collapsing ceiling crushed them all. In modern Israel's case, the plan would be to launch a massive, preemptive nuclear strike against Moscow, Tehran, Damascus, Tripoli, Khartoum, and other enemy cities, despite the fact that Russia—at the very least—would unleash her nuclear missiles as well, leaving no one standing on either side.

Regardless of first-strike plans being made by either side, the War of Gog and Magog will be unlike any other war in human history. The intelligence Ezekiel provides clearly indicates that God himself will go to war on behalf of Israel and against her enemies, with devastating results.

Ezekiel 38:18-20 indicates that "on that day, when Gog comes against the land of Israel," the Lord God says, "My fury will mount up in My anger. In My zeal and in My blazing wrath, I declare that on that day there will surely be a great earthquake in the land of Israel. The fish of the sea, the birds of the heavens, the beasts of the field, all the creeping things that creep on the earth, and all the men who are on the face of the earth will shake at My presence" (NASB).

The earthquake will be epicentered in Israel, but its shock waves will be felt around the world. Clearly, Israel's enemies will be directly and immediately affected by the quake, as "the mountains . . . will be thrown down, the steep pathways will collapse and every wall will fall to the ground" (Ezekiel 38:20, NASB). But does the text also mean that literally every person on the planet will physically shake as if he or she were standing at the epicenter? Or does it mean that the destruction will be so great throughout the Middle East that everyone on earth will be affected personally by fear, by higher gas and oil prices, or by other less physical but no less powerful forces? It is not quite clear, but one should be prepared for all of the above.

This massive earthquake, however, is only the beginning.

"I will call for a sword against him on all My mountains," declares the Lord God in Ezekiel 38:21 (NASB). "Every man's sword will be against his brother." In other words, in the ensuing chaos, the enemy forces arrayed against Israel will begin fighting each other. The war will begin all right, but Russian and Muslim forces will be firing at *one another*, not at the Jews.

"With pestilence and with blood I will enter into judgment with him," the Lord God continues in Ezekiel 38:22, referring to the Russian dictator known as Gog. "And I will rain on him and on his troops, and on the many peoples who are with him, a torrential rain, with hailstones, fire and brimstone" (NASB).

This will be the most terrifying sequence of events in human history to date. On the heels of a terrifying supernatural earthquake that will undoubtedly take many lives will come a cascading series of other disasters. Pandemic diseases will sweep through the troops of the Russian coalition as well as through "the many peoples" who support these troops in their war of annihilation against Israel. Additional judgments will be leveled against the attackers such as have rarely been seen since the cataclysmic showdown in Egypt between Moses and Pharaoh (Exodus 7–11).

Deadly and devastating hailstorms will hit these enemy forces and their supporters (reminiscent of Exodus 9). So, too, will apocalyptic firestorms that will at once call to mind both the terrible judgment of Sodom and Gomorrah (Genesis 19) and the most frightening of Hollywood's long list of disaster films. But such events will be neither ancient history nor fiction. They will be all too immediate, real, and tragic.

Such firestorms will be geographically widespread and thus exceptionally deadly. In Ezekiel 39:6, the Lord says, "I will rain down fire on Magog and on all your allies who live safely on the coasts. Then they will know that I am the LORD."

This suggests that targets throughout Russia and the former Soviet Union, as well as Russia's allies, will be supernaturally struck on this day of judgment and partially or completely consumed. These could be limited to nuclear missile silos, military bases, radar installations, defense ministries, intelligence headquarters, and other government buildings of various kinds. But such targets could very well also include religious centers, such as mosques, madrassas, Islamic schools and universities, and other facilities that preach hatred against Jews and Christians and call for the destruction of Israel. Either way, we will have to expect extensive collateral damage, and many civilians will be at severe risk.

THE AFTERMATH

The devastation will be so immense that Ezekiel 39:12 tells us it will take seven full months for Israel to bury all the bodies of the enemies in her midst, to say nothing of the dead and wounded in the coalition countries. What's more, the process would actually take much longer except that scores of bodies will be devoured by carnivorous birds and beasts that will be drawn to the battlefields like moths to a flame.

"Call all the birds and wild animals," the Lord God tells his prophet in Ezekiel 39:17-19. "Say to them: Gather together for my great sacrificial feast. Come from far and near to the mountains of Israel, and there eat flesh and drink blood! Eat the flesh of mighty men and drink the blood of princes as though they were rams, lambs, goats, and bulls. . . . Gorge yourselves with flesh until you are glutted; drink blood until you are drunk. This is the sacrificial feast I have prepared for you."

A more gruesome sight is hard to imagine, but again, this is not the stuff of fiction. Ezekiel is giving us an intelligence report of the future, a future that is steadily approaching.

Ezekiel 38:22 says that one of the weapons God will use against the enemies of Israel is disease. When I see reports about the threat posed by the avian flu, it is hard not to think about this passage and its implications. The H5N1 virus is sweeping through the bird populations of Russia, the Middle East, central Asia, and east Asia, and it has begun to penetrate Africa as well, forcing officials in these regions to slaughter more than 200 million birds in an attempt to head off a possible global pandemic. European nations are just beginning to find cases of infected birds. U.S. officials say they expect birds in North America to be hit with the deadly disease soon and are working feverishly to produce and stockpile vaccines for human consumption.

By early 2006, over 100 people had died from this strain of avian flu worldwide. But health experts warn that millions more could die if the flu successfully leaps from birds to humans, from humans to humans, and then accelerates into a pandemic.

One worst-case scenario from an Australia-based think tank projected 142 million deaths and global economic losses of $4.4 trillion. But researchers warned that even a "mild" pandemic could result in 1.4 million deaths and $330 billion in economic losses.[7] The report also found that U.S. deaths alone could range from 20,000 in a "mild" scenario to more than 2 million in an "ultra" or severe scenario.[8]

We don't yet know, of course, if there is a connection between the H5N1 virus and the approaching fulfillment of Ezekiel's prophecy. There may be none. But when one watches how much fear the virus is striking in the hearts of government leaders and public health officials, one can begin to imagine how quickly and how terribly a modern pandemic could sweep across the world and take the lives of millions, just as Ezekiel has predicted will happen in the last days.

REASONS FOR HOPE

Ezekiel's prophecy raises many troubling questions. Will *all* of Russia be supernaturally destroyed? Will *all* of Iran and Libya and Sudan and other Islamic countries in central Asia and elsewhere be destroyed?

What about Germany and Austria? Will everyone in these countries be killed as well?

Without a doubt, the devastation described in the text will be beyond compare in human history. It is clear that God intends this War of Gog and Magog as a divine judgment of Israel's mortal enemies. It is also clear from the text that the countries certain to be affected by this judgment include those that have in recent times warred against the very existence of God (Moscow-driven Communism and atheism) and those that have warred against the One True God, the God of the Bible, the God of Abraham, Isaac, Jacob, and Jesus (Mecca-driven Islam).

One may reasonably conclude, therefore, that the judgment will bring both political and spiritual systems to their stunning ends. The wrath of God will fall on the Kremlin and the Red Army. And the world will witness the end of radical Islam as we know it.

As discussed earlier, Germany and perhaps Austria may find themselves facing calamity too. We do not know for certain that this will be the case, but we can't rule out the possibility either.

That said, however, there are also strong indications in the text that the devastation will not be complete and that God will show mercy.

In the Masoretic Text—the ancient Hebrew manuscript of the Old Testament upon which the King James Version of the Bible is based—we find an interesting passage in Ezekiel 39:2. The Lord says to Gog, "I will turn thee back, and leave but *the sixth part of thee*, and will cause thee to come up from the north parts, and will bring thee upon the mountains of Israel" (emphasis added). This suggests that five-sixths of Gog's forces and his coalition's forces will be destroyed but that one-sixth—about 17 percent—will remain behind and survive. We should hold out hope that many will be spared, but the truth is we simply do not know for sure.

Throughout history, God has acted in ways that humans don't always understand but that bring to fruition some part of his perfect plan. I must say I don't fully understand what is coming, and much of me wishes that God in his providence would find some other way to protect Israel and chasten the nations who oppose him. At the same time, I do see signs of hope that will come out of the disastrous judgment described in Ezekiel.

Several verses in the biblical text indicate that a great, global spiritual awakening will result from this unprecedented day of judgment. In Ezekiel 38:23, for example, the Lord God says, "I will magnify Myself, sanctify Myself, and make Myself known in the sight of many nations; and they will know that I am the LORD" (NASB). In Ezekiel 39:21-22, the Lord God provides more detail: "I will set My glory among the nations; and *all* the nations will see My judgment which I have executed and My hand which I have laid on them. And the house of Israel will know that I am the LORD their God from that day onward" (NASB, emphasis added).

Dr. Charles Ryrie, editor of the *Ryrie Study Bible*, once noted, "The twofold purpose of this judgment is that the nations might acknowledge God's glory and that Israel might know God's grace."[9]

I agree. It is entirely consistent with God's character and his plan and purpose throughout history for him to use times of judgment against some to shake up—and wake up—others to their need for a personal relationship with him. In John 3:16, we read: "God loved the world so much that he gave his one and only Son [Jesus Christ], so that everyone who believes in him will not perish but have eternal life." 1 Timothy 2:3-4 tells us that "God our Savior . . . desires all men to be saved and to come to the knowledge of the truth" (NASB). 2 Peter 3:3-9 tells us that "in the last days mockers will come" to cynically dismiss the words of the prophets since their forecasts have not yet come true. But "the Lord is not slow about His promise, as some count slowness, but is patient toward you, not wishing for any to perish but for all to come to repentance" (NASB).

It's important to note that just because the leaders of Russia, Iran, Germany, and the other coalition countries have set themselves in opposition to God does not mean God does not love them and the people under their rule. To the contrary, Christ died to save his enemies. The apostle Paul—himself once a chief enemy of Jesus Christ—wrote in Romans 5:8-9 that "God demonstrates His own love toward us, in that while we were yet sinners, Christ died for us" and that "we shall be saved from the wrath of God" and be saved from condemnation if we turn to Christ and ask Him to be our Savior (NASB). Jesus said in Matthew 5:44, "I say to you, love your enemies and pray for those who persecute you" (NASB). The apostle Peter said in Acts 2:21 that "everyone who calls on the name of the Lord will be saved." There is, therefore, hope for all, including those in nations aligned with Gog. But Russians, Iranians, Germans, and others cannot choose to follow Christ if they have all perished. Thus, the God of Israel has given the world a warning about the coming judgment *before* it occurs to give individuals in these target countries time to repent of their personal and national sins and to receive Jesus Christ by faith as their personal Savior and Lord. What's more, I believe that he will also allow many people in these countries to survive these judgments so they have a second chance to understand and accept his love and grace.

A GLOBAL STORY

When my father and I were in Moscow in 2005, we met with the senior pastor of one of the largest evangelical churches in Russia. Through an interpreter, we talked for more than an hour about the spiritual and political climate in Russia and the former Soviet Union and about the biblical prophecies of the last days. He told me he firmly believes that Ezekiel 38–39 refer directly to Russia's future and that the War of Gog and Magog is rapidly approaching. He said he had just preached a sermon on the topic a few months before my visit and was trying to prepare the believers of Russia for the dark days ahead for their country.

This is not an easy task, he said. The younger pastors of the country—many of whom came to faith in Christ only after the collapse of the Soviet empire and have little or no formal Bible college or seminary training—do not know much about such prophecies. But he insisted that it is an important task and one to which he is deeply committed. "We need to wake up the church before it happens so Christians can turn Russians' hearts back to God. And we need to be ready for after it happens since so many Russians will be in such great need."[10]

The War of Gog and Magog will not be the most important day in history. That was the resurrection from the dead of the crucified Jesus of Nazareth. But Ezekiel's war will certainly be the most tragically dramatic moment in modern history, and it will be witnessed by billions. Some five hundred people personally witnessed the resurrected Jesus in the forty days after his resurrection. But Ezekiel 39:21 tells us that "all the nations will see" God's judgment (NASB). With the proliferation of televisions and satellite dishes around the globe, we are now living in the first age in history when this prophecy could truly be fulfilled.

This really struck home with me when my father and I were in Moscow and the school in Beslan was seized by radical Islamic terrorists. Few had ever even heard of this obscure town in southern Russia, much less seen pictures of its people and its streets. We certainly hadn't. But no sooner had the crisis erupted than live images were being beamed from Beslan to televisions all over the world. This will be the case when God's judgment falls. It will be the most televised, most reported story ever, giving every nation on earth the opportunity to see the God of Israel display his glory.

What will happen when the smoke clears from the War of Gog and Magog? This is the subject of our final chapters.

IRAQ EMERGES FROM CHAOS AS REGION'S WEALTHIEST COUNTRY

When it comes to the future of Iraq, there is no shortage of naysayers.

Senator Ted Kennedy of Massachusetts, a Democrat, says America may have won the war in Iraq but warns "we may lose the peace."[1]

Senator Robert Byrd, the Democrat from West Virginia, says "the cost of the war has spiraled," yet "the situation in Iraq has gone from bad to worse" and "the level of violence only keeps growing, week after week, month after month."[2]

Democratic senator John Kerry of Massachusetts says that "invading Iraq has created a crisis of historic proportions, and, if we do not change course, there is the prospect of a war with no end in sight." He adds that President Bush "misled, miscalculated, and mismanaged every aspect of this undertaking and he has made the achievement of our objective—a stable Iraq, secure within its borders, with a representative government—harder to achieve."[3]

Democrats are not alone in their lack of hope for Iraq.

Senator Chuck Hagel, the Nebraska Republican, says, "Things aren't getting better; they're getting worse" and warns point blank:

"The reality is, we're losing in Iraq."[4] He adds, "I think our involvement there has destabilized the Middle East. And the longer we stay there, I think . . . further destabilization will occur."[5]

Tucker Carlson, formerly one of CNN's Republican commentators, was once a big supporter of "regime change" and getting rid of Saddam Hussein and his thugs. Now he says, "I am embarrassed that I supported the war in Iraq."[6]

The list of such doubting Thomases in Washington and in the media goes on and on, as do the list of books preemptively declaring defeat. Among them:

LOSING IRAQ: INSIDE THE POSTWAR RECONSTRUCTION FIASCO
BY DAVID L. PHILLIPS

SQUANDERED VICTORY: THE AMERICAN OCCUPATION AND THE BUNGLED EFFORT TO BRING DEMOCRACY TO IRAQ
BY LARRY DIAMOND

HOW AMERICA LOST IRAQ
BY AARON GLANTZ

IMPERIAL HUBRIS: WHY THE WEST IS LOSING THE WAR ON TERROR
BY MICHAEL SCHEUER

Such pessimism is shortsighted in my view, but to be fair, it is understandable. The third anniversary of the liberation of Baghdad in April 2006 was, after all, marked not by a full withdrawal of U.S. forces but by a ferocious insurgency launching wave upon wave of suicide bombings. Vehicles were being blown up regularly by roadside bombs. American casualties were rising. Iraqi civilian casualties were rising. Iraq seemed to be teetering on the edge of civil war, and calls by American politicians and editorial boards to withdraw our forces and let the Iraqis take care of the mess themselves were increasing.

But those who argue that Iraq's liberation will not succeed in bringing about a season of stability and prosperity are making the mistake of viewing current events through only political and economic lenses. As such, they are unable to see the big picture. For when one views Iraq's future through the third lens of Scripture, a much different picture emerges.

IRAQ THROUGH THE THIRD LENS

The truth is that Iraq will form a strong, stable, and decisive central government. Iraq's military and internal security forces will be well trained, well equipped, and increasingly effective. The insurgency will be crushed, support for it will evaporate, and foreign terrorists will stop flowing into the country.

As the situation stabilizes, Iraqi roads and airports will become safe, and people will finally be able to move freely about the country. Tourists will pour in to visit the country's many ancient archeological sites and national treasures. Business leaders will also pour into the country, as will foreign investment, particularly to get Iraq's oil fields, refineries, and shipping facilities up to twenty-first-century standards.

In short order, Iraq will emerge as an oil superpower, rivaling Saudi Arabia. Trillions of petrodollars will flood into the country, and as this happens, Iraq will become a magnet for banks and multinational corporations that will set up their regional and international headquarters in the country.

High-rise office buildings, luxury apartments, and single-family homes will be constructed. Theaters, concert halls, parks, and malls will be built. The ancient city of Babylon will emerge virtually overnight like a phoenix rising from the ashes to become one of the modern wonders of the world.

As I described in *The Last Days*, *The Ezekiel Option*, and most recently *The Copper Scroll*, Iraq is about to see a political and economic renaissance unparalleled in the history of the world. The people of Iraq are about to experience a level of personal and national wealth and power they have never dreamed possible. The pundits who have written the country off to failure and chaos will be absolutely stunned by such a dramatic turn of events, much as those who said the Berlin wall would never come down and the Soviet empire would never collapse found themselves scratching their heads in disbelief just a few years later.

How can I be so sure? By looking at Iraq through the third lens and analyzing the advance intelligence the Bible provides.

Iraq is described by the Hebrew prophets Ezekiel, Isaiah, Jeremiah, and Daniel, as well as by the apostle John in the book of Revelation, as a center of unprecedented wealth and power in the last days before the return of Christ. The city of Babylon not only literally comes back from the dead in the last days, but the writers of Scripture portray her as Iraq's future capital. In Revelation 18, Babylon is described as a "great city" and a center of "extravagant luxury."

Iraq is described as one of the world's great commercial hubs, where "the merchants of the world" come to trade "great quantities of gold, silver, jewels, and pearls," along with all kinds of other "expensive" goods and services that entice "the kings of the world" and draw ships from everywhere on the planet (Revelation 18:9-12). When the people of the world think about the great wealth of Iraq's future capital, they will ask themselves and each other, "Where is there another city as great as this?" (Revelation 18:18).

To be sure, we also learn from the book of Revelation that Iraq will eventually become a center of great evil as well and will one day face a judgment similar to the War of Gog and Magog. But the Scriptures are clear: before that, Iraq will be rich and powerful.

What's more, the judgment of Russia, Iran, and other Middle Eastern countries will work to Iraq's advantage. Oil and gas exports from those countries will be slowed or halted altogether because of the terrible destruction described by Ezekiel. Iraq, meanwhile, as one of the few Middle Eastern countries not having participated in the attack on Israel, will be one of the few oil powers (besides Israel) left intact when the smoke clears. As oil and gas prices skyrocket due to severe shortages, the world will become increasingly dependent upon Iraq for energy, and money will pour into the country's coffers like never before.

But first, Iraq must become stable, peaceful, and free. Only then can the physical and financial infrastructure for such explosive growth be set into place. Only then will international oil companies invest heavily in refurbishing Iraq's drilling, refining, and export equipment and facilities. Only then will the merchants of the world begin establishing headquarters in Iraq and dramatically increasing the level of trade done in and through Iraq. What's remarkable is that those who are watching carefully can see the early stages of such developments happening right now.

A MODERN-DAY DANIEL

Few people are more qualified to talk about the future of his country than Iraqi general Georges Sada, for he knows firsthand how far his people have come already.

Now in his sixties, Sada has served as the chief spokesman for the Iraqi prime minister and as a senior advisor to the Iraqi president, and he was one of the chief architects of the new Iraqi military. But he was once Iraq's top fighter pilot, his country's air vice-marshal, and a top military advisor to Saddam Hussein—a role he did not seek and one that almost cost him his life.

In November 1990—only two months before U.S. and coalition forces liberated Kuwait—Saddam ordered Sada and his colleagues to plan a massive attack against Israel using every plane in the Iraqi air force. If the U.S. dared to attack Iraq, Saddam vowed, then he would order a retaliatory strike against Israel that would involve dropping chemical weapons on Jerusalem, Tel Aviv, Haifa, and other Israeli population centers, killing hundreds of thousands if not millions of Israelis.

Sada was horrified. As a devout evangelical Christian working for a ferociously anti-Christian regime, he had refused to join the Baath Party and was deeply pained to see what Saddam was doing to his beloved country. Yet, remarkably, he had been promoted through the ranks anyway, partly because of his flying ability and leadership skills, partly because of his reputation for telling his superiors the truth no matter what the consequences, and partly because Saddam did not see him as a direct and personal threat to him and his regime.

Now Sada faced the most difficult moment of his life. If he expressed even doubt—much less opposition—to the plan, he could be signing his own death warrant. But how could he keep silent? He abhorred the thought of annihilating Jews. In his eyes, the Jews were God's chosen people and the authors of the Scriptures he had loved since growing up in the ancient Assyrian city of Nineveh (modern-day Mosul). What's more, he knew that since most of Iraq's bombers and fighter jets would no doubt be shot down before entering Israeli airspace, most of Iraq's chemical-weapon-laden bombs would likely land on Jordan and Syria, killing thousands if not millions of Iraq's neighbors.

So when Saddam asked for his counsel, Sada said a silent prayer asking God for mercy, braced himself for the worst, and refused to support the plan. In fact, in front of at least ninety other senior military officers, he actually sought to dissuade Saddam from attacking Israel by launching into a highly technical description of Israel's air-defense systems and the enormous challenges Iraqi pilots would have going up against superior technology and training. His presentation lasted an hour and forty-one minutes, and when it was over, the room was dead silent.

Not many men disagreed with Saddam and lived to tell about it. Several of Sada's colleagues told him later that they had been certain he was going to be executed on the spot. But by God's grace, he survived. So, of course, did Israel.

On December 17, 1990, Saddam did, in fact, sign the order for the massive chemical-weapons attack against the Jewish state if the U.S. attacked Iraq first. But when the Gulf War began on the night of January 16, 1991, American and coalition forces destroyed Iraq's air force so quickly that Saddam never had the chance to implement his order.

I first heard about Sada while living in Cairo, working on this book. Sada's memoir, *Saddam's Secrets: How an Iraqi General Defied and Survived Saddam Hussein*, had just been released in the U.S., and a friend had e-mailed me to suggest that I read it as soon as possible.

When I got back to the States, I read Sada's book in a single day and tracked him down for an interview. What I found was a man who understands both his country's past and its future far better than any American journalist or politician, because he has been at the center of events there for decades and has viewed them all through the third lens of Scripture.

In my view, Sada is a modern-day Daniel, a man of faith and prayer whom God used to speak truth to a modern-day Nebuchadnezzar.

IRAQ'S NEW RELIGIOUS FREEDOM

In his book Sada describes working with Iraq's new civilian leadership in Baghdad to help plan their nation's recovery from the Saddam era. He also describes his meetings in Washington with various high-ranking White House, State Department, and Pentagon officials. It is all interesting and important material, but when I interviewed Sada, one of the first things I wanted to know was what it was like to stand before Saddam Hussein and actually hear him say, "Georges, I've decided that the air force will attack Israel and wipe her out with chemical weapons."

"I was thinking of it in two ways," he told me. "One, as a Christian, as a believer. Second, as a national officer that belonged to the Iraqi forces. . . . As a Christian, I could not accept [this order] to send two waves of fighters to attack Israel, one wave through Jordan and one through Syria. I knew the capabilities of the Israeli air force and their air defenses and their plans to destroy all aircraft coming from the east before entering the Israeli borders. So this means the bombs were [mostly] going to drop on Jordan and Syria. . . . But with ninety-eight aircraft, some of them would still penetrate to Israel. Just imagine as a Christian [the deaths that would result] as all three countries were going to be hit by chemicals."[7]

Sada could not bear the thought of having to stand before Jesus Christ on the Day of Judgment with such a sin on his conscience. Nor could he bear to see the destruction that would be unleashed upon his own people if Saddam's plan was successful.

What's more, "as a tactical general and a strategist, I also knew the Israelis would have the right to retaliate with nuclear weapons and they would destroy our big cities like Baghdad, Mosul, Basra, and the others. So what was the benefit of doing this?"

"What gave you the courage to try to dissuade Saddam?" I asked.

"Believe me, only Jesus. *Only.* I know how brave I am. I am not a coward. But to be that brave—to put your life in front of Saddam—he could shoot you at any second—there were some people who said, 'Georges is finished. Today his head is gone' . . . but you see, it was Jesus who gave me the courage."

Twelve years later, it was Saddam Hussein, not Sada, who was finished.

American and coalition forces liberated Baghdad on April 9, 2003. Iraqis cheered in the streets in those heady first days. They sang and danced and wept as they tore down the forty-foot statue of Saddam in Fardus Square.

Sada described for me the scene as he returned to Baghdad on May 8, 2003, and entered Saddam's main palace a few days later. The multi-million-dollar gold-and-marble compound no longer had any doors or windows. Everything was covered in dust. These hallways had been ground zero of the republic of fear only weeks before. But now here he was, a free man, walking around in a free country.

Slowly, cautiously, Sada entered Saddam's throne room. It took a few moments to grasp the enormity of what he was seeing, or rather not seeing. Saddam was not there. Saddam's sons were not there. Saddam's henchmen were not there. They ruled no longer. They could issue their evil, murderous decrees no longer. Iraq was free. Yes, troubles and trials lay ahead. Yes, life would be very hard for some time to come. But the Butcher of Baghdad was gone. And Sada told me that when that truth sunk in, he began to weep.

Before long, at Sada's urging, Saddam's throne room was being used for evangelical church services. In the very room where just a few months earlier Saddam had ordered Iraqis to their deaths, Christians were now gathering to worship the name of Jesus. What could be more fitting, Sada thought, than to turn Saddam's house of evil into a house of God?

"Did you ever imagine when you were in a meeting with Saddam Hussein that one day you would actually be worshipping Jesus in that very room?" I asked him.

"No, no," he said, laughing like a man from whom a great burden has been lifted. "I would never have dreamt that."

And yet it happened.

Religious freedom has come to Iraq for the first time in centuries. New churches are opening. Bibles are being printed. Muslims are converting to Christianity in record numbers. And nominal Christians are experiencing a spiritual revival, becoming excited about their faith in a way that Sada and other evangelical leaders I have spoken with have never seen before.

I will describe this in more detail in chapter 14 and put it in the context of the evangelical revolution that is sweeping through the post-9/11 Middle East. But for now it is important to note that this newfound religious freedom is a significant part of why Sada and many of his colleagues are hopeful about their country's prospects. They have come so far so fast from the dark days of Saddam that, unlike the naysayers in the West, they have no doubt even more dramatic and positive changes are coming.

A NATIONAL CONVERSATION

"I am a man who is very, very optimistic about the future of Iraq," Sada says with a sense of passion that is at once believable and contagious.

Newfound religious freedom is part of the answer. So, too, is the new political freedom Iraqis are experiencing for the first time in their lives. Despite the violence of the insurgency, each new round of elections has drawn more Iraqis to the polls than the one before. In January 2005, 8.5 million citizens voted—58 percent of all those eligible to do so. By October of that year, turnout had climbed to 9.8 million Iraqis—63 percent of all eligible voters. And by December, more than 12 million Iraqis came out to the polls, a stunning 77 percent of all those eligible.[8]

What's more, turnout has increased dramatically even in provinces racked by violence and those where large numbers of Sunni Muslims live, many of whom have been either wary of participating in the political process or outright hostile to doing so.

Does this mean that voters in these provinces are satisfied with the results of the elections? Not necessarily. But it does mean that they are beginning to see the electoral process as a way to achieve their personal and political objectives, and this is a very hopeful sign.

The fact is, a national conversation is under way inside the country. Iraqis now have the freedom to think, to speak their minds, and to discuss and debate ideas unlike ever before. And despite the severe violence in the streets of some provinces, the conversation has not stopped. It has only intensified.

"There is a great, dramatic change if we compare it with the Saddam Hussein regime," Sada told me. "Whatever happens now, it will still be much, much better than that. Because now if you have fifty people killed, you have tremendous reaction of newspapers, TV channels. Everybody will speak [about their deaths]. But in the time of Saddam, if he will kill 5,000 people, nobody will know. They will be killed and they will be taken to a mass grave. This will not happen in Iraq anymore. . . . We have many newspapers, many radios, many TVs, everybody has got a [satellite] dish, everybody is watching everything, and this was impossible at the time of Saddam."

THE NEW IRAQI ECONOMY

Yet another reason for optimism is the fact that Iraq's new economy has nearly doubled since liberation and is already beginning to attract some of the largest companies in the world that increasingly believe the country has a very prosperous future.

In April of 2006 I had the privilege of having lunch with Ali Abdul Ameer Allawi, Iraq's finance minister, and Dr. Sinan Al-Shabibi, the governor of Iraq's Central Bank. They had come to Washington to explain to journalists and policy makers the impressive untold story of Iraq's rapidly expanding economy.

"We are talking about the restructuring of an entire country," Minister Allawi told me. "We're doing it in an atmosphere of violence. . . . But Iraq is moving. It's growing. And once the security situation settles down, it is poised to have enormous economic growth. There are a lot of pent-up energies ready to be released."[9]

Dr. Al-Shabibi heartily agreed. "We are making a transition from a war economy to a peace economy. We're making a transition from a dictatorship to a democracy, and from a centrally planned economy to a market economy. It will take time. But we are already making real progress."[10]

Sure enough, after declining by two-thirds after the invasion of Kuwait, the country's economy surged from $18.9 billion in 2002 to $33.1 billion in 2005. In 2006, growth has been expected to hit 10.4 percent. It has been projected to surge by 15.5 percent in 2007. The new Iraqi dinar is stable, and annual inflation has dropped from 32 percent to around 10 percent today.[11]

Such a trajectory is catching the eye of corporate executives around the globe. Visa proved it really is "everywhere you want to be" when it opened for business in Iraq in June 2003. The credit-card company was the first to process payments in Iraq since economic sanctions were imposed.[12]

FedEx began door-to-door pickup and delivery in Baghdad, Basra, and Mosul in August of 2003. A press release noted that "the company's role as one of the world's leading drivers of international trade and growth will be a significant asset to Iraq and its business community as the country works towards rebuilding its infrastructure and economy. Access to the FedEx Express international network also helps facilitate the transportation of humanitarian aid into the country, including working with Water Missions International and International Aid."[13]

Hamdi Osman, FedEx's regional vice president, said, "Iraq has the potential to be one of the fastest growing economies. There is no question that the country faces a tough business climate, but nothing that can't be overcome."

Coca-Cola began joint venture talks with several Iraqi bottling companies in November 2003, eventually striking a deal and launching a new front in the cola wars against Pepsi, their biggest rival. Coke had been exiled from Iraq for thirty-seven years for choosing to do business in Israel and thus facing Saddam's anti-Zionist wrath.[14]

In December 2003, Iraq's previous finance minister, Kamel al-Gailani, wrote an essay for the *Wall Street Journal* entitled "Iraq: Open for Business!" He noted that foreign companies operating in Iraq are now finally permitted to have "direct ownership, joint ventures, or branches as they see fit. We will guarantee equality of legal standing for all foreign firms as well as full and immediate remittance of profits, dividends, interest, and royalties. The investment process will be quick and clear with no bureaucratic hurdles to get in the way."[15]

Since then, hundreds of foreign companies, including General Electric, General Motors, Nokia, Lucent Technologies, Motorola, and Canon, have entered Iraq.

What's more, some 33,000 new Iraqi businesses have been registered, and about 1.5 million Iraqis have been employed to build or rebuild schools, health clinics, police stations, roads, bridges, and numerous other infrastructure projects.[16] A U.S. government report to Congress in the spring of 2006 noted that "over 20,000 microfinance loans with a value of $44 million have been disbursed to small entrepreneurs creating an estimated 30,000 jobs" and "over 2,400 businessmen and women have taken advantage of training programs for small and medium sized enterprises."[17] The report also noted that "countries other than the U.S. have pledged some $13.5 billion worth of support to Iraq."

Iraq's oil industry, meanwhile, is slowly coming back on line and holds tremendous promise for the country's future. Iraq is currently producing about 2.1 million barrels a day and is exporting an average of 1.5 million barrels a day, says Finance Minister Allawi.[18] More than 350 pipelines have been repaired since the end of major combat operations, and U.S. officials report that Iraqi oil revenues have climbed from $5.1 billion in 2003 to an impressive $24.5 billion in 2005.[19]

But, again, this is only the beginning. Minister Allawi notes that while Iraq currently has the second-largest reserves of oil in the region, behind the Saudis, the country still has not discovered all of its reserves and desperately needs new oil rigs and production facilities to maximize production. "Our technology is not much better than Soviet era," Allawi told me. "We can do much better."

Allawi conservatively estimates that Iraq will be exporting 3 million barrels of oil a day within the next few years. But he and Central Bank governor Al-Shabibi also told me that a new internal Iraqi study found that by 2010, Iraq could be exporting 6 million barrels a day.

Western oil executives and energy experts I consulted for this book concurred with this assessment. A Congressional Research Service study found that "only 17 of 80 [Iraqi] oil fields have been developed" and that "Iraq could potentially produce far more oil than has been realized in its history. Given a stable security situation, very large amounts of capital investment, and the involvement of one or more large oil companies, it would be realistic to suggest potential output ramping up to 5 or 6 million barrels per day over the period of several years."[20]

After a speech I delivered at an executive conference in 2005, the vice president of a large North American oil company told me that he had just finished reading *The Last Days* and wanted to tell me I was significantly *understating* the oil wealth that Iraq would soon find. While Iraq was currently believed to possess about 115 billion barrels of oil reserves, he said, Saddam's reign of terror and more than a decade of UN economic sanctions meant that it had been years since anyone had done a serious survey of the country's oil wealth using the latest geological mapping techniques and technology. Once the violence settles down and companies like his can safely rebuild Iraq's wells and do more exploration, he and his colleagues are sure Iraq's proven reserves will be found to be much higher.

"We're already sending in survey teams," he told me. "We're building alliances in the government and with local leaders. We're ready to move in and make a major investment in Iraq, as soon as the violence settles down. And we're not alone."[21]

INSIDE THE NEW IRAQI MILITARY

The question is, how soon will things settle down in Iraq?

General Sada hesitates to make a hard-and-fast prediction. He concedes that at times his country seems "close to civil war," and he does not rule out the possibility of such a war erupting. But he is convinced that in ten years or less, Iraq will be quiet, stable, and immensely prosperous, and he personally believes it will be much sooner than that.

The key, he says, is getting the new Iraqi military recruited, trained, equipped, and combat ready. It's a project he has been work-ing on from the moment he returned to his newly liberated country. "In May 2003, I told [American general] Garner, 'Let us Iraqis start tak-ing [charge of] the internal security. Because you have done a great job in battle. You have removed the regime of Saddam. Now let us take the responsibility of the security.'"

The U.S. originally envisioned only three Iraqi army divisions—one in the north, one in the center, and one in the south. Sada did not think this was nearly enough to crush the insurgency or to keep Iraq safe from Iran or other potentially hostile neighbors. He recom-mended nine divisions, with reserves of about 150,000 men. As the violence of the insurgency intensified, Sada increased his original recommendation to eleven divisions, and U.S. officials eventually re-alized that he and his Iraqi military colleagues were right. Later, it was decided to create a new counterterrorism division as well, bring-ing the total number to twelve Iraqi divisions. Each is now comprised of about 12,000 men, for a total of about 160,000 men in the Iraqi armed forces, separate from police and internal security forces.

"Twelve divisions are already functioning," Sada says. "Half of them are well-trained by the Americans. The Americans are doing a great job training the others, and I am sure that soon all the Iraqi army will be well-trained."

As this increasingly battle-hardened force matures, Sada says Iraqis will be able to take charge of their own security and allow American and coalition forces to go home. He also says the new Iraqi military is being trained solely for defense purposes and will have no territorial or ideological designs on neighboring countries as in the past, even vis-à-vis Israel.

"From the early beginning when I was forming the forces," Sada in-sists, "the principle was to build these forces on the basis of freedom and democracy, and [that] these forces should be not trained in a way to do violence in the region and for the world. . . . The nature of the forces will be defensive, not offensive."

As much as I respect General Sada, I have to disagree with him on those last comments. I have no doubt he and others are training Iraq's new military for defense-only operations. But the Scriptures are clear that Iraq will one day be the headquarters for the Antichrist, a dictator who will wield unprecedented global authority and will set up his power base in the city of Babylon. We know, therefore, that while Iraqi forces today are being trained by U.S. and NATO commanders—the best in the world—and outfitted with the latest state-of-the-art military gear, someday such forces will be drafted into a final showdown with Israel at Armageddon and ultimately with God himself.

Some Christians I know have asked if the effort to liberate and re-build Iraq is worth it, knowing the evil that lies ahead. In other words, are all our blood, toil, tears, and sweat making Iraq safe for democracy or safe for the Antichrist?

The answer, honestly, is both. But yes, I believe it's worth it. After all, the Iraqi people desperately need a time of religious, political, and economic freedom, even if it is only for a season. They deserve the op-portunity to think and read and debate and travel. They should also have the opportunity to hear the good news of God's love for them and the way of salvation offered to them through Jesus Christ. Followers of Christ outside of Iraq need the opportunity to get the gospel inside and to strengthen the faith of our brothers and sisters there—especially if a greater evil is rising.

Think of it this way: Ronald Reagan believed that after the collapse of the Evil Empire, another evil dictator—Gog—would one day arise. But that did not stop Reagan from pursuing the collapse of the Soviet Union and the tearing down of the Berlin wall. Why? Because he saw the future of that part of the world through the third lens of Scripture. He knew what was coming, but he didn't know when. So he wanted the Russian people to taste freedom, if only for a time. He wanted them to have an opportunity to hear the gospel and respond before prophetic events overwhelmed them.

In Russia's case, it has been a decade and a half since the demise of the USSR. We don't know when the window of freedom in Russia will fully close, but it is certainly closing now. Likewise, we don't know how long a window we will have in the new Iraq, but we should make the most of every opportunity while we can.

BABYLON RISING

Those who do not view world events through the third lens of Scripture will, understandably, have a difficult time imagining a season of peace and prosperity emerging in Iraq. They will also have a difficult time imagining the rebuilding of the ancient Iraqi city of Babylon, at least on the scale described in the Left Behind series or my novels.

Former Republican strategist turned best-selling author Kevin Phillips is one such skeptic among many. "Evil Babylon, the antithesis of Jerusalem, the good city, prompted its own literature in the 1990s, and [Tim] LaHaye's tens of millions of readers praised his series as making the Bible and its supposed predictions 'come alive,'" sniped Phillips, citing like-minded authors mocking "prophecy believers" who accept the biblical view that Babylon will one day actually be rebuilt "on its ancient ruins."[22]

Historically, such cynicism has been understandable. For nearly two thousand years, the city of Babylon, located about sixty kilometers south of Baghdad, has been all but extinct. This has led to speculation that the Babylon described in the book of Revelation actually refers to New York or Washington or Rome or Moscow. How could it refer to an Iraqi city that doesn't exist?

Except that now it does.

"More than 2,500 years ago, a fabulous city rose here on a bend in the Euphrates River," wrote *New York Times* correspondent John Burns in the fall of 1990. "Under King Nebuchadnezzar, Babylon and its hanging gardens became as fabled, and as much a seat of imperial power, as Rome became later. Under President Saddam Hussein, one of the ancient world's most legendary cities has begun to rise again."[23]

Burns explained that Saddam had invested millions of dollars to build replicas of Nebuchadnezzar's buildings—including palaces and throne rooms—"on the original sites." He described Saddam's efforts to rebuild the city's roads, lakes, canals, and bridges, and even to build new museums, souvenir shops, and fast-food restaurants. And he reported that Saddam had offered "a $1.5 million reward to anybody who can produce a satisfactory plan for rebuilding the Hanging Gardens."

The article didn't even make the paper's front page. It was buried on page 13 of the A section. But to me, as well as to millions of evangelical Christians who believe in Bible prophecy, it was hugely significant.

The following year Charles Dyer, senior VP at Moody Bible Institute in Chicago, published *The Rise of Babylon: Sign of the End Times*. In it he described his experience attending an international festival held in Babylon in 1987 and provided even more firsthand details of the efforts of the Iraqi government to make the ancient city a symbol of the country's future.[24]

Both Burns and Dyer noted that construction in Babylon had stalled after Iraq's invasion of Kuwait because Saddam ran out of cash. But what was so significant about these and similar reports over the next few years was that they provided fresh evidence that a Bible prophecy so difficult for so many to believe for so long—a prophecy concerning the resurrection of an entire ancient city to modern power and prosperity—was actually beginning to come to pass. They also strongly suggested that when Iraq is flush with new petrodollars, Babylon will rise even more rapidly.

That day may be sooner than most people think.

On April 18, 2006, the *New York Times* reported in a front-page story that "Babylon, the mud-brick city with the million-dollar name, has paid the price of war. It has been ransacked, looted, torn up, paved over, neglected and roughly occupied. . . . But Iraqi leaders and United Nations officials are not giving up on it. They are working assiduously to restore Babylon, home to one of the Seven Wonders of the World, and turn it into a cultural center and possibly even an Iraqi theme park." The mayor of the area says that, "God willing," they will even build a Holiday Inn.[25]

"The United Nations Educational, Scientific and Cultural Organization is pumping millions of dollars into protecting and restoring Babylon and a handful of other ancient ruins in Iraq," noted correspondent Jeffrey Gettleman. "UNESCO has even printed up a snazzy brochure, with Babylon listed as the premier destination, to hand out to wealthy donors."

"Cultural tourism could become Iraq's second biggest industry, after oil," said Philippe Delanghe, a United Nations official helping with the project.

Gettleman noted, "What makes the project even conceivable is that the area around Babylon is one of the safest in Iraq, a beacon of civilization, once again, in a land of chaos."

"One day millions of people will visit Babylon," said Donny George, head of Iraq's board of antiquities. "I'm just not sure anybody knows when."

I asked Iraqi finance minister Allawi about this project when I met with him in Washington a few days after the article was published. He loved the idea of rebuilding Babylon—anything to attract investors and their capital and get the Iraqi economy growing again.

"Cultural, religious, archeological, and biblical tourism is a big opportunity for Iraq," he told me. "I think rebuilding Babylon is a wonderful idea, as long as it is not done at the expense of the antiquities themselves." Then he added, "I don't know about a theme park, though—maybe, as long as it's done outside of Babylon, away from the archeological sites."[26]

It all sounded so natural, but what Minister Allawi was telling me was really quite historic. The highest levels of the new Iraqi government want to rebuild the ancient city of Babylon and make it a great center of commerce. The Hebrew prophets and the book of Revelation told us it was going to happen. Now it really is.

That said, people like General Sada and his fellow Christians in Iraq have little time to think about the prophetic implications of their work at the moment. They are solely focused on making Iraq secure, creating jobs and economic opportunities, and getting the gospel of Jesus Christ to every Iraqi who is willing to listen.

"What's going to happen in the future?" Sada asks. "I am a man who believes in God's promises 100 percent. I believe what's in the Bible. Those [prophecies] will happen whether somebody will like it or not like it. . . . We believers see what is happening [in Iraq today], and the first thing that comes to our heads is that we are living in the last days. But how God thinks—his ways and his methods and his thoughts—are not like our own. It is very difficult for a human being to know and understand the thoughts and the ways of God. The most important thing is to believe in the [prophecies] that are going to happen."

JEWS BUILD
THIRD TEMPLE
IN JERUSALEM

Jewish reaction to the War of Gog and Magog will take several forms.

First and foremost, widespread atheism and secularism will collapse essentially overnight within the Jewish world in light of the supernatural protection of Israel. In turn, the world will see an unprecedented resurgence of religious expression among Israelis and among Jews worldwide. The question will no longer be "Is there a God in Israel?" The question will become "How can I know the God of Israel?"

Some will join the Orthodox and ultra-Orthodox communities in their newly urgent quest. Others may turn to more mystical forms of Judaism such as the Chabad-Lubavitch movement and the practice of Kabbalah, made famous by a number of Hollywood stars, including Madonna, in recent years. Still others will turn to faith in Jesus as Messiah and join the rapidly growing movement of messianic Jews in Israel and around the world. But nearly all Jews will become united around one central mission: rebuilding the Holy Temple in Jerusalem.

It is difficult for most people in the early years of the twenty-first century to envision either the First Temple built by King Solomon or the

Second Temple begun in the time of Nehemiah and Ezra after the Jews began to return from captivity in Babylon in 538 BC and later expanded by King Herod into the Temple of Jesus' day. And it is nearly impossible for most people to imagine a Third Temple soon standing where the Dome of the Rock and the Al-Aksa Mosque stand today. But when one looks at current and future events through the third lens of Scripture, the image of the coming Temple is clear.

Ezekiel spends two chapters describing the War of Gog and Magog, but the next nine chapters describe the future "house of the Lord." And Ezekiel was by no means alone. The Hebrew prophet Isaiah tells us, "In the last days, the mountain of the LORD's house will be the highest of all—the most important place on earth" (Isaiah 2:2). The prophet Micah echoes this statement. Daniel speaks of an end-times Temple that will be desecrated by a future enemy of God (known by Christians as the "Antichrist"), and this view was verified in the New Testament by the apostles Paul and John and by Jesus Christ himself.[1]

The question Jews and Christians have been asking themselves since the Second Temple was destroyed by the Romans in AD 70 is, how in the world will the Temple be rebuilt?

In recent years, prominent Palestinian leaders—including Yasser Arafat—have fiercely denied that a Jewish Temple ever even existed in Jerusalem and have explained in no uncertain terms that they bitterly oppose the building of a future Temple. Among the recent statements made by Palestinian leaders:

- "Jews never had any connection to Jerusalem."
- "The Jews never lived in ancient Israel."
- "There never was a Jewish Temple in Jerusalem."
- "The Temple didn't exist in Jerusalem. . . . It was in Nablus."[2]

Jewish leaders counter that Israel, Jerusalem, and the Temple Mount were given to them by God and that God's plans cannot be thwarted by the Palestinian Authority or radical Islamic terror masters in Iran, Saudi Arabia, or anywhere else. The Temple Mount has, therefore, become a flash point in the Israeli-Palestinian conflict and the site of numerous violent clashes since the Israelis took control of the Mount during the Six Days' War of 1967.

Security experts now believe that the Temple Mount is the most dangerous square mile on the planet. Israeli police and intelligence forces maintain tight security around the site to prevent Jewish or other extremists from trying to blow up the Dome of the Rock and the Al-Aksa Mosque. After all, not only would such an attack be morally wrong, it would be incredibly dangerous. For if the dome and the mosque were somehow destroyed by a terrorist attack, this could unleash a war of horrific proportions as the wrath of a billion Muslims turned against Israel.[3]

The vast majority of Christians and Jews oppose such violence. I do too. We are convinced that the Temple will be built because the Bible says it will. We simply are not sure how it will happen. But the "War of Gog and Magog" may provide the answer.

One possibility is that the God of Israel will use the supernatural judgment involving a massive earthquake, hailstorms, and firestorms from heaven to destroy the Dome of the Rock and the Al-Aksa Mosque, clearing the Temple Mount for the building of a Holy Temple to worship him. This is the scenario I put forth in *The Ezekiel Option* and *The Copper Scroll*.

Another possibility is that while the supernatural events do not destroy these Islamic sites directly, the destruction of Israel's most dangerous enemies could make it possible for the government of Israel to dismantle the dome and the mosque when the smoke of the war clears and to then rebuild the Temple.

Still another possibility is that the postwar environment will create a situation of such religious tolerance that the Jewish Temple, the dome, and the mosque will all be able to somehow coexist side by side.

Do we know for certain *how* it will happen? No, we don't. But we do know for certain that something will happen to make construction of the Third Temple possible—maybe within our lifetime. And we know that there is a growing movement of Israeli Jews urgently preparing for that day.

A MOVEMENT TO REBUILD

Gershon Salomon is a descendant of ten generations of Jerusalemites and an Israeli military officer who became convinced in the 1960s that the Messiah was coming soon and that God had chosen him to help prepare the way. So in 1967, after Israel reunified Jerusalem, Salomon formed an organization known as the Temple Mount Faithful with seven provocative objectives.

Among them: "liberating the Temple Mount from Arab (Islamic) occupation . . . consecrating the Temple Mount to the Name of G-d[4] so that it can become the moral and spiritual center of Israel, of the Jewish people and of the entire world according to the words of all the Hebrew prophets . . . [and] rebuilding the Third Temple" for the "coming of the King of Israel, Messiah Ben David."[5]

Salomon believes that Israel is the epicenter of the world, Jerusalem is the epicenter of Israel, and the Temple is the epicenter of Jerusalem, and it is there in the Holy of Holies that the Messiah will reign. So for the past forty years, he has been writing and speaking all over Israel and around the world, trying to teach people about the centrality of the Temple in Jewish life and the importance of establishing the Third Temple before the coming of the Messiah. And more than ever, Salomon is convinced that day is increasingly close at hand.

In 1998, for example, Salomon told his followers that as Israel's fiftieth anniversary approached "we see how events are steadily moving toward the fulfillment of G-d's end-time promises to the people of Israel." He specifically noted that "the prophet Ezekiel prophesied that in the end-times of the redemption of the people of Israel, a terrible war will break out in the land when Gog and Magog with many other nations come to the land of Israel and try to destroy the people and State of Israel" and that "G-d said that He would bring this enemy from the far north against the mountains of Israel."

Salomon went on to explain that "the coming war will be the final war undertaken against Israel by her enemies," for "in it G-d will terribly defeat them." After this war, he concluded, "the new era will start" and "the Third Temple will be the House of G-d, the only building on the Temple Mount. . . . Mashiach Ben David [the Messiah, Son of David] will be the King of Israel and all mankind."[6]

In July of 2001, on the Jewish holiday that marks the destruction of the first two Temples (Tisha B'Av), Salomon and his supporters tried to enter the Temple Mount to lay a four-and-a-half-ton cornerstone they had carved out of limestone to serve as the beginning of the Third Temple. The Israeli authorities denied them access, but Salomon, convinced that he was on the winning side of history and that victory was near, was undeterred. So every year since, he and his group have repeated their efforts, only to be stopped by the local police as well as Israel's Supreme Court, none of whom want an Islamic revolt on their hands.[7]

"G-d expects Israel to rebuild the Temple now and then He will send Mashiach Ben David," wrote Salomon. "Our activities and struggle brought this idea very close to fulfillment, and we know that time is short and that it will soon come to pass."[8]

Rabbi Yisrael Ariel is another Israeli building a movement dedicated to rebuilding the Temple. As one of the first Israeli paratroopers to reach the Temple Mount during the Six Days' War, Ariel became gripped with the notion that he was part of prophecy coming to pass. He went on to immerse himself in the study of Scripture and became one of Israel's leading rabbis.

"It is so very difficult to describe the feeling that filled us during that extraordinary time in the life of the nation," Ariel once wrote, so expectant was he that the Messiah's appearance was imminent and so disappointed over the next few years when nothing happened. He would later explain that "in the passing of time as I pursued my studies, I discovered that our expectations were simply misplaced. . . . The more I studied the more I began to understand that we had only ourselves and our own inaction to hold accountable: G-d does not intend for us to wait for a day of miracles. We are expected to act. We must accomplish that with which we have been charged—to do all in our power to prepare for the rebuilding of the Holy Temple."[9]

So Ariel founded the Temple Institute in 1987 "to rekindle the flame of the Holy Temple in the hearts of mankind through education" and "to do all in our limited power to bring about the building of the Holy Temple in our time." The institute, whose headquarters I have visited in the Jewish Quarter of the Old City (not far from the Western Wall), thus serves an educational function similar to the Temple Mount Faithful. But it also goes an important step further.

Ariel and his team are conducting meticulous historical research to understand the look and size and function of the sacred vessels and implements the Scriptures say were once used in the Temple. What's more, with the understanding that these same sacred utensils will one day be used in the Third Temple, Ariel's team is rebuilding them using the same materials of gold, silver, copper, and wood, and they are doing so with the finest craftsmanship. Though many of the items can be seen on display at his headquarters, Ariel insists that these are not showpieces. He and his team expect them to be used . . . and soon.

"These are authentic, accurate vessels, not merely replicas or models," his Web site explains. "All of these items are fit and ready for use in the service of the Holy Temple. Among the many items featured in the exhibition are musical instruments played by the Levitical choir, the golden crown of the High Priest, and gold and silver vessels used in the incense and sacrificial services. After many years of effort and toil, the Institute has completed the three most important and central vessels of the Divine service: the seven-branched candelabra, or Menorah, made of pure gold, the golden Incense Altar, and the golden Table of the Showbread." Ariel and his team are also "currently creating the sacred uniform of the Cohein Gadol, the High Priest. This project, the culmination of years of study and research, has been underway for several years. To date, the High Priest's Choshen (Breastplate) and Ephod [the High Priest's garment] have already been completed."[10]

Meanwhile, a dramatic new effort has been launched in Israel to rebuild the Temple—the re-creation of the Sanhedrin.

"A unique ceremony—probably only the second of its kind in the past 1,600 years—is taking place in Tiberias today: the launching of a Sanhedrin, the highest Jewish-legal tribunal in the Land of Israel," read a story in the Israeli press in January 2005. The Sanhedrin was "a religious assembly that convened in one of the Holy Temple chambers in

Jerusalem" and was made up of "71 sages" in ancient times.[11] Organizers of the new Sanhedrin also announced their intention to convene seventy-one rabbis, meet regularly, solicit architectural plans to build the Temple, and examine ways to restart animal sacrifices, something not done in Israel since the first century.

"It is appropriate that the Sanhedrin convened to discuss this lofty matter [of the Temple's location] this week," Sanhedrin spokesman Rabbi Chaim Richman told Arutz-7, an Israeli news service, "as the Torah portion is *Terumah*—the portion of the Bible which begins to deal with the preparations for the Tabernacle. Though seemingly esoteric, the preparations for building a Tabernacle and the Temple are at the center of who we are as a people."[12]

A RED HEIFER

One specific headline to be watching for amid such preparations will center on the birth of a red heifer, one that according to Jewish law must be sacrificed prior to the purification and consecration of the Temple and those entering it.

In Numbers 19 we learn that the Israelites were required to bring "a red heifer, a perfect animal that has no defects and has never been yoke to a plow" and give it to the high priest, whereupon it would be slaughtered and burned. "Then someone who is ceremonially clean will gather up the ashes of the heifer and deposit them in a purified place outside the camp. They will be kept there for the community of Israel to use in the water for the purification ceremony. This ceremony is performed for the removal of sin" (Numbers 19:2, 9).

"For the lack of a red heifer's ashes, there is simply . . . no way for Jews to purify themselves to enter the sacred square, no way for Judaism to reclaim the Mount, no way to rebuild the Temple," wrote one Israeli journalist on the intensifying interest in Israel in finding such a red cow.[13]

When a red cow named Melody was born in August 1996 and briefly believed to be "the one," a veritable media avalanche ensued. TV crews from ABC, CBS, CNN, and others from Japan, Holland, and

France covered the event, as did print journalists from around the world. Most of the media found Israeli interest in the cow and the rebuilding of the Temple quaint or bemusing. But *Haaretz* columnist David Landau "argued that the security services should see the red heifer as a 'four-legged bomb' potentially more dangerous than any terrorist: 'It's equal, in its ability to set the entire region on fire, to the power of non-conventional weapons in the hands of Iranian ayatollahs.'"[14]

Ultimately, Melody was pronounced "unclean" by Israeli rabbis. She grew several white hairs at the tip of her red tail and thus proved that she was not the one. Now efforts are being made by some to genetically engineer a perfect red heifer.

OTHER FUTURE HEADLINES?

All this constitutes further evidence that the building of the Third Temple is increasingly close at hand and that the events of Ezekiel 38–39 are as well. They are like strobe lights along an airport runway at night, guiding a pilot in for a landing. When we see such lights, we are not yet at our final destination, but we know we are closer than ever. On this final approach, therefore, we would be well advised to keep our eyes peeled for other events that, while not explicitly promised in Scripture, would certainly be consistent with the rebuilding of the Temple.

In my fourth novel, *The Copper Scroll*, I write about the possible discovery of the Second Temple treasures. I cannot point to biblical prophecies that assure us with any finality that such treasures will be found. But there are a number of intriguing Scriptures that seem to hint that such discoveries could happen in the last days.

In Jeremiah 27:21-22 we read that during the Jewish exile in Babylon, the Lord planned to safeguard the First Temple treasures and would restore them to the children of Israel when it was time to build the Second Temple. "Yes, this is what the LORD of Heaven's Armies, the God of Israel, says about the precious things still in the Temple and in the palace of Judah's king: 'They will all be carried away to Babylon and will stay there until I send for them,' says the LORD. 'Then I will bring them back to Jerusalem again.'"

Likewise, the prophet Isaiah promised the children of Israel that the First Temple treasures would be restored to them when it was time to build the Second Temple. In Isaiah 52:11, instructing the Israelites to return from their captivity in Babylon, the prophet wrote, "Purify yourselves, you who carry home the sacred objects of the LORD."

Do such verses, as well as others found in the books of Nehemiah and Ezra, provide a precedent that God is safeguarding the Second Temple's treasures for the children of Israel and will reveal them when it is time to build the Third Temple? Some Jewish and Christian scholars think so. We simply do not know for sure. But the notion is tantalizing.

I, for one, would not be surprised at all if it happened. The discovery of these priceless treasures—each more than two thousand years old—would make huge headlines around the world. Would they not also cause many to have to reconsider their skeptical and/or negative views about God and the Bible?

Imagine the international uproar that would be caused by the sudden rediscovery of the Ark of the Covenant—so long as it was not locked away in some U.S. government storage facility, the way it is at the end of *Raiders of the Lost Ark*. We have no definitive prophecies that say the Ark will be found in the last days. But again, a number of Jewish and Christian scholars believe the Temple treasures and the Ark will be rediscovered when it is time for the Third Temple to be built.

As with the other Temple treasures, there is biblical precedent for the Ark of the Covenant being hidden from those who would destroy or desecrate the Temple, only to be restored to the Temple when the time was right and the coast was clear. In 2 Chronicles 35:3, for example, we read that "[King Josiah] issued this order to the Levites, who were to teach all Israel and who had been set apart to serve the LORD: 'Put the holy Ark in the Temple that was built by Solomon son of David, the king of Israel. You no longer need to carry it back and forth on your shoulders. Now spend your time serving the LORD your God and his people Israel.'"[15]

Some are convinced they already know where the Ark is but cannot yet reach it. "Tradition records that even as King Solomon built the First Temple, he already knew, through Divine inspiration, that eventually it would be destroyed," notes Rabbi Ariel on his Temple Institute Web site. "Thus Solomon, the wisest of all men, oversaw the construction of a vast system of labyrinths, mazes, chambers, and corridors underneath the Temple Mount complex. He commanded that a special place be built in the bowels of the earth, where the sacred vessels of the Temple could be hidden in case of approaching danger. Midrashic [Jewish commentaries] tradition teaches that King Josiah of Israel, who lived about forty years before the destruction of the First Temple, commanded the Levites to hide the Ark, together with the original menorah and several other items, in this secret hiding place which Solomon had prepared."[16]

Rabbi Ariel goes on to claim that "this location is recorded in our sources, and today, there are those who know exactly where this chamber is. And we know that the Ark is still there, undisturbed, and waiting for the day when it will be revealed. An attempt was made some few years ago to excavate towards the direction of this chamber. This resulted in widespread Moslem unrest and rioting. They stand a great deal to lose if the Ark is revealed—for it will prove to the whole world that there really was a Holy Temple, and thus, that the Jews really do have a claim to the Temple Mount."

Imagine, then, what might be found after the War of Gog and Magog.

EZEKIEL AND THE MESSIAH

One of the things that has struck me while writing my novels is the growing number of Jews, regardless of their specific religious traditions, who see the landing lights as well, who are convinced that the Messiah is coming soon.

In the late 1980s and early 1990s, belief that Chabad-Lubavitch rabbi Menachem Schneerson (known as "the Rebbe") was the Messiah reached a fever pitch among hundreds of thousands of Jews around the world. "Schneerson purportedly has healed the sick, restored fertility to barren women and averted family tragedies," said a 1988 *Washington Post* profile. "He has never claimed publicly to be the messiah, but critics say he has been slow to deny the claim when made by his followers. They contend that this is why Schneerson has never set foot in Israel; under Jewish tradition, the messiah will arrive only when the era of redemption begins."[17]

Even when Schneerson suffered a massive stroke in 1992, there were still those who refused to give up their beliefs. "The Rebbe will surprise all," one follower told *U.S. News & World Report*, claiming that the Messiah would announce himself after doctors gave up. "The Rebbe will lead all of us to Jerusalem," he said, "and you and I may find ourselves standing shoulder to shoulder."[18]

After Schneerson's death in 1994 at the age of ninety-two, his supporters praised him for at least having prepared the way for someone else. "In virtually every talk the Rebbe gave, every letter he wrote and every action he initiated, the theme, the sign-off and the objective was: the coming of *Moshiach* [the Messiah], the attainment of the Redemption," notes the Chabad.org Web site, adding that "perhaps no leader in history emphasized the urgency and immediacy of Moshiach as did the Rebbe."[19]

Today Rabbi Ariel and his colleagues at the Temple Institute are not only convinced that the Messiah is coming soon; they are convinced the Third Temple is coming sooner. In one article posted on his Web site, Ariel wrote, "Which comes first, the Messiah or the Temple? There seems to be ample indication that the building of the Holy Temple will precede the Messiah's arrival. Various biblical verses and statements made by the great sages prove this. This is actually the opinion of Maimonides, a Jewish rabbi and philosopher, who quotes an astounding verse from the prophecy of Malachi (3:1) in his classic Letter to Yemen: 'For suddenly the master whom you are seeking will come to the sanctuary.' It appears that this prophecy, referring to the arrival of the Messiah, specifies that he will indeed arrive at the already built Temple."[20]

While I was writing this book, I came across this headline from the *Times* of London: **"Old Shack Will Give Madonna Front-Row Seat for Arrival of her Messiah."** According to the article, the pop singer was "trying to buy a house overlooking the Sea of Galilee at the place where followers of her Kabbalist faith expect the Messiah to reappear to herald world peace. . . . The star—who was raised an Italian Catholic but adopted the Hebrew name Esther several years ago—wants the house to turn it into a Kabbalah study centre where followers can pore over the mystical texts. Kabbalists believe that the Messiah will appear at Safed and walk to Tiberias on the shores of the Sea of Galilee."[21]

There is also a growing sense among the Jewish community worldwide that the cataclysmic events of recent decades are signs of the last days and the Messiah's nearing appearance as well. The famed twentieth-century Jewish writer Martin Buber, for example, wrote an entire novel called *Gog and Magog* (it was much different from my novels). In it, he spoke of the "three hours of speechless terror after the tumult of the wars of Gog and Magog and before the coming of the Messiah," which will be "more difficult to endure than all the tumult and thunder" that had gone before, and "only he who endures them will see the Messiah."[22]

Elie Wiesel, the widely beloved Jewish Nobel laureate, also wove Ezekiel's prophecies into his work and has long believed their fulfillment will signal the Messiah's arrival. In his moving 1972 novel *Souls on Fire,* he wrote of Jewish communities watching unfolding world events in great fear. "Frontiers, thrones, loyalties, and systems change overnight. The earth trembles. Nations discover new passions, liberating but deadly. History moves and bursts into flame. And the blood flows. . . . In the rabbinical courts, these events are endowed with a messianic dimension. One speaks of Gog and Magog, of their gigantic, apocalyptic war. . . . The Jews needed the Messiah, perhaps more than ever."[23] Years later, Wiesel told an interviewer that "Messianism is the gift of the Jew to the world, but in our tradition we believe that before redemption there will be a huge catastrophe. We call it the war of 'Gog and Magog.'"[24]

I agree. The war of which Ezekiel wrote will precede the appearing of the Messiah on earth. But it will be his second appearing, not his first, and his name will be *Yeshua HaMoshiach*, Jesus the Messiah.

Few people have any idea just how many Jewish people have come to faith in Jesus in recent years, but the numbers are dramatic. Indeed, more Jews are coming to faith in Jesus today than at any time since the first century.

In 1967, when I was born, there were only five or six native Israeli believers in Jesus and fewer than 250 Jewish believers in Jesus in all of the Holy Land. Today there are more than 1,000 "sabra" believers—native-born Israeli Christians—and some 10,000 messianic Jews total in Israel.[25]

Worldwide in 1967, there were fewer than 2,000 Jewish followers of Jesus. Today conservative estimates say there are at least 100,000 Jewish believers, while some put the number at over 300,000.[26] One respected international Christian research agency says there are 132,000 Jewish believers connected to messianic congregations and 200,000 Jewish believers in Jesus attending Gentile churches worldwide.[27]

For a follower of Jesus from an Orthodox Jewish heritage like myself, not only is this exciting, it is also startling evidence of an ancient prophecy coming to pass before our eyes. Jesus once spoke to the Jews of Israel, saying, "For I say to you, from now on you will not see Me until you say, 'Blessed is He who comes in the name of the LORD'" (Matthew 23:39, NASB). In other words, until Jewish people turn to him in dramatic numbers—and get excited about his Second Coming—Jesus said he would delay his return.

How many are enough to trigger the Second Coming? I have no idea. But the trend lines are exciting, and I believe many, many more Jews will turn to Jesus in the time leading up to the War of Gog and Magog and in its immediate aftermath.

MUSLIMS TURN TO CHRIST IN RECORD NUMBERS

Charles Sennott was the Middle East bureau chief for the *Boston Globe* from 1997 to 2001. As he left that role to cover events in Europe, he published a book that became a best seller in the Boston area entitled *The Body and the Blood: The Middle East's Vanishing Christians and the Possibility for Peace.*

The book purported to document "the dramatically diminishing Christian presence" in the Middle East, a veritable "Christian exodus" that has left the Christian community there "withering" and "imperiled" in the face of war, persecution, and radical Islam. "What will happen if those [Christian] ideas and those institutions are abandoned, if they become barren, empty, echoing halls of the past?" Sennott asked. "Is Christianity truly going to die out in the land where it began?"[1]

The *Christian Science Monitor* called the book "a powerful and moving narrative. . . . Valuable and timely, it illuminates the human struggles while providing the in-depth historical context essential to understanding today's conflicts." *Foreign Affairs* called the book a "touching account of a venerable community whose numbers are sharply declining." The

Hartford Courant called it "profound and moving . . . a major achievement of insight, understanding, and interpretation."[2]

Sennott's book on the potentially imminent death of Christianity
echoes a prevailing media worldview. **"Christians Leaving Middle
East,"** declared a CNN headline.[3] **"Christians Quit Christ's Birthplace,"** proclaimed the BBC.[4] A National Public Radio story talked of
"the dwindling number of Christians in the Middle East."[5] A *Denver Post*
article claimed that "once significant Christian communities" in the
Middle East "have shrunk to a miniscule portion of their former robust
selves" and "in 50 years they may well be extinct."[6] An article in the
Guardian newspaper in London suggested the Christians of the Middle
East have become "an endangered species."[7] A story in the *Toronto Sun*
suggested that "a time might come, unless the political situation dramatically improves, when Christian communities of the Middle East
no longer exist."[8]

This Christianity-is-dying theme is complemented by the Islam-is-
taking-over-the-world theme, so fashionable in academic and media
circles over the past decade. In his 1996 book *The Clash of Civilizations
and the Remaking of World Order*, for example, Samuel P. Huntington argued that the percentage of Christians in the world will fall sharply in
the twenty-first century and will be overtaken by the explosive growth
of Muslims. "In the long run," wrote Huntington, "Mohammed wins
out."[9] CNN, meanwhile, called Islam the world's "fastest-growing religion."[10] PBS called Islam "the world's fastest growing faith."[11] If you do
a Google search of *Islam* and *fastest-growing religion*, you will find dozens of Muslim Web sites that abound with similar quotes from sources
ranging from ABC News to Mike Wallace of *60 Minutes* to *USA Today*.[12]

There is just one problem with such stories. They are not quite accurate. Not anymore, at least.

THE BIG (UNTOLD) STORY IN THE MIDDLE EAST

The War of Gog and Magog, as we have seen, will bring about a shat-
tering of radical Islam that will trigger a spiritual crisis for Muslims all
around the world as they see, to their shock, the hand of the God of

Israel defending—not demolishing—the Jewish people. The soul-searching that results will be intense. As they monitor saturation coverage on radio, television, and the Internet, Muslims will hear followers of Christ explaining what will happen and why, and they will see the prophecies of the Bible—not the Koran—coming true before their own eyes. What's more, they will see the power of the God of the Bible displayed before the eyes of the world.

In the process, many will realize for the first time that Jesus Christ did, in fact, die on the cross *for them.* He also rose again *for them*—to give them assurance of salvation, a place in heaven for eternity, and an abundant, joyful life here on earth, if they will only receive his free gift of salvation. When that happens, Muslims will turn to Jesus Christ en masse.

But even today, an exciting and dramatic spiritual revolution that is being completely missed by the mainstream media is under way throughout the Islamic world. The big (untold) story in the Middle East is that more Muslims are turning to Christ *today* than at any other time in human history, and much of it has happened since 9/11.

Over the past several years, I have had the privilege of interviewing more than three dozen Arab and Iranian pastors and Christian leaders throughout North Africa, the Middle East, and central Asia. In sharp contrast to the picture the media is painting, the picture they present is one of Christianity being dramatically resurrected in the lands where the Bible was written.

While I was writing this book, for instance, my wife and kids and I lived for two months in Egypt, where scores of Arabs are coming to Christ in the most amazing ways. During our time there we visited the largest church of born-again believers in the Middle East, which meets in a cave on the outskirts of Cairo beside what is known as the "garbage village." Some 10,000 new and growing believers worship there every weekend. In May of 2005, more than 20,000 Arab believers gathered for a day of prayer for their unsaved Muslim friends to become followers of Christ. The event was broadcast throughout the Middle East on a Christian satellite-television network, allowing millions more to see God powerfully at work.

This extraordinary church ministry began in 1972 when a young Egyptian businessman named Farahat lost an $11,000 watch and was stunned when a garbageman found it and gave it back to him.

"Why didn't you take the watch for yourself?" Farahat asked.

"My Christ told me to be honest until death," replied the man, dressed in filthy rags.

"You are a Christian?" Farahat asked.

The garbageman said he was.

"I didn't know Christ at the time," Farahat would later tell a reporter, "but I told him that I saw Christ in him. I told the garbage collector, 'Because of what you have done and your great example, I will worship the Christ you are worshiping.'"[13]

Over the next few years, Farahat began to study the Bible and grow in his faith, but when the garbageman asked Farahat to help him reach his fellow garbage collectors for Christ, Farahat always said he was too busy. For the next two years, in fact, the man begged him to come and start a church among his friends, but Farahat resisted.

Finally, in 1974, Farahat visited the garbage village outside of Cairo and couldn't believe what he found. He had never seen (or smelled) anything like it before—a series of rickety concrete tenement buildings built over massive dumps where men, women, and even the smallest children sift through thousands of tons of trash, sorting bottles, cans, glassware, and other goods for recycling and looking for items of even miniscule value to be sold for cash or bartered for food or clothing. There was no running water, no electricity, and no hope. Many turned to alcohol, drugs, gambling, and prostitution to find some meager escape from the deeply depressing environment. But even more appalling to Farahat were the numbers. Somewhere between 15,000 and 30,000 people were living amid the most gut-wrenching squalor he could possibly imagine.

The more Farahat and his wife, Su'aad, saw, the more they found themselves gripped by the words of Jesus in Matthew 5:3: "Blessed are the poor in spirit, for theirs is the kingdom of heaven" (NASB), and the words of the apostle Paul in 1 Corinthians 4:13, "We have become as the scum of the world, the dregs of all things" (NASB). Soon a small ministry was born. Farahat and his wife began preaching the gospel in the garbage village and caring for people's spiritual and material needs, and people started turning to Christ in droves.

In 1978, Farahat was officially ordained by the Coptic (Orthodox) Church, and he became known as Father Sama'an. The congregation met in a cave in the Muqattam Mountains beside the garbage village. By 1993, they had to expand the cave to fit all the new believers and seekers who wanted to attend. What they have now is an amazing testimony to God's grace in a region where many believe Christianity is dying.

My wife and kids and I visited the garbage village. We also toured the cave that houses the church facilities with a man who told us how he had been an alcoholic and hashish user until he heard Father Sama'an preach. He gave his life to Christ in 1992. You should have heard the passion in his voice and seen the gleam in his eyes. He had been at the bottom of the barrel, and now he was on top of the world. And he was the first to tell us: only the love and power of Jesus Christ had made the difference.

Such stories of lives transformed are spreading throughout Egypt and North Africa. Despite government restrictions and Muslim attacks against churches and believers, Christianity there is growing like wildfire. "I've never seen such hunger for God's Word and the message of Jesus as I do today," one North African Arab Christian leader told me.

In 1996 the Egyptian Bible Society sold just 3,000 video copies of the JESUS film, based on the Gospel of Luke and produced in the late 1970s by Warner Brothers and Campus Crusade for Christ. In 1997 the Bible Society decided to sell the videos at the famed Cairo International Book Fair. Sales surged to 35,000 in just a few weeks. In 2000 the group sold 600,000 copies of the JESUS film and a children's version of the video. Today annual sales top 750,000 copies of the Bible on audio-cassette, 200,000 to 300,000 full Bibles, and between 300,000 and 500,000 New Testaments.[14]

"We don't give these away," one Bible Society leader told me. "We don't charge a lot, but we charge something, and many, many people are buying them. Think about what that means. . . . Egyptians certainly don't have the money or the interest to buy a Bible or a JESUS film or any other piece of Christian literature unless they are really serious about finding God. I believe these sales are leading indicators of growing spiritual interest throughout this country, and particularly among Coptic Christians, of which there are some ten million. . . . There is a revival going on among Orthodox Christians."

CHRISTIANITY SURGING ACROSS NORTH AFRICA

Egypt is not alone.

When I was in Casablanca and Rabat in 2005, I found the Moroccan media up in arms about the "phenomenon of Moroccans converting to Christianity." Newspaper and magazine articles estimated that 25,000 to 40,000 Muslims have become followers of Jesus Christ in recent years. These numbers are overstated, church leaders in the country tell me, but the fact that they are being published and widely discussed says a lot about the dynamic that is at work and how rapidly the church is growing there.[15]

The government of Morocco—which has long worked to prevent missionaries and Bibles, JESUS films, and other Christian materials from entering the country—has begun taking a series of small but important steps to reach out to evangelicals and to project an image of religious openness. In 2004, for example, top officials began an ongoing dialogue with Richard Cizik of the National Association of Evangelicals and Rob Schenck of the National Clergy Council, among others. In 2005, King Mohammed VI invited American evangelist Josh McDowell and other Christian leaders and musicians for a series of high-level talks, public-speaking events, and even a Christian concert in Marrakech. The concert alone attracted more than 80,000 Moroccan young people, and a similar event was held in May of 2006.

When I visited with Ahmed Kostas, an aide to the king, in his office at the Ministry of Islamic Affairs in Rabat, he insisted that the kingdom was opening up and becoming more friendly to Christians. "You can buy *The Passion of the Christ* in shops all over Morocco. Moroccans can watch Christian television on their satellite dishes. We don't care what people watch. They can see whatever they want. They can choose whatever they want. . . . [In the past] the West has tried to force Christianity on us—it's the feeling of force that is the real tension."[16]

"What about efforts by Arab and Western Christians to get more Bibles and Christian literature into Morocco?" I asked.

"Officially, it's not a concern," he said. "But the way it is done is. . . . The big concern is any activities that cause unrest."

"You're worried that public, visible efforts to promote Christianity in Morocco will infuriate radical fundamentalists, who could cause trouble for the regime?" I pressed.

"We don't want anything that causes unrest."

A few months later I met with Mr. Kostas's boss, Dr. Ahmed Abaddi, who was appointed by the king to serve as Morocco's director of Islamic affairs, responsible for overseeing the country's 33,000 mosques. Abaddi, a soft-spoken, gentle-mannered former professor of comparative religion, told me that the king wants to build bridges of friendship with evangelical Christians in the United States because he knows the "real" America is not Hollywood and the pornography industry but people of faith. "Historically, it has been the Christians who have held America together," Abaddi said. "Anyone who traces the history of America knows that evangelicals are behind it."[17]

The king also wants all Moroccans—and particularly his country's Islamic leaders—to develop more friendly relations with Christians, Abaddi explained. "We need our people to know the real West, to understand that the West ain't no angel, but it ain't no demon either."

Why would Morocco reach out to evangelicals, though, when one of the central goals of such Christians is to evangelize, a practice frowned upon in his country? Abaddi said evangelicals are "gentlemen" whom you can trust. "We are trying to reach out to the real America. . . . Evangelicals are serious people, helpful people."

Abaddi acknowledged that the idea of Muslims converting to Christianity is a very sensitive subject in his country. But he also told me that he had recently published a book in Lebanon about the importance of encouraging religious freedom within Islam and even suggested that "Muslims have the right to change their religion," if they so desire.

Unfortunately, not all leaders in the region are as open as Dr. Abaddi and his colleagues. The church is growing as never before all across North Africa, and most Muslim leaders are up in arms.

In neighboring Algeria—the birthplace of St. Augustine but for many centuries almost devoid of a Christian presence—more than 80,000 Muslims have become followers of Christ in recent years.[18] The situation has become so alarming to Islamic clerics that in March of 2006, Algerian officials passed a law banning Muslims from becoming Christians or even learning about Christianity. Christians trying to share their faith with Muslims face two to five years in jail and fines of 5,000 to 10,000 euros for "trying to call on a Muslim to embrace another religion." In a move to stamp out the rapidly growing house-church movement, the law also forbids Christians from meeting together in any building without a license from the government.[19]

In Sudan, meanwhile, one of the biggest stories in modern Christendom is unfolding—a spiritual awakening of almost unimaginable proportions amid civil war, radical Islam, rampant persecution, and outright genocide. More than one million Sudanese have turned to Christ just since the year 2000—and not in spite of persecution, war, and genocide but *because* of them. "People see what radical Islam is like," one Sudanese Christian leader told me, "and they want Jesus instead."[20]

When Sudan received independence in 1956, there were only five or six born-again Anglican priests in the entire country. Today there are some 3,500, caring for more than 5 million followers of Christ affiliated with the Anglican Church alone. Other denominations are also growing rapidly. "The growth of the church is really tremendous," says Daniel Bul, bishop of the Episcopal Church of Sudan. "We hope . . . in the southern Sudan . . . everybody is going to be a Christian."[21]

Muslim clerics throughout the region have been watching this dramatic movement toward Christianity for some time and have been horrified. Now the trend is rapidly accelerating.

In 1993, a Saudi sheikh by the name of Salman Al-Odeh delivered a sermon entitled "Christian Missionaries Sweeping the Islamic World." He argued that "in Spain [Christians] have the biggest center of missionaries to Africa. They are trained really well and their efforts lead many Moroccans to convert." He then cited the *World Christian Encyclopedia*—which he described as a "dangerous survey"—and warned his fellow Muslims that "the number of Christians in Africa was 9 million only in 1900 A.D., or 9 percent of the whole population. In the year 1980 they became 200 million! They jumped from 9 to 200 million in 80 years [and the survey's authors] expected them to reach 390 million in the year 2000, or 48 percent of the whole population of Africa."[22]

Eight years later, in December 2001, Sheikh Ahmad Al Qataani, another leading Saudi cleric, appeared on a live interview on Aljazeera satellite television to confirm that, sure enough, Muslims were turning to Jesus in alarming numbers. "In every hour, 667 Muslims convert to Christianity," Al Qataani warned. "Every day, 16,000 Muslims convert to Christianity. Every year, 6 million Muslims convert to Christianity."

Stunned, the interviewer interrupted the cleric. "Hold on! Let me clarify. Do we have 6 million converting from Islam to Christianity or converting from Islam *and* other religions?"

Al Qataani repeated his assertion.

"So 6 million Muslims a year convert?" said the interviewer.

"Every year," the cleric confirmed, adding, "a tragedy has happened."[23]

GOD AT WORK IN CENTRAL ASIA

God is also on the move in central Asia, and Muslims there are turning to Christ in record numbers.

Before September 11, 2001, there were only seventeen known followers of Christ in all of Afghanistan. Today Afghan Christian leaders tell me there are more than 10,000 believers in the country, and Afghan Muslims are open to hearing the gospel message like never before. Dozens of baptisms occur every week. People are snatching up Bibles and other Christian books as fast as they can be printed or brought into the country. The JESUS film was even shown on television in one city before police shut down the entire TV station.

The enormous controversy over the case of Abdul Rahman, a

Muslim convert to Christianity facing execution for apostasy by a court in Kabul, became the talk of the nation in the spring of 2006, with saturation coverage by Afghani TV, radio, and newspapers. The event shined a huge spotlight on the fact that Afghans are turning to Christ in such numbers that Islamic leaders are furious. It also showed the fledgling Afghan church that fellow believers around the world are praying for them and eager to see them grow and flourish.

By God's grace, and with pressure from American, Canadian, British, Italian, and other leaders, the case against Rahman was dropped. He was set free and left the country.

But persecution of believers in Afghanistan has hardly diminished. Just days after Rahman's release, two more Afghani believers were arrested, and according to the Compass Direct News service and Open Doors International, a Christian ministry to the "closed" countries of the Middle East, "One young Afghan convert to Christianity was beaten severely outside his home by a group of six men, who finally knocked him unconscious with a hard blow to his temple. He woke up in the hospital two hours later but was discharged before morning." Compass and Open Doors also reported that "several other Afghan Christians have been subjected to police raids on their homes and places of work in the past month, as well as to telephone threats."[24]

Yet none of this has stopped the Afghan church from growing. "God is moving so fast in Afghanistan, we're just trying to keep up," one Afghani believer told me. "The greatest need now is leadership development. We need to train pastors to care for all these new believers."[25]

Afghanistan is not alone.

As I mentioned earlier in this book, I went to Alma-Ata (now Almaty), a city in southern Kazakhstan, near the Chinese border, on a missions trip in 1986. At the time there were no known Kazakh believers in Christ in a country of some 15 million people. By 1990, there were only three known believers. But today evangelical leaders in the country report that there are more than 15,000 Kazakh Christians and more than 100,000 Christians of all ethnicities.

On that same trip, I went to Tashkent, the capital of Uzbekistan. At the time, there were only a handful of Uzbek believers in a country of

27 million people. Today there are some 30,000 Uzbek followers of Christ, and hunger for the gospel is at an all-time high.

While these may seem like small numbers in comparison to the overall populations of these Muslim countries, the immensity of their importance cannot be overstated. These are historic developments, unprecedented in the fourteen hundred years since the Islamic religion was founded, especially when one considers the tremendous social, religious, legal, and economic persecution faced by Muslim converts from Islam. In many of these countries, a new believer in Christ risks being ostracized from his or her family, fired from a job, attacked verbally and physically by Islamic fundamentalists, imprisoned by authorities, and even executed.

INSIDE THE FIRES OF IRAQ

In Iraq, the hunger for Christ is also at an all-time high, say Iraqi pastors and other Arab Christian leaders who have been inside the country.

More than one million Arabic New Testaments and Christian books have been shipped into Iraq since the fall of Saddam Hussein's regime. More are being printed inside the country, and pastors say they cannot keep up with the demand. What's more, Iraqis today are turning to Christ in numbers unimaginable at any point during Saddam Hussein's reign of terror.

Iraqi general Georges Sada, who in addition to serving as a senior advisor to Iraq's president has served as president of the National Presbyterian Church in Baghdad and chairman of the Assembly of Iraqi Evangelical Presbyterian Churches, says that at least 5,000 Iraqis have publicly identified themselves as new followers of Christ just since the fall of Saddam Hussein. The number of secret believers may be much higher, he told me, since conditions are not yet safe enough in the country for all believers to gather together for worship and prayer.

The Kurds in the north of Iraq are especially receptive to the gospel message and are converting to Christianity "by the hundreds," Sada reports. One evangelical church recently started in Kurdistan now has more than 800 people worshipping there every week, most of whom are new converts from Islam. What's more, Nechirvan Barzani, the prime minister of the Kurdistan Regional Government in Irbil, has vowed to protect the ancient Assyrian Christian community there as well as new followers of Christ from persecution and violence. Sada and Dr. Terry Law, president of World Compassion, a Christian relief organization based in Oklahoma, met with Barzani in May of 2006. "I would rather see a Muslim become a Christian than a radical Muslim," Barzani told them, an absolutely remarkable statement by a Muslim leader in a land racked by sectarian violence.[26]

Despite the fact that numerous Iraqi churches have been fire-bombed and converts from Islam have been attacked and killed, at least fourteen new evangelical churches have opened in Baghdad alone since the war. Other evangelical congregations are forming all around the country, some with as many as 500 to 600 people attending every Sunday. In 2004–2005, more than 160 Iraqi believers began training to become new pastors and lay leaders. Iraqis are also flooding back into the ancient Christian churches.

"Catholic and Orthodox Christian priests are seeing their faith in Christ revitalized," one Iraqi pastor, who asked not to be named, told me. "They want to see their churches restored to the first-century kind of activity—evangelism, discipleship, and miracles."[27]

Why such spiritual hunger? Every Iraqi Christian I have interviewed has given me the same two answers: war and persecution.

"The security in Iraq is deteriorating," explained one of the leaders of the Iraqi evangelical movement over breakfast, "but the ministry is increasing compared to any time in church history. It's not that complicated really, Joel. When human beings are under threat, they look for a strong power to help them—a refuge. Iraqis look around and when they see believers in Jesus enjoying internal peace during a time of such violence and fear, they want Jesus too."[28]

But, I asked, how can you share your faith and lead people to Christ with all the suicide bombings, car bombings, snipers, and other troubles?

"We're doing what we can, and especially getting Bibles into the hands of people who want them," he explained. "And people can now watch Christian preaching and teaching on satellite television and get our Bible studies and other materials off of the Internet. But the truth is, God is doing something else that is amazing.

"People are being healed. Many of them. We don't have much experience with that but we're seeing it happen anyway. . . . And that's not all. Muslims are seeing visions of Jesus Christ. He is coming to them and speaking to them, and they are repenting and giving their lives to him. *Shiites!* I'm talking about Shiite Muslims seeing visions of Jesus and becoming his followers. In fact, I actually haven't personally met any Shiites who have come to Christ who were converted because someone shared the gospel with them. They have all come to faith through dreams and visions. They are coming to us already persuaded. Our job, then, is to help them study the Bible, meet other believers, and grow in their faith."

This pastor was not alone in telling me about the enormous number of Muslims who are coming to Christ through dreams and visions. It is a message I heard from nearly every Middle East Christian leader that I interviewed. What's more, they believe all this is a fulfillment of God's message through the Hebrew prophet Joel and the apostle Peter. In Acts 2:17-20 Peter, quoting Joel 2:28-31, says, "'In the last days,' God says, 'I will pour out my Spirit upon all people. Your sons and daughters will prophesy. Your young men will see visions, and your old men will dream dreams . . . before that great and glorious day of the LORD arrives.'"

One night in a Middle Eastern country I cannot name, I had dinner with an Iraqi pastor from Baghdad. I asked him to paint me a picture of what he was seeing God do in his country. He graciously agreed.

"You know, Joel, the best way to think about Iraq right now is to think of Shadrach, Meshach, and Abednego," he said, referring to the famous story found in Daniel 3. "Remember, they were captives in Babylon, and they refused to bow down and worship the idol that King Nebuchadnezzar had built. So the king ordered that the fiery furnace be heated seven times hotter than usual, and then he threw the men in there. But when the king looked into the furnace, he was stunned. He asked his officials, 'Didn't I throw three men in there?' And they said, 'Certainly, O king.' And then he said, 'But look! I see four men walking around in there, without chains on their hands, and without being harmed—and the fourth is like a son of the gods!'

"This is what we are facing today. When you look at the news, you see Iraq on fire—seven times hotter than before—and that's true. Things are very difficult. There is much violence and bloodshed. But that is only part of the story. That was the view from the outside. On the inside, it looked much different for Shadrach, Meshach, and Abednego. Yes, they were inside the flames. But they were also free, and they were walking with Jesus. That's our situation today. For the first time in our lives, we are free, and Jesus is walking with us, guiding us, helping us be a blessing to our fellow Iraqis who need his love and his salvation so desperately. We couldn't be more excited about the miracles God is doing here. We just ask the church outside to keep praying that we are brave enough and worthy enough to bear the name of Jesus."[29]

THE PASSION IN PERSIA

Perhaps the most dramatic story unfolding in the Middle East is the explosion of Christianity inside Iran, arguably the most fiercely Islamic and diabolically anti-Christian country on the face of the planet, certainly on par with Saudi Arabia.

"In the last 20 years, more Iranians have come to Christ [than in] the last 14 centuries," said Lazarus Yeghnazar, an Iranian-born evangelist now based in Great Britain. "We've never seen such phenomenal thirst. . . . I believe this phenomenon [will] snowball into a major avalanche. This is still a rain. This is not the avalanche coming . . . but it will be happening very, very soon."[30]

At the time of the Islamic Revolution in 1979, there were only about 500 known Muslim converts to Jesus inside the country. By 2000, a survey of Christian demographic trends reported that there were 220,000 Christians inside Iran, of which between 4,000 and 20,000 were Muslim converts.[31] But according to Iranian Christian leaders I interviewed for this book, the number of Christ followers inside their country has shot dramatically higher since 2000.

In fact, the head of one leading Iranian ministry, who agreed to speak on the condition of anonymity, told me, "Based on all the things we are seeing inside Iran today, I personally believe that if every Iranian who secretly believes in Jesus could come forward right now and declare his or her faith publicly, the number would top a million."[32]

Such numbers are impossible to verify given the current political conditions, but the trend lines are clear, and the increasingly panicked reaction of Iranian authorities in recent years does point to unprecedented growth of the Iranian church.

In April 2004, Iranian Shiite cleric Hasan Mohammadi delivered a stunning speech at a high school in Tehran. He urged the students to "safeguard your beloved Shiite faith" against the influence of the evangelicals and other so-called apostate religions, and warned, "Unfortunately, on average every day, fifty Iranian girls and boys convert secretly to Christian denominations in our country."[33]

Mohammadi had been hired by the Ministry of Education to teach fundamental Shiite Islam to the country's youth, who are increasingly dissatisfied with the Islamic Revolution and are looking elsewhere for fulfillment. But as one father whose son was in the audience told a reporter, Mohammadi "unknowingly admitted the defeat of the Islamic Republic of Iran as a theocratic regime in promoting its Islam."

By September of that year, the Iranian regime had arrested eighty-six evangelical pastors and subjected them to extended interrogations and even torture.

In October 2004, Compass Direct reported that "a top [Iranian] official within the Ministry of Security Intelligence spoke on state television's Channel 1, warning the populace against the many 'foreign religions' active in the country and pledging to protect the nation's 'beloved Shiite Islam' from all outside forces." The news service went on to report that this security official had helped interrogate ten of the arrested evangelical pastors, had complained that Christian activities in Iran had gone "out of control," and was "insisting that their church do something to stop the flood of Christian literature, television, and radio programs targeting Iran."[34]

The rise of Mahmoud Ahmadinejad led to a dramatic acceleration of government-directed persecution of Iranian Christians—particularly pastors, many of whom have been arrested, interrogated, beaten, and even worse.

Compass Direct reported in November 2005:

An Iranian convert to Christianity was kidnapped last week from his home in northeastern Iran and stabbed to death, his bleeding body thrown in front of his home a few hours later. Ghorban Tori, 50, was pastoring an independent house church of covert Christians in Gonbad-e-Kavus, a town just east of the Caspian Sea along the Turkmenistan border. Within hours of the November 22 murder, local secret police arrived at the martyred pastor's home, searching for Bibles and other banned Christian books in the Farsi language. By the end of the following day, the secret police had also raided the houses of all other known Christian believers in the city. According to one informed Iranian source, during the past eight days representatives of the Ministry of Intelligence and Security (MOIS) have arrested and severely tortured ten other Christians in several cities, including Tehran.[35]

Only a few days before the pastor's murder, Ahmadinejad met with thirty provincial governors and vowed to shut down the country's growing house-church movement, reportedly saying, "I will stop Christianity in this country."[36]

Nevertheless, evangelical leaders inside Iran say they are seeing Jesus' words in Matthew 16:18 come true before their very eyes: "I will build my church; and the gates of hell shall not prevail against it" (KJV).

"Before the [Islamic] Revolution, there was a very small response to the gospel," one Iranian pastor told me. "In the summer of 1975, our ministry shared Christ with nearly 5,000 people. Only two people showed any interest. But [in 2005], 98 out of every 100 people we shared with showed interest, and we saw many decisions for Christ."[37]

He added that a Farsi-language broadcasting ministry he works with received 50,000 calls in 2005 from Iranians wanting to receive

Christ despite the fact that they had to make long-distance calls at their own expense, knowing the lines could be tapped and facing the threat of persecution, jail, and torture.

Radio and satellite-television evangelism ministries are big factors in getting the gospel to millions of Iranians who would otherwise have no access to the truth. And God is using other creative methods to reach Iranians as well. Back in 2003, for example, when Iranians heard that Mel Gibson's *The Passion of the Christ* was anti-Semitic, they couldn't wait to see it. Neither, apparently, could the mullahs and the government authorities, thinking that anything negative about the Jews had to be good for Muslims. So despite the fact that Islam forbids the visual depiction of Jesus—and teaches that Judas was crucified in Jesus' place, and thus was never resurrected—*The Passion* actually played in Persia. True, only one theater ran it. But there was a ten-day waiting list for tickets. What's more, tens of thousands of bootlegged copies of *The Passion* are now circulating throughout Iran, and the official version is actually available in Iranian stores, as it is in most Muslim countries throughout the region.[38]

Ultimately, though, I'm told that many Iranians are not coming to Christ primarily through *The Passion* or the JESUS film or radio and satellite-TV ministries or even the work of the mushrooming house-church movement. These resources are vitally important. They are giving many unbelievers initial exposure to the gospel, and they are certainly strengthening the faith of new believers and those who have been following Christ for some time. But they are not enough to bring some Iranians to a point of decision. What is bringing these Iranians to Christ is dreams and visions of Jesus, just as in Iraq, though in much larger numbers.

As one Iranian pastor explained, "A factory manager recently showed up at a church. We didn't need to share the gospel with him. We didn't need to persuade him of anything, which was good, in a way, because many in our congregation are terrified to share their faith. But this man already believed because Jesus had spoken to him in a dream. In fact, he said that Jesus had been personally teaching him the way to follow him for two hours a day for an entire year. Now he finally had the courage to identify himself with other believers, and he wanted to worship Christ with us. It was amazing. But things like this are happening all the time in Iran."[39]

In my third novel, *The Ezekiel Option*, I tell the story of two Christians driving through the mountains of Iran with a carful of Bibles. Suddenly their steering wheel jams and they have to slam on the brakes to keep from driving off the side of the road. When they look up, they see an old man knocking on their window asking if they have the books. "What books?" they ask. "The books Jesus sent me down here to get," the old man replies.

He goes on to explain that Jesus recently came to him in a dream and told him to follow. When he awoke, he found out that everyone in his mountain village had had the same dream. They were all brand-new followers of Jesus, but they did not know what to do next. Then the old man had another dream in which Jesus told him to go down the mountain and wait by the road for someone to bring books that would explain how to be a Christian. He obeyed, and suddenly two men with a carful of Bibles have come to a stop right in front of him.

This was one of my favorite passages in *The Ezekiel Option*, but it's not fiction. I didn't make it up. It's true. I got it directly from a dear friend of mine who is the head of a ministry in the Middle East. He personally knows the men involved. I simply asked if I could change their names for use in the novel, and my friend agreed.

Yet for all the good news that is happening in Iran today, it is just the beginning. The avalanche of God's grace is coming, and it may be coming very soon. A few years ago, while I was writing *The Ezekiel Option*, my wife and I invited some friends to dinner, a dear couple; the wife is Iranian and a passionate Muslim convert to Christ. She had actually never heard of the War of Gog and Magog or the prophecies of Ezekiel 38–39. However, as she listened to me explain them, she said they struck her as very similar to a prophecy all the Iranian believers on the Internet were talking about from Jeremiah 49:34-39.

In "the last days," Jeremiah says, God will scatter the people of Elam—ancient Iran—to "the four winds" and "there will be no nation to which the outcasts of Elam will not go" (NASB). Our friend explained that this is exactly what happened after the Islamic Revolution in 1979: Iranians found themselves scattered all over the world, unable to return home, and today the Persian diaspora tops 5 million. Next, the prophecy says God will bring his "fierce anger" against Elam "and destroy out of it king and princes" (Jeremiah 49:37, 38, NASB). But then, declares the Lord, "it will come about in the last days that I will restore the fortunes of Elam" (Jeremiah 49:39, NASB).

The buzz among Iranian Christians today is that this prophecy is about to be fulfilled, that the leaders and deputies of Iran will be destroyed by the God of the Bible, who will then pour out his Holy Spirit and bring the people of Persia into the Kingdom of Jesus Christ in a manner that will stun the world. What's more, many believe this prophecy may be directly connected to the events of Ezekiel 38–39.

REACHING HAMAS FOR JESUS

There are many, many more wonderful stories of what Jesus is doing in the Middle East that I wish I could share with you, but space does not permit. As the apostle John once wrote, "Jesus also did many other things. If they were all written down, I suppose the whole world could not contain the books that would be written" (John 21:25). Still, I would be remiss if I did not end this chapter with the amazing story of how one man set out to reach the leadership of Hamas for Jesus.

In October of 2004, my wife and I had the privilege of having lunch in Southern California with a man named Brother Andrew, one of the most remarkable missionaries of this century and the last.[40] He is the founder of Open Doors International and the author of the mega–best seller *God's Smuggler,* describing his efforts to penetrate the Evil Empire with the gospel. Brother Andrew is now the author (with Al Janssen) of a powerful and unforgettable book called *Light Force: A Stirring Account of the Church Caught in the Middle East Crossfire,* which describes his efforts to penetrate the Muslim world with the gospel.

What struck us first about meeting him in person—aside from what a kind and gentle and grandfatherly figure he has become—is the man's boldness and incurable confidence. He doesn't just say he believes in a God who can "open doors" to the most closed countries and the most closed hearts on earth. He really means it.

Over salads and iced tea, Andrew humbly told us how he personally shared the gospel with Yasser Arafat, with Islamic ayatollahs, and with Palestinian terrorists exiled to Lebanon. But the story that affected me most was about his unforgettable experience of preaching the gospel to four hundred Hamas leaders in Gaza City. I did not take notes at that lunch, so let me just quote here from Brother Andrew's book.

"I can't change the situation you face here in Gaza," Brother Andrew told the Hamas leaders. "I can't solve the problems you have with your enemies. But I can offer you the One who is called the Prince of Peace. You cannot have real peace without Jesus. And you cannot experience Him without forgiveness. He offers to forgive us of all our sins. But we cannot receive that forgiveness if we don't ask for it. The Bible calls this repentance and confession of sin. If you want it, then Jesus forgives. He forgave me and made me a new person. Now I'm not afraid to die because my sins are forgiven and I have everlasting life."[41]

Hearing the story, I felt both amazed at this man's faith and ashamed at my own lack of faith. I had to confess to Brother Andrew that it had never dawned on me to pray for—much less preach the gospel to—Hamas leaders. But isn't that what Jesus tells his followers to do—to love our enemies and bless those who persecute us? What made the story all the more remarkable was that rather than lynching Andrew for trying to convert them to Christ, the Hamas leaders actually invited him to speak to other Muslims.

"Andrew, I believe you know that I teach at the Islamic University," said one. "To my knowledge, we have never had any lectures about Christianity. While you were talking, I was thinking that it would be helpful for our students to know about real Christianity. Would you consider coming to the university and giving a lecture about the differences between Christianity and Islam?"

Even the Palestinian Christian leaders who accompanied Brother Andrew to the event were taken aback.

"I think my God is too small," said the head of the Palestinian Bible

Society. "I never thought that a Christian could speak to radical, fanatical fundamentalists. But even if someone did have a chance, it never occurred to me that they would actually want to sit and listen to the gospel. Today God showed me how big He is."

Such are not the stories being told by the mainstream media today, and they are only the beginning of what God will do in fulfillment of Ezekiel 38–39. But they raise an important question with which I would like to close this chapter.

How big is your God?

CHAPTER FIFTEEN

TRACKING THE TREMORS

Hurricane Katrina struck Louisiana and the U.S. Gulf Coast in late August 2005. At the time, I was in the middle of a seventeen-city book tour for *The Ezekiel Option* across the U.S. and Canada, but like everyone else in North America, I was horrified as I watched television coverage of the disaster and the enormous human toll it left in its wake.

Like the Asian tsunami in December 2004, Katrina was a sudden and sobering reminder of the enormous devastation that can be unleashed by an "act of God." But this time it was not in some faraway place. An *American* city had been virtually wiped out overnight. Americans of all ages, races, and income levels saw their homes and businesses and memories swept away forever. Local, state, and federal officials from both political parties found themselves overwhelmed by the magnitude of the destruction and seemed all but paralyzed to respond quickly or effectively enough to meet the growing needs of the residents of New Orleans and other Gulf Coast communities.

And then the questions began: Why did so many people ignore the storm warnings? Why didn't the mayor and the governor do more to explain to people just how powerful this storm was going to be? Why weren't more people evacuated? Why were whole fleets of school buses not used for such an evacuation? And so forth.

A few days after the hurricane hit, I was preparing to give a speech in Winnipeg, Canada, to 250 business leaders about *The Ezekiel Option* and the coming War of Gog and Magog. Right before the speech began, I felt my BlackBerry buzz, alerting me to a new e-mail. I don't know what compelled me to read it just then. I was about to step onto the stage. But something caught my eye.

The automated e-mail alert from NBC News was written by Brian Williams, describing an eerie experience he'd had on the day before Katrina reached land. "I was on the phone with my wife while at the check-out area [of a local Wal-Mart] when a weather bulletin arrived on my Blackberry, along with a strong caveat from our New York producers," Williams explained. "The wording and contents were so incendiary that our folks were concerned that it wasn't real . . . either a bogus dispatch or a rogue piece of text. I filed a live report by phone for Nightly News (after an exchange with New York about the contents of the bulletin) and very cautiously couched the information. Later, we learned it was real, every word of it. Below are actual excerpts, in the urgent, all-capital-letters style of the medium. Note the time on the message . . . but more importantly . . . note the content."[1]

URGENT — WEATHER MESSAGE

NATIONAL WEATHER SERVICE NEW ORLEANS LA

1011 AM CDT SUN AUG 28 2005

. . . DEVASTATING DAMAGE EXPECTED . . .

HURRICANE KATRINA . . . A MOST POWERFUL HURRICANE WITH UNPRECEDENTED STRENGTH . . . RIVALING THE INTENSITY OF HURRICANE CAMILLE OF 1969.

MOST OF THE AREA WILL BE UNINHABITABLE FOR WEEKS . . . PERHAPS LONGER.

AT LEAST HALF OF WELL CONSTRUCTED HOMES WILL HAVE ROOF AND WALL FAILURE. ALL GABLED ROOFS WILL FAIL . . .

```
ALL WOOD FRAMED LOW RISING APARTMENT BUILDINGS WILL
BE DESTROYED . . . ALL WINDOWS WILL BE BLOWN OUT.

THE VAST MAJORITY . . . OF TREES WILL BE SNAPPED OR
UPROOTED. ONLY THE HEARTIEST WILL REMAIN STANDING
. . . BUT BE TOTALLY DEFOLIATED.

POWER OUTAGES WILL LAST FOR WEEKS . . . AS MOST POWER
POLES WILL BE DOWN AND TRANSFORMERS DESTROYED. WATER
SHORTAGES WILL MAKE HUMAN SUFFERING INCREDIBLE BY
MODERN STANDARDS.[2]
```

"The last sentence in that statement is as concise a summation of conditions in New Orleans as is possible," Williams wrote. "It turned out to be an *advance copy of the script for this storm,* predicting in unbelievable detail the level of destruction that was by now less than 24 hours away. To me it conjured up the image of a lone forecaster, known but to his or her co-workers, struggling to merge decades-old boilerplate Weather Service wording with the most vivid language possible in a final attempt to warn an entire region" (emphasis added).

AN ADVANCE SCRIPT FOR THIS STORM

As I headed to the podium, I kept chewing over those last few sentences, and I found myself reminded that Ezekiel 38:9 says that the War of Gog and Magog will "come like a storm" upon Israel and the world (NASB). And it struck me at that moment that God himself was giving us an advance script for this terrible and powerful global storm.

So as I began speaking, I walked the audience through the prophecies of Ezekiel 38–39, and then I read them Williams's e-mail and the National Weather Service bulletin. I explained that when Ezekiel's "storm" hits, it will make the devastation caused by the Asian tsunami and Hurricane Katrina pale by comparison, and then I tried as best I could to help the audience understand how their lives would be changed forever.

In the run-up to the war, for example, a wave of fear will sweep across the world as a nuclear cataclysm draws near. We will see our leaders feverishly trying to negotiate a peaceful solution that will never come. We may very well see the American military mobilized as a defensive posture against Russian, Iranian, and other Islamic forces streaming toward Israel.

At the same time we will likely experience unprecedented price shocks at the pumps as oil and gas prices reach new record heights. At the very least, the markets will be traumatized by the prospect of World War III in the oil-rich region. But there may also be a cutoff of the very oil supplies upon which we so depend. We will see American citizens and business leaders fleeing the Middle East, eager for a safe haven. We may see terrorist attacks increase abroad and even here at home.

When the war itself begins, the world will experience the great earthquake of which Ezekiel wrote, "and all the men who are on the face of the earth will shake" at God's presence (Ezekiel 38:20, NASB). If this does, in fact, mean that all people around the globe will experience a physical shaking as opposed to an emotional and spiritual shaking, we could well see catastrophic casualties and property damage here in North America. The "big one" Californians and particularly San Franciscans have feared for so long could be triggered, bringing unspeakable devastation, though it would by no means be isolated to the American West Coast.

Simultaneously, we should expect to see pandemic diseases sweep through Russia, the Middle East, central Asia, North Africa, and southern Europe, putting the entire world at risk of such pestilence and plagues. Is this a massive outbreak of the avian flu? Or is it something else, like Ebola or some other pandemic? We do not know for certain, but we can conclude that casualties will be high. What's more, we will see massive hailstorms and torrential rains and a firestorm unlike anything the world has ever experienced, and again, casualties and property damage and psychological trauma will overwhelm all the emergency systems our nation and our fellow nations have ever put into place.

Air and shipping traffic will be disrupted indefinitely. Depending on the magnitude of the earthquake, roads and railways may be impacted across the U.S. and Canada. But even if not, global commerce will be severely affected, and though Americans and others will no doubt be exceedingly generous with their financial contributions to the

Red Cross, Salvation Army, and other emergency-relief agencies, none of it will be enough. Not in the near term, anyway.

The safest place in the world to be, ironically, will be Israel, though it, too, will be impacted by the effect of the "Day of Devastation" on its neighbors and the rest of the world. If the oil industry in Israel is fully up and running by that point, the energy resources and services of the Jewish state will be a desperately needed blessing for the rest of the world. If not, God may use the aftermath of the war to bring those oil resources on line at last. Either way, we know Israel will be the center of global attention and a blessing to the world at that difficult hour.

Soon afterward, churches will be overflowing around the world as masses turn to Jesus Christ and his followers for wisdom and comfort amid such cataclysmic events. Synagogues will also be overflowing as many Jews turn not to Jesus (though many will) but back to their roots in the Hebrew Scriptures. Mosques, on the other hand, will be increasingly deserted—if they survive this day of judgment at all—as Muslims begin an intense period of soul-searching in the shadow of the sudden global demonstration of the power of the God of Israel. New Age and other forms of spirituality will also surge in popularity as many seek explanations for events from sources other than the Bible. And the Internet will become a primary source in the global search for news, analysis, and answers.

Unfortunately, Ezekiel's war is not the end of such global trauma. The Bible states that it is only the beginning. It will be followed eventually by an event known as the Rapture, in which followers of Jesus Christ suddenly disappear and meet Christ in the sky. This will lead to the rise of the Antichrist and a seven-year period described in the book of Revelation as "the great tribulation" (Revelation 7:14), the worst seven years in the history of mankind.

I realize there are many skeptics reading this book, people who are certain all this is a fairy tale, not something to be taken seriously. As I stated in the introduction, I am not trying to persuade you that these events are going to happen. I am simply trying to explain what the Bible says will happen, why it matters, and how it will change your world.

And what if it is true? What if God has given us in the Scriptures a sneak preview of the terrible things to come? None of us want these things to happen. I certainly don't. But for those of us who believe the Bible is the actual Word of God and therefore have no doubt that these events are actually going to happen—perhaps in our lifetime—should we be silent? Should we keep such information to ourselves?

I don't see how. I would rather be criticized or even ridiculed than be asked after the fact how I could have known such traumas were coming and given people no warning. So I asked the audience in Winnipeg that night—and many audiences since—these questions: Are you going to heed the Bible's warnings of this coming storm and take the necessary precautionary steps to protect yourself and your loved ones and neighbors? Or are you going to try to ride out the storm and suffer its unspeakable consequences?

"WE DIDN'T THINK IT WOULD COME THIS SOON"

It is easy to ignore such warnings or to think that we have more time. But history suggests this is a mistake. This point was really driven home to me on the September 15, 2005, broadcast of the *NBC Nightly News*, when Brian Williams followed up his story by doing an on-camera interview with Robert Ricks of the National Weather Service, the "lone forecaster" who had written that prescient warning tragically disregarded by so many.

WILLIAMS: *Did a part of you want to be wrong?*
RICKS: I would much rather have been wrong in this one. I would much rather be talking to you and taking the heat and crying wolf. But our local expertise said otherwise. You know, "Hey, let's gear up for the Big One, this is going to be the Big One."

WILLIAMS: *How much of you is in that statement? What of you is in that wording?*
RICKS: I also had to validate each one of those statements and . . . in my mind, I was saying, "I'm not going to take this out, it sounds valid. I'm not going to take this part out, it sounds valid."

WILLIAMS: *So you went through point by point?*
RICKS: Yeah, I read each one. I was trying to find things to actually take out. And I said, "I cannot find it in myself to take these out, because they seem very valid for the situation." And I came from the experience of going through [hurricanes] Betsy and Camille myself in the Lower Ninth Ward [of New Orleans].

WILLIAMS: *If you knew the damage was going to be like this, you did everything in your power to tell people a monster was coming, did the response break your heart?*
RICKS: Yes, it did. Because we always prepare for the Big One; we just didn't think it was going to come this soon.[3]

As I watched that interview, I felt great sadness for the people who had chosen not to take the warnings seriously and had paid the ultimate price for their disbelief or inaction. At the same time, I thought about how many more would have suffered and died if Ricks had known such a terrible storm was coming and said nothing or chosen to temper his sense of urgency for fear of sounding like an alarmist. In such a scenario, Ricks would not have been responsible for Katrina itself. But he certainly would have been guilty of knowing the truth—however terrible—and doing little or nothing to alert those who would be most impacted by it. Thank God he did what he could.

The more I thought about it, the more it struck me that Ezekiel wrote chapters 38 and 39 for the same reason Robert Ricks wrote his weather bulletin—not because he *wanted* to, but because he *had* to. Both men saw terrible events coming. Both men felt morally and ethically compelled to tell people what they knew. And both men were willing to risk their public reputations in order to give people time to get to safety.

I wrote *Epicenter* and the Last Jihad series for the same reason. Some may ignore them. Others may be offended or even angered by their content. But with more than one million copies now in print in multiple languages, I am struck by how many people around the world are eager to view world events through the third lens of Scripture and to make sure they are spiritually safe before the storms Ezekiel described arrive with full force.

REAL-TIME INTEL

A book, however, can only lay out the basic elements of the story. It cannot keep pace with rapidly moving events. To track the tremors in real time, therefore, I have created a weblog at www.joelrosenberg.com, where I write about the latest political, economic, military, and spiritual developments in Washington, DC, Moscow, and the Middle East.

The site allows me to link to breaking news—like when Iranian president Mahmoud Ahmadinejad announced, "Like it or not, the Zionist regime is heading toward annihilation. . . . The Zionist regime is a rotten, dried tree that will be eliminated *by one storm*," echoing the very language of Ezekiel 38:9.[4] It also allows me to link to stories a casual observer might have missed, often from foreign media and intelligence sources, and to analyses by a wide range of Jewish, Muslim, and evangelical Christian writers with their own unique insights and perspectives.

The latest technology also makes it possible for me to post from almost anywhere in the world in real time, and I have done so from Jerusalem, the Golan Heights, Moscow, Istanbul, Amman, Cairo, and other Middle Eastern locations.

What's more, readers of the site can post their own comments and give me and others a heads-up on intriguing stories they have found. They can also e-mail me with intelligence they have gleaned from their own experiences. This can prove exceptionally useful. One reader, for example, was an F-16 weapons-systems officer flying combat missions over Iraq during the war. He didn't provide any classified information, of course, but he did give my readers and me intriguing insights into the war effort that we weren't getting anywhere else. A former CIA undercover officer operating in central Asia occasionally e-mails me details on the growing turmoil in that region. A Palestinian pastor e-mailed me from inside Gaza when Hamas won the elections there. A Wall Street investment banker (a real-life Jon Bennett) sends me the latest inside news from Russia and the Middle East. When I can, I post these or weave the pertinent information into the articles I write.

One of my favorite examples comes from a radio producer in California who became intrigued with *The Ezekiel Option,* began reading my weblog, and started studying the Scriptures more closely for himself. At one point, he came across Ezekiel 38:4-8, where God says to the dictator of Russia, "I will turn you around and put hooks in your jaws to lead you out . . . to the mountains of Israel." The passage suddenly reminded him of an article he had read in *U.S. News & World Report.* He contacted me and asked me if I'd read "Moscow's Mad Gamble," a column by Mort Zuckerman. I had not. "You should," he said. "It's pretty spooky in light of your books."

He was right. Zuckerman wrote that when it came to Iran's nuclear ambitions, "Russia has become part of the problem, not the solution." Why? Because Moscow is selling nuclear power plants and nuclear technology to Iran and has thus become inextricably linked to Iran's fate. As one American diplomat told Zuckerman, this Russian-Iranian nuclear business is a *"giant hook in Russia's jaw"* that will lead to serious dangers for both countries.[5] The story had been written three months earlier, in January of 2006, but I would have missed it if not for an alert reader now tracking events through the third lens of Scripture.

>>FLASH TRAFFIC<<

Another way I try to help people track the tremors is through the e-mail alerts I send out from Washington called >>FLASH TRAFFIC<<, to which people can subscribe for free at joelrosenberg.com.

These are typically brief interviews with key players in Washington and the Middle East, my own analysis of breaking news, or advance notice of important upcoming events, films, or media appearances. Sometimes they are geopolitical in nature; sometimes they are more spiritual. But whereas I update the weblog every day or two (and sometimes several times a day), FLASH TRAFFIC e-mails only go out about once every week or two. They are designed for people who may not have the time to check the weblog every day but want to have the most important stories delivered directly to their desktops, Palm Pilots, or BlackBerrys without having to be reminded.

One dispatch dated March 30, 2006, described my experience at a dinner put on by the Radio and Television Correspondents Association, where conversation at my table centered on the three *I*'s—Iran, Iraq, and Israel.

I quoted Frank Gaffney, who served as assistant secretary of defense in the Reagan administration and is now head of the Center for Security Policy. Frank told me that Iran worried him for several reasons, and not just because of its nuclear program. "First: Iran now has the capability of firing a Scud missile off the back of a commercial container ship, making it possible to deliver a nuclear warhead into the U.S. without having an ICBM. Second: Iran is working on building an electromagnetic-pulse bomb, which could detonate over an American, European, or Israeli city, fry all electronics and communications, and render a country virtually defenseless."

I also quoted Lt. General Thomas McInerney—former assistant vice chief of staff of the U.S. Air Force and author of *Endgame: The Blueprint for Victory in the War on Terror*—who told me that the Iranians were near or past the point of no return in developing a nuclear bomb and that Bush had a narrow window of time to shut down the mullahs' military capability and decapitate the regime.

McInerney's insights turned out to be quite prescient, as my readers would soon find out. Eleven days after I sent out that FLASH TRAFFIC, Iran announced that it had successfully enriched uranium and had joined the nuclear club. The following day a high-ranking State Department official warned that once Iran could perfect the use of 50,000 centrifuges, it could produce a nuclear bomb in sixteen days.

A year earlier, my wife and I had the wonderful privilege of attending the National Prayer Breakfast in Washington, DC, for the first time. It was a remarkable event, with 4,000 guests from all over the U.S. and around the world, and we were moved by what we saw and heard. When I got home that afternoon, I wrote a FLASH TRAFFIC to describe the importance various leaders were placing on the power of prayer during a time of war and terrorism. In the dispatch, I quoted from leaders of both political parties, including President Bush and Senator Dianne Feinstein, the California Democrat, who read from the writings of the Hebrew prophet Micah.

But the most interesting talk of the morning was given by Tony Hall, the former Democratic congressman from Dayton, Ohio, who had been appointed by the president to serve as the U.S. ambassador to the United Nations food and agriculture agencies, based in Rome. In his gentle, understated way, Hall urged religious men and women of both parties not to be shy about bringing their faith to the office and letting it be part of who they are in public. In fact, he described a trip he took to an Islamic country where he was greeted by the U.S. ambassador at the airport.

"Congressman Hall," said the unnamed ambassador, "I just want to remind you that you're in a Muslim country. Please don't talk about religion, or it could really set back what we're trying to accomplish here."

Hall said he just nodded politely, but when they arrived at the office of the king, he was asked by the king why he had come to the country.

"I would like to be your friend," Hall replied. "I would like our countries to be friends. And I would like to invite you to the National Prayer Breakfast, in the name of Jesus."

The U.S. ambassador went pale. But the king got very excited. He slapped his knee and said, "That is remarkable. You have come all this way to be my friend and to talk to me about Jesus. That is wonderful. My mother used to talk to me a lot about Jesus when I was a child. We should talk about Jesus more often." And then the king turned to the ambassador and said, "Why don't you talk about Jesus?"

The audience howled, as did my wife and I, and though his remarks were not reported in the major news media, I thought Hall's point was one worth passing on to my readers: those who say they are followers of Jesus Christ should never be ashamed of speaking his name. Nor should they be hesitant to bless people in his name or invite them to church or to a prayer breakfast or to read and study the Scriptures together. After all, they may be surprised just how interested even presidents, prime ministers, and kings—not to mention their own friends and neighbors—are to hear Christ's message of hope and love, especially during times of great turmoil and unrest.

GETTING READY

In his book *Saddam's Secrets,* Iraqi general Georges Sada cites an Arab proverb that says, quite bluntly, "Don't be a mute Satan." As Sada explains, "It means, if you have important information that may help someone in a difficult situation, say something. Don't be a devil and keep silent when you can say something to help."[6]

I would feel remiss, therefore, to walk you through these ten headlines and explain how such events will change our lives forever without providing some practical suggestions of ways that you and your family can act on such intelligence and be ready when these dramatic events occur. Allow me, then, to conclude with three simple points.

First, have an exit strategy.
Regardless of precisely when the fulfillment of Ezekiel 38–39 occurs, none of us have any guarantee that we will wake up tomorrow morning or even make it through this day. You may feel healthy and vibrant at any given moment, but the truth is you don't know how much time you have left in this life, and neither do I. Anything can happen. It is, therefore, vitally important that we have an exit strategy, that we know with absolute certainty where we are going to go when we die.

The good news is that the Bible says we can know for certain that we are going to heaven if we put our faith in Jesus Christ. One of the clearest explanations of this good news or gospel message that I have ever read—and one that had a great impact on my parents and me—was written by Dr. Bill Bright, one of the twentieth century's most prominent evangelical Christian leaders. In *The Four Spiritual Laws,* Bright explained that "just as there are physical laws that govern the physical universe, so there are spiritual laws which govern our relationship with God."[7]

- **Law One: God loves you and has a wonderful plan for your life.** Jesus said, "For God loved the world so much that he gave his one and only Son, so that everyone who believes in him will not perish but have eternal life" (John 3:16). Jesus also said, "I came that they may have life, and have it abundantly," that it might be a full and meaningful life (John 10:10, NASB).
- **Law Two: Man is sinful and separated from God.** Therefore, people cannot know and experience God's love and plan for their lives. The apostle Paul wrote, "Everyone has sinned; we all fall short of God's glorious standard" (Romans 3:23) and that "the wages of sin is death" (Romans 6:23), that is, eternal separation from a holy and perfect God.
- **Law Three: Jesus Christ is God's only provision for sin.** Through Christ you can know and experience God's love and plan for your life and be assured of going to heaven. Jesus died on the cross in Jerusalem—the epicenter of the epicenter—in our place, and the Bible says that "God showed his great love for us by sending Christ to die for us while we were still sinners" (Romans 5:8). Jesus also rose from the dead. The apostle Paul wrote, "Christ died for our sins, just as the Scriptures said. He was buried, and he was raised from the dead on the third day, just as the Scriptures said. He was seen by Peter and then by the Twelve [disciples]. After that, he was seen by more than 500 of his followers at one time. . . . Then he was seen by James and later by all the apostles" (1 Corinthians 15:3-7). What's more, Jesus is the only way to get to heaven. Jesus said, "I am the way, the truth, and the life. No one can come to the Father except through me" (John 14:6).
- **Law Four: We must individually receive Jesus Christ as Savior and Lord.** Only then can we know and experience God's love and plan for our lives. The Bible says, "To all

who believed him [Christ] and accepted him, he gave the
right to become children of God" (John 1:12). We receive
Christ through faith. "God saved you by his grace when
you believed," wrote the apostle Paul in Ephesians 2:8-9.
"And you can't take credit for this; it is a gift from God.
Salvation is not a reward for the good things we have
done, so none of us can boast about it." When we receive
Christ, we experience a new birth, as Jesus described in
John 3:1-8. And we receive Christ by personal invitation.
"Look!" Jesus said. "I stand at the door and knock. If
you hear my voice and open the door, I will come in"
(Revelation 3:20).

Bright explained that "receiving Christ involves turning to God from
self (repentance) and trusting Christ to come into our lives to forgive
our sins and to make us what He wants us to be. Just to agree intellectually that Jesus Christ is the Son of God and that He died on the cross for
our sins is not enough. Nor is it enough to have an emotional experience. We receive Jesus Christ by faith, as an act of the will."

What was particularly helpful about *The Four Spiritual Laws* for me
and my family was that it concluded with a very simple and clear explanation that you can receive Jesus Christ right now through prayer.
"God knows your heart and is not so concerned with your words as He
is with the attitude of your heart," Dr. Bright noted. And then he offered a suggested prayer:

Lord Jesus, I need You. Thank You for dying on the cross for
my sins. I open the door of my life and receive You as my Savior and Lord. Thank You for forgiving my sins and giving me
eternal life. Take control of the throne of my life. Make me the
kind of person You want me to be.

My father, Leonard Rosenberg—an Orthodox Jew— prayed that exact
prayer in 1973 and thus accepted Jesus as his Messiah. My mother,
Mary, did too. I prayed a similar prayer a few years later. It transformed

our lives. We didn't become perfect. Nor did our personal troubles and trials disappear. To the contrary, in many ways they have increased, as they will continue to do as we rapidly approach the end of days and the War of Gog and Magog. But now we have God's love and forgiveness to protect us. Now we know God's purpose for creating us and the plan he has for us to honor him in these last days. And now we have this prayer-hearing and prayer-answering God in our hearts and at our sides as we head into mankind's darkest days.

Does this prayer express the desire of your heart? If so, I encourage you to pray it right now. If you do, Jesus Christ will come into your heart, forgive your sins, and give you eternal life, just as he promised. Then you can know for certain—beyond any shadow of a doubt—that you are going to heaven when you die. In fact, the apostle John explained that the New Testament was written for this very reason. "I have written this to you who believe in the name of the Son of God, so that you may know you have eternal life" (1 John 5:13).

When we receive Christ as our Savior, we receive absolute assurance that we will spend eternity with God. That assurance gives us the hope and the courage to endure sorrow, disappointment, and dangerous, difficult times. The Bible puts it this way: "This hope is a strong and trustworthy anchor for our souls" (Hebrews 6:19). It assures us, "Whatever was written in earlier times was written for our instruction, so that through perseverance and the encouragement of the Scriptures we might have hope (Romans 15:4, NASB). And it gives us the comforting promise that God really does have a wonderful plan for our lives, no matter what lies ahead: "'For I know the plans I have for you,' says the LORD. 'They are plans for good and not for disaster, to give you a future and a hope'" (Jeremiah 29:11).

As soon as you receive Christ as your personal Savior, start reading the Bible and talking to God in prayer every day. I recommend beginning with the Gospel of John and then reading Matthew, Mark, and Luke to really get to know the life and person of Jesus Christ. Also, begin attending a good church that preaches the salvation message of the Cross, teaches the Bible, and can help you learn how to become a fully devoted follower of Christ.

Second, have a neighborhood strategy.

As important as it is to know what storms are coming and make sure we and our own families are spiritually prepared, this is only the beginning. Compassion must also compel us to share what we know with those around us so they can become informed and prepared. Both Moses (Leviticus 19:18) and Jesus (Matthew 22:39) said, "Love your neighbor as yourself." Such an instruction certainly applies to the times in which we live. Here are a few suggestions:

- Invite your neighbors to your home for a four- or five-week study of Ezekiel 38–39 and its implications in light of current events. Remember, the goal is not to persuade people that these events are going to happen but to help them understand such events through the third lens of Scripture and become spiritually prepared.
- Begin a weekly prayer meeting in your home. In times of "war and rumors of war," gathering for prayer is a wonderful way to draw on the strength of God and build a strong community. Certainly pray for each other—for wisdom, for courage, and for each other's practical needs and spiritual growth. Pray, too, for the president, his advisors, Congress, our military, and leaders around the world to make wise decisions during these difficult hours. The apostle Paul urges: "Pray for all people. Ask God to help them; intercede on their behalf, and give thanks for them. Pray this way for kings and all who are in authority so that we can live peaceful and quiet lives marked by godliness and dignity. This is good and pleases God our Savior, who wants everyone to be saved and to understand the truth" (1 Timothy 2:1-3).
- If *Epicenter* has been helpful to you, consider giving a copy to your pastor, rabbi, or imam. Arrange some time to discuss it with them and get their take, especially in light of current events in Russia, Iran, Israel, and throughout the Middle East. Consider, too, discussing

the themes of this book with friends, neighbors, class-
mates, colleagues at work, and your extended family;
ask them for their feedback, thoughts, and opinions.
You may also consider suggesting that *Epicenter* be part
of your next book-club discussion. Again, remember
that the key is to encourage discovery and dialogue,
not dissension and debate.

Third, have a global strategy.

While it is vitally important to act locally, compassion must also compel us to act globally. After all, the events described in this book are
going to affect those in other regions even more than those of us in
North America, and we would be truly remiss if we did not find a way
to help others understand what is coming and know God's love and
plan for the people who live in the epicenter.

One of the ways my wife and I are trying to do this is by founding
the Joshua Fund, a nonprofit educational and charitable organization
designed "to bless Israel and her neighbors in the name of Jesus, according to Genesis 12:1-3."

Many wonderful and effective organizations with a similar
passion are already working in Israel and throughout the Middle
East. Over the years and through the writing of this book, we have
gotten to know many of the leaders of such groups who are doing
great work. Our goal is not to reinvent the wheel or duplicate their
efforts but rather to draw attention and direct resources to such
work. As such, one of the objectives of the Joshua Fund will be to
identify worthy projects run by credible, Christ-centered organizations and then raise funds that will be invested into accomplishing
those projects.

> The Lord had said to Abram . . . "I will make you into a great
> nation. I will bless you and make you famous, and you will be a
> blessing to others. I will bless those who bless you and curse
> those who treat you with contempt. All the families on earth
> will be blessed through you." (Genesis 12:1-3)

According to the Scriptures, blessing Israel means

- praying for the peace of Jerusalem (Psalm 122:6);
- bringing good news of God's love to the afflicted (Isaiah 61:1);
- rebuilding the ancient ruins (Isaiah 61:4);
- caring for the poor (Deuteronomy 15:11);
- being a "light to the nations" of the Middle East (Isaiah 49:6, NASB)—that is, blessing Israel's neighbors and her enemies, not just Israel herself.

The driving force of the Joshua Fund, therefore, is to help evangelical Christians

- pray knowledgeably and consistently for Israel and the Middle East;
- take vision trips to—and attend conferences in—Israel and other Middle Eastern countries;
- invite speakers from Israel and other Middle Eastern countries to help your community, company, or church better understand the issues facing the epicenter;
- publish Christian books and music in Israel and the Middle East that raise awareness of God's love and plan for the epicenter;
- print and distribute Bibles, copies of the New Testament, and copies of the JESUS film in Arabic, Farsi, Turkish, Russian, and other epicenter languages;
- invest in the rebuilding of Israel to welcome more Jewish people back to their ancient, God-given homeland;
- assist the poor and needy in Israel in the name of Jesus Christ;
- support the evangelical church in Israel and the Middle East as the only true hope for peace and reconciliation.

If blessing the nations of the epicenter in the name of Jesus is an effort you and/or your family, church, or company are interested in helping with and investing in, please visit www.joshuafund.net for more information. You can also send a check payable to The Joshua Fund to

The Joshua Fund
P.O. Box 3468
McLean, Virginia 22103-3468

May God richly bless you for doing so.

CONCLUSION

The history of mankind began in the Middle East, and it will end there too.

The Garden of Eden was located in the land we now know as Iraq. The last two cities mentioned in the Bible before the second coming of Christ are Jerusalem and Babylon. And the prophets tell us that before Christ returns the earth will suffer through the War of Gog and Magog.

Though these events and prophecies were written thousands of years ago, they are as real and as relevant today as this morning's headlines. Pick up any newspaper and you will find the countries of the Middle East shaking our world and shaping our future. You will find Russia and Iran forming a military alliance. You will find Babylon rising out of the deserts of Iraq. What's more, you will find Israel at the epicenter of the world, Jerusalem at the epicenter of Israel, and the Temple Mount at the epicenter of Jerusalem.

This intense focus on the Middle East generally and on the State of Israel specifically will only accelerate in the days and months ahead. Those who view the world through the third lens of Scripture know it. The people living in the Middle East sense it too, though they may not always know why.

If you ever visit Saddam Hussein's main palace in Baghdad, be sure to visit Saddam's throne room and look up, for there you will see a large dome. Painted on this dome are images of the Dome of the Rock on the Temple Mount in Jerusalem. Beside these are paintings of horses attacking Jerusalem. Painted on the walls are Scud missiles pointed at

Jerusalem. And at the center of it all is an image of Saddam himself, riding a white horse into the Holy City.

One day not long from now, someone actually will come from the clouds, riding on a white horse, leading his armies into battle in Israel. But his name will not be Saddam Hussein or Mahmoud Ahmadinejad or that of any other Middle Eastern dictator or warrior. Rather, Revelation 19 tells us that his name will be Jesus—Messiah and Savior of Jews and Gentiles, the Prince of Peace, the Risen One who loved us and gave his life for us, that we might live a full and abundant life, both now and forever. May you experience his amazing love and forgiveness before that day, for that is his greatest wish, and mine.

AFTERWORD

M uch has happened in Russia, Israel, and the Islamic world since I completed the original *Epicenter* manuscript in June 2006 that may, in fact, have prophetic significance. What follows is a summary and analysis of the most dramatic developments.

THE SECOND LEBANON WAR

The thirty-four-day war between Israel and Hezbollah was not in and of itself a prophetic event. That is, there are no passages of Scripture in either the Old or New Testament that forewarned this specific conflict was coming. That said, the Second Lebanon War was hugely significant for several reasons.

First, the war was consistent with the Bible prophecies suggesting a series of traumatizing wars in the Middle East that will serve as the "birth pangs" before the return of Jesus Christ. In Daniel 9:26, the Hebrew prophet tells us that "even to the end [of history] there will be war" and that "desolations are determined" (NASB). In Matthew 24:6-7, Jesus tells us that in the last days before his return, "you will be hearing of wars and rumors of wars" and that "nation will rise against nation and kingdom against kingdom" (NASB). In Matthew 24:8, Jesus specifically indicates that such wars will be the "birth pangs" of even greater traumas to come. In many ways it was startling, therefore, to hear U.S. Secretary of State Condoleeza Rice state on July 29, 2006—right in the middle of the Second Lebanon War—that such events were the "birth pangs of a new Middle East."[1] Though Secretary Rice has in the past described herself as a Bible-believing Christian, it is not clear whether she specifically meant to reference this Bible prophecy or whether she simply used a phrase that seemed to accurately capture the moment. Either way, I believe she was right.

Second, the war was consistent with the overall arc of Bible prophecy, which says that Israel will increasingly be the focal point of world attention in the last days. As I have sought to explain throughout this book, the Bible teaches us that in the end times the eyes of the world will once again be riveted upon Israel and the fate of the Jewish people and Jerusalem. That seemed virtually impossible for most of the past two thousand years. After all, Israel was not even a nation and only a handful of Jews lived in the Holy Land. Yet today, Israel dominates headlines around the globe. Thousands of international journalists are stationed in Jerusalem and Tel Aviv. Satellite television beams images from Israeli wars into living rooms on every continent. The Second Lebanon War was fresh evidence of just how thoroughly the resurrected State of Israel captivates the attention of people from every nation and language on the face of the earth.

Third, the war suddenly thrust Rome—of all cities in the world—into the center of the Mideast peace process, capturing the attention of Bible students and prophecy scholars around the world. For ages, Christians have believed, based on their reading of Bible prophecy, that Israel will be reborn in the "last days," and so will the Roman Empire. What's more, many evangelical Christians have believed that a political leader from Rome will one day emerge to finalize a comprehensive peace treaty between Israel and her neighbors. While not all Christians have believed this in the past, nor do all Christians believe this today, those who do point to Daniel 9:26-27 and a fascinatingly detailed and specific trajectory of future events.

1. First, the Messiah will come to Israel.
2. The Messiah will then seem to be "cut off" from his people.
3. After the Messiah is gone, Jerusalem will be destroyed.
4. The Temple will then be destroyed.
5. War will continue until the end of history.
6. "Desolations are determined" until the end of history.
7. Then, in the end times, a leader will emerge from the people who destroyed Jerusalem and "will make a firm covenant" between Israel and her neighbors for seven years (Daniel 9:27, NASB).
8. Other events will make it clear that this leader is actually profoundly evil, opposed to God, opposed to the Jewish people, opposed to peace, but the Scriptures promise that this leader will eventually come to destruction.

In the judgment of millions of Bible-believing Christians around the world, six of these eight prophetic events and trends have already been fulfilled.

1. Jesus was born in Israel at the beginning of the first century and proved to be the Messiah by teaching the people, performing miracles, loving his neighbors and his enemies, caring for the poor, and conquering death by his resurrection.
2. To those who did not believe in him, Jesus was seemingly "cut off" from his people when he was crucified around AD 33.
3. Then, in AD 70, the Roman army destroyed Jerusalem.
4. The Romans also destroyed the Jewish Temple, directly fulfilling Daniel's prophecy.
5. Wars have continued for the past two thousand years.
6. Desolations have continued for the past two thousand years.

Now millions of Christians around the world are watching for Rome to emerge as the focal point of Mideast peacekeeping efforts. Why? Because Daniel 9:26 indicates that the leader or "prince" who will eventually finalize the comprehensive peace treaty between Israel and her neighbors will emerge from the people who destroy Jerusalem, we can deduce that the future leader Daniel describes will be of Roman origin. It is, therefore, reasonable to expect that even before this leader's identity is known, Rome will become a key player in the Middle East peace process.[2]

In that context, one can understand why the following headlines during the Second Lebanon War captured the attention of so many Christians, myself included:

RICE TO VISIT ISRAEL, ROME FOR TALKS ON MIDEAST CRISIS:
Secretary of State Calls for Plan to Ensure Stable, Enduring Peace in Region
U.S. STATE DEPARTMENT, AMERICA.GOV, JULY 23, 2006

FOREIGN MINISTERS GATHER IN ROME FOR CONFERENCE ON LEBANON
Voice of America News, JULY 25, 2006

SECRETARY-GENERAL IN ROME CALLS FOR POLITICAL FRAMEWORK, ECONOMIC AID TO ADDRESS "HORRENDOUS AND DANGEROUS" SITUATION IN LEBANON
UNITED NATIONS DEPARTMENT OF PUBLIC INFORMATION, UN.ORG, JULY 26, 2006

CNN reported on June 26 that "leaders and representatives of countries around the world are meeting in Rome to discuss how to bring an end to the conflict in Lebanon and ease the humanitarian crisis. Pressure is on to achieve a swift cease-fire, but disagreements are expected as the U.S. pushes for a longer term solution to conflict in the Middle East."[3]

Italian foreign minister Massimo D'Alema then stated during a press conference in Rome that "an international force in Lebanon should urgently be authorized under a U.N. mandate to support the Lebanese armed forces in providing a secure environment. The Rome conference pledged its support for Lebanon's revival and reconstruction." What's more, D'Alema noted that the world leaders who had gathered in Rome had pledged "their full commitment to the people of Lebanon, Israel and throughout" to bring about "a comprehensive and sustainable peace."[4]

Rome, however, was not satisfied to simply host a Middle East peace conference. That was only the beginning. Italian prime minister Romano Prodi then publicly offered to lead a UN peacekeeping force of some 15,000 soldiers in southern Lebanon and quickly persuaded the Italian parliament to send up to 3,000 troops, the largest contingent of forces sent by any country.

The move was a dramatic and unexpected one. Not since the fall of the Roman Empire had Rome stationed military forces in or near the Holy Land. Now Rome was suddenly playing a central role in the Arab-Israeli peace process, consistent with Bible prophecy, and heads were turning.

A further note about the Middle East peace process: Is it possible that we will see dramatic breakthroughs for peace before the final, comprehensive treaty that Daniel 9 describes? Or, put another way, might we see more peace treaties and truces in the epicenter—as well as an even more impressive surge in Israeli prosperity—in the months or years before the War of Gog and Magog? Yes, I think that is possible, and desirable. Jesus said, "Blessed are the peacemakers," and he was right, of course. Well-crafted treaties with the Syrians, the Lebanese, and the Palestinians—treaties that truly respect both Arab and Israeli rights and protect the honor and national security of both sides—should be signed, sealed, and delivered, if at all possible. But we should be on guard against offers of false peace, deals that vastly overpromise and tragically underdeliver. We should also be aware that more violent convulsions could consume the region before good deals are signed. Let me simply caution readers to be prepared for any number of twists and turns on the road from here to the fulfillment of the prophecies described in this book.

Fourth, Russian president Vladimir Putin stunned the world by sending military forces and equipment to Lebanon in the fall of 2006, putting hundreds of Russian troops close to the border of Israel for the first time in two hundred years. True to form, however, Putin insisted that this was a unilateral action by Moscow and that Russian forces would not be under the command of the Italian general running the UN peacekeeping operation. What's more, the Kremlin stated that Russia's role in Lebanon could grow over time.

Agence France-Presse (AFP), noting the historic nature of Putin's move, reported that this was "Russia's first military intervention in Lebanon since the early 1770s, when Russia, under Empress Catherine the Great, defeated Ottoman forces and a naval detachment landed in Beirut." Russian military spokesman Vladimir Cherepanov told AFP that this was "the first time that Russia, or the former Soviet Union, publicly puts boots on the ground in the Middle East, apart from military advisors who have for decades served and trained customers of Moscow's weaponry."[5]

To be sure, the Russian contingent sent to Lebanon in 2006 was small—about four hundred specialists and engineers, some of whom were helping rebuild bridges that would enable humanitarian relief supplies and UN forces to move southward toward the Israeli border. To some, therefore, Russia's actions were perfectly consistent with assisting the international community in bringing peace to this troubled region.

To others, Putin's move was a classic case of the camel's nose getting under the tent. A modern diplomatic and military precedent had suddenly been set for Russian forces to be stationed in Lebanon. But Moscow was not then—nor had it ever been—a neutral player in the region. Dating back to Czar Peter the Great and as recently as 1982, Russia has sought to dominate or fully control the Middle East, as I have described earlier in this book. Russia has historically and consistently armed Israel's most dangerous enemies, even to this very day. That is why for decades it has been bedrock U.S. and Israeli foreign policy to keep Russian forces out of the region. Why then did the Israeli government agree to the presence of Russian forces so close to the Jewish state? Why did the U.S. government agree? Wasn't this move paving the way for more Russian forces to be pre-positioned in Lebanon in the future? Wasn't it possible that these Russian forces could eventually be used to execute the War of Gog and Magog?

Fifth, Turkey raised eyebrows by contributing military forces to the peacekeeping mission in Lebanon—the first time Turkish troops have been stationed on the borders of the Holy Land since the collapse of the Ottoman Empire in 1922. On the face of it, Turkey's move appeared consistent with the UN's declared mission to create and maintain peace and stability in the epicenter. Turkey is, of course, a member of NATO, a close American ally, and a predominately Muslim nation that has actually maintained peaceful ties with Israel in the six decades of the Jewish state's modern existence. The Israeli government, therefore, did not seem bothered in the slightest. The Associated Press reported that "Israeli Foreign Ministry spokesman Mark Regev said Israel was especially interested in having Turkey in the force because it is a largely Muslim country and a regional power."[6]

But the notion of Turkish military forces suddenly moving to the northern border of Israel stirred serious concerns among those tracking Ezekiel's prophecies. Why? For precisely the same reason the sudden presence of Russian military forces along Israel's northern border raised concerns. It established a contemporary and internationally sanctioned precedent for positioning even more forces from Magog and Gomer to Israel's north, and it did so at a time when so many other events consistent with Ezekiel 38–39 were occurring throughout the epicenter.

Sixth, Germany also shocked many—especially within Israel—by sending military forces to join the UN peacekeeping mission in southern Lebanon. When 2006 began, the notion of German military forces anywhere close to the borders of the Jewish state seemed absolutely inconceivable. At the time, one German lawmaker who had opposed the mission put it this way: "After the killing of millions of Jews there could be no way German soldiers should participate in such a mission."[7] A German TV correspondent noted that "only a few years ago the attitude in both Germany and in Israel would have been more or less the same: After the Holocaust, German soldiers anywhere near Israel—never!"[8]

Yet by the end of 2006, some 1,000 German naval and police forces were involved in the peacekeeping efforts, including patrolling the coast of Lebanon right up to Israeli sovereign waters, with the full approval of the Israeli government. In August 2007, the German government agreed to extend its maritime mission at least until September 2008. Israeli critics and some Jewish groups in Germany warned from the beginning that the UN was creating a scenario in which German forces could end up firing upon Jews. But the thinking in Prime Minister

Olmert's government went, *Why wouldn't we want to encourage Germany to do whatever they can to help defend the Jewish people?*[9]

The prophetic significance of Germany's involvement in Lebanon remains to be seen. As noted earlier in this book, some Bible scholars believe German military forces will join the War of Gog and Magog against Israel one day. Others are not so convinced. But one thing is certain: such historic and unexpected developments bear watching closely.

Seventh, with the help of Iran, Syria, and possibly Russia, Hezbollah is rapidly arming itself for a new, apocalyptic war with Israel. On September 2, 2004, the UN Security Council passed Resolution 1559. The vote was passed 9-0 with six abstentions, including Russia. It called for free and fair elections in Lebanon and for the withdrawal of all foreign forces in Lebanon (referring namely to Syria, given that all Israeli forces had been withdrawn in 2000). What's more, it called for the "disbanding and disarmament of all Lebanese and non-Lebanese militias."[10]

Not that it did any good.

Neither the UN, the Lebanese, the Syrians, nor anyone else in the international community paid much attention. Hezbollah continued importing weapons, building up its arsenal, training its forces, and preparing for the war it launched against Israel in July 2006 in which it fired more than 4,000 rockets and missiles at the Jewish state.

On August 11, 2006, the UN Security Council unanimously passed Resolution 1701. The resolution called for an immediate cease-fire and authorized the dramatic expansion of a UN peacekeeping force to 15,000 soldiers. Perhaps more importantly, at least to Israel, the resolution ordered this expanded peacekeeping force to prevent the rearming of all Lebanese militias and to disarm all such militias.[11]

Israeli prime minister Olmert's government readily accepted the resolution, believing that the arms embargo and disarmament provisions of Resolutions 1559 and 1701 would truly be enforced. In the end, however, it was all just so much talk. Not only did the United Nations Interim Force in Lebanon (UNIFIL)—which has been claiming to keep the peace in that beautiful but war-torn country since 1978—not disarm Hezbollah, it actually allowed Hezbollah to import advanced new

missiles and other weapons systems from Iran and Syria, in direct violation of its mandate. Consider this headline:

UN REPORT: ISRAEL SAYS HEZBOLLAH'S ARSENAL INCLUDES 30,000 ROCKETS

ASSOCIATED PRESS, MARCH 4, 2008

"Israel says Hezbollah is rearming and has an arsenal including
10,000 long-range rockets and 20,000 short-range rockets in southern
Lebanon, Secretary-General Ban Ki-moon told the Security Council in
a report," noted the AP. "While Ban's report did not confirm Israel's
claim, the U.N. chief reiterated his concern about Hezbollah's public
statements and persistent reports pointing to breaches of a U.N. arms
embargo, which bans weapons transfers to the militant Shiite Islamic
militia. Ban also expressed concern at 'the threats of open war against
Israel' by Hezbollah leader Hassan Nasrallah."

But that was not all. In his previous report to the Security Council,
"Ban alleged that Hezbollah had rearmed with new long-range rockets capable of hitting Tel Aviv and tripled its arsenal of C-802 land-
to-sea missiles since the 2006 war. He also drew attention to alleged
breaches of the arms embargo and the transfer of sophisticated weapons from Iran and Syria—both strong backers of Hezbollah—across
the Lebanon-Syria border. Syria disputed the claim and countered that
the allegations of weapons smuggling are motivated by political rather
than security considerations, Ban said, but Hezbollah's leaders have
admitted on several occasions that their military capacity had been
replenished after the war with Israel."[12]

Also deeply disturbing was both the presence and the use of
Russian arms on the Lebanon battlefield in 2006, arms that apparently
had been sold originally to Iran and Syria but were later either sold or
given to Hezbollah. No sooner did Israeli ground forces enter the theater than they found themselves facing Russian antitank missiles that
were being used against them to deadly effect. "The anti-tank missiles
proved to be one of Hezbollah's most effective weapons in combat in
south Lebanon, killing many of the 118 Israeli soldiers who died in the
clashes," reported the Associated Press.[13]

In mid-August 2006, a senior Israeli delegation was sent to Moscow by Prime Minister Olmert to give the Kremlin evidence that Russian arms were being used to kill Jews. Publicly, the Russian government initially denied this was even possible. But Shimon Peres, then Israel's vice premier, stated flatly, "We saw these weapons, they had certain markings."[14]

Have the Russians since convinced Israel they are complying with UN Security Council Resolutions 1559 and 1701 not to rearm militias in Lebanon? Hardly. On March 21, 2008, as I was finishing this update for *Epicenter*, a new headline popped up in *Haaretz*, one of Israel's leading daily newspapers: **"[Israeli] PM Says Worried Russian Arms Will Reach Hezbollah."**

A CZAR IS BORN

The most significant development that has occurred since the completion of the first edition of *Epicenter* is the fact that Vladimir Putin has chosen to stay in office and further centralize all power and wealth unto himself and is, in fact, fashioning himself as a twenty-first-century czar, an absolute dictator who can barely be criticized much less stopped.

Am I saying that Putin is Gog, the Russian dictator described by the Hebrew prophet Ezekiel who will form an alliance with Iran and other Middle Eastern countries and attack Israel in "the last days"? I am not. As of this edition of *Epicenter*, it remains too early to draw such a firm conclusion. But I maintain that such a possibility cannot be ruled out. For though it is not yet clear that Putin is Gog, he most certainly is Gog-esque.

Though his formal title has changed from president to prime minister, there is no doubt that Putin has more power than ever before. It is Putin who runs the Kremlin. It is Putin who runs the Russian military. He runs the Russian economy, Russia's domestic policy, Russia's foreign policy, and he appears willing to run down anyone who stands in his way, be they an opposition political leader or a critical journalist. More than two hundred journalists have been killed since the fall of Communism in 1991. Yet, while Russian police reportedly solve 80 percent of all murders, the number drops to only 6 percent when the victim is a journalist.[15]

Among the highest-profile unsolved cases in Moscow is the murder of Anna Politkovskaya, Russia's most famous investigative reporter. In December 2005, Politkovskaya published a book entitled *Putin's Russia: Life in a Failing Democracy*, a scathing and highly detailed attack on Putin's antidemocratic, dictatorial behavior both as head of the Russian intelligence services and as president of the Russian Federation that made headlines around the world. In the book she pulled no punches about her deep disdain for Putin. "I dislike him for . . . his cynicism, for his racism, for his lies . . . for the massacre of the innocents which went on throughout his first term as president."[16] Less than a year later, on October 7, 2006, she was found shot to death in the elevator shaft of her Moscow apartment. Former Soviet leader Mikhail Gorbachev denounced the crime as "a blow to the entire democratic, independent press. . . . It is a grave crime against the country, against all of us."[17]

One month later, the assassination in London of Alexander Litvinenko—an ex–KGB operative turned critic of Putin and a man who was investigating the murder of Anna Politkovskaya—stunned the West and raised chilling new questions about who Putin is, what he wants, and how far he is willing to go to get it.

"The story would be fit for a spy novel if it weren't so implausible," reported Bob Simon in a *60 Minutes* story. "A Russian ex-KGB agent turns against the Kremlin and flees Moscow. He continues his attacks from exile in London, until he is poisoned with a rare radioactive isotope and dies a slow painful death."[18]

British authorities concluded Litvinenko was killed by swallowing polonium-210, an almost impossible to obtain radioactive substance that was traced back to Russian nuclear facilities. It was as if a small nuclear bomb had been detonated in a man publicly accusing Putin of becoming an all-powerful dictator. "Litvinenko was fired in 1998 from the FSB security police, post-Soviet successor to the KGB, which Putin ran before becoming president," reported the *Daily Mail*, a London newspaper. "He spent the next eight years trying to publicise his belief that Putin was presiding over a return to a KGB-style state."[19]

But why would Litvinenko's enemies—or enemy—choose to launch a highly targeted nuclear attack? Why would they choose a weapon of micro destruction? Some believe, as do I, that someone was trying to send a message, not just to Litvinenko but to anyone and everyone choosing to criticize the Kremlin and the man at its helm: there is nowhere we cannot find you and kill you.

Was Putin actually and ultimately responsible for Litvinenko's death? Litvinenko certainly believed so. The Associated Press reported that "in a dramatic statement written before he died, Litvinenko . . . blamed [Putin] personally for the poisoning. The 43-year-old Litvinenko, who fiercely criticized Putin's government from his refuge in London since 2000, told police he believed he was poisoned November 1 while investigating the October slaying of Russian journalist Anna Politkovskaya." Litvinenko's last words accused Putin of having "no respect for life, liberty or any civilized value," and he added, "You may succeed in silencing me but that silence comes at a price. You have shown yourself to be as barbaric and ruthless as your most hostile critics have claimed. . . . You may succeed in silencing one man but the howl of protest from around the world will reverberate, Mr. Putin, in your ears for the rest of your life."[20]

British investigators announced in 2007 that they believed they had solved the case and requested that Russia extradite a former FSB official to stand trial for Litvinenko's murder. The Putin government denied the extradition request.[21]

Given the moves made by Putin, his advisors, and his government in recent years—as well as those actions Putin's team is suspected though not proven of—there is a steadily growing consensus among international journalists and analysts that a new czar is, in fact, emerging in Moscow, the first since the reign of Nicholas II ended disastrously in the October Revolution of 1917. Consider these headlines:

CZAR VLADIMIR

CBS News.com, October 3, 2007

CZAR VLADIMIR

New York Post, October 7, 2007

CZAR PUTIN

CNN SPECIAL REPORT, NOVEMBER 20, 2007

PUTIN, THE CZAR

Pravda (MOSCOW), NOVEMBER 26, 2007

PUTIN FOR CZAR?

Khaleej Times (DUBAI), DECEMBER 2, 2007

A CZAR IN THE MAKING:
The Cold War Is Dead, but Vladimir Putin Is Very Much With Us

Air Force Magazine, DECEMBER 2007

On December 4, 2007, *Time* magazine named Putin its "Person of the Year." The title of the cover story that followed? **"A Tsar Is Born."**

In the story, *Time* reported:

To achieve stability, Putin and his administration have dramatically curtailed freedoms. . . . Yet this grand bargain—of freedom for security—appeals to his Russian subjects, who had grown cynical over earlier regimes' promises of the magical fruits of Western-style democracy. Putin's popularity ratings are routinely around 70%. "He is emerging as an elected emperor, whom many people compare to Peter the Great," says Dimitri Simes, president of the Nixon Center and a well-connected expert on contemporary Russia. . . .

How do Russians see Putin? For generations they have defined their leaders through political jokes. It's partly a coping mechanism, partly a glimpse into the Russian soul. In the oft told anecdotes, Leonid Brezhnev was always the dolt, Gorbachev the bumbling reformer, Yeltsin the drunk. Putin, in current punch lines, is the despot. Here's an example: Stalin's ghost appears to Putin in a dream, and Putin asks for his help running the country. Stalin says, "Round up and shoot all the democrats, and then paint the inside of the Kremlin blue." "Why blue?" Putin asks. "Ha!" says Stalin. "I knew you wouldn't ask me about the first part."[22]

Despite his cruel and heavy-handed tactics, by the beginning of 2008, Putin's approval rating was a stunning 81 percent. It was not, therefore, difficult in the slightest for Putin to effectively install a puppet president and promote himself to the unequalled Ruler of Russia, regardless of specific rank or title.[23]

Mikhail Kasyanov, who once served as prime minister under Putin, was fired in 2004, and is now a fierce Putin opponent, warned: "The person who sits in the Kremlin is a czar. . . . De facto Putin is going to keep all the presidential powers. This will prolong the current political crisis which will lead the country along the path to destruction."[24]

Could Dmitry Medvedev, the baby-faced former law professor whom Putin handpicked and personally anointed to take his place as president, eventually find a way to ice his benefactor out of the way and seize full control of Russia himself? It is conceivable, perhaps, but as of this writing seems unlikely.

For starters, Medvedev is in every way Putin's junior. He is twelve years younger than Putin, just forty-two at the time of his "landslide" victory in a rigged election in March 2008. Medvedev is three inches shorter than his mentor, clocking in at five foot four as compared to Putin's already diminutive five foot seven. What's more, while Medvedev has spent the last several years running Gazprom for Putin—the behemoth state-run gas monopoly that supplies 30 percent of Europe's gas and has a market capitalization of $345 billion—he has precious little experience in the cutthroat, winner-take-all worlds of FSB intelligence or Kremlin palace politics.

No sooner did Putin select Medvedev for the job of president than his puppet blurted out that Putin would and should run the country anyway. "In order to stay on this path [of foreign and economic policy strength], it is not enough to elect a new president who shares this ideology," Medvedev told reporters. "It is not less important to maintain the efficiency of the team formed by the incumbent president. That is why I find it extremely important for our country to keep Vladimir Vladimirovich Putin at the most important position in the executive power, at the post of the chairman of the government."[25]

Putin, for his part, has made no bones about how long he plans to stay in power or whether he will be subservient to Medvedev. "I formulated the objectives for the development of Russia from 2010 to 2020," he has told reporters, and "if I see that I can realize these goals in this position [of prime minister], then I will work as long as this is possible." Will he hang President Medvedev's portrait in his office? "I do not have to bow to [Medvedev's] portraits," Putin stated without apparent humor.[26]

RUSSIAN LEADERS FUEL FEARS OF A NEW COLD WAR

It is not simply the fact that Vladimir Putin is systematically centralizing all power in Russia to himself that worries Western leaders and geopolitical analysts. It is the fact that Putin seems intent on projecting power in all kinds of new and destabilizing ways. Both by his words and his actions, Putin is fueling fears of a new Cold War in Europe, in the Middle East, and around the globe.

Consider, for example, these headlines, published since the original edition of *Epicenter* was completed:

PUTIN'S SPEECH: BACK TO COLD WAR?
BBC, February 10, 2007

PUTIN THREAT RAISES COLD WAR SPECTRE
Times of India, April 27, 2007

RUSSIA'S COLD WAR HANGOVER
Time magazine, April 27, 2007

PUTIN INVOKES THE LANGUAGE OF THE COLD WAR
London Telegraph, April 28, 2007

RUSSIA-BRITISH TIES HIT POST COLD WAR LOW

Gulf Times, MAY 1, 2007

RICE, PUTIN TRADE COLD WAR WORDS

Washington Post, JUNE 1, 2007

PUTIN RAISES SPECTRE OF NUCLEAR WAR IN EUROPE

London Times, JUNE 4, 2007

GATES TO PUTIN: "ONE COLD WAR IS ENOUGH"

China Daily, DECEMBER 2, 2007

What is driving such headlines?

The list of provocative statements and actions by Putin and his Kremlin team grows longer by the month. Consider a sampling:

- **February 2007:** Putin launches a vehement attack on Washington for pursuing, in his view, a U.S.-dominated "uni-polar" world. "What is a uni-polar world?" he asks. "No matter how we beautify this term, it means one single centre of power, one single centre of force and one single master. . . . The United States has overstepped its borders in all spheres—economic, political and humanitarian, and has imposed itself on other states. . . . Local and regional wars did not get fewer, the number of people who died did not get less but increased. We see no kind of restraint—a hyper-inflated use of force."[27]
- **February 2007:** News reports indicate that Russia is preparing "to sell Syria thousands of advanced anti-tank missiles, despite Israeli charges that in the past Syria has transferred those missiles to Hezbollah guerrillas in Lebanon."[28] The following month, a Russian journalist working on the story of Russian arms sales to Iran and Syria is found dead in Moscow.[29]
- **April 2007:** Putin threatens to pull out of a major arms-

control treaty if the U.S. and NATO build a missile defense system in Europe.[30]

- **May 2007:** Putin and his aides refuse to extradite the suspect British authorities have accused of murdering leading Putin critic Alexander Litvinenko.[31]

- **June 2007:** Putin threatens to aim Russian missiles armed with nuclear warheads at European cities if the U.S. and her allies proceed with building a ballistic missile defense system to protect the Western alliance from rogue regimes such as Iran and North Korea. "It's obvious that if part of the strategic nuclear potential of the U.S. is located in Europe, which in the opinion of our military experts represents a threat, we will take the corresponding steps in response," Putin told reporters at the time. "Of course we will have to get new targets in Europe."[32]

- **June 2007:** Russia begins delivery of "top-of-the-line fighter jets to Syria under a new deal estimated to be worth U.S. $1 billion," reports the Associated Press.[33]

- **June 2007:** That same month, Russia unveils and successfully tests a new breed of sea-based ballistic missiles with a range of 6,200 miles and capable of carrying six nuclear warheads each. Putin declares the missiles capable of penetrating any ballistic missile defense shield.[34]

- **June 2007:** Putin stuns the world by declaring that Russia owns the North Pole and the entire Arctic circle. "Russian President Vladimir Putin is making an astonishing bid to grab a vast chunk of the Arctic—so he can tap its vast potential oil, gas and mineral wealth," reports the U.K's *Daily Mail.* "His scientists claim an underwater ridge near the North Pole is really part of Russia's continental shelf. One newspaper printed a map of the 'new addition,' a triangle five times the size of Britain with twice as much oil as Saudi Arabia. . . . Observers say the move is typical of Putin's muscle-flexing as he tries to increase Russian power."[35]

- **July 2007:** Word leaks that Russia is preparing to sell "250 advanced long-range Sukhoi-30 fighter jets to Iran in an unprecedented billion-dollar deal."[36]

- **July 2007:** Putin and his aides declare they are breaking with the Conventional Forces in Europe Treaty, a major peace accord signed with NATO in 1990. They threaten to move large numbers of conventional forces from the Asian sectors of Russia back into the European sectors, raising fears throughout Georgia, Poland, the Czech Republic, and the rest of Europe of a possible future Russian invasion. The Associated Press notes that the move "threatened to further aggravate Moscow's already tense relations with the West."[37]

- **August 2007:** News leaks out of Moscow that "for [the] first time since [the] fall of [the] Iron Curtain, Russia plans to build permanent bases on Syrian soil as part of [a] large arms deal between [the] two countries," including two ports for the Russian navy in Tartus and Latakia.[38]

- **August 2007:** Putin meets with Iranian president Mahmoud Ahmadinejad in Bishkek, Kyrgyzstan, to oversee a series of large-scale war games in Central Asia involving some 6,000 troops and more than 100 aircraft from nations that could prove to be Ezekiel 38 coalition countries. Putin proposes the war games occur on an annual basis. Joining Russian forces are troops from Kazakhstan, Kyrgyzstan, Tajikistan, and Uzbekistan. Communist China also participates in the military exercises, as founding member of the new alliance. In Bishkek, Ahmadinejad is merely an observer. But Iran has applied to be a full-fledged member of the Shanghai Cooperation Organization (SCO), the umbrella organization of this Central Asian military alliance that was officially announced on June 15, 2001. Turkmenistan also holds observer status. As the SCO event ends, Putin announces that the 2009 summit will be held in Moscow.[39]

- **October 2007:** Putin and the other heads of the SCO sign an agreement effectively joining forces with another (and at times overlapping) Russian-dominated military and political alliance known as the Collective Security Treaty Organization (CSTO).[40] As one Russian news agency noted: "CSTO members . . . use the organization as a platform for fighting drug trafficking, terrorism, and organized crime, and have pledged to provide immediate military assistance to each other in the event of an attack. The bloc has a Collective Rapid Reaction Force deployed in Central Asia, and is continuing to build up its military forces."[41]

- **December 2007:** Immediately after anointing Dmitry Medvedev as his presidential successor, Putin makes a state visit to neighboring Belarus. This prompts the Kremlin to strenuously deny that Putin is planning to "swallow" the country and preside over a Russia-Belarus union, but given that high-level discussions between the governments of both countries have been occurring on and off since the late 1990s, rumors of a back room deal continue to fly.[42]

- **December 2007:** With Putin's blessing, Russia begins delivering enriched uranium to Iran's Bushehr nuclear power plant.[43]

- **December 2007:** The day after Christmas, Iranian officials announce that the Putin government has agreed to sell Iran a high-tech new antiaircraft missile defense system. According to news reports, "the S-300 anti-aircraft missile defense system is capable of shooting down aircraft, cruise missiles and ballistic missile warheads at ranges of over 90 miles and at altitudes of about 90,000 feet" and "Russian military officials boast that its capabilities outstrip the U.S. Patriot missile system."[44]

- **February 2008:** Putin threatens to target Ukraine with Russian missiles armed with nuclear warheads if the democratic former Soviet republic proceeds with joining NATO and allows Western missile defense batteries to be positioned on Ukrainian territory. Said Putin in a Kremlin press conference: "It is horrible to say and even horrible to think that, in response to the deployment of such facilities in Ukrainian territory, which cannot theoretically be ruled out, Russia could target its missile systems at Ukraine. Imagine this just for a second."[45]

- **April 2008:** Putin becomes the first Russian leader in history to visit the north African country of Libya, an Ezekiel 38 country, creating a strategic alliance, signing numerous agreements, and negotiating a multibillion-dollar arms deal with this enormous historic enemy of Israel. The Russian president met with Libyan leader Mu'ammar Al-Qadhafi, who described the visit as "historic, strategic, and very important."[46]

PUTIN VISITS TEHRAN AS AHMADINEJAD DISCUSSES THE END OF THE WORLD

On October 16, 2007, Vladimir Putin made history by becoming the first Russian leader to visit Iran for the purposes of forging an alliance with the Islamic republic and her neighbors, an alliance emerging for the first time in the 2,500 years since Ezekiel wrote down the prophecy given to him by God.

Why did Putin do it? And why at this particular moment in history?

The last leader from the Kremlin to visit Iran at all was Joseph Stalin in 1943. But he went to hold meetings with U.S. president Franklin Delano Roosevelt and British prime minister Winston Churchill in a neighboring country the Soviet Union partially occupied at the time. Stalin did not go to meet specifically with the leaders of Iran. He certainly did not go to forge an alliance.

Putin's trip was by no means conclusive proof of Gog getting his alliances ready to attack Israel one day. But it was another example of a move made by Putin that turned heads and raised eyebrows because it was so provocative against Israel and Western powers and so consistent with biblical prophecy. What did Putin do the moment he arrived in

Tehran, for example? He began threatening Israel, the U.S., and every other country even remotely considering taking military action to stop Iran's alleged program to develop nuclear weapons.

"Vladimir Putin issued a veiled warning Tuesday against any attack on Iran as he began the first visit by a Kremlin leader to Tehran in six decades—a mission reflecting Russian-Iranian efforts to curb U.S. influence," reported the Associated Press. "He also suggested Moscow and Tehran should have a veto on Western plans for new pipelines to carry oil and natural gas from the Caspian Sea, using routes that would bypass Russian soil and break the Kremlin's monopoly on energy deliveries from the region. Putin came to Tehran for a summit of the five nations bordering the Caspian, but his visit was aimed more at strengthening efforts to blunt U.S. economic and military ties in the area."[47]

If the historic and dramatic Putin trip to Iran was not evocative enough of a biblical end times scenario, the next day President Bush delivered his own apocalyptic remarks back in Washington. During a press briefing at the White House, the president was asked about Putin's visit with Ahmadinejad and the threat posed by this emerging Russian-Iranian nuclear alliance.

The president could have ducked the question or answered in vague generalities. Instead, he told reporters, "I believe that if Iran had a nuclear weapon, it would be a dangerous threat to world peace. We've got a leader in Iran who has announced that he wants to destroy Israel. So I've told people that if you're interested in avoiding World War III, it seems like you ought to be interested in preventing them from [having] the knowledge necessary to make a nuclear weapon."[48]

Plenty of skeptics disagree, to be sure. But President Bush made it crystal clear that day just how high he believed the stakes are, and I for one agreed with him.

As the president was speaking to reporters at the White House the morning of October 17, I actually had the privilege of speaking to a group of more than one hundred military leaders at the Pentagon at an event that had been on the schedule for several months, long before Putin's travel plans to Iran were known. The event was off the record, and thus I am not at liberty to share who was in the meeting or to quote any of the participants in the room. I can say that the title of the talk was "How Mahmoud Ahmadinejad's Eschatology Is Driving Iranian Foreign Policy: An Evangelical Christian Perspective." The next day, I delivered the same talk to an off-the-record meeting of members of Congress on Capitol Hill. In both meetings, I shared an executive summary of the material in this book, discussed the potential significance of the prophecies found in Ezekiel 38–39 in light of unprecedented trend lines vis-à-vis Russia and Iran, and answered the many questions that such a discussion necessarily provokes.

I urged those military and political leaders I spoke with to consider that Mr. Putin may not simply be rattling a saber in hopes of gaining political advantage with the U.S. or our European allies. He might, in fact, be preparing Russia for a major military move in the Middle East sometime in the not-too-distant future. At the same time, I urged these leaders to examine more closely the dangerous religious beliefs of Ahmadinejad and his allies and to track very carefully Ahmadinejad's actions as well as his speeches in the weeks and months ahead.

In the summer of 2005, for example, the newly elected Ahmadinejad told followers the end of the world was just two or three years away and that the way to hasten the coming of the Islamic messiah known as the Mahdi or the Twelfth Imam was to annihilate Israel and the United States.[49] By the summer of 2007, two years into his cryptic but apocalyptic countdown, Ahmadinejad was telling the Muslim world that the return of the Mahdi was "imminent."

In an address to the "International Seminar on the Doctrine of Mahdism" in Tehran in August of that year, Ahmadinejad warned that the West's day was almost finished and that the preparations for the Twelfth Imam "will soon be complete." Consider these excepts from Ahmadinejad's speech, translated from Farsi by the Middle East Media Research Institute:

> The current situation in the world has led the nations to reject in disgust the rule of the oppressors. Now is the time to invite people to accept the rule of the righteous, and [especially that] of the most righteous of [rulers]—the Hidden Imam. . . . The

oppressors and tyrants are responsible for all the difficulties and problems currently faced by the nations, and the only way to establish justice is through popular uprising and determined resistance in the face of these oppressors. . . . *[The day] of these aggressors . . . who are oppressing and controlling the nations, is now coming to an end.* . . . The time of the righteous rulers will come, and the most righteous of rulers [the Hidden Imam] will form a government and thereby instate the monotheism of Abraham [throughout the world]. *That day is not far away.* . . . Our enemies naturally feel threatened by the call to [believe in] the Mahdi, for they do not want people to think about justice. But our reply to them is that *the era of the aggressive [powers] has come to an end*. We believe that it is time for the righteous to rule.[50] (emphasis added)

A few days later, during a speech he delivered on August 28, Ahmadinejad went a step further.

The current problems faced by the world result from [the rule] of unworthy rulers. The ultimate solution is to replace these unworthy regimes and rulers, and to establish the rule of the Hidden Imam. . . . Those who are not versed in [the doctrine of Mahdism] believe that the return [of the Hidden Imam] will occur only in a very long time, but, *according to the divine promise, [his return] is imminent.*[51] (emphasis added)

Then came his curious addresses in September 2007 to the United Nations General Assembly and to students and faculty at Columbia University. Rather than end his remarks with a prayer that Allah would hasten the coming of the Islamic messiah as he did in his 2005 and 2006 speeches to the UN, Ahmadinejad actually began both speeches with these words: "Oh, God, hasten the arrival of Imam al-Mahdi and grant him good health and victory and make us his followers and those to attest to his rightfulness."[52]

Why had the Iranian leader moved the prayer from the end of his remarks to the front? Was it because the month earlier he had been telling conferences in Iran that the arrival of the Mahdi was imminent?

At the time, I told the Pentagon leaders and members of Congress it was not clear to me. As of this writing, it remains unclear. Maybe a false prophet known as the Mahdi will appear in Mecca and Medina and try to perform the duties that Shia scholars say would befit the Twelfth Imam. Maybe not. The point is not whether such things are true but that Ahmadinejad and his allies in Iran—and millions more like them throughout the Islamic world—believe they are true. These beliefs are driving Ahmadinejad to seek the arms and alliances he thinks he needs to bring more chaos and carnage to the world and to create what are in his mind the ideal conditions for the Islamic messiah to arrive.[53]

Why would a leader like Vladimir Putin do business with such a man rather than seek to isolate him, as the U.S. and our closest allies are doing? Why would Putin sell arms to a radical leader of a historically radicalized country? Why would Putin take time out of his schedule to travel away from Russia to visit such a man? Why would he build regional military, political, and economic alliances around such a man? Are these prophetic events, or are there simpler reasons?

Putin—along with a wide variety of political leaders in the U.S., Europe, the Middle East, and Asia who believe we should negotiate with or even do business with Ahmadinejad and his regime—is missing the big picture. Ahmadinejad is not operating by the norms of conventional, civilized behavior. He is actively trying to bring about the end of the world. He believes it is his mission, his divine calling. We should not expect any amount of diplomatic logic to dissuade or distract him.

The sobering conclusion we must draw is that more war is coming to the Middle East. Even setting aside a prophetic war for the moment, either the West will launch an attack to stop Iran from becoming a nuclear-armed nightmare or some combination of Iran, Syria, Hezbollah, Hamas, and Al-Qaeda will launch a cataclysmic war against the Jewish state, and possibly against U.S. targets and/or interests. When would such a war or series of attacks occur? No one knows for sure, but millions of innocent civilians are likely to be caught in the cross fire when it happens.

HOW SOON WILL IRAN HAVE THE BOMB?

In December 2007, a ferocious international debate erupted over just how soon Iran could go nuclear against Israel or any other country.

The debate was triggered by the release of an American document known as the "National Intelligence Estimate," or NIE. Written in co-operation with sixteen U.S. spy agencies, the NIE suggested that the U.S. had hard evidence that Iran halted its program to develop nuclear weapons back in 2003.

"Tehran is most likely keeping its options open with respect to build-ing a weapon," but intelligence agencies "do not know whether it cur-rently intends to develop nuclear weapons," reported the *International Herald Tribune*, drawing upon the unclassified version.[54] The article continued:

> Iran is continuing to produce enriched uranium, the report says, a program that the Tehran government has said is designed for civilian purposes. The new estimate says that the enrichment program could still provide Iran with enough raw material to produce a nuclear weapon sometime by the middle of next decade, a timetable essentially unchanged from previous esti-mates. But the new estimate declares with "high confidence" that a military-run Iranian program intended to transform that raw material into a nuclear weapon has been shut down since 2003, and also says with high confidence that the halt "was directed primarily in response to increasing international scru-tiny and pressure."[55]

The big question: was this U.S. intelligence assessment correct that Iran has given up trying to build nuclear weapons?

"Maybe," I told audiences at the time, "and let's hope so." It would, after all, be wonderful to know that Iran is not the steadily, increasingly worrisome nuclear threat that U.S. and other intelligence agencies had been saying it was right up to the release of the NIE. But there is, of course, always the possibility that the U.S. assessment is wrong.

The accuracy of some of our intelligence reports in the Middle East has certainly been called into question in recent years, and rightly so. What's more, we must always remember May 1998, when India and Pakistan conducted multiple nuclear weapons tests, stunning U.S. and Western intelligence agencies that had absolutely no idea either country was so close to getting the bomb. At the time, Senator Richard Shelby, then the chairman of the Senate Intelligence Committee, called this a "colossal failure" of the U.S. intelligence community, and he was right.[56]

God forbid we should have a similar failure with regards to Iran. A new intelligence failure concerning the current apocalyptic regime in Tehran could be cataclysmic, not merely "colossal." After all, even if Iran did briefly halt development of nuclear weapons in 2003, much has happened since then that could have changed the calculus in Tehran.

For one thing, the United States and our allies liberated Iraq from the thuggish regime of Saddam Hussein, who was later caught, tried, convicted, and hanged. Is it possible Iran restarted its nuclear weapons program for defensive reasons after 2003, trying to prevent Iran from ever being "liberated" by the U.S. or any other country or coalition?

Mahmoud Ahmadinejad came to power in June 2005, convinced it was his God-given mission to hasten the coming of the Mahdi and breathing genocidal threats against Israel and the United States as a result. Is it also possible, then, that Iran restarted its nuclear weapons program for offensive reasons after 2003, seeking to eventually annihilate Jewish and Christian infidels in hopes of setting the stage for the Islamic messiah to appear and restore order on the earth?

NIE skeptics abounded then and still do now. Numerous former U.S. diplomats, intelligence analysts, and military experts at home and abroad doubted whether the assessment of Iran's intentions and capabilities was accurate.[57] But in a rare convergence of agreement, so did the editorial pages of the *New York Times,* the *Wall Street Journal,* and the *Washington Post.*

The *Times* warned that the NIE "is not an argument for anyone to let down their guard when it comes to Iran's nuclear ambitions."[58]

The *Journal* pointed out that "as recently as 2005, the consensus estimate of our spooks was that 'Iran currently is determined to develop nuclear weapons' and do so 'despite its international obligations and international pressure.' This was a 'high confidence' judgment. The new NIE says Iran abandoned its nuclear program in 2003 'in response to increasing international scrutiny.' This too is a 'high confidence' conclusion. One of the two conclusions is wrong, and casts considerable doubt on the entire process by which these 'estimates'—the consensus of 16 intelligence bureaucracies—are conducted and accorded gospel status."[59]

The *Post,* curiously as skeptical as the others, highlighted the fact that "while U.S. intelligence agencies have 'high confidence' that covert work on a bomb was suspended 'for at least several years' after 2003, there is only 'moderate confidence' that Tehran has not restarted the military program." Furthermore, the *Post* noted—somewhat ominously, I might add—that "Iran's massive overt investment in uranium enrichment meanwhile proceeds in defiance of binding U.N. resolutions, even though Tehran has no legitimate use for enriched uranium" and "the U.S. estimate of when Iran might produce enough enriched uranium for a bomb—sometime between late 2009 and the middle of the next decade—hasn't changed."[60]

So where does this leave us? Is the Iranian threat growing, or has it stalled? Should we feel safer, or just confused? Senior Israeli leaders are convinced Iran could have enough highly enriched uranium to create a nuclear bomb by 2010.[61] Senior White House officials are convinced that if Iran gets the bomb, we could see a "nuclear holocaust."[62] The 2008 Republican nominee for the presidency warns that if Iran gets the bomb, "we could have Armageddon."[63]

Only time will tell, but clearly the clock is ticking.

WHAT DOES IT ALL MEAN?

I have said it before, but I will say it again: it remains too early to draw definitive conclusions about whether we will witness the fulfillment of Ezekiel 38–39 in our lifetime, much less in the next few years. But one thing is clear: awareness of—and curiosity about—these biblical prophecies has grown considerably and will continue to do so as long as world events consistent with these coming events continue to occur.

Epicenter—in English and in Spanish—was reviewed in or profiled by dozens of publications and Web sites around the world and featured on several hundred radio and TV shows, including CNN, FOX, and MSNBC, and an *Epicenter* documentary film released on DVD for the fortieth anniversary of the Six Days' War has been shown in hundreds of churches and conferences in the U.S. and abroad.

In November 2006, Rush Limbaugh devoted an issue of his newsletter, *The Limbaugh Letter* (for which I used to write), to considering the themes and claims of the book. In December 2006, a leading Israeli news service ran a story with this headline:

MODERN DAY GOG AND MAGOG: SIMILARITIES BETWEEN EZEKIEL'S PROPHECIES, TODAY'S MIDEAST REALITY UNCANNY

YNET NEWS, DECEMBER 10, 2006.

The article noted that *"current world events are beginning to increasingly resemble the 2,500 year old Bible prophecy made by Ezekiel in chapters 38-39"* and that *"in Joel C. Rosenberg's book . . . the author points to Ezekiel's prophecies in chapters 36-37, which have largely come true.* Rosenberg then asks the obvious question: If prophecies such as 'the rebirth of the State of Israel, the return of the Jews to the Holy Land after centuries in exile, the re-blossoming of desolate desert land to produce abundant food, fruit and foliage, and the creation of an exceedingly great army' materialized in the late 19th and early 20th centuries, then why shouldn't the next prophecies come true in our lifetime?"[64]

On March 30, 2007, Glenn Beck of *CNN Headline News* devoted an entire one-hour prime-time special to addressing current events in the Middle East in light of Bible prophecy, using *Epicenter* as one of his featured books. "We are having a conversation for a full hour tonight about the end of days," Glenn told his audience as the special began. "It might sound nuts, but I encourage you to listen and, at the end of the hour, judge for yourself. Is this nuts, or is it possible that this is happening?" During that show, which also included Tim LaHaye and Jerry Jenkins as guests, Glenn asked me to decode Ezekiel 38 and 39 for his viewers and to talk about how allusions to Bible prophecy are even popping up in the language of major world leaders. That special, which his producers later told me they had implored Glenn not to tape (because they were unable to imagine who would watch it), drew such high ratings it aired a total of three times in 2007.[65]

In October 2007, when Putin visited Iran and President Bush warned a nuclear Iran could trigger World War III, a leading Israeli news site ran the following headline:

ISRAEL WARNS WORLD WAR III MAY BE BIBLICAL WAR OF GOG AND MAGOG
ARUTZ SHEVA, OCTOBER 18, 2007

What's more, "Israeli newscasts featured Gog and Magog maps of the likely alignment of nations in that potential conflict," the article noted. "Channel 2 and Channel 10 TV showed the world map, sketching the basic alignment of the two opposing axes in a coming world war, in a manner evoking associations of the Gog and Magog prophecy for many viewers. The prophecy of Gog and Magog refers to a great world war centered on the Holy Land and Jerusalem and first appears in the book of Yechezkel (Ezekiel)."[66]

On April 10, 2008, some 2,000 pastors and evangelical Christians from around the world met for the first-ever Epicenter Conference. Held at the International Convention Center in Jerusalem, the event was sponsored by the Joshua Fund—the relief organization I described in the "Tracking the Tremors" chapter—and webcast around the globe. Together, we:

- celebrated the sixtieth anniversary of the prophetic rebirth of the State of Israel in 1948;
- examined the geopolitical threats to the Jewish state and her neighbors;
- discussed the biblical mandate Christians have to love Israel, her neighbors, and her enemies;

- studied the Bible prophecies regarding the future of Israel, Iran, and Russia;
- released an exclusive poll of American Christian attitudes toward Israel, Iran, and Mideast issues (see the results in Appendix 3);
- explained the Joshua Fund's new relief strategy called "Operation Epicenter," aimed at blessing Israel and her neighbors with $120 million worth of humanitarian relief aid over the next few years, including food, clothing, and medical supplies to care for the poor and needy as well as victims of war and terrorism (learn more at www.joshuafund.net); and
- mobilized tens of thousands of Christians around the world to pray knowledgeably and consistently for the peace of Jerusalem and for all the people of the epicenter, because the God of the Bible loves them all.

Along the way, I have had the privilege of meeting with and discussing the book with hundreds of Jewish leaders, Islamic clerics, Arab and Iranian pastors, foreign ambassadors, Russian pastors and foreign policy experts, White House staffers, administration officials, generals and other military officials at the Pentagon and around the world, and high-level officials in a variety of U.S. and foreign intelligence agencies. Two members of Congress sent a letter to their colleagues urging them to read *Epicenter* over the August recess in 2007. In February 2008, I even had the extraordinary opportunity to give a signed copy of *Epicenter* to Iraqi president Jalal Talabani through his spokesman, during a research trip a colleague and I made to the Republic of Iraq.

Not all who have read this book, watched the film, or heard me discuss the subject have agreed with my conclusions. To be sure, some strongly disagreed. But I am deeply grateful for the fact that, all told, in the first two years since *Epicenter* was published, millions of Americans, Canadians, Israelis, Russians, Iranians, Arabs, and others have begun to be introduced to a series of once-obscure and little-discussed prophecies tucked away at the end of the book of Ezekiel.

The reason for this explosion of interest in Bible prophecy has nothing to do with me or the quality (or lack thereof) of the book you hold in your hands. The reason has everything to do with the growing fear people around the world have regarding the future of the Middle East, the growing fascination people have with what the Bible says about the future of their lives and their world, and the growing curiosity people have over whether there is really a correlation between the two. Based on what I see happening in the world, and in the hearts of men and women around the globe, I suspect that interest will continue to grow, and for good reason.

APPENDIX 1
FREQUENTLY ASKED QUESTIONS

Q: *Do the prophecies in Ezekiel 38–39 mean that the U.S. should simply accept the inevitable and give up its attempts to stop Iran from acquiring nuclear weapons?*

A: The answer to this question is no. Even though the Bible makes it clear that Iran will join forces with Russia and attack Israel, that doesn't mean the U.S. should sit idly by and wait for it to happen. Stopping Tehran from building or acquiring nuclear weapons is essential for the stability and security of the Middle East and the entire world.

Keep in mind that the Bible doesn't specifically say that Iran must acquire nuclear weapons for Ezekiel's prophecy to be fulfilled. And Iran could do a horrendous amount of damage and snuff out a horrific number of lives with a nuclear bomb before the War of Gog and Magog takes place. That's why I believe Iran's nuclear ambitions must be stopped. And the longer we wait, the greater the danger we face.

So what is to be done? Can the U.S. rely on sanctions and other diplomatic strategies to force Iran to desist in its efforts to become a nuclear power? Can we rely on our intelligence agencies to tell us when we're approaching the point of no return?

Unfortunately not.

There is no question that Iran—particularly under Mahmoud Ahmadinejad—is a dangerous regime. As we have seen, Iran is currently enriching uranium. When they successfully build 50,000 centrifuges they will be able to build a nuclear bomb in sixteen days. Will we know when that day is? Or will the smoking gun be a mushroom cloud in Washington, New York, Chicago, or Los Angeles? Remember that back in 1998 India tested a nuclear weapon and in so doing completely stunned the CIA and most of the world's intelligence agencies, who had no idea that India was so close to getting the bomb. And India is a friend. I personally have little confidence that our intelligence agencies will be able to be more precise with the Iranian nuclear program, especially with the Russians helping Tehran.

Combine that with the fact that Ahmadinejad has vowed to wipe Israel off the face of the map and has asked Muslims to envision a world without the United States. He believes that Israel is the Little Satan and the U.S. is the Great Satan. He believes the end of the world is just a few years away and that it is his mission to bring it about. Deterrence, therefore, will not work. Negotiations are not working. And the time to foment a popular uprising to overthrow Ahmadinejad and the mullahs before they go nuclear is rapidly running out.

President Bush has done an excellent job defending the U.S., and I have strongly supported the U.S. war effort in Afghanistan and Iraq in light of the 9/11 attacks. But let's be clear: if Iran goes nuclear on President Bush's watch, *all* the gains that have been made thus far in the War on Terror will be wiped out virtually overnight.

We absolutely cannot let Iran go nuclear. To do so would put Americans and all freedom-loving people in existential danger. It is time to prepare for war. It is not my best-case scenario, but prudence demands we move before it's too late.

Q: *Doesn't Ezekiel's scenario rule out any attack on Iran by the U.S. or a Western-led coalition?*

A: Not necessarily. Ezekiel rules out the possibility that any country—including the United States—will come to Israel's defense once Russia and Iran and their allies have surrounded Israel. Only God will come to Israel's defense in the final throes of this prophecy. But a number of scenarios could unfold between now and then:

- The U.S. could effectively use preemptive military force against Iran, defusing the crisis for a number of years and buying the world more time before the day of judgment Ezekiel foretold.
- Likewise, Israel could use preemptive military force against Iran, with the same result. (Remember that Israel's invasion of Lebanon in 1982 resulted in the capture of massive amounts of Soviet weaponry, thus forestalling a Russian invasion of Israel.)
- In yet another scenario, Israel might use preemptive military force but not destroy all of Iran's weapons of mass destruction. In the process, Israel could trigger international condemnation against them and give Russia a pretext to take Iran's side and form a coalition against Israel.

U.S. foreign policy cannot be expected to be based on biblical prophecy. It should, however, be based on U.S. national interests. Stopping Iran from going nuclear is in our supreme national interest. Protecting the oil fields of Saudi Arabia, Kuwait, Iraq, and the United Arab Emirates—on which we depend—from Iranian domination is in our supreme national interest. Safeguarding against an Iranian takeover of Turkey, Jordan, and Iraq is also in our supreme national interest, as is protecting Israel, our most faithful and effective ally in the region and the first and strongest democracy in the Middle East. We should, therefore, act accordingly.

That said, there is very little political support in the United States for another war in the Middle East. Most Americans want to pull out of Iraq, not invade Iran. And members of Congress and the intelligence services note very real and serious risks of launching any sort of military strike against the mullahs. We could get all of their nuclear sites but one, and the retaliation could be devastating. Iran could also—as Ahmadinejad has vowed to do in the event of an attack against Iran—

launch thousands upon thousands of new terrorist insurgents into Iraq, worsening the violence there. They might also send suicide bombers into the U.S., possibly through the all-too-porous U.S. borders with Mexico and Canada (scenarios I wrote about in *The Last Days*). Or they could unleash their missiles on the oil fields of Saudi Arabia and the other Gulf states, destroying pumping, refining, and shipping facilities and driving the price of oil—already at record highs—through the roof.

I can, therefore, envision a scenario in which the current president or the next takes no military action against Iran or plans to do so but waits too long, even as Russia develops a full-blown military alliance with Iran. We could then see Ezekiel's prophecy play out in the not-too-distant future.

I can also envision a scenario in which, under great international pressure, Iran announces that it will dismantle its nuclear weapons program if Israel agrees to give up its nuclear weapons as well. Diplomatic pressure would then begin to grow for the adoption of a "Middle East nuclear-free zone" resolution at the United Nations.

Israel would surely resist such a diplomatic ploy, insisting (rightfully, in my view) upon the need to retain its arsenal as a matter of self-defense. In such a scenario, Russia might then begin building a coalition to force Israel to comply with the UN demands, much like the U.S. built a coalition to force Iraq to comply with UN demands. This was the scenario I used in *The Ezekiel Option*. The Egyptians in particular have been pushing a nuclear-free-zone option in the Middle East. As the crisis with Iran intensifies, their proposal may pick up widespread support.

The thing to remember is that there are many roads that could ultimately lead us to the events described in Ezekiel 38–39. As individual believers (as opposed to national policy makers), we should keep our eyes on the big picture—praying for peace and working to communicate the good news of Christ's redeeming love to the nations of the epicenter as this terrible drama unfolds.

Q: *Are you really certain that the West, particularly the U.S., will not come to Israel's defense during the War of Gog and Magog?*

Given the historically strong and strategic relationship between our two countries, that just doesn't seem possible.

A: Unfortunately, Ezekiel's account is clear—no one comes to Israel's defense. By definition, that includes the United States. I agree that is difficult to imagine, especially when one considers how consistent American public opinion has been in favor of the Jewish state over the past four decades. During the Six Days' War in June 1967, for example, 56 percent of Americans told the Gallup poll that their sympathies lay with Israel, while only 3 percent sided with the Arab states. In February 2006, 59 percent of Americans told Gallup they sided with Israel, compared with 15 percent who said they sympathized more with Palestinian Arabs.[1]

What's more, the number of Americans who view Israel as a reliable ally has climbed from only 33 percent in 1982 (when Israel bombed Iraq's nuclear reactor and invaded Lebanon to stop terrorism and a massive buildup of Soviet armaments) to 41 percent in 2005, though it has fluctuated along the way.[2]

American support for Israel stands in marked contrast to Europe, however, where anti-Semitism and anti-Israel sentiments are rising rapidly. Synagogues and Jewish schools and cemeteries throughout Europe are being burned, vandalized, or otherwise desecrated in ever-increasing numbers. Jews are being verbally and physically assaulted throughout Europe. Rockwell Schnabel, the U.S. ambassador to the European Union, said at a dinner of the American Jewish Committee in Brussels in 2004 that anti-Semitism in Europe "is as bad as it was in the 1930s."[3] European polls increasingly show antagonism toward Israel and Israeli policies. In November 2003, a majority of Europeans actually named Israel as the greatest threat to world peace, ahead of Iran and North Korea.[4]

It seems like a safe bet, therefore, that Europe would not raise a hand to help protect Israel against attack. But would the U.S.? Even given historical trends and current indications of American support for Israel, we should expect that the closer we get to the War of Gog and Magog, the fewer Americans we will see strongly supporting the Jewish state. I'm already beginning to pick this up anecdotally on radio interviews in which a surprising number of callers say things like, "Why should we spend a dime to save Israel?" and "Let the Jews fight their own battles" and "The only reason we as Americans are getting attacked by Muslims is because we support Israel—the sooner we stop, the sooner there will be peace."

The real test, of course, will come when Russia and Iran and their allies begin to move forces toward Israel. How many Americans would be willing to risk nuclear war with Russia and Iran to protect even a loyal ally like Israel—especially if Moscow and Tehran argue that they have no desire for a confrontation with the U.S. if we will just stay out of the way? Sadly, I suspect the number today is much lower than most supporters of Israel are willing to admit.

Those who already want American forces out of Iraq and Afghanistan are not likely to support a new war. Nor will undecided voters or those who believe we should finish the job in Iraq but then be done with the Middle East. Under such circumstances, it will be extremely difficult for any American president to commit forces to defend Israel.

Q: *What should be the attitude of Christians toward Israel in the days leading up to the showdown with Russia and Iran?*

A: I believe the vast majority of evangelical Christians will maintain support of Israel to the bitter end. Many Catholics and Christians from other denominations who are also passionate about their love for Jesus and their understanding of God's plan and purpose for the Jewish people will also stand with Israel. Indeed, true followers of Jesus Christ may be the only friends Israel and the Jewish people have left as this terrible war approaches.

It is vitally important, therefore, that Christians become faithful in praying for the peace of Jerusalem every day, visit and tour Israel while they still can, and find new and creative ways to show Israel and the Jewish people how much the church loves and cares for them. If at all possible, it would be my hope to take my family to Israel and live there in the run-up to the war as a show of solidarity.

At the same time, it is vitally important to remember that God loves the Muslim people of the Middle East as well as the Russians and others living in the former Soviet Union. Jesus made it clear that he died in order to give eternal life to *everyone* who believes in him (John 3:16), regardless of nationality or heritage. Thus, followers of Christ must show love and compassion to all the people of the region, both now and as the war approaches. That does not mean excusing the actions of certain hostile or anti-Christian governments or troops. But Christ died on the cross to save sinners from *every* country, even countries he has, in his sovereignty, chosen to judge. Our job is to find a way to demonstrate and communicate Christ's love during mankind's darkest hours. This is the reason my wife and I formed the Joshua Fund (see chapter 15).

Q: Will the War of Gog and Magog happen before or after the Rapture?[5]

A: The truth is we simply do not know the answer for certain, because Ezekiel does not say. Many of the theologians I have cited in this book believe the war will occur after the Rapture. In the novel *Left Behind*, Tim LaHaye and Jerry B. Jenkins describe the War of Gog and Magog as having already happened before the Rapture takes place. In *The Ezekiel Option*, I also chose to portray the war occurring before the Rapture.

In Matthew 24:14, Jesus says, "This gospel of the kingdom shall be preached in the whole world as a testimony to all the nations, and then the end will come" (NASB). We also know from Ezekiel that God will use the War of Gog and Magog to display his glory to all nations and to pour out his Holy Spirit, particularly on the nation of Israel. As a result of the entire world seeing God defend Israel from the onslaught of the Russian-Iranian coalition, a dramatic spiritual awakening will occur around the globe. It would certainly be consistent with God's heart for humanity that he would cause this cataclysmic moment to occur *before* the Rapture in order to shake people out of their spiritual apathy and/or rebellion and give them at least one more chance to receive Christ as their Savior before the terrible events of the Tribulation occur.

But let me be clear: I believe that the Rapture could occur at any moment, and I would certainly not be surprised in any way if it occurred before the events of Ezekiel 38 and 39 come to pass.

Christian theologians speak of the "doctrine of imminence." This means that according to the Bible there is no prophetic event that has to happen before Jesus snatches his church from the earth. That is, the Bible teaches us that we should be ready for Jesus to come for us at any moment. I fully believe that. But it should be noted with regard to this doctrine that while no major prophetic event *has* to happen before the Rapture, that doesn't mean no such event *will* happen first. Perhaps the clearest evidence of this truth is the rebirth of Israel. This major prophetic event was foretold in Ezekiel 36–37, yet its fulfillment happened *before* the Rapture. Thus, it is certainly possible that other events—such as the events of Ezekiel 38–39—could happen before the Rapture as well.

Q: *Ezekiel says the War of Gog and Magog will happen in the last days. Doesn't that by definition mean it will happen during the seven years of the Tribulation?*

A: Ezekiel 38:16 does say these events will happen in the "last days" (NASB), but this term is not necessarily limited to the period of the Tribulation. The apostle Peter, for example, used the term in Acts 2 to refer to the period he was living in, and that was nearly two thousand years ago. Likewise, consider the words of another apostle in 1 John 2:18: "Dear children, the last hour is here. You have heard that the Antichrist is coming, and already many such antichrists have appeared. From this we know that the last hour has come." Again, John was writing nearly two thousand years ago. It's important to note that the Hebrew term translated as "the last days" can also be translated as "in the distant future" (NLT) or "in days to come" (NIV). Thus, it is reasonable to conclude that the term *the last days* refers to an indeterminate period of time leading up to the second coming of Jesus Christ. This period includes—but is not limited to—the seven years of the Tribulation.

Q: *Isn't it possible that events look like they are leading up to the War of Gog and Magog but that the war won't actually happen for hundreds or thousands of years?*

A: God could certainly forestall the fulfillment of this prophecy for some time until he, in his sovereignty, is ready to move.

But he will not postpone it for hundreds or thousands of years. We know this because of what Jesus said in Matthew 24:32-34: "Now learn a lesson from the fig tree. When its branches bud and its leaves begin to sprout, you know that summer is near. In the same way, when you see all these things, you can know his return is very near, right at the door. I tell you the truth, this generation will not pass from the scene until all these things take place." In other words, when we see certain events happening, we can know that the Rapture and the Second Coming are imminent.

So what are "all these things" that we should be watching for?

Jesus described the signs in detail in Matthew 24 and Luke 21: the rise of false prophets and false messiahs, wars and rumors of wars, revolutions, famines, earthquakes, persecution of believers, the spread of the gospel, and the rebirth of the State of Israel (described as a "fig tree" in the Jewish Scriptures[6]).

Today, for the first time in two thousand years, we are seeing all of these signs come true, and the rebirth of Israel is the most dramatic sign of them all. We can, therefore, have confidence that Jesus' return is closer than ever. What's more, we can be confident that our generation will not pass away before we see this remarkable event occur. No other generation in history has been able to say that, but we now can. It is true that Jesus cautions us not to speculate on the exact day and hour of his return. But we are encouraged to watch current events closely and know when the clock is running out.

In this regard, I often think of the words of Gandalf from the last film of the Lord of the Rings trilogy, *The Return of the King*. As events unfold and the clouds of war are brewing, Gandalf says, "The board is set. The pieces are moving." As I write this, I would say the board is almost set, and God is putting the pieces in place for the final drama to begin.

Q: Doesn't the Bible tell us that the War of Gog and Magog will happen at the very end of time—after the Rapture, after the Tribulation, after the Battle of Armageddon, and after the thousand-year reign of Christ on earth—not before all these things as you have described?

A: Revelation 20:7-10 does speak of another War of Gog and Magog that occurs at the end of time, after all these other events. But this is a second war, not the war referred to by Ezekiel 38–39. We know this for several reasons.

First, Ezekiel's war is described as occurring relatively soon after the rebirth of the State of Israel and the ingathering of the Jewish people from around the world (Ezekiel 36–37). The war in Revelation, by contrast, occurs after Jesus has reigned on earth for a thousand years.

Second, Ezekiel's war involves a fearsome but *limited* coalition of countries that surround Israel, as we learned in earlier chapters. The war in Revelation involves all the nations from "every corner of the earth" coming to attack Israel (Revelation 20:8).

Third, after Ezekiel's war, life continues. Bodies are gathered and buried for seven months, weaponry is gathered and burned for seven years, and Ezekiel 40–48 describes the Temple that will be built. By contrast, the war in Revelation is followed immediately and literally by the end of the world. Satan and his followers are judged and thrown into the "lake of fire" (Revelation 20:10). The heavens and earth are destroyed. A completely new heaven and a new earth are created, and followers of Christ will live on this new earth for the rest of eternity.

Q: *You wrote in The Ezekiel Option that Ronald Reagan was fascinated with the coming War of Gog and Magog. Is that really true?*

A: It is. In 1971, Reagan—then governor of California—attended a banquet to honor State Senator James Mills. After the main course, he asked Mills if he was familiar with "the fierce Old Testament prophet Ezekiel." He went on to explain that Russia was the Magog described in Ezekiel's prophecy and was thus doomed to destruction.

"In the thirty-eighth chapter of Ezekiel it says God will take the children of Israel from among the heathen [where] they'd been scattered and will gather them again in the promised land," Reagan told Mills. "Ezekiel says that . . . the nation that will lead all the other powers into darkness against Israel will come out of the north. What other powerful nation is to the north of Israel [besides Russia]? None. But it didn't seem to make sense before the Russian revolution, when Russia was a Christian country. Now it does, now that Russia has become communistic and atheistic, now that Russia has set itself against God. Now it fits the description perfectly." Reagan conceded that "everything hasn't fallen into place yet," but he strongly believed the end of the Soviet empire and the second coming of Christ were increasingly close at hand.[7]

In his 1997 book *Dutch: A Memoir of Ronald Reagan*, Edmund Morris—the president's official biographer—revealed that Ezekiel was actually Reagan's "favorite book of prophecy."[8] Morris also recounted an intriguing scene he personally witnessed in the Oval Office in which Reagan discussed the Ezekiel option with White House Chief of Staff Howard Baker and National Security Advisor Colin Powell.[9]

"We talk mainly about religion," read the notes of Morris's meeting with Reagan on February 9, 1988. "I have been reading a book about his Armageddon complex, and, when I mention the subject, am rewarded by an animated speech, full of jovial doom, that lasts the rest of the half hour. . . . [White House chief of Staff] Howard Baker and [National Security Advisor] Colin Powell arrive, impatient for their own thirty minutes. 'We're having a cozy chat about Armageddon,' I say. They stand grinning nervously as he continues."

"When it comes [Ezekiel 38–39]," Reagan explained to his senior staff, "the man who comes from the wrong side, into the war, is the man, according to the prophecies, named Gog, from Meshech, which is the ancient name of Moscow—"

"I tell you, Mr. President," Baker replied. "I wish you'd quit talking about that. You upset me!"

But Reagan continued to talk about such things, as he had for many years.

I once asked Michael Reagan, the president's son, if such accounts rang true. He confirmed that they did, noting that his father firmly believed he was living in history's last days and thought that he might even see the return of Christ in his lifetime.[10]

Ronald Reagan was a devout Christian. He was a student of the Bible. He was fascinated with end-times prophecies. He believed they were true. He talked about them with friends and colleagues. They helped shape his view that the Soviet Union, and the system of evil it advanced and perpetuated, was not long for this world. For a movie actor turned president like Ronald Reagan, the Bible was indeed the greatest story ever told. He had read the last chapter, and thus he knew for certain that a day of reckoning—a day of justice—was coming.

Q: *I understand you and your family lived in Egypt while you were researching and writing this book. But if Egypt will not play a role in the War of Gog and Magog, why did you choose to live there?*

A: You're right; we did live in Egypt for several months while I was working on this book, and it was a wonderful experience for my wife and kids, as well as for me. Egypt, with a population of 70 million, is the largest Arab country. It is also the intellectual and cultural center of the Arab world, and by extension of the Islamic world. It is strategically located close to several Ezekiel 38 coalition countries (Sudan, Ethiopia, Libya, Algeria, and Tunisia) and it is, of course, a direct neighbor of Israel.

While Egypt has historically been a great enemy of Israel and the Jewish people, it does currently have a peace treaty in place, which is no small thing. In fact, I took my boys to the gravesite of the slain Egyptian president Anwar Sadat to pay tribute to the courage he displayed in visiting Israel, speaking to the Knesset, cutting a deal for peace, and telling his people that no good could be achieved for the Arab people through war.

Egypt was an excellent place, therefore, to immerse myself in Islamic culture, to meet players in this unfolding drama, and to conduct interviews that have strongly affected this book, though nearly all of them were off the record or on "deep background."

One of the things that struck me most about living there was how many Bible characters crisscrossed through Egypt during their lives. Abraham and Sarah did, as did their sons, and later Joseph, who rose to become the country's first and only Jewish prime minister. But many others were there as well, including Mary, Joseph, and Jesus. The more I studied the Scriptures while I was there, the more I realized that God has a special place in his heart for the Egyptian people. Indeed, the prophet Isaiah says that one day God will shower his grace upon the Egyptians and the Assyrians (including the people of Syria, Lebanon, Jordan, and northern Iraq) and draw them to himself and to peace with Israel in a way few can currently imagine.

> In that day there will be an altar to the LORD in the heart of Egypt, and there will be a monument to the LORD at its border. It will be a sign and a witness that the LORD of Heaven's Armies is worshiped in the land of Egypt. When the people cry to the LORD for help against those who oppress them, he will send them a savior who will rescue them. The LORD will make himself known to the Egyptians. Yes, they will know the LORD and will give their sacrifices and offerings to him. They will make a vow to the LORD and will keep it. The LORD will strike Egypt, and then he will bring healing. For the Egyptians will turn to the LORD, and he will listen to their pleas and heal them.
>
> In that day Egypt and Assyria will be connected by a highway. The Egyptians and Assyrians will move freely between their lands, and they will both worship God. And Israel will be their ally. The three will be together, and Israel will be a blessing to them. For the LORD of Heaven's Armies will say, "Blessed be Egypt, my people. Blessed be Assyria, the land I have made. Blessed be Israel, my special possession!" (Isaiah 19:19-25)

Q: *Jordan currently has a peace treaty with Israel. Why, then, do you believe Jordan will participate in the War of Gog and Magog?*

A: To be clear, I am not certain that Jordan will participate. I sincerely hope not. I had the privilege of visiting that beautiful, historic country in 2005 and have many friends among the Jordanian people. The late King Hussein was a man of character and courage who deserves great respect for signing a peace treaty with Israel in 1994. His son, King Abdullah II, has impressively carried on in his father's tradition. He sided with the West against Al-Qaeda and Saddam Hussein after the 9/11 attacks. He is working hard to fight radical

Islamic insurgents inside his country. He is also building bridges of friendship with evangelical Christians and Jews, even speaking at the National Prayer Breakfast in February 2006—the first Muslim king ever to do so.

That said, however, I fear Jordan may tragically wind up being part of the Russian-Iranian coalition. Not only did the Hashemite kingdom of Jordan participate in numerous wars against Israel prior to the treaty that currently exists, its present leadership is increasingly at risk of a coup or revolution. Terrorist forces from Iran, Al-Qaeda and Hamas, and others are trying to gain a foothold in Jordan. They would like nothing more than to assassinate or overthrow the current king and create a new radical Islamic regime there that could help them in their battle to annihilate Israel.

In April 2004, Jordanian authorities narrowly stopped a terrorist attack in the capital city of Amman meant to decapitate the Jordanian government as well as destroy the U.S. Embassy. An astounding 20 tons of explosives and chemical weapons were discovered. Authorities said that if the poison gas attack had been successful, more than 80,000 people could have been killed and over 160,000 wounded. The Jordanian-born Abu Musab al-Zarqawi (who until his death in June 2006 was Al-Qaeda's top man in Iraq) was believed to have been behind the attack.[11]

Iraqi general Georges Sada told me the only place Al-Qaeda could have gotten 20 tons of chemical weapons for that attack was from Syria, which he says now possesses Iraq's weapons of mass destruction. Sada explains that Saddam Hussein moved all of his WMD to Syria in the summer of 2002—several months before U.S. and coalition forces invaded—a charge now being followed up by U.S. and British intelligence.[12]

On November 9, 2005, Al-Qaeda struck in Jordan again, launching three attacks on hotels in Amman—including one where a wedding party was taking place—killing 57 people and wounding more than 150 others. Zarqawi further vowed to behead King Abdullah II.

"These people are insane," the king responded, vowing to hunt down and destroy radical Islamic forces trying to use his kingdom as a base camp. Jordanian authorities said they had thwarted fifteen separate terrorist plots since April 2004 but noted that the hotel bombings were further evidence of just how determined the jihadists were to destabilize the kingdom.[13]

Al-Qaeda isn't the only threat, of course. At a luncheon I attended in Washington as I was finishing this book, I asked Bernard Lewis—the renowned Middle East scholar and author of numerous important books about the region including *The Crisis of Islam*—to assess the potential impact of Hamas coming to power in the post-Arafat environment. "The Hamas-Palestinian government may pose more of a danger to Jordan than to Israel," he said.[14]

Lewis is right. Some 70 percent of Jordanian citizens are Palestinians, and Hamas would love to radicalize them and use them to help overthrow the king and unify Jordan, the West Bank, and Gaza into one jihadist state poised at Israel's throat.

The good news is that King Hussein was one of the longest-serving monarchs in modern Middle Eastern history, and we can and should hope and pray that King Abdullah II is likewise able to maintain stability, defeating the radicals while continuing to give the Jordanian people more freedom and building bridges to Christians and Jews.

But we must acknowledge this is by no means certain. Should Jordan fall into the hands of the jihadists, Israel will be in grave danger, as will the newly democratic government in Iraq, and the nominally pro-Western government of Egypt.

Q: *Why do you believe Morocco plays no role in the War of Gog and Magog?*

A: Okay, this isn't a frequently asked question, but it is a question important to me and one that can shed some light on this whole issue of God blessing those who bless Israel.

The truth is I don't know for certain whether Morocco will join the Russian-Iranian coalition against Israel or not. In *The Ezekiel Option*, Morocco does not participate in the war, and I think that is a reasonable conclusion. That's certainly my hope.

I have had the privilege of visiting Morocco a number of times over the years, and I have really fallen in love with the country. I have always been treated with great warmth and kindness as an American and as a Jewish person, as well as a follower of Christ. Indeed, the kingdom has a long and impressive history of protecting the Jewish people and of trying to broker a series of peace deals between Israel and the Arab world.

When I visited Casablanca and Rabat in the fall of 2005, I had the privilege of meeting with a man named Serge Berdugo, a Jew who has served as one of the top advisors to a number of recent Moroccan kings. He gave me some fascinating insights.

He noted, for example, that the first thing King Mohammed V did when he returned from exile in 1956 and led his country to independence was to declare that the "Jews are equal citizens." From 1956 to 1961, the king made a point to install at least one or two Jewish leaders into senior-level positions in each cabinet ministry. He also allowed Jews to freely emigrate when they wanted, and there are now some 600,000 Moroccan Jews living in Israel.

Berdugo told me that Morocco's relationship with Israel began in the late 1960s with top secret meetings with Yitzhak Rabin and Moshe Dayan, who at that time were two of Israel's leading defense officials.

In 1984 the king invited fifty Jewish and Israeli leaders to Rabat, Morocco's capital, for an interfaith conference—and then decided that the entire senior leadership of the Moroccan government, including the crown prince, should attend the conference's gala dinner.

In 1986, the king invited Israeli prime minister Shimon Peres to Morocco for a highly publicized visit, a move that stunned most of the rest of the Muslim world.

When a series of bombings ripped through synagogues and Jewish clubs in Morocco in 2003, the new king—Mohammed VI—blessed a series of candlelight vigils and later a rally in which one million Moroccans, including more than a thousand Jews, marched in unison to denounce the radical jihadists and called for peace. "We were applauded as Jews," Berdugo told me. "We were kissed. People came up to us and said, 'You are our brothers.' It was extraordinary."

All of this suggests two things: First, secret talks between Israel and her Arab neighbors have been going on for years, and there may be other countries willing to make peace with Israel before or immediately after the War of Gog and Magog. And second, Morocco's relationship with Israel and the Jewish people could prove to be a model for other Arab and Islamic countries to follow, particularly if the fulfillment of Ezekiel 38–39 is still some years away. After all, my sources inside the Moroccan government say the king is seeking to play a "bridge builder" role between the Israelis and Palestinians and can do so with considerable authority since Morocco has proven that Jews and Muslims can live and work together in peace and harmony.

Q: *Joel, would you tell me more about your spiritual journey?*

A: This is by far my most frequently asked question. I appreciate it every time, for it goes to the core of the things that matter most in life. In 2005 I posted on my Web site a response to the many e-mails I receive every week on this topic. Here is an excerpt from that response:

First some background: My grandparents and great-grandparents were Orthodox Jews who fled from the pogroms of czarist Russia. As they hid in a hay wagon that was crossing a border into an Eastern European country, czarist soldiers drew their swords and plunged them into the hay, in case any Jews were trying to escape. By God's grace, none of the children coughed or sneezed or said, "Are we there yet?" By God's grace, no one was injured. And by God's grace, my family didn't succeed in escaping the vicious anti-Semitism of Russia only to say, "Phew, let's settle in Poland. Or Germany. Or Austria." They made their way across Europe, got on a ship to the New World, landed at Ellis Island, and like any good Jewish family, set up shop in Brooklyn.

That's where my father was raised, in the Bedford-Stuyvesant section, in a devoutly religious home—religious, but sadly, almost devoid of love. Every meal was kosher but served without the kind of warm and engaging family conversations children should grow up enjoying. Every day my father attended Hebrew school, and every Sabbath he and his family went to synagogue, but he was never taught what the words he recited each week meant or why they mattered. His family celebrated every Jewish holiday, from Passover to Hanukkah, but such times were often spent with arguing relatives, and the holiday meaning was lost.

My father's father was angry and abusive. His mother was distant toward him. The public schools my father attended were scarred by violence, gangs, and drugs. His was certainly nothing like the healthy, inviting Orthodox families I have come to know here in the United States and in Israel. In fact, for years my father refused to talk much about the days of his youth because there was so much pain and alienation wrapped up in those memories.

My father left home when he was eighteen. He moved as far away as he could, studying architecture in California under John Lloyd Wright (son of famed architect Frank Lloyd Wright). He eventually found a job in Syracuse, New York, where he met and fell in love with my non-Jewish mother, further deepening the ever-growing rift with his parents.

How could he even consider marrying a Gentile? It was unthinkable to his parents. But my father had already left behind the religious trappings of his childhood, which held nothing for him but bad memories. He did not feel compelled to marry someone of a faith he did not share.

To make matters worse for my grandparents, my mother wasn't just a Gentile. She was of English descent—a white Anglo-Saxon Protestant. A Methodist, of all things!

My Jewish grandmother couldn't bear the thought. She actually offered to buy back the engagement ring my father had given to my mother—*at a profit to him*—if my father would call the wedding off. He refused, and they were married in August of 1965.

Two years later, in April of 1967, I was born. Though agnostic, my parents were both intrigued with the idea of finding God. They would take long walks through the streets of suburban Syracuse and later a little town called Fairport, New York, just outside of Rochester, where they moved in 1969. As they walked they would talk about whether there really was a God and, if there was, how one could know him.

They read the Koran and the Bhagavad Gita and the Bible. They talked to neighbors and friends about their spiritual journeys. One Sunday they happened to visit a church where a group of visiting lay-people explained how they had found a personal relationship with God through Jesus Christ and how becoming followers of Jesus had transformed their lives.

For the first time, someone simply and clearly explained that God loved my parents. They heard the New Testament verse John 3:16: "For God so loved the world that He gave his only begotten Son [Jesus Christ], that whoever believes in Him shall not perish [be eternally separated from God] but have eternal life" (NASB). They heard that a person must make a conscious, willful choice to receive Jesus as Savior and Lord in order to experience God's love and plan for his or her life.

It was all new to my parents, but it resonated instantly with my mother. Suddenly she knew that a personal relationship with God through Jesus—not through some sort of devotion to a religious code—was exactly what she had been looking for. When one of the speakers invited people who wanted to ask Jesus to become their Savior to come to the front of the church and be led through a short prayer, my mother went forward immediately, just assuming my father was right behind her. But he wasn't.

This was too big a leap, even for an admittedly lapsed Orthodox Jew from Brooklyn. My father wasn't sure how one got to God, but he couldn't believe that the path led through Jesus. That was one thing that had been drilled into his head as a kid, and it had stuck.

He agreed, however, to begin attending a Bible study with my mother because he was curious and wanted to support her. The weekly study took a small group of young married couples like themselves through the Gospel of Luke, the third book of the New Testament, nd there, week after week, my father began to read and increasingly understand the life and work and person of Jesus of Nazareth.

He began to learn that according to the Hebrew prophet Micah, the Messiah would be born in Bethlehem. He learned that the Hebrew prophet Isaiah said the Messiah would be born of a virgin, and live and minister in the region of the Sea of Galilee, and that he would suffer and die to pay the penalty for our sins. "We considered him [the Messiah] stricken by God, smitten by him, and afflicted," wrote Isaiah in chapter 53, verses 4 and 5. "But he was pierced for our transgressions, he was crushed for our iniquities; the punishment that brought us peace was upon him, and by his wounds we are healed" (NIV). And over time, my father saw that each of these messianic prophecies was fulfilled in the person of Jesus.

Jesus, who was Jewish.

Jesus, who was born in Bethlehem and preached in Galilee and lived in Israel.

Jesus, whose disciples were all Jewish.

One day while riding home from work on a bus, my father read two little booklets published by an organization known as Campus Crusade for Christ. One was called *The Four Spiritual Laws*. It explained God's plan of salvation simply and clearly. The second was a little blue pamphlet that explained that when a person chooses to turn away from his own way of living and prays to receive Jesus Christ as his personal Savior and Lord, he or she can experience a new life through the transformational power of God's Holy Spirit.

Suddenly, it all seemed to make sense. It all rang true.

My father walked into our house, into our kitchen, and announced to my mother that he believed Jesus was in fact the Messiah and that he had prayed to become a follower of this Son of the living God.

I was six years old and didn't think much of it at first. Then Mom and Dad started dragging my sister and me off to church every Sunday morning. They made us go to Sunday school. Worse, they sent us to something called Vacation Bible School. Ugh. I can't sing. I hate crafts. And that's all you do in VBS. That and listen to stories about Jesus. It was horrible. Pretty much. Except those stories . . .

I listened to those stories. I was curious about Jesus. He seemed so loving, so kind, and he could do the coolest miracles. It began to sink in that he was more than a man; he was and is the Messiah. I came to know this not just because of what I heard in VBS, but over the years as I saw the lives of my parents changing before my eyes. My mother was no longer racked with anxiety and fear or stricken with constant migraine headaches. She had a peace that I couldn't explain. My father was no longer the bitter man with a quick temper that I had long feared. He was becoming gentle and kind, a man who loved to study the Bible—and to teach it, especially to kids.

Who were these people? They were followers of Jesus. That was the only explanation I could come up with. God was real to them. They knew him, and he was changing their lives.

As a teenager I began to hope that he could change my life too. Perhaps Jesus could give me the purpose and direction I so desperately wanted and needed.

In January of 1984, the winter of my junior year of high school, I became a deeply convinced and devoted follower of Jesus. And yes, my life began to change in ways I never dreamed possible, and I began to see my place in God's plan and purpose for his chosen people.

One of the most welcome but least expected changes God made in me was a sudden and growing interest in all things Jewish. With a name as distinct as Joel Rosenberg everybody I knew in my little town knew that I was Jewish. But I'd had little idea what that really meant. I hadn't been raised going to Hebrew school or synagogue or celebrating the Jewish holidays. I never had a bar mitzvah. But the more I read the Bible, the more intrigued I became by the fact that Jesus and his disciples were Jewish. I began asking my father a thousand questions, and to my surprise, he began answering them. We began celebrating Passover as a family. We began studying the Jewish Scriptures together, especially the Hebrew prophets, with whom I became intrigued.

In 1987, I had the opportunity to study for six months in Israel at Tel Aviv University, and I jumped at the chance to see the Holy Land for myself. It is hard to describe the deep sense of connection I felt when I arrived in the land of Abraham, Isaac, Jacob, and Jesus. It was as if I had come home—studying Hebrew (six hours a day!), eating falafel, and visiting the ancient sites where the Bible was written and passed down through the ages.

I had a powerful sense that Israel was the epicenter of human history—a land chosen by God for the most important event of human history (the death and resurrection of the Messiah); a land reborn in modern times, as foretold by the prophets; and the stage upon which the cataclysmic final events of history would be acted out. I knew then and there that I wanted to write. And not just about Israel, but about her enemies, about the forces of freedom and tyranny in the Middle East. And I wanted to write about the clues the prophets told us to watch for so that we would know beyond the shadow of a doubt when the final chapter of history was about to be unveiled.

It was exciting, but a little lonely. To my knowledge, I was the only Jewish believer in Jesus on the Tel Aviv campus. My American room-mates insisted I was no longer Jewish because I had "converted" to Christianity.

"Nonsense," I said. "I didn't convert to anything. Jesus is the Jewish Messiah. I've simply believed in the Anointed One God sent to us."

When they still insisted I wasn't Jewish, I'd shoot back, "What are you talking about? You guys barely believe God *exists*, much less fol-low the Jewish Scriptures." It was true. They were good guys, but they didn't read the Bible and weren't interested in living lives of faith.

It has been almost twenty years since my first visit to Israel, and I still remember that semester so vividly. When I go back these days, I am amazed that people are still asking me the same question that dogged my roommates: "How can you be Jewish and believe in Jesus?" Some ask because it's a theme woven through my novels. They also ask, I think, because they sense I am willing to answer. And I am. It's an important question, and one that deserves a thoughtful, hon-est reply.

When my father became a follower of Jesus in 1973, he thought he was the only Jewish person on the planet since the apostle Paul to be-lieve Jesus is the Messiah. Besides my father, I certainly don't remember knowing any Jewish believers in Jesus in my childhood. But in the past few decades, the number of Jewish believers has spiked dramatically— as Jesus said it would.

Just before his crucifixion, Jesus told his Jewish followers, "For I tell you, you will not see me again until you say, 'Blessed is he who comes in the name of the Lord'" (Matthew 23:39, NIV). In other words, Jesus is coming back—at a time when lots of Jewish people will not only believe in him, but will be ready and waiting with excitement.

Not long ago I was in Israel doing research for my fourth novel, *The Copper Scroll*. I was having coffee at the King David Hotel with the head of a messianic Jewish congregation. As we looked out over the Old City and the Mount of Olives, I asked him, "In 1967, when I was born, how many Israeli Jews believed in Jesus?"

"Maybe a handful," he said.

"How many Jews worldwide in 1967 believed Jesus was the Messiah?" I asked.

"Based on my research, less than 2,000," he said.

How much has changed since then. Today there are some 10,000 Israeli Jewish believers in Jesus. Worldwide, conservative estimates put the number around 100,000. Some believe the number is closer to 300,000. What a startling increase—and my father and I and my sons are part of those numbers, part of that dramatic trend. Jews are turning to Jesus in record numbers, and they are getting excited about his Second Coming.

So I write my books and I answer the question of how a Jew can believe in Jesus. And no, I'm not a psychic and I don't have access to secret government information. But I do have access to the Jewish prophets— *and so do you*. God has told us what the future holds for Israel, for the world, and for you as biblical events continue to unfold. It's all in the book . . . not mine, but his.

He is coming back soon. Maybe sooner than you think.

APPENDIX 2
AMERICAN ATTITUDES
TOWARD BIBLE PROPHECY

Exclusive National Survey for Joel C. Rosenberg
Conducted by McLaughlin & Associates
1,000 randomly selected adults
February 13, 2006

In February of 2006, I commissioned a national survey to get a sense of how Americans feel about the question of whether we are living in the last days. The survey was conducted by a nationally respected polling organization. I found the results intriguing. I include them here for your interest as well.

ISRAEL: A PROPHECY COME TRUE?

The polling firm asked people whether they agreed or disagreed with the following statement: The rebirth of the State of Israel in 1948 and the return of millions of Jews to the Holy Land after centuries in exile represent the fulfillment of biblical prophecies.

52% of all Americans agree

Only 22% disagree

26% say they don't know

Israel Prophecy—Gender
- 54% of women agree; 18% disagree; 28% don't know
- 49% of men agree; 27% disagree; 24% don't know

Israel Prophecy—Religion
- 70% of evangelical/born-again Christians agree; 12% disagree
- 59% of all Protestant Christian affiliations agree; 16% disagree
- 52% of Catholics agree; 24% disagree
- 56% of Jewish Americans agree; 22% disagree

Israel Prophecy—Ideology/Party Affiliation
- 44% of liberal Democrats agree; 21% disagree
- 50% of self-described moderates agree; 28% disagree
- 65% of conservative Republicans agree; 18% disagree

Israel Prophecy—Party Affiliation
- 47% of Democrats agree; 24% disagree
- 61% of Republicans agree; 19% disagree

Israel Prophecy—Race
- 60% of African-Americans agree; 17% disagree
- 52% of whites agree; 22% disagree
- 46% of Hispanics agree; 41% disagree
- 29% of Asians agree; 29% disagree; 42% don't know

Israel Prophecy—Income
- 62% of Americans earning under $20,000 per year agree; 15% disagree

- 55% of Americans earning between $60,000 and $75,000 a year agree; 22% disagree
- 37% of Americans earning $100,000 or more per year agree; 37% disagree; 26% don't know

Israel Prophecy—Region
- 45% of Americans living in the East agree; 29% disagree
- 52% of Americans living in the Midwest agree; 23% disagree
- 58% of Americans living in the South agree; 15% disagree
- 48% of Americans living in the West agree; 29% disagree
- 47% of New Englanders agree; 20% disagree

Israel Prophecy—Age
- 61% of Americans age 18–25 agree; only 7% disagree; 32% don't know
- 37% of Gen Xers age 26–40 agree; 33% disagree; 30% don't know
- 53% of Americans age 41–55 agree; 19% disagree
- 56% of Americans age 56–65 agree; 22% disagree
- 59% of Americans over age 65 agree; 21% disagree

ARE WE LIVING IN THE LAST DAYS?

The polling firm asked people whether they agreed or disagreed with the following statement: Events such as the rebirth of the State of Israel, wars and instability in the Middle East, recent earthquakes, and the tsunami in Asia are evidence that we are living in what the Bible calls the last days.

42% of all Americans agree

44% disagree

14% say they don't know

Last Days—Gender
- 50% of women agree; 37% disagree; 13% don't know
- 34% of men agree; 52% disagree; 14% don't know

Last Days—Religion
- 58% of evangelical/born-again Christians agree; 30% disagree
- 50% of all Protestant Christians agree; 35% disagree
- 38% of Catholics agree; 52% disagree
- 31% of Jewish Americans agree; 56% disagree

Last Days—Ideology/Party Affiliation
- 30% of liberal Democrats agree; 57% disagree
- 39% of self-described moderates agree; 47% disagree
- 51% of conservative Republicans agree; 39% disagree

Last Days—Party Affiliation
- 39% of Democrats agree; 47% disagree
- 48% of Republicans agree; 39% disagree

Last Days—Race
- 75% of African-Americans agree; 16% disagree
- 39% of whites agree; 47% disagree
- 33% of Hispanics agree; 56% disagree
- 14% of Asians agree; 86% disagree

Last Days—Income
- 60% of Americans earning under $20,000 per year agree; 26% disagree
- 43% of Americans earning between $60,000 and $75,000 per year agree; 49% disagree
- 16% of Americans earning $100,000 or more per year agree; 77% disagree

Last Days—Region
- 37% of Americans living in the East agree; 49% disagree
- 39% of Americans living in the Midwest agree; 48% disagree
- 51% of Americans living in the South agree; 35% disagree
- 35% of Americans living in the West agree; 50% disagree
- 35% of New Englanders agree; 51% disagree

Last Days—Age

- 57% of Americans age 18–25 agree; 39% disagree
- 32% of Gen Xers age 26–40 agree; 49% disagree
- 43% of Americans age 41–55 agree; 47% disagree
- 42% of Americans age 56–65 agree; 44% disagree
- 46% of Americans over age 65 agree; 39% disagree

APPENDIX 3
AMERICAN CHRISTIAN ATTITUDES
TOWARD ISRAEL AND EPICENTER ISSUES

Exclusive National Survey for Joel C. Rosenberg
Conducted by McLaughlin & Associates
1,000 randomly selected American Christians
March 16-18, 2008

On May 14, 2008, Jews and Christians the world over celebrated the sixtieth anniversary of the dramatic and prophetic rebirth of the State of Israel.

In light of this historic anniversary, I commissioned a second national survey to examine more closely the attitudes of American Christians toward Israel, the future of Jerusalem, the Iranian nuclear threat, and other Middle East issues. Whereas the first survey looked at the views of Americans as a whole, this survey focused exclusively on Americans who identified themselves as Protestants or Catholics and was conducted by the same nationally respected firm that did the first poll.[1]

On April 10, 2008, I had the honor of releasing these results to 2,000 Christian and Jewish leaders from all over the world at the inaugural

Epicenter Convention. They found the results intriguing. I think you will too.

EXECUTIVE SUMMARY

Among the major findings of this survey:

- The overwhelming majority of American Christians love the State of Israel and its people, and 82% believe they have "a moral and biblical obligation to support Israel and pray for peace in Jerusalem."
- American Christians also desire to demonstrate their unconditional love and compassion for the people of Israel and the epicenter in real and practical ways. Fully 75% of all Christians in the U.S.—and 81% of evangelical Protestants—believe that "in addition to caring for the poor and needy in our own country, Christians have a moral and biblical obligation to provide humanitarian relief to the poor and needy and to victims of war and terrorism in Israel and the Middle East."
- Half of all American Christians—and 57% of evangelical Protestants—desire to one day take a tour of Israel, walk where Jesus walked, and visit the Christian and Jewish holy sites.
- That said, however, American Christians are worried about the threat posed by Iranian president Mahmoud Ahmadinejad and his government—65% are convinced that if Iran develops nuclear weapons, Iran's leaders will eventually try to use them to attack Israel and wipe her "off the map," as Ahmadinejad has threatened.
- What's more, though recent U.S. presidents have pushed hard diplomatically for a final status peace deal between Israel and her neighbors, American Christians are deeply conflicted about the goal of creating a sovereign

Palestinian state in the West Bank and Gaza. They share the desire for peace in the Middle East but fear that a Palestinian state could become a base camp for terrorism, not the home of a peaceful new democracy.

- American Christians feel strongly about the Holy City of Jerusalem—they want Jerusalem to remain the undivided capital of the Jewish State of Israel and overwhelmingly oppose dividing the Holy City to become the capital of a Palestinian Muslim state.
- Finally, the survey found that the manner in which U.S. presidential candidates handle epicenter issues could be a key factor in how American Christians decide whom they will vote for.

CHRISTIAN LOVE FOR ISRAEL

The polling firm asked people whether they agreed or disagreed with the following statement: Christians have a moral and biblical obligation to show love and support for the people of Israel and pray for peace in Jerusalem.

82% of American Christians agree

Only 10% disagree

8% say they don't know

Historically, American Protestants and Catholics have been divided on a host of social and political issues. But standing in solidarity with Israel turns out to be one of the great unifiers among Christians, the poll found.

Evangelical Christians—defined as those who describe themselves as "born again"—are the biggest supporters of Israel (89% said they agree). But strong pro-Israel convictions were by no means limited to evangelicals. They actually cut across all key demographics. Regardless of age, gender, race, political ideology, political party, region of the country, and denomination (Protestant or Catholic), the vast majority of Christians in the U.S. believe at a core level that the Bible teaches them to love Israel and pray for peace in Jerusalem.

	TOTAL	PROTESTANT	CATHOLIC	EVAN. PROT.	NON-EVAN. PROT.	EVAN. PROT. REP.	EVAN. PROT. DEM.	EVAN. PROT. MOD.	EVAN. PROT. CONS.
AGREE	82	84	76	89	78	92	87	87	90
DISAGREE	10	8	16	5	12	3	6	4	6
DON'T KNOW	8	8	7	6	9	5	7	9	5

CHRISTIAN COMPASSION FOR ISRAEL AND HER NEIGHBORS

The polling firm asked whether people agreed or disagreed with the following statement: In addition to caring for the poor and needy in our own country, Christians have a moral and biblical obligation to provide humanitarian relief to the poor and needy and to victims of war and terrorism in Israel and the Middle East.

75% of American Christians agree
16% disagree
9% say they don't know

Based on the answers to the previous poll question, it should not be surprising that Christians want to demonstrate their love in real and practical ways to victims of war and terrorism in Israel. But significantly, they also want to demonstrate biblical love and compassion to Israel's neighbors, such as the Palestinians living in the West Bank and Gaza and the people of Lebanon, Iraq, Sudan, and the rest of the Middle East.

The issue of providing humanitarian aid—food, clothing, medical supplies, and the like—to those in real and serious need is a unifying issue among Christians. Evangelicals feel strongest about the importance of doing relief work (89% said it is a biblical mandate), but they are not alone. A full 76% of Christians who say they are not "born again" also say they want to care for the poor, and this conviction turned out to be widely held among all Christians.

For example:

- 77% of Christians who identified themselves as "very liberal" said they agreed with providing humanitarian relief to the needy in Israel and the Middle East.
- 82% of Christians who identified themselves as "very conservative" agreed as well.

	TOTAL	PROTESTANT	CATHOLIC	EVAN. PROT.	NON- EVAN. PROT.	EVAN. PROT. REP.	EVAN. PROT. DEM.	EVAN. PROT. MOD.	EVAN. PROT. CONS.
AGREE	75	77	72	81	70	87	76	82	85
DISAGREE	16	14	19	11	20	8	14	10	10
DON'T KNOW	9	9	9	8	10	5	11	9	6

CHRISTIAN DESIRE TO VISIT THE HOLY LAND

The polling firm asked, Do you have an interest in someday taking a tour of Israel, walking where Jesus walked, and visiting the Christian and Jewish holy sites?

49% of all American Christians said yes

58% of Evangelical Christians said yes

52% of Catholics said yes

We probed deeper to determine how many had a "strong interest" in touring Israel and how many simply had "some interest." The numbers were still strikingly high. Nearly one-fourth of all American Christians (24%) have a "strong interest." Among Catholics, the number jumps to 28% with "strong interest." And among evangelicals, the number jumps to nearly one in three (32%) with "strong interest."

In the end, however, what was particularly striking about these results was not so much the percentage of Christians who said they would like to visit Israel but how that percentage translates into sheer numbers of potential tourists to the Jewish state. There are an estimated 100 million evangelical Christians in the U.S., according to the Institute for the Study of American Evangelicals at Wheaton College.[2] That translates into some 32 million American evangelicals who have a "strong interest" in visiting Nazareth, Bethlehem, the Sea of Galilee, the Mount of Beatitudes, and the Temple Mount in Jerusalem.

At the same time, there are an estimated 64 million Catholics in the U.S., according to the U.S. Conference of Catholic Bishops.[3] That translates into nearly 18 million Catholics who have a "strong interest" in walking the Via Dolorosa and visiting the Church of the Holy Sepulcher, the Garden of Gethsemane, and other sites where Jesus and his disciples walked and ministered.

All told, there are about 91 million American Christians who want to visit Israel, and at least 50 million who strongly desire to walk where Jesus walked.

	TOTAL	PROTESTANT	CATHOLIC	EVAN. PROT.	NON-EVAN. PROT.	EVAN. PROT. REP.	EVAN. PROT. DEM.	EVAN. PROT. MOD.	EVAN. PROT. CONS.
YES	49	48	52	57	35	59	53	56	56
STRONG	24	23	28	30	12	29	32	27	32
SOME	25	25	24	27	23	29	22	29	24
NO	47	49	45	41	60	40	43	38	42
DON'T KNOW	4	4	3	3	5	2	4	6	2

CHRISTIAN CONCERN OVER THE "IRANIAN BOMB"

The polling firm asked, If Iran develops nuclear weapons, do you believe the leaders of Iran will eventually try to use those nuclear weapons to attack Israel?

65% of American Christians said yes

13% said no

23% said they don't know

While strong majorities fear Iranian use of nuclear weapons—and those majorities cut across all demographics—there are notable differences:

- 60% of Christians who identified themselves as "very liberal" fear Iranian nuclear weapons will be used to attack Israel, compared to 83% of those who describe themselves as "very conservative."
- 60% of Christians who are registered Democrats said yes, compared to 77% of Christian Republicans. (55% of self-identified Independents said yes.)
- Only 55% of Christians 40 and under said yes, while 66% of Christians 55 and over said yes.
- Non-white Christians are more worried than white Christians (71% said yes, vs. 64%).

It should be noted that nearly a quarter of American Christians (23%) told the polling firm they were not yet sure how to evaluate the Iranian threat to Israel, suggesting they are perhaps watching events in the Middle East to see if Iranian leaders are prepared to make good on their threats or whether the U.S., Israel, or other Western allies will take decisive diplomatic, economic, or military action to neutralize the threat.

	TOTAL	PROTESTANT	CATHOLIC	EVAN. PROT.	NON-EVAN. PROT.	EVAN. PROT. REP.	EVAN. PROT. DEM.	EVAN. PROT. MOD.	EVAN. PROT. CONS.
YES	65	64	65	68	60	77	64	65	75
NO	13	11	17	7	15	4	9	9	7
DON'T KNOW	23	25	18	25	25	19	28	27	18

CHRISTIAN CONCERNS ABOUT A PALESTINIAN STATE

The polling firm asked, If a Palestinian state were established in the West Bank and Gaza, do you believe it would more likely be a peaceful, moderate democracy or a terrorist state?

32% of American Christians said "a terrorist state"

24% said a "peaceful democracy"

44% said they don't know

American Christians who believe in the words spoken by Jesus—"Blessed are the peacemakers"—certainly hope that the Middle East peace process will produce a just and fair solution to the Arab-Israeli conflict. But they are deeply conflicted about what would be "just and fair" and about the potential unintended consequences of a comprehensive treaty.

By an eight-point margin (32% to 24%) American Christians fear that if a Palestinian state was established, it would more likely be a terrorist state than a peaceful, moderate democracy. However, a striking 44% doesn't know.

There are some clear demographic distinctions. For example, Protestants lean toward saying a Palestinian state would be a terrorist state, but Catholics are virtually split. Evangelical Protestants say a Palestinian state would be a terrorist state by a twenty-point margin but non-evangelical Protestants lean toward saying it would be a peaceful, moderate democracy. The opinion that a Palestinian state would be a terrorist state is strongest among Republican and conservative evangelical Protestants.

	TOTAL	PROTESTANT	CATHOLIC	EVAN. PROT.	NON-EVAN. PROT.	EVAN. PROT. REP.	EVAN. PROT. DEM.	EVAN. PROT. MOD.	EVAN. PROT. CONS.
PEACEFUL	24	22	30	16	32	16	15	18	14
TERRORIST	32	32	32	36	26	43	29	25	49
DON'T KNOW	44	46	38	48	42	41	56	57	36

CHRISTIAN VIEWS ON DIVIDING JERUSALEM

The polling firm asked the following question: Throughout history Jerusalem has never been the capital of any state except the Jewish State of Israel. Now, the international community is pressuring Israel to divide Jerusalem. Do you believe that Jerusalem should remain the united capital of Israel, or be divided and become the capital of a Palestinian Muslim state as well?

> 50% say Jerusalem should remain the united capital of Israel
> Only 17% think Jerusalem should be divided
> 33% say they don't know

While by a 3 to 1 ratio (50% to 17%) American Christians believe that Jerusalem should remain the united capital of Israel, curiously, Protestants and Catholics are somewhat divided. A majority of Protestants (53%) support a united Jerusalem, but only 44% of Catholics do. The biggest split, however, comes between evangelical and non-evangelical Christians.

- 70% of evangelical men support a united Jerusalem, while only 37% of non-evangelical men share that view.
- 55% of evangelical women support a united Jerusalem, versus only 45% of non-evangelical women.
- 71% of evangelical Republicans support a united Jerusalem, while only 42% of non-evangelical Republicans share that view.
- 58% of evangelical Democrats support a united Jerusalem, versus only 41% of non-evangelical Democrats.

That said, fully one in three American Christians say they don't know enough to take a position one way or the other, suggesting that there is still quite a bit of education to be done by those who advocate keeping Jerusalem the united capital of the Jewish state. After all, among those who feel they have the knowledge to have a firm opinion, 75% of American Christians support a united Jerusalem, while 25% think it should be divided. Among evangelical Protestants, a stunning 85% say Jerusalem should stay united under Jewish control, while only 15% say it should be divided with Muslims.

	TOTAL	PROTESTANT	CATHOLIC	EVAN. PROT.	NON-EVAN. PROT.	EVAN. PROT. REP.	EVAN. PROT. DEM.	EVAN. PROT. MOD.	EVAN. PROT. CONS.
REMAIN	50	53	44	62	39	71	59	59	72
DIVIDE	17	16	19	11	25	8	15	13	8
DON'T KNOW	33	31	37	27	36	21	26	28	21

HOW EPICENTER ISSUES MAY AFFECT CHRISTIAN VOTERS

The polling firm also asked, Would you be more likely or less likely to vote for a candidate for president of the United States if you knew that candidate would strongly advocate policies to protect America from radical Islamic terrorism; protect Israel from a nuclear attack by Iran; protect the capital of Israel, Jerusalem, from being divided with Palestinian Muslims; and refuse to pressure Israel to make diplomatic concessions that could endanger Israel's national security? If it would make no difference, just say so.

45% of American Christians said they would be more likely
to vote for a U.S. presidential candidate who advocated
such positions on Middle East issues

Only 9% said they would be less likely

29% said such positions would make no difference
in their voting behavior

The survey results suggest that American Christians are looking carefully for a presidential candidate who understands the magnitude of the threat posed to the U.S. and its allies by radical Islamic extremists and who strongly advocates policy positions to defend U.S. national security as well defend strategic allies such as Israel in the winner-take-all battle with radical Islam.

Americans Christians can be expected to watch epicenter-related issues closely, and the survey results suggest a presidential candidate's position on these issues will strongly affect Christians' behavior at the ballot box.

- By a nearly an 11 to 1 margin (64% to 6%), Republican Christian men would be more likely to vote for a candidate with a strong position on these epicenter issues.
- Republican Christian women would also be strongly swayed (56% said more likely, while only 3% said less likely).
- Democrat Christian men would not be swayed as strongly as Republican Christian men, but by more than 2 to 1, they are also looking for a candidate taking such epicenter positions (35% to 15%).
- Democrat Christian women are even more open to persuasion (37% say they are more likely, while only 11% say they are less likely).
- Perhaps most intriguing is that epicenter issues matter significantly to Christians who describe themselves as Independents. A full 44% of Christian Independent men say they are more likely, while only 6% say less likely. The numbers are similar for Christian Independent women (44% to 11%).

	TOTAL	PROTESTANT	CATHOLIC	EVAN. PROT.	NON-EVAN. PROT.	EVAN. PROT. REP.	EVAN. PROT. DEM.	EVAN. PROT. MOD.	EVAN. PROT. CONS.
MORE LIKELY	45	45	44	52	35	66	41	45	64
LESS LIKELY	9	9	9	7	12	4	8	9	6
NO DIFFERENCE	29	29	28	24	38	18	28	26	19
DON'T KNOW	18	17	18	18	15	13	23	21	11

CHAPTER 38

And the word of the LORD came to me saying, [2]"Son of man, set your face toward Gog of the land of Magog, the prince of Rosh, Meshech and Tubal, and prophesy against him [3]and say, 'Thus says the Lord GOD, "Behold, I am against you, O Gog, prince of Rosh, Meshech and Tubal. [4]I will turn you about and put hooks into your jaws, and I will bring you out, and all your army, horses and horsemen, all of them splendidly attired, a great company with buckler and shield, all of them wielding swords; [5]Persia, Ethiopia and Put with them, all of them with shield and helmet; [6]Gomer with all its troops; Beth-togarmah from the remote parts of the north with all its troops—many peoples with you.

[7]"Be prepared, and prepare yourself, you and all your companies that are assembled about you, and be a guard for them. [8]After many days you will be summoned; in the latter years you will come into the land that is restored from the sword, whose inhabitants have been gathered from many nations to the mountains of Israel which had been a continual waste; but its people were brought out from the nations, and they are living securely, all of them. [9]You will go up, you will come

like a storm; you will be like a cloud covering the land, you and all your troops, and many peoples with you."

¹⁰"Thus says the Lord GOD, "It will come about on that day, that thoughts will come into your mind and you will devise an evil plan, ¹¹and you will say, 'I will go up against the land of unwalled villages. I will go against those who are at rest, that live securely, all of them living without walls and having no bars or gates, ¹²to capture spoil and to seize plunder, to turn your hand against the waste places which are now inhabited, and against the people who are gathered from the nations, who have acquired cattle and goods, who live at the center of the world.' ¹³Sheba and Dedan and the merchants of Tarshish with all its villages will say to you, 'Have you come to capture spoil? Have you assembled your company to seize plunder, to carry away silver and gold, to take away cattle and goods, to capture great spoil?'"'

¹⁴"Therefore prophesy, son of man, and say to Gog, 'Thus says the Lord GOD, "On that day when My people Israel are living securely, will you not know it? ¹⁵You will come from your place out of the remote parts of the north, you and many peoples with you, all of them riding on horses, a great assembly and a mighty army; ¹⁶and you will come up against My people Israel like a cloud to cover the land. It shall come about in the last days that I will bring you against My land, so that the nations may know Me when I am sanctified through you before their eyes, O Gog."

¹⁷"Thus says the Lord GOD, "Are you the one of whom I spoke in former days through My servants the prophets of Israel, who prophesied in those days for many years that I would bring you against them? ¹⁸It will come about on that day, when Gog comes against the land of Israel," declares the Lord GOD, "that My fury will mount up in My anger. ¹⁹In My zeal and in My blazing wrath I declare that on that day there will surely be a great earthquake in the land of Israel. ²⁰The fish of the sea, the birds of the heavens, the beasts of the field, all the creeping things that creep on the earth, and all the men who are on the face of the earth will shake at My presence; the mountains also will be thrown down, the steep pathways will collapse and every wall will fall to the ground. ²¹I will call for a sword against him on all My mountains," de-

clares the Lord GOD. "Every man's sword will be against his brother. [22]With pestilence and with blood I will enter into judgment with him; and I will rain on him and on his troops, and on the many peoples who are with him, a torrential rain, with hailstones, fire and brimstone. [23]I will magnify Myself, sanctify Myself, and make Myself known in the sight of many nations; and they will know that I am the LORD.""""

CHAPTER 39

"And you, son of man, prophesy against Gog and say, 'Thus says the Lord GOD, "Behold, I am against you, O Gog, prince of Rosh, Meshech and Tubal; [2]and I will turn you around, drive you on, take you up from the remotest parts of the north and bring you against the mountains of Israel. [3]I will strike your bow from your left hand and dash down your arrows from your right hand. [4]You will fall on the mountains of Israel, you and all your troops and the peoples who are with you; I will give you as food to every kind of predatory bird and beast of the field. [5]You will fall on the open field; for it is I who have spoken," declares the Lord GOD. [6]"And I will send fire upon Magog and those who inhabit the coastlands in safety; and they will know that I am the LORD.

[7]"My holy name I will make known in the midst of My people Israel; and I will not let My holy name be profaned anymore. And the nations will know that I am the LORD, the Holy One in Israel. [8]Behold, it is coming and it shall be done," declares the Lord GOD. "That is the day of which I have spoken.

[9]"Then those who inhabit the cities of Israel will go out and make fires with the weapons and burn them, both shields and bucklers, bows and arrows, war clubs and spears, and for seven years they will make fires of them. [10]They will not take wood from the field or gather firewood from the forests, for they will make fires with the weapons; and they will take the spoil of those who despoiled them and seize the plunder of those who plundered them," declares the Lord GOD.

[11]"On that day I will give Gog a burial ground there in Israel, the valley of those who pass by east of the sea, and it will block off those who would pass by. So they will bury Gog there with all his horde, and

they will call it the valley of Hamon-gog. [12]For seven months the house of Israel will be burying them in order to cleanse the land. [13]Even all the people of the land will bury them; and it will be to their renown on the day that I glorify Myself," declares the Lord GOD. [14]"They will set apart men who will constantly pass through the land, burying those who were passing through, even those left on the surface of the ground, in order to cleanse it. At the end of seven months they will make a search. [15]As those who pass through the land pass through and anyone sees a man's bone, then he will set up a marker by it until the buriers have buried it in the valley of Hamon-gog. [16]And even the name of the city will be Hamonah. So they will cleanse the land."'

[17]"As for you, son of man, thus says the Lord GOD, 'Speak to every kind of bird and to every beast of the field, "Assemble and come, gather from every side to My sacrifice which I am going to sacrifice for you, as a great sacrifice on the mountains of Israel, that you may eat flesh and drink blood. [18]You will eat the flesh of mighty men and drink the blood of the princes of the earth, as though they were rams, lambs, goats and bulls, all of them fatlings of Bashan. [19]So you will eat fat until you are glutted, and drink blood until you are drunk, from My sacrifice which I have sacrificed for you. [20]You will be glutted at My table with horses and charioteers, with mighty men and all the men of war," declares the Lord GOD.

[21]"And I will set My glory among the nations; and all the nations will see My judgment which I have executed and My hand which I have laid on them. [22]And the house of Israel will know that I am the LORD their God from that day onward. [23]The nations will know that the house of Israel went into exile for their iniquity because they acted treacherously against Me, and I hid My face from them; so I gave them into the hand of their adversaries, and all of them fell by the sword. [24]According to their uncleanness and according to their transgressions I dealt with them, and I hid My face from them."'"

[25]Therefore thus says the Lord GOD, "Now I will restore the fortunes of Jacob and have mercy on the whole house of Israel; and I will be jealous for My holy name. [26]They will forget their disgrace and all their treachery which they perpetrated against Me, when they live se-

curely on their own land with no one to make them afraid. [27]When I bring them back from the peoples and gather them from the lands of their enemies, then I shall be sanctified through them in the sight of the many nations. [28]Then they will know that I am the LORD their God because I made them go into exile among the nations, and then gathered them again to their own land; and I will leave none of them there any longer. [29]I will not hide My face from them any longer, for I will have poured out My Spirit on the house of Israel," declares the Lord GOD.

APPENDIX 5
INTERVIEW TRANSCRIPTS

The following interviews were conducted in 2007 for the *Epicenter* documentary film released for the fortieth anniversary of the Six Days' War.

BENJAMIN NETANYAHU
Former Prime Minister of Israel

JOEL ROSENBERG: *Mr. Prime Minister, thank you for spending time with us. First question I want to ask you: In your 1995 book,* **Fighting Terrorism,** *you said, "It's only a matter of time before the U.S. gets hit by radical Islam." You had talked about the World Trade Center and kamikazes. What is it you were able to see in the mid-1990s that so many analysts, like the leaders in the West, couldn't see?*

BENJAMIN NETANYAHU: I think the West misunderstood, and still misunderstands, the threat of radical Islam. It is a fanatic messianic ideology that seeks to have an apocalyptic battle for world supremacy with the West. It seeks to correct what it sees—its disciples see—as an accident of history, where the West has risen and Islam has declined. The correction is supposed to be done by the reselection of an Islamic empire and the acquisition of nuclear weapons and the use of nuclear weapons, if necessary, to obliterate Islam's enemies, and to subjugate the rest.

This is a pathological ideology, much like Nazism was. And it poses a threat, in my judgment, in many ways bigger than Nazism because Hitler embarked on a world conflict and then sought to achieve nuclear weapons, whereas the leading radical Islamic regime, Iran, is seeking to first acquire nuclear weapons and then embark on a world conflict. And that is what is not yet understood in the West, and certainly, if it's understood, it's not acted upon.

ROSENBERG: *[Iranian president Mahmoud] Ahmadinejad has an apocalyptic theory. . . . In your view, how is that driving Iranian foreign policy? Because that's not something that Western analysts are talking much about. They're starting to, but this seems to be animating where they're headed and their timetable.*

NETANYAHU: I think the world changes once Iran acquires nuclear weapons. With this fanatic regime, it's almost akin to the Branch Davidians under David Koresh acquiring nuclear weapons. You know, it's one thing if you have a crazy sect stuck up in some commune in Oregon or in a ranch in Waco, Texas. But when the wacko from Waco gets nuclear weapons and he wants to obliterate the United States and its allies, then you start worrying. And that's what is happening in Iran.

You think that these people are normal; you think that Iran would conform to the conceptions of deterrents and careful calculation of cost and benefit. But in fact, it is part of that stream of radical Islam, in this case [the] Shiite stream, but you've already seen what the Sunni stream does, which is to smash into buildings in Manhattan with collective suicide, to smash into the Pentagon with collective suicide. And there's no reason to believe that the militant Shiites, once they have atomic weapons, will not be suicidal. They say openly that they intend to remove Israel, the first position of the West, really "little Satan," but remember that their goal is to get the United States, the "big Satan." We're just a station, one station, on the way to world conquest. And to have such a regime that believes in apocalyptic Armageddon with the West—in which millions will die on both sides, but the Muslim millions go to a Muslim heaven with all the trappings—to have that crazy ideology in charge of a country that is developing atomic weapons is unbelievably dangerous, and it should stop. Everything else is secondary to this.

I find it hard saying this, because I said in the early nineties that the radical Muslims would bring down the World Trade Center and the response was no response at all. And I am saying here, now, in the beginning of the first decade of the twenty-first century, that the world faces an enormous danger, should Ahmadinejad's Iran acquire atomic weapons. It is not merely a danger to my own country—and for the reasons of full disclosure I tell you, yes, it is a danger to my own country—but it's a danger to my own country the way Hitler was a danger to the Jews. Yes, of course, he went after the Jews, but then he went after everyone else. And that's exactly what you have with Iran. It has to be stopped. Now.

ROSENBERG: *Can you negotiate with, or even successfully deter, someone who believes that it is his God-given mission to eliminate millions of people?*
NETANYAHU: No, it's very hard to rely on deterrents. It is not the same as Soviet Russia. It is not the same as China, or India, or any one of the nuclear powers today, that you're fairly comfortable understanding what they think in terms of cost and benefit. In the case of an extreme religious cult, that has no such calculations. You could, in fact, face a suicidal regime. Therefore you can't rely on deterrents; you should work on prevention, that is, preventing them from acquiring the weapons and mass death.

ROSENBERG: *How much time does the West have to make a decision to act decisively to stop Iran?*
NETANYAHU: Not much. We are running out of time. I can't tell you if it's a period of months or a few years. It's certainly no more than a few years.

ROSENBERG: *When you were prime minister, both India and Pakistan tested nuclear weapons. As I understand from my research, Western intelligence agencies—I don't know about the Mossad—were startled that they were ready at that moment. What was your assessment at the time?*

NETANYAHU: Well, the first thing I did, or among the first things I did, after I was elected prime minister, was, I think some three weeks later, to speak before a joint session of the U.S. Congress. And I said at the time that the greatest danger that the world faces is the arming of Iran with nuclear weapons. What was true ten years ago is doubly true today—not doubly, *triply*. I couldn't get the leading powers of the world, including the U.S. administration at the time, to focus on this danger and to stop the shipment of nuclear and ballistic technology to Iran from many countries, including Russia. I could not get the U.S. to focus on this. I think today people understand the danger. It's much more advanced. It has moved forward.

Could we be surprised tomorrow? Well, we were surprised by the extent of Libya's advancement in its nuclear program, and happily it was dismantled, probably as a result of the deterrent effect of [Mu'ammar] Al-Qadhafi's seeing Saddam [Hussein] at the end of a hole—realizing that he too could hang by the end of a rope. But no such deterrent necessarily works on the true believers in Tehran. And therefore, our focus should not be on deterrents, which may not work, but on prevention, which can obviate the need for deterrents.

ROSENBERG: *Natan Sharansky was telling me a story a couple of years ago when I was working with him, about how you sent him back to Moscow, to meet with then KGB chief Vladimir Putin to talk about this specific threat. And he repeated it, of course, for the cameras, a couple days ago. Why? Why did you send him? What message were you trying to send Putin and the leaders of Russia? Because this relationship—Russia and Iran—takes this thing to a new level.*

NETANYAHU: I think there is a fundamental contradiction in Russia's policy. On the one hand, it gives free rein, or almost free rein, to Iran; giving it political support, giving it antiaircraft weapons, and so on, vetoing stiff measures in the Security Council. But on the other hand, it's building, inadvertently, a powder keg that could explode the soft underbelly of Russia, its own Muslim populations, and the Muslim republics, former Soviet republics, that gird Russia's southern belly. So I think this is a big mistake. I think that nuclear weapons in the hands of an Iranian, fervently Islamic regime is a danger to Russia. But Russia is perhaps acting on short-term gains at the cost of long term-interest, and this is something that I wanted to bring to their attention when I asked Sharansky to go there. And something that I sought to deal with by getting the U.S. administration at the time to apply sanctions on Russian companies, and the Russian government itself, for selling ballistic and nuclear technology to Iran.

We were unsuccessful then because the U.S. did not focus on this. And the question is, what will the U.S. do today? It has probably in Washington today, I think, a clear understanding of the dangers. But . . . there are really [three] steps here: One is understanding . . . the danger. Two is preparing a response to it. And third is acting. And of all the things that are difficult for statesmen and political leaders, preemption is the hardest because you can never prove what would happen if you don't preempt. So had the West preempted against Germany in the 1930s, there would have been a lot of controversy and a lot of argument against excessive violence. But of course, millions, tens of millions of people, let alone the six million Jews, would have been saved. And it's the same thing today; to take strong action against Iran, first in the form of sanctions, and second, if those don't work, using other means, is something that would be criticized, perhaps severely criticized, by some of the rest of the Arab or Muslim world. They just want it to happen; they are begging it to happen. . . . In the West you'd be criticized, but you'd be saving the world, and probably saving millions and millions of lives.

ROSENBERG: *So what's Putin's objective, in your assessment of him, personally, of where he's taking Russia, in submarines, missiles, nuclear technology—*

NETANYAHU: I think it's very clear that there is a monetary gain [for Russia] in the contract with Iran. [But] I think it's folly to take a perspective of short-term financial gain at the expense of your vital strategic interest, like the survival of your cities. That is not a good trade-off. And I think that it would be prudent for Russia to take a second look.

It may not, so the U.S. action—U.S.-led action—should take into account the fact that the U.S. will not have Russian support, will not have Chinese support. And then there are things that could be done to put pressure on the Ahmadinejad regime today that [don't] require anything [from] governments. [Things like] pension funds [withdrawing] their funds from companies that invest in this genocide regime of Iran, just the way they stopped investing in the apartheid regime of South Africa. That would create a snowball effect that would seriously pressure the regime. So these things, non-governmental, and governmental sanctions, and governmental action, whether you have a common front with Russia and China, or without them. That is what leadership is about today; you have to act in time, before the radical Muslims arm themselves with atomic bombs.

ROSENBERG: *One more question on radical Islam and then just a couple on relationships between evangelicals and Israel. But on this, to finish up on the radical Islam side, Hezbollah, Hamas, Syria, and their relationship to Iran—are you looking at a war here, '07, '08? I mean, this is looking like what happened [in 2006], maybe just the prelude. Whether it's the apocalyptic version that Iran is preparing for, or something intermediate?*

NETANYAHU: No, I don't think [so]. I think a repeat of the Second Lebanon War would only happen if it's in Iran's interest. That is, I think their interest right now is just to proceed to complete their nuclear program, and they don't want anything to interfere with it. So I'm not sure that they would use their proxies—Hezbollah in Lebanon or Hamas in Gaza—to activate another war. That may not be in their interest if they think that such a war could escalate to an armed activity against Iran. So I don't necessarily think that they will pull this lever. On the other hand, they might want to, if pressures accumulate on the Iranian nuclear program [and] they want to deflect pressure.

But on balance, my guess is they'll be very careful right now. They want to concentrate on completing their nuclear program, because once they have that, then they could threaten the West in ways that are unimaginable today. They could take over the Persian Gulf on all its sides and take control of the oil reserves of the world, most of them. They could topple Saudi Arabia and Jordan in short order. And of course, Iraq. All your internal debates in America on Iraq would be irrelevant because [a] nuclear-armed Iran would subordinate Iraq in two seconds. And of course, they threaten to create a second Holocaust in Israel and proceed on their idea of a global empire, producing 25 atomic bombs a year, 250 bombs in a decade, with missiles that they are already working on and they want to develop to reach the eastern seaboard of the United Sates. This is something that just—Everything else pales in comparison to this development. This has to be stopped. For the sake of the world, not only for the sake of Israel.

ROSENBERG: *So is it your assessment that it's very possible that the next war, if it's not launched by the West to stop Iran, will be Iran trying to eradicate Israel?*

NETANYAHU: I don't think necessarily that Iran will go through another exercise with Hezbollah or Hamas. It may ignite itself, but I don't think they'll necessarily ignite it unless they think it helps deflect attention [from] their nuclear program. If, in fact, it draws attention to their nuclear program, that's the last thing they have in mind. In other words, what will happen—because Hezbollah is a wholly owned subsidiary of Iran, and [Hezbollah Secretary-General Hassan] Nasrallah doesn't decide on anything, it's decided in Tehran—whether or not they'll enflame the area is really dependant on Iran's goals. Right now its goal is to turn Lebanon into a second Iran. That's what they're concentrating on. I'm not sure they'd want another exchange with Israel necessarily. They will if they think it helps the Iranian nuclear program. They won't if they don't think that.

ROSENBERG: *We took a survey; we used [McLaughlin & Associates] as our pollster [to survey] American attitudes toward Israel, toward Bible prophecy, [and] 52% of American [Christians] say that they believe the rebirth of Israel in the modern era is a result of Bible prophecy. . . . [In] your own assessment—I mean you, the prime minister of Israel—is Israel* *simply a political re-creation of Political Zionism [or] do you see it also in biblical or prophetic—*

NETANYAHU: Well, I'm not an Orthodox Jew—although I have respect for our traditions. But those traditions have had a tremendous thrust in our history. Because you have to ask yourself, "How is it that the Jews are able to, really, to resist the iron laws of history?" You know, you had a lot of people who were exiled. In fact most peoples of the world were either exiled or conquered. All the ancient nations, most of them, something happened to them that they were dispersed, or they were conquered, or they were decimated. So the Jews were not any different in that sense.

But what is different about the Jews is that they refuse to conform to the patterns of destruction and disappearance that afflicted other nations that were overtaken. And in our dispersal we said year after year, "Next year in Jerusalem." We wanted to come back to this land you see around you. And it's defying of these laws of history with the faith and purpose that we had that enabled us to get back here. So obviously you can't just discount it and say, "Well, it's just a blanket political process." It has enormous reservoirs of faith and hope [without which the rebirth of Israel] would not have [been] possible.

The rebirth of Israel is deeply embedded in our traditions. It's said that the Jewish people, the Jewish exiles, will come back and rebuild their land, their ancestral homeland, here in Israel and create an independent life. And that weaves together both religious and secular traditions in ways that probably are not found anywhere else in the world or in any other people.

That's why it's such a powerful story; it's like a parable. You know, this is why the establishment of America was premised on the story of the people of Israel. This is why the view of the United States, this new America, was called the City on the Hill. Well, the [original] City on the Hill is—If you look outside the window, you'll see those hills. That city is Jerusalem. And this is the fundamental belief, that they can create a new life, really, for an old people in the "old new land," as [Austrian writer Theodor] Herzl called it. This is a very powerful theme that obviously resonated from the Jewish people to many, many others.

There is hope; there is redemption for mankind. And if the Jews can make it, then anybody else can.

ROSENBERG: *So along those lines then—this is the last two questions— Shiites have this end times theology; it's radical. Obviously evangelicals have an end times theology, but Jews as well, from the prophet Ezekiel. Right after he says Israel will be reborn in the future, he also talks about Russia and Iran forming an alliance. That probably can't—those type of prophecies probably don't guide Israeli foreign policy but—*
NETANYAHU: Well, there's a huge difference, and I would be careful to make the analogy between the Judeo-Christian traditions and prophecies and the radical Islamic traditions, for two reasons. One, the radical Islamists have a very violent tradition. In other words, it's not something that will happen, but it will happen by destruction that *we* effect. *We* effect. That is, we—the radical Muslims—should unsheathe our swords and embark on a great jihad of fire and blood, first against nonbelieving Arabs and then against the Muslims, and then against everyone else. That is not present in the evolution of Judeo-Christian theological thinking. Secondly, it's the immediacy of the idea of, you know, of an "End of Days," so to speak. At least in the Jewish tradition, this is something that you strive for; it may not necessarily happen in our time, but it is a day in which people will do—what? What will they do? They won't take their swords and cut off other people's heads. In fact, they'll take their swords and turn them into plows. So it's the exact opposite. It's [not] immediate; it is something to strive [for], and it's a vision of peace, not a vision of apocalyptic war.

These are two traditions which are very different, and I would be very, very, careful in equating the two because they're not the same. In any case, the impact of the Jewish messianic thinking was benign. That is, it was merely an idea that the dispersed Jews would come back and purchase empty lots in a wasteland that was here—what you see around you is basically sand, and bog, and desert. There's nothing. And we basically built it up and never sought to make war with anyone. Including the many Arabs that [came] into this country as a result of the Jewish rebirth. We accepted them too. It's they who didn't accept us. Having immigrated, many of them, into this country as a result of the Jewish restoration. So, it's basically a benign conception of rebirth and redemption, as opposed to a very warlike cult of blood that seeks to destroy. It's construction versus destruction. It's peace versus war. It's beating your swords into plowshares as opposed to beating your plowshares into swords. And it's a very, very different conception.

ROSENBERG: *You are sitting under a picture of Menachem Begin, [who] probably took the lead in building alliances and friendships with evangelicals, but you have really continued that legacy—*
NETANYAHU: Yeah, I did.

ROSENBERG: *Why, and where do we go from here? Where would you like us to go from here?*
NETANYAHU: It's important to understand that the partnership between Jewish Zionists and Christian Zionists is actually over a century and a half old. I don't think it's possible to understand the rebirth and growth of Jewish Zionism without [recognizing] the tremendous backing we had in the Christian world, in Britain and the United States in the nineteenth century. Societies were established to help the Jews come back here. [The writer] Mark Twain visited the Holy Land and wrote rather realistically of the forlorn state of the country, saying that it'll only come back to life when the Jews come back here. Queen Victoria, in England, set up the Palestine Exploration Fund, which was intended to do scientific archeological expeditions to find out the locations of the biblical cities and towns, which, by the way, they did. And they too came to the conclusion that the country will only come back to life when the Jews come back here in great numbers.

And so this was the background of Christian Zionism that presaged Jewish political Zionism by a full half century. And so this is a very deep partnership which I understand, I respect. And today, I see it not merely as a partnership for Israel, that's very clear, but as a partnership for the defense of our common values against those who would obliterate our lives. Initially, the danger came from Soviet totalitarianism. But increasingly, especially after the demise of Communism as a creed, the danger is from militant Islam that seeks to obliterate those values that our traditions hold dear: individual freedom, democratic life, the respect for an individual. These things are anathema to the militant Muslims. It's not so much that they hate the West because of Israel; it's that they hate Israel because of the West. Because we represent to them this hated culture and civilization that they want to annihilate. And of course they hated the West for centuries before the State of Israel was reborn. So I think there is a natural partnership out there with the citizens of all the democracies. Many of them, especially in Europe, they don't get it. Some of them do, especially in Eastern Europe, increasingly they get it. In Western Europe, increasingly they get it. But in the United States, they *get it*. The secular and religious citizens of America, they pretty much get it, and they get it right.

ROSENBERG: *So one follow-up, and I have to ask you. There were tensions for a long time between the followers of Jesus and Jews, though in many ways that's evaporating. But how can we continue to help in the last days? Are there specific ways you'd love to see evangelicals do more?*

NETANYAHU: The transformation that has taken place in the evangelical community is quite impressive. The first transformation is that it doesn't seek to proselytize among the Jews; it seeks to support the state of the Jews. And that is a growing tendency which I think has made a big difference. And secondly, political leaders like myself have said that the greatest partners, the greatest supporters we have are those who view Israel as an asset in itself, who have a deep attachment to it. And unquestionably those include first and foremost the evangelical community which is in the United States, and Northern Europe, and Scandinavia, and probably in seventeen, eighteen countries and growing. And I think that setting aside the theological hairsplitting about what'll happen in the end of days, and focusing on what we have to do in these present days, has been the source of great support.

And I think that this should radiate beyond the evangelical community to [the] non-evangelical community. Because, you know, it's the same thing, when these terrorist bombs of militant Islam hit Israel, they don't distinguish between religious and secular, between left and right. To them, we're all marked for death. And the same thing is true in America. When they slammed into the World Trade Center, they didn't really care who was there. For them, we are all marked for death. So for me, it would be important that this basic partnership today that you see between the evangelical community in the United States and Israel would turn into a broad partnership, which I think it is turning into. Between Americans, period, and Israel because we're in the same boat; we have the same goals and the same values and we're threatened by the same enemies.

NATAN SHARANSKY
Former Deputy Prime Minister of Israel

JOEL ROSENBERG: *How serious is the Iranian nuclear threat, in your assessment?*

NATAN SHARANSKY: I think what makes it so serious is it's nonconventional weapons in the hands of nonconventional government. [Iran's] leaders [view] life in this world only as the introduction to the next world. And their success in the next world depends on how many unfaithful people they will kill in this world and how successful they will be with Small Satan and Big Satan. This is very dangerous. We have to understand that nuclear weapons in the hands of this regime changes not only the chances of Israel for survival, it changes the chances of the Free World. Free World will never be free again. It will never be led by the spiritual freedom of the United States of America or other free nations. It is all about appeasement and how to save your life [by] sacrificing your freedom. That's in fact the challenges of nuclear weapons in the hands of this regime in Iran. And that's why it is the highest moral obligation— moral interest and practical interest of the Free World—to mobilize for two aims: to prevent this regime from having nuclear weapons and to encourage the democratic opposition to replace this regime.

ROSENBERG: *How much time do we have?*

SHARANSKY: I believe that 2007 is the last year to do something.

ROSENBERG: *And if 2008 begins and we haven't done anything?*

SHARANSKY: Then our situation and our opportunities to deal with the problem will be much more limited. You have to understand, I don't want to say that in 2007 Iran can try to use nuclear weapons against Israel, America, or whatever. But I am saying that if this problem will not be solved in 2007, the chances for success later will be far less, and the scope or efforts which have to be undertaken will be simply incomparable.

ROSENBERG: *Mahmoud Ahmadinejad is denying the Holocaust, yet he seems to be preparing for another one. Do you see a scenario in which Iran could get to the point where they're capable of doing in six minutes what it took Hitler six years to do—to kill six million Jews?*

SHARANSKY: I think that for leaders of Iran, there is no problem to launch a new holocaust as long as the holocaust is connected with the right idea. Maybe where they can have disagreement with the Nazi regime [is] that [the Nazis] don't show that it was done for the right idea, to [gain entrance] in the right way to paradise. . . . Another problem [is that a] holocaust can happen only when there are enough people who are ready to think about it, who are not afraid of it, and for whom it is legitimate to kill the others [whom they consider] less than human beings. And it took quite an effort for [the] Nazi regime to create [a] nation where so many people believed that Jews [were] less than human beings; [that it was] okay to view them in [a] different way. In fact there was a whole history of [a] double standard [regarding] Jews which helped. For these leaders of Iran, you don't need [to make] any [such] efforts, [a holocaust is] already justified. For them there is no doubt they have the right and that they are obliged to do it, to do everything in their power to finish with the Satans of this world and to pave the way for the new world of faithful people. In fact, their children study in their schools that all the unfaithful will turn to be Muslims or will disappear from this world.

ROSENBERG: *Why is Russia selling weapons, selling nuclear technology, and building nuclear facilities inside Iran?*

SHARANSKY: All the history of leakage of Russian technologies toward Iran is a very sad story showing how short-range interests can prevail over the strategic thinking; showing how dangerous it is when the regimes are not building the real cooperation built on mutual desire to live in freedom and democracy.

I was sent by Israel in the name of Netanyahu to warn [the] Russians about the dangers of leakage of that technology in January '97. In fact, I was the first minister to start this, and then I happened to be the first former prisoner of conscience in the Soviet Union ever who came back to visit his own prison and then to meet the head of new KGB, [Vladimir] Putin.

For Russia in the beginning, it was all about the markets. They felt that America and the West [were] trying to put them out of the markets, and here where [Russia] can have [an] important market, we have not room to give up. For them it was also belief—once Putin told me, "You'll see even if you don't trust us that we are doing our best to prevent this leakage of technologies. You will see one day that the best technology [is] coming from Europe." And unfortunately to great extent, they happened to be right, that it's not only Russian technologies but very sophisticated German, French, English, Dutch technologies which came through Pakistan to Iran.

But also for Russia today, when they believe that America is not willing to become a very strategic partner, what is important for them today is whether America is really serious about fighting Iran. I remember in the past, when [it] became clear that America [was] striking Iraq, [the Russians] were very critical about this. When they understood that it [was] inevitable, they started seriously discussing with America, thinking, what will be their role? What will be their possible cooperation the day after? But they are thinking that America is not suitable, it's too big. Then all their interest is how to prevent [America's] role in this: how to make clear to Arabs, and to Iran, and to the others, that if America is not strong enough against them it's only because of Russia. So Russia has here economical interests which are shortsighted; they are not taking into account [the] strategic danger of Muslim fundamentalists for Russia itself, but they also—they attempt to play their usual game, how to make best of their relations with America and with Arab countries at the same time. So I think it is very important for America to have clear, big stick and big carrot at the same time. And unfortunately, very often, America doesn't have either of these.

ROSENBERG: *Talk to me a little bit more about your meeting with Putin. . . . When you met with him [in 1997], what was it that you were trying to convey on behalf of the president?*

SHARANSKY: Look, my main message to all the leaders [in] Russia was yes, we want world cooperation . . . and yes, we are interested in all forms of cooperation. But all this will mean nothing if, really, Russia will help Iran to have nuclear weapons and missiles. We were saying . . . that if these policies will continue, the way it goes now, with all the leakage of Russian technologies, with the assistance of the others, in ten years Iran will have missile and bomb. [For us, this is a] question of death and life. That's why all our talks, expressions of friendship and so on, mean nothing. We will fight against this, we will fight against Iran, we will fight against your interest if you will be helping Iran to [acquire nuclear capability]. So the private conversations were respectful but very tough. . . . [They assured me] there [would] be no more leakages. Unforunately, [that] didn't happen. Probably they took care of some of the most obvious leakage of technologies, but in general, cooperation in this field continued, and they [maintain] that the leakage from the West continues [as well].

Putin again and again was saying that he understands—that was my second message—that he understands that [in] the long run, Iranian power in [the] Muslim world can be very dangerous for Russia. . . . On theoretical level, from time to time, it would seem that we are on the same wavelength. [But on a practical level, according to] our intelligence, Russia continued the same policy.

I think Putin never felt confidence that he can build real partnership with the West and with America, which will be protecting his long-range interests. And also he was never sure that America will have enough chutz-pah, if you want, enough strength, really, to fight with Iran if it would be needed. And of course Russia is not going to fight Iran. So I personally believe that the more forceful, the more determined is America, the more there is a chance to get cooperation of Russia in this issue.

ROSENBERG: *However, is it possible that we have passed some point of no return with the Russian and Iranian cooperation? I mean, one could make a case that Russia is building a military alliance with Iran.*

SHARANSKY: Look, I personally believe it's all dysfunctional. Russian leaders are different from Iranian leaders because they are not thinking about the next world. I don't think they believe in the next world. Definitely for them, the real value is this world. . . . They will have different set of policies. Definitely there are forces in each [country] to restrict democracy, and we should not be happy with this. But [the Russian] forces, these people, are much more realistic, much less fanatical, much less fundamental—not fundamentalists like in Iran—and that's why we can play in this difference of interest. . . .

But if we want to [achieve] cooperation on this issue, [Russia] should have no doubts that America is absolutely determined to solve the problem of Iran. [Either] with Russia or without Russia. And the [stronger] the message, the more there is a chance that Russia will be at least passively cooperative with America on this issue.

ROSENBERG: *How determined do you think the United States is to stop Iran at all costs?*

SHARANSKY: I personally think that the president of the United States of America is very determined. But once I told him, during our first meeting, that Mr. President, you are really a dissident [more than a politician] because politicians are [given to posturing]. They are saying and doing many things which are popular. This isn't loyal to the ideas in which they believe. You believe in the ideas of the power of freedom to overcome tyranny and terror. You believe the evilness of the Iranian threat, and you are fighting it. But I want to warn you that dissidents have to be ready to be lonely, and only [in the long term is] history on the side of dissidents.

So my concern is the president is determined but he is very lonely in his determination. And no doubt developments in Iraq didn't make him stronger in implementation of this. I believe this is a threat for all the Free World, not for one or another candidate, not for one or another country, but for all the Free World to remain free. And that's why there is no reason why [the] president should be alone in this. There is no reason why this cause [should] not be [a bi-]partisan cause of Republicans and Democrats. After all, the Soviet Union was defeated in [the] Cold War only when . . . Democrats like Senator [Henry] Jackson or even Edward Kennedy on one hand and Republicans like President Reagan could work together and fight together. So that is [the] type of unity which is needed today.

ROSENBERG: *Let me ask you about—I'm gonna wrap up soon—Christians and Jews—Evangelical Christians, Jews, Israelis—how important are these two communities to work together against Radical Islam?*
SHARANSKY: I think they are natural allies. I tell you, in Soviet prison, I was an activist of two worlds at the same time; I was Zionist, Jewish nationalist, and human rights activist. And some people saw that as contradiction. I was filled with contradiction. In fact, in prison, there were different dissidents of different types: Catholics from Lithuania, and Pentecostals from Siberia, and Russian monarchists, Ukrainian nationalists, Jewish Zionists. Very quickly we [came] to the understanding that we—with all our differences, with all passions, with all our political disagreements, we are all fighting the same struggle, the same war. Our mutual enemy is KGB, and we all want to live in the society where people are not punished for their views. And the secret of your inner power to resist KGB was this feeling or fear of God. Understanding that we are created in the image of God and to remain free people, we have to fight KGB together.

In fact, some of the most moving moments of my imprisonment experience [were those] which I spent with my Christian friend. He was fighting that his Bible would be returned to him; I was fighting to have my Torah to be returned. . . . After many days of hunger strikes, they returned to us our books and we were together once—we started reading. We called it Reagan's ecumenical readings. Why? Because it was just published that Reagan declared that year [1983] the year of [the]

Bible. . . . And we decided that it's because of pressure of Americans that suddenly they are giving us these books. And he start reading key chapter from New Testament, and I from Psalms, we were reading together, and it was very powerful feeling that with all the differences, we are praying to the same God. We are praying to the God in whose image we are created, as free people. And that's what was giving us lot of power.

And I think for people who are so strongly connected today that—and they are connected not with [the] idea that all the other identities have to be erased, that those who don't agree with you aren't faithful and you are paving your way to paradise by killing them, but to the contrary, you believe that you are not doing to others what you don't want to do to yourself. This is the power of people who are believing in freedom. That's why I think it's [a] very natural alliance. I think we have mutual interest and today, the biggest challenge of course is to fight this evil which threatens all of us, people who want to live in freedom.

GENERAL MOSHE YA'ALON
Former Israeli Defense Forces Chief of Staff

JOEL ROSENBERG: *Your assessment that we are in World War III right now—talk to us about that.*

MOSHE YA'ALON: Yes, we are engaged now in World War III, in which radical Islamists—I call them jihadists—[intend] to wipe Israel off the map on their way to defeat the West. They [want] to impose Islam all over the world, either by convincing people or by sword. This is the case with the Iranian ideology, Al-Qaeda ideology, as well as Muslim Brotherhood ideology. And the challenge is for the rest of the world, not just for the State of Israel.

ROSENBERG: *Describe the apocalyptic thinking that's driving Iranian foreign policy.*

YA'ALON: The turning point in history, when it comes to this wave of radical Islam or jihadist ideologies, is 1979—the success of the Iranian Revolution. The Iranian Revolution success inspired and empowered other radical Islamists like Al-Qaeda, Sunni-Wahabi, these Muslims, and Muslim Brotherhood, Sunni Muslims. And Hamas is part of it. They believe they're winning. They believe that they are able to impose Islam all over the world and they feel like they are winning, first of all because of lack of determination on behalf of the West. They feel like they are winning because they believe they defeated the Soviet Union and they are responsible for the Soviet Union collapse as a result of the war in Afghanistan. They feel like they are winning because they feel like they defeated us in Lebanon because of our withdrawal in 2000. They feel like they are winning because we [withdrew] unilaterally from Gaza and they believe that Hamas defeated us. And they feel like they are winning because Iran is the driving force behind this wave [and] the Iranian regime hasn't paid any price for . . . deploying proxies all over the world against Israel [and] against the United States. . . . Going back to the devastating attacks in Beirut, 1983, in which 241 [U.S.] Marines were killed [and] 69 French servicemen were killed—Iran didn't pay any price for it. The Iranian regime didn't pay any price for the two attacks in Argentina against the Israeli Embassy and the Jewish Center in Argentina. The Iranian regime didn't pay any price for . . . killing U.S. servicemen in [the Khobar Towers bombing in] Saudi Arabia in 1996. They didn't pay any price for it.

And they feel like they are winning because [of] the lack of determination regarding the international community, regarding the International Institute [for Strategic Studies], when it comes to their determination to acquire military nuclear capabilities. Violating all understanding and agreements in order to win this kind of capability without paying any price.

And they feel like they are winning because they are behind the scenes. Succeed in destabilizing Iraq, supporting both Sunnis and Shiites to kill each other, to generate the sectarian violence, not to allow stability in Iraq. To allow democratization in Iraq. So they gain confidence because of this lack of determination on behalf of the West.

ROSENBERG: *What is Mahmoud Ahmadinejad's endgame, in your view?*

YA'ALON: It's very clear. Ahmadinejad says what he means and means what he says. He believes in the messianic apocalyptic worldview, in which the Hidden Imam, which is his Islamic messiah, in the end should appear. In the end of the days, when he appears, all the world, all people all over the world, will become Muslims. There is no room for infidels. Neither Jews, nor Christians, Buddhists, whatever. All the world will become Muslim.

But according to his belief . . . he is a messenger of this idea. He should be proactive. . . . And he believes that in two years' time, he might reach it by wiping Israel off the map and defeating the West. And actually, according to his talks, talking about his eighteen-page letter to President Bush, actually recommending him to be converted to Islam, otherwise he may be full of remorse. This is an Islamic expression. According to the jihadist principle, you should offer your enemies—the infidels, non-Muslims—the option to be converted to Islam. When they refuse, then you are allowed to use the sword. And that is his terminology when he speaks [to] Europeans as well [as to] the Jews, Israel. . . . Israel should be wiped off the map on the way to defeat the West. This is not just Israel, it is Europe, it is the United States; the Western culture should be defeated. All the world should become Muslim.

ROSENBERG: *You're a military general; you were the head of the Israeli Defense Forces. What's your military assessment of how much time the West has to make a decision about how to stop Iran?*

YA'ALON: When it comes to the Iranian Military Nuclear Project, it is in terms of a couple of years, might be a couple of months, to reach capabilities. . . . Having said that, even without the bomb, we see [that the] Iranian regime is operating today [by] proxies. In the war in Lebanon, actually Hezbollah was a proxy. Iran was the mastermind. In the military campaign in the Gaza Strip, June 2006, Hamas was a proxy; Iran was the mastermind. When it comes to Iraq, Iran is the mastermind behind the Shia violence as well as part of the Sunni violence today. Iraq equips them with IEDs, improvized explosive devices; terror know-how; weapons; money; to kill each other to avoid stability in Iraq, which is the Western interest. And this is the case when it comes to moderate regimes in our region: Jordan, Egypt, the Russian Gulf States.

The Iranian interest is to gain hegemony and the idea of having military nuclear capabilities. First of all, they use it as an umbrella to blackmail and to undermine those orderly regimes in the region which are linked to the West and act, to their mind, according to Western interest. This is the role of this Iranian regime.

In military terms, they are not so strong. To compare with the Western strengths when it comes to the United States, NATO . . . they are not so strong. But the West [lacks] determination and this is the big one. . . . There are few leaders today who really understand that we are engaged in World War III and try to deploy this kind [of] strategy. President Bush is one of them.

ROSENBERG: *Talk about your experience [with Russia].*

YA'ALON: Russian leadership is playing a very negative role when it comes to Iran. Not just Iran, actually. I know, I was head of intelligence here in Israel. And Russian engineers, Russian experts, were involved in the Iranian Missiles Project, the Shahab Project. Talking about the nuclear reactor in Bushehr, it's very clear, it's Russian assistance. And in the last summer, we faced, in the military campaign in Lebanon, antitank guided weapons provided by Russia to Syria. But the end user was Hezbollah, [the] Iranian arm. Russian interest, to my mind, is first of all to become a player [again] in the superpower games; to become superpower. And as long as they don't have positive assets to play with, they use negative assets to challenge the United States and Israel as well. This is one reason, or one explanation for the Russian support to the Iranian regime.

Another explanation is the kind of understanding between Russia and Iran. We support you when it comes to the military nuclear project and the missiles project. Don't deal with us in our court when it comes to the Islamic former Soviet Union states—Chechnya, Uzbekistan, Kurdistan, and so forth. . . . The Russian government is blackmailed by the Iranian regime. The Iranian regime has proven its capability to support radical Islamic elements, in Chechnya, in Iraq today, in Lebanon, in the Palestinian arena, so they might do it against Russian interest in former Soviet Union Islamic states. It's a kind of modus operandi.

Don't deal with us in our court; we will support you when it comes to your interest, in this case the nuclear capability.

ROSENBERG: *In your view, has Russia therefore joined the axis of evil?*
YA'ALON: It's playing with the axis of evil, yes. Supporting Syria, Iran, is all [leading] to actually challenging the international world order. Denying accountability and operating proxies against Western states— Israel, the United States.

ROSENBERG: *So what has Russia been selling, in terms of military hardware, to Iran?*
YA'ALON: Russian experts actually were involved in the Iranian Shahab, the missile port. And I had the opportunity, as head of intelligence, to meet at that time [with] Russian Foreign Affairs Minister [Yevgeny] Primakov. Fighting proves that Russian engineers and Russian institutes were involved in the Iranian missile port. Actually he denied it. He was interested in my sources, as a former KGB agent. But Russia didn't do anything, and you know the Israeli government asked the Russian government to stop it. And that was the reason that I met Minister Primakov. They didn't hide it; they denied it. But they went on supporting and assisting the Iranian missile port. And this is the case when it comes to the nuclear mission as well. And when it comes to selling arms and anti-guided weapons that we faced in Hezbollah in the last military campaign. And a defense system to Iran, the most sophisticated of defense systems to Iran in the current situation. Yes, this is a Russian interest today.

ROSENBERG: *If Iran gets nuclear weapons and is able to fit their missiles with them, how much time would Israel have from a launch before an impact here?*
YA'ALON: The time is a couple of minutes. The time between launching a missile from Iran to the target Israel, a couple of minutes. It's enough time to deal with it when it comes to our active defensive measure. But it is not the key point. The key point is to prevent Iran, this nonconventional regime, from having a nonconventional plan. This is a noncon-

ventional regime, this messianic, apocalyptic worldview. And it would be a nightmare, not just for us [but] for moderate [states] in the Persian Gulf, Jordan, Egypt. So this is the key point. It's not a military question whether we are able to intercept the missile or not, it's to prevent this kind of capability from this nonconventional regime.

ROSENBERG: *How much time does the West have to make a decision to stop Iran?*

YA'ALON: The decision has to be made as soon as possible. Actually without defeating Iran, there is no way to stabilize Iraq. There is no way to stabilize Lebanon. There is no way to stabilize [the] situation around Israel, in the Palestinian society or anywhere. So it should have been done as soon as possible. The problem is lack of clarity in the West. Actually, Western people are sleeping. People in the West do not feel like they are engaged in World War III. But they are now, attacked. They are under a jihadist defense. Only [a] few leaders understand it. And we need to wake up. We need awakening. Otherwise it will be too late. And because of this lack of clarity, which is lack of clear understanding of situation, lack of moral clarity and lack of clear strategy, [Iran] will go on with a way to challenge us. And we are stronger, when it comes to military might, when it comes to economy. But, yes, they are determined so far, they are determined more than Western like-minded people today.

ROSENBERG: *Last question. Do you see any way to stop Iran from going nuclear?*

YA'ALON: I thought in the past that political isolation and economic sanctions to be imposed on this regime in Iran might be helpful to trigger or to generate the inevitable internal change in Iran. I believe that in the end, we will face internal change in Iran. Today, those who actually avoid political isolation or economic sanction promote the military ops. The confrontation with this regime is inevitable, and it is going to be a military one, rather than political one, because of the lack of determination when it comes to [the] international community to deal with it by political or economic means. And we can't avoid it. Unless we are going to give up our way of life, our values, our culture. And I don't believe that the West is going to give up.

DORE GOLD
Former Israeli Ambassador to the United Nations

JOEL ROSENBERG: *Describe the threat that [Mahmoud] Ahmadinejad poses to Israel, the United States, and the West. I'm talking about the apocalyptic thinking that's driving Iranian foreign policy.*

DORE GOLD: In 1979, it was Ayatollah Khomeini who launched at the time an Islamic revolution in Iran that basically chased out the old shah of Iran and set up an Islamic government. There was tremendous momentum at the time, in the late seventies and early eighties, for this Islamic revolution. It was exported into Bahrain, into Kuwait, into the Shiite areas of Saudi Arabia. But then it lost steam. It continued to support terrorism quietly, but it put up in the front people like [Akbar Hashemi] Rafsanjani and [Mohammad] Khatami, who were the presidents of Iran. With the election of Mahmoud Ahmadinejad at the end of 2005, the old Islamic revolution gained new steam. But in fact, it became much worse. Ahmadinejad comes out of a cult in the Shiite Islamic world, which was actually illegal in Khomeini's time. And this cult believes in the impending return of the Twelfth or Hidden Imam, a kind of messianic savior for the Shiites, who is supposed to come to power in the aftermath of tremendous wars, an Armageddon-type scenario. The danger of Ahmadinejad is that he believes that this apocalyptic scenario can be accelerated by men. And he believes that the destruction of Israel is part of the key first steps to realizing this apocalyptic scenario that will lead to Islamic rule over the whole world.

ROSENBERG: *Ahmadinejad, in your view, is inciting genocide. Talk to me about the case for that.*

GOLD: Well, back in 1948, the international community was concerned with creating new international laws that would prevent another replay of the Holocaust that had just occurred. And it adopted the [Convention on the Prevention and Punishment of the Crime of Genocide]. In the convention, there was an article, known as Article 3, which specifically states that incitement to genocide is a crime under international law. Now this convention has been adopted by most of the countries of the world, including Iran and Israel and, of course, the United States. What Ahmadinejad has been doing, he has been calling to erase Israel off the map of the earth. You cannot erase a country off a map without erasing its people. A number of years ago, right after the genocide in Rwanda, it was discovered that there was a Hutu radio station which was broadcasting genocidal messages to the Hutu population of Rwanda, to kill off the Tutsi population. Once the United Nations set up an international tribunal for trying of various Hutu leaders of Rwanda for war crimes, they also tried individuals for inciting genocide under the genocide convention, so that this convention has been actually used in legal cases against those inciting genocide. The group that I put together here at the Jerusalem Center for Public Affairs firmly believes that Ahmadinejad is violating this article of the genocide convention and ought to be tried by the United Nations or any of its organs as a result.

ROSENBERG: *Talk then about Ahmadinejad denying the Holocaust yet calling for another, essentially.*

GOLD: Well, one of the ironies of the rhetoric of Ahmadinejad is [that] on the one hand, he denies the Holocaust, and yet he seems to be calling for yet another holocaust in order to trigger the return of the lost Imam. It's as though he thinks that if he can get away with Holocaust denial, which is such a patently false assertion, he believes that he can also get away with another holocaust. And so the two seem to be linked.

There's a third aspect, of course, to the whole thing: Ahmadinejad understands that Shiites only make up 15 percent of the Islamic world and he has to reach over the heads of Arab governments to the Arab street. And so he's hoping to use these messages of destroying Israel, of Holocaust denial, to arouse the support of Shiite Iran among the Sunni Arab masses. And therefore, he's engaging in a very dangerous game.

ROSENBERG: *Can't we just say, Ahmadinejad has got hot rhetoric but who really cares; he can't possibly accomplish these objectives of wiping Israel out? Actually, let me back up and ask you, does Ahmadinejad represent a threat only to Israel?*

GOLD: Well, first of all, the best way to look at whether Ahmadinejad is only a threat to Israel is to look at both his intentions and his capabilities. He speaks about a war of Iran against the world of arrogance. Now Persian experts understand that the "world of arrogance" is the West. So his declared intentions seem to be directed at a much larger target than just Israel. But second of all, you have to look at his capabilities. If Ahmadinejad just wanted to wipe out Israel, he would develop a Shahab-3 missile, which they now have operational, that has a 1,300-kilometer range, and he would stop there. Why waste defense budget resources on longer-range missiles? But alas, we see that Ahmadinejad and the Iranian establishment is developing extended-range Shahab-3 missiles that have [a] 2,000-kilometer range, well beyond Israel. They have bought a missile called the BM-25 from North Korea, which comes in two varieties: a 2,700-kilometer missile and a 3,700-kilometer-range missile. It's also known that Iran is determined to achieve space-lift capability—putting a Sputnik in orbit. Now once you have a multistage missile that can put a payload into orbit from some Iranian testing ground, you have the capability of reaching intercontinental-range targets.

Back in 1998, the U.S. Congress, both the Democrats and the Republicans, put together a commission analyzing the vulnerability of the United States to ballistic missile attack from third world countries. This commission, which received material from American intelligence sources and which had bipartisan backing—it was called the Rumsfeld Commission, he headed it at the time—concluded that the Iranians could build an intercontinental-range missile that could strike the eastern seaboard of the United States within five years of making the decision of doing so. And it wouldn't be clear to American intelligence and military leaders that, in fact, the Iranians had [made] that decision. So when you look at the whole development of the Iranian missile program, their procurement of cruise missiles from the Ukraine, their development of multistage missiles down the road, it is clear that Iran is looking far beyond Israel and far beyond Tel Aviv. Their aim is the West as a whole.

ROSENBERG: *What's the furthest city, let's say, in Europe right now, that can be hit by an Iranian missile?*
GOLD: Well, if we are looking at the 2,700-kilometer-range missile or 3,700-kilometer-range missile, I would assert that they could probably strike in the very near future Central Europe, certainly Germany, Italy, Austria.

ROSENBERG: *Talk to me just for a moment, in terms also of capability, about Iran testing, firing SCUD missiles, or missiles off the back of commercial container ships, and the threat that could pose.*
GOLD: There are thousands of container ships moving around the world today as part of international trade. And certainly one of the scenarios that defense officials in the West have considered is the placement of shorter-range missiles, which the Iranians already have, on a container ship near the coastline of the United States or of another Western country, which it might seek to threaten. Just imagine the announcement that there is a container ship afloat, somewhere in the Atlantic Ocean, containing either weapons of mass destruction or containing even short-range missiles. It would certainly set off a panic among many people. And if the United States was considering military action against [Iran at] some point in the future, and the Iranians could boast that they had container ships with missiles, this might forestall action by the U.S. or any of its allies.

ROSENBERG: *Or you could have a first strike.*
GOLD: Certainly a first strike is a physical possibility. The question is how that would fit into the Iranian strategy at that particular period.

ROSENBERG: *Let's go back to Ahmadinejad's Shiite Islamic eschatology. Is that his alone? How widespread is this view that the end of the world is near and that the way to hasten the coming of the Islamic messiah is to launch this annihilating war against Israel?*
GOLD: There is, in fact, a well-developed eschatological literature that

exists not only on the Shiite side of Islam but [also] on the Sunni side of Islam. And one can affect the other. One of the noticeable developments over the last ten years has been the proliferation of sort of cheap books that do not have any accreditation or support from Islamic religious authorities that call for action against the antichrist, in Arabic known as the *dajal*. And we're seeing the proliferation of these books in Jordan, in Egypt, in the Palestinian Authority. They envision sometimes the end of the world, they envision the end of Israel. And what's troubling is that many of these apocalyptic books are runaway best sellers in many Arab countries. And therefore, those who speak about end of times scenarios in Islamic terms have a certain popularity today.

One of the most important individuals in spreading radical Islamic thinking is Yusuf al-Qaradawi, who might be described as the spiritual head of the Muslim Brotherhood. He's Egyptian in origin but now he lives in Qatar. And he has a regular television program on Aljazeera. And there he speaks about everything from U.S. forces in Iraq to how women should be treated in Islam. In my book *The Fight for Jerusalem*, I disclose a talk that al-Qaradawi gave on Aljazeera in which he spoke about a group called, in Arabic, al-Ta'ifa al-Mansura, and this group is a kind of Mahdist group that is supposed to be in Jerusalem for the fight between the Sunni Islamic Mahdi and the antichrist, known as the dajal. The problem for me, and I convey it in my analysis, is that al-Qaradawi believes that this worldwide group, al-Ta'ifa al-Mansura, is already in Jerusalem today. And therefore, they are not seeing these scenarios of the end of days as something that'll occur in one thousand years, but as something that might occur tomorrow, and is something that could be triggered tomorrow.

A second theme that I raise in *The Fight for Jerusalem* is that in Islamic apocalyptic thought, Jerusalem has a special role as triggering global jihad. Back in the times of Saladin, when the crusaders were in control of Jerusalem, there was an Islamic thinker in Damascus who put forward the thesis that if Saladin will retake Jerusalem, Constantinople—now today called Istanbul—the capital of Eastern Christendom, will fall into the hands of Islam. So there is a kind of causality created in Islamic thought between the fall of Jerusalem, the retaking of Jerusalem, and the fall of other centers of Christendom around the West. In fact, much of the apocalyptic thought of al-Qaradawi includes somehow recovering Istanbul yet again, but specifically, the fall of Rome. And, you know, how this exactly physically works, I don't know. But it's certainly expressing itself in the apocalyptic literature, that, again I repeat, is extremely popular today in much of the Islamic world.

ROSENBERG: *And your case is that this is surging—this interest in apocalyptic thinking—in the Islamic world?*
GOLD: If you speak to many Arab intellectuals and you mention these things about apocalyptic thought, they may not know what you're talking about. But if you check book sales in bookstores, or in various countries—in Egypt, in Jordan, in the Palestinian Authority—you'll find much of this literature to be very popular. Again, even though it does not have the backing of Islamic religious authorities.

ROSENBERG: *Talk to me about why Russia, under Vladimir Putin, is selling nuclear technology to Iran. Walk me through the series of actions that Russia is taking to strengthen Iran.*
GOLD: When I served under Prime Minister Benjamin Netanyahu, we were aware at the time that Iran was receiving missile technology from the Russians. We thought this was insane policy. And in fact, many in the Israeli government and in the Clinton administration warned the Russians that this activity was going on. Today you also have the issue of nuclear technology. There's the Bushehr reactor along the Persian Gulf, where the Russians have been very active in selling technology. Now one thesis, of course, put forward to understand the Russian policy, is that the Russians need money and nuclear reactors are one of the best export items in their sort of arsenal of exports.

I have my own personal feeling, or personal view, that I can't prove, but it's one of those intuitions. The Russians understand that they are increasingly at war with radical Sunni Islam. And it is perhaps their hope that they can divide the Islamic world between the Shiites and the Sunnis; they can help a Shiite radical government, and somehow that will serve their interests, while they fight in Chechnya against Sunni radicals that are funded by wealthy businessmen in Saudi Arabia and in the Gulf. But I think it's a mistake in policy, because frequently, when you start feeding one part of radical Islam, the other part gets fed as well.

ROSENBERG: *List for me some of the types of weapon systems that Russia has been selling. It's my understanding we're talking about anti-missile systems, submarines, obviously nuclear technology.*

GOLD: One of the surprising Russian sales to Iran back in the 1990s were Kilo class submarines, which the Iranian navy has now deployed. It's clear that the Iranians have generally invested in two areas of their military capability. Number one, their naval forces. And number two, their missile and potential nuclear forces. If you look at the Iranian air force, the Iranian ground forces, they've actually suffered a number of setbacks and are not as equipped as they were in the past. Now the Iranian interest at this point is to make sure that the Persian Gulf becomes a Persian lake—one where they will have naval dominance. And even though the U.S. Navy puts carriers and battleship groups into the Gulf, the Iranians have experience using small speed boats with revolutionary guards, who are willing to shoot anti-ship missiles, either bought from China or from other sources, against the U.S. Navy. That's one scenario.

The second scenario has to do with the Russian contribution to the Iranian missile program. The Iranian missile program certainly has been built around North Korean technology, but there is a kind of movement with missile technology that begins in Russia, reaches North Korea, and comes back to Iran. And that is the sort of loop that we are suffering from today. If the Russians would cut back their assistance to the missile programs of Iran and to the nuclear program of Iran, I think the world would be in much better shape.

ROSENBERG: *One of the cases that I make in* Epicenter *is that Russia, by selling arms and nuclear technology to Iran, has joined the axis of evil. Is it a fair assessment to make at this point, that Russia—under Putin—has joined the axis of evil?*

GOLD: Well, what has happened is that Russian policy may have gone further than the Russians intended or were prepared to go. For example, when Russian antitank missiles . . . were sold to Syria or sold to Iran and ended up in the hands of Hezbollah, we saw advanced weapons now in the hands of an international terrorist organization. And what is likely is that if Russia continues its policy, it will in effect be supplying organizations which are viewed as terrorist organizations by most of the international community. That would be a sad development for Russia; it would make it very difficult to develop an international standard for fighting terrorist organizations, which ultimately hurt Russia itself.

ROSENBERG: *Is it your assessment that Putin is building a military alliance with Iran?*

GOLD: I think Russian policy is torn today. On the one hand, the Russians are concerned with the rise of radical Islam, which is spreading beyond Chechnya and Pakistan to much of the upper Volga regions of Russia. And the threat is a real threat to the future existence of the Russian Federation. That should put Putin alongside of President George W. Bush as an ally on the war on terrorism. But on the other hand, there is an old establishment in Russian military circles and in Russian intelligence circles that would like to see Russia assume the great power status of the Soviet Union. The Russians no longer have a strong position in Eastern Europe. Eastern European countries are now joining the EU or joining NATO, and therefore the only area for Russian expansion to recover its great power status is Iran and the Middle East. But if Russia attempts to recover the great power status of the Soviet Union by means of expansion into the central Middle East and towards Iran, it will ultimately be hurting itself as well as linking up with the axis of evil.

ROSENBERG: *Last question for you. Given the threat of radical Islamic eschatology, Ahmadinejad—take just the last few moments here to talk about how evangelicals and Israel can and should be working together—if your view is that they should be. . . . It seems like we have a common enemy, so how do we deal with it by uniting?*

GOLD: You know back in the second century, the Jewish people were facing a terrible threat from the Roman Empire. And in fact at the time, according to Dio Cassius, the Roman historian, the Jews and early Christians may have worked together to defeat the oppression of imperial Rome, which was threatening both Christianity—early Christianity—and threatening the future of Judaism. What's necessary in international relations is a capacity to draw [a] distinction between good and evil, between those who support security and peace and those who wish to undermine it. And what Jewish values and Christian values provide is an ability to make that distinction. And therefore, the alliance that we once had back in the second century is an alliance which should be restored again today. . . .

There is a terribly mistaken belief that is widespread in many intellectual circles in the United States and especially in Europe that somehow, if Israel will undertake further withdrawals in the Israeli-Palestinian peace process, that this will lower the flames of radical Islam. My analysis in *The Fight for Jerusalem* is that rather than lower the flames of radical Islam, further withdrawals would actually elevate those flames. And Israel has real experience; we withdrew from Lebanon in the year 2000 and [we] got the [al-Aqsa] Intifada, Arafat's attacks against Israel, in return. Israel withdrew from the Gaza Strip in 2005, and we got a Hamas election victory in 2006 and the entry of Al-Qaeda into the Gaza Strip in return. The assertion I put forward in *The Fight for Jerusalem* is that—given the widespread nature of Islamic apocalyptic thought, which pins on Jerusalem a crucial role in the launching of a new global jihad—if Israel would withdraw from parts of the Old City of Jerusalem, we would set off a terrorist tsunami that would spread well beyond the Middle East to the heart of Western Europe and even to the United States. And therefore Jerusalem has to be treated very specially. Only a free and independent Israel can protect Jerusalem as a city that will be open to all faiths. That should be the policy, in my judgment, of every country in the Western alliance, and it certainly should be the policy of the State of Israel.

ENDNOTES

EPICENTER 2.0: INTRODUCTION TO THE SOFTCOVER EDITION

1. Hanan Greenberg, "Halutz: Abducted Soldier Alive," Ynet News, June 25, 2006.
2. For more, see Joel C. Rosenberg, "Reporters and Politicians Ask: Are These the End Times?", joelrosenberg.blogspot.com, weblog, July 23, 2006.
3. Associated Press, "Ahmadinejad: Israel pushed self-destruct button in Lebanon," July 28, 2006.
4. Aviram Zino and Roni Sofer, "Winograd: Political, Military Leadership Failed during War," Ynet News, January 30, 2008.

INTRODUCTION: ALL EYES ON THE EPICENTER

1. Nora Boustany, "For Arab World, a Sea Change," *Washington Post*, August 19, 1990.
2. Nadia Abu el-Magd, "Egypt Ponders Regional Role After War," Associated Press, May 7, 2003. Other examples: In April 2003, Israeli Military Chief of Staff Moshe Ya'alon told senior Israeli commanders that the Middle East was "undergoing a political earthquake . . . that would take months, and possibly years, before the full effects are realized." See "Israeli Security Perceptions to Change After Iraq War," *Voice of Israel Radio/BBC Worldwide Monitoring*, April 14, 2003. In his March 8, 2005, column in the *New York Times*, David Brooks wrote of "political earthquakes now shaking the Arab world." Steve Forbes wrote in his "Fact and Comment" column in *Forbes* magazine on March 28, 2005, "Our overthrow of Saddam Hussein and the resultant elections in Iraq have set off a political earthquake: elections in Afghanistan that extended the vote to women; free elections in Iraq; a free presidential election among the Palestinians, with the winner pleading for an end to violence and negotiating deals with Israel; a popular uprising in Lebanon; and Egypt's President Hosni Mubarak suddenly calling for a free presidential election when his term expires."
3. Agence France-Presse, "Hardline Win in Iran Sparks Fears on Nukes and Extremism," June 25, 2005.
4. Search of the Lexis-Nexis news database conducted on February 21, 2006.
5. President Mahmoud Ahmadinejad, address to the United Nations General Assembly

(speech, New York, September 17, 2005), translated and distributed by the Islamic Republic News Agency, posted on www.globalsecurity.org.

6. Golnaz Esfandiari, "President Sees Light Surrounding Him," Iran Press Service, November 29, 2005.

7. Iranian president Mahmoud Ahmadinejad, text of address to Tehran conference, reported by the Iranian Students News Agency, October 26, 2005, cited by the Middle East Media Research Institute, Special Dispatch Series No. 1013, October 28, 2005.

8. See Reuters, "Iran Says It Joins Nuclear Club,"April 12, 2006. See also Amos Harel, "MI Chief Warns That Iran Will Produce Nuclear Bombs by 2010," *Haaretz*, May 10, 2006; Agence France-Presse, "Iran 2–3 Years from Nuclear Bomb," April 11, 2006; Con Coughlin, "Iran 'Could Go Nuclear within Three Years,'" *Daily Telegraph* (London), January 16, 2006; Bloomberg News, "Iran Could Produce Nuclear Bomb in 16 Days, U.S. Says," April 12, 2006.

9. John Mintz, "U.S. Called Unprepared for Nuclear Terrorism," *Washington Post*, May 3, 2005.

10. Graham Allison, *Nuclear Terrorism: The Ultimate Preventable Catastrophe* (New York: Times Books, 2004). See excerpts in Graham Allison, "Nuclear Terrorism," *Blueprint* magazine, Democratic Leadership Council, October 7, 2004.

11. See Associated Press, "Iran Leader: Israel Will Be Annihilated," April 14, 2006. See also Chris Brummitt, "Iran Leader Calls Israel an 'Evil Regime,'" Associated Press, May 11, 2006.

12. President George W. Bush, State of the Union Address (speech, United States Capitol, Washington DC, January 29, 2002).

13. Glenn Kessler, "Bush Says U.S. Would Defend Israel Militarily," *Washington Post*, February 2, 2006.

14. Edmund Blair, "Bush Won't Rule Out Nuclear Strike on Iran," Reuters, April 18, 2006.

15. Sen. John Kerry, for example, said during the September 30, 2004, presidential debate that "Iran is moving toward nuclear weapons and the world is more dangerous." (http://www.debates.org/pages/trans2004a.html). His campaign Web site stated that "a nuclear armed Iran is an unacceptable risk to the national security of the United States and our allies in the region" (http://www.globalsecurity.org/military/library/report/2004/kerry_natl-security-plans_strategy.htm). Sen. John Edwards told the *Washington Post* in an interview published August 30, 2004, that "a nuclear Iran is unacceptable for so many reasons, including the possibility that it creates a gateway and the need for other countries in the region to develop nuclear capability—Saudi Arabia, Egypt, potentially others" (http://www.washingtonpost.com/wp-dyn/articles/A45216-2004Aug29.html). Sen. Joe Lieberman delivered a speech in Munich on February 5, 2006, warning, "Iran will test us all. If we ignore the threat it poses, or cover it with endless and hopeless negotiations, we will regret it" (http://lieberman.senate.gov/newsroom/release.cfm?id=251200).

16. Senator Hillary Clinton, address to the American Israel Public Affairs Committee annual conference (speech, May 24, 2005), http://clinton.senate.gov/~clinton/speeches/2005524910.html.

17. John Zogby, "Zogby: 66% Say Iran A Threat To U.S." (e-mail alert from Zogby. com, based on poll by John Zogby). See http://www.zogby.com/news/ReadNews.dbm?ID=1109.

18. Agence France-Presse, "Khatami Warns U.S. of 'Burning Hell' as Iran Marks Islamic Revolution," February 10, 2005.

19. See "Tehran Threatens West with Homicide Attacks," *Sunday Times*, April 16, 2006; see also Ali Nouri Zadeh, "Iran's Secret Plan if Attacked by U.S. Codenamed 'Judgment Day,'" *Asharq Al-Awsat*, April 27, 2006.

20. Associated Press, "Russia Agrees To $1 Billion Arms Deal With Iran," December 2, 2005.
21. Anton LaGuardia, et al., "We Will Use Force, Blair Warns Iranians," *Daily Telegraph*, October 28, 2005. See also Philip Webster, "Blair Hints at Military Action after Iran's 'Disgraceful' Taunt," *Times* (London), October 28, 2005.
22. Hilary Leila Krieger, "Olmert: Ahmadinejad Is a Psychopath," *Jerusalem Post*, April 29, 2006.
23. "Peres: 'Ahmadinejad Represents Satan,'" *CNN.com*, April 15, 2006.
24. Transcript, NBC's *Meet The Press*, April 2, 2006.

CHAPTER 1: PREDICTING THE FUTURE

1. President George W. Bush, State of the Union Address (speech, United States Capitol, Washington, DC, January 29, 2002).
2. Associated Press, "3 Americans Killed in Gaza Blast," October 15, 2003.
3. Paul Bedard, "Washington Whispers: Modern Nostradamus," *U.S. News & World Report*, November 3, 2003.
4. Associated Press, "Gunfight at Arafat Mourning Tent," November 14, 2004.
5. Asia News, "Civil War Looms over Palestine After Arafat's Death," November 15, 2004; Arutz Sheva, "Rival Gangs Violently Vie for Control in PA," *IsraelNationalNews.com*, November 15, 2004. See also Daniel Pipes, weblog, "Palestinian Anarchy, Post-Arafat," November 14, 2004.
6. Agence France-Presse, "Palestinian PM Called for End to 'Armed Chaos,'" November 18, 2004.
7. See "Bush Pledges to Spread Democracy," CNN, January 20, 2005; Peter Baker and Michael A. Fletcher, "Bush Pledges to Spread Freedom: Global Focus on Rights Would Be a Shift in Policy," *Washington Post*, January 21, 2005; Barbara Ferguson, "Bush Again Calls for Democracy in Middle East," Arab News, February 4, 2005; "Rice Calls for Mid-East Democracy," BBC News, June 20, 2005. See also Joel C. Rosenberg, "Two Great Dissidents: Natan Sharansky's Vision, and President Bush's," *National Review Online*, November 19, 2004.
8. Joel C. Rosenberg, interview by Sean Hannity, *Sean Hannity Show*, June 24, 2005.
9. Henry Meyer, "Putin Amendment May Allow Third Term," Associated Press, June 24, 2005.
10. See Agence France-Presse, "'Street Sweeper' Ahmadinejad Promises New Era for Iran," June 24, 2005; Associated Press, "Ahmadinejad Vows Strong Islamic Iran After Election Triumph," June 25, 2005; BBC News, "Iran Hardliner Sweeps to Victory," June 25, 2005; Roxana Saberi, "Iran's New Leader Vows to Restart Nuclear Program," National Public Radio, June 27, 2005.
11. See John Daniszewski, "Hard-Liner Wins Decisively in Iran Presidential Election; Ahmadinejad's victory signals the return of an Islamic fundamentalist government and is likely to alter the dynamic in nuclear negotiations," *Los Angeles Times*, June 25, 2005; see also Kathy Gannon, "Iran's New Leader to Pursue Nuclear Plans," Associated Press, June 27, 2005.
12. Vladimir Isachenkov, "Putin Offers Iran's President-Elect to Continue Nuclear Cooperation," Associated Press, June 25, 2005.
13. Associated Press, "Novel Written By Saddam to Be Published," June 24, 2005.

CHAPTER 2: THE GENESIS OF JIHAD

1. To better understand the case he was making at the time, see Natan Sharansky, "'Too Eager to Close the Deal," *New York Times*, June 6, 2000; Natan Sharansky, "No Justice, No Peace," *Wall Street Journal*, July 6, 2000; Natan Sharansky, "And Israel's Task," *Washington Post*, July 30, 2000.

2. Daniel Klaidman and Jeffrey Bartholet, "The Fate of Jerusalem," *Newsweek* cover story, July 24, 2000.

3. Statement by Natan Sharansky, July 25, 2000.

4. Putin served as head of the FSB—*Federal'naya Sluzhba Bezopasnosti Rossiyskoi Federatsii*—from July 1998 to August 1999 and was then promoted by Boris Yeltsin to the role of Russia's prime minister.

5. See articles and studies by Joel C. Rosenberg: "Land of Promise: Restoring Israel's Economic Miracle," *Policy Review* (Fall 1991; Joel C. Rosenberg with Edward L. Hudgins, "Economic Reform, Not Loan Guarantees, Israel's Only Path to Prosperity," *Heritage Backgrounder* #881, The Heritage Foundation, February 13, 1992 ; "Still Time to Say No," *Jerusalem Post*, August 10, 1992; "Why Economic Growth Is Critical to Arab Israeli Peace," *Heritage Backgrounder* #920, The Heritage Foundation, November 5, 1992; "Economics and the Middle East," *Journal of Commerce*, November 25, 1992.

6. Tim LaHaye, *The Coming Peace In The Middle East* (Grand Rapids: Zondervan, 1984), 9.

7. For 1948 data, see Israel Ministry of Foreign Affairs "Independence Day" press release, April 25, 2004. For current data, see Israel Central Bureau of Statistics press release, "The Population of Israel Has Reached About 7 Million," October 2, 2005 (actual number: 6,955,000). For future projections, see analysis by the Jewish Policy Planning Institute, cited by Amiram Barkat, "Greater TA Replaces NY As World's Largest Jewish City," *Haaretz*, January 17, 2006.

8. Jon Felder, "Focus on Israel: Israel's Agriculture in the 21st Century," Israel Ministry of Foreign Affairs, December 24, 2002, 2. See also *Statistical Abstract of Israel: 2005*, Agriculture section, chart 19.19, 654.

9. "Country Studies: Israel," Agriculture section, U.S. Library of Congress, countrystudies. us/israel/76.htm.

10. Jon Felder, "Focus on Israel: Israel's Agriculture in the 21st Century," Israel Ministry of Foreign Affairs, December 24, 2002.

11. Ibid.

12. *Statistical Abstract of Israel: 2005*, Agriculture section, chart 19.19, 654.

13. Ibid.

CHAPTER 3: CONNECTING THE DOTS

1. It was widely reported by the international media and interpreted in capitals around the world that Sharon's stroll across the Temple Mount sparked spontaneous Arab protests. But even top Palestinian officials later acknowledged the "Al-Aksa Intifada," as it came to be known, had been carefully planned and shrewdly orchestrated. "Whoever thinks the intifada broke out because of the despised Sharon's visit to the Al-Aksa Mosque is wrong," Palestinian communications minister Imad Al-Faluji told an Arab newspaper in the spring of 2001. "This intifada was planned in advance, ever since President Arafat's return from the Camp David negotiations." Another Arafat advisor told a French newspaper that "a few days before the Sharon visit to the mosque . . . Arafat requested that we be ready to initiate a clash." Indeed, a closer look at official Palestinian media in the days and even months leading up to Sharon's visit revealed such preparations. See Dore Gold, publisher, "One Year of Yasser Arafat's Intifada: How It Started and How It Might End," *Jerusalem Issue Brief*, 1, no. 4, Jerusalem Center for Public Affairs (October 1, 2001).

2. See "Palestinian Violence and Terrorism Since September 2000," Fact Sheet, Israel Ministry of Foreign Affairs, www.mfa.gov.il (accessed March 2, 2006); Martin Asser, "Lynch Mob's Brutal Attack," BBC News, October 12, 2000; "Attack on USS Cole," U.S. State Department fact sheet, www.usinfo.state.gov (accessed March 2, 2006).

See also, "Will Saddam Hussein Attack Israel?" Special Dispatch Series No. 136, Middle East Media Research Institute, October 13, 2000; "U.S. Calls Iraqi Troop Movement 'All Show,'" CNN, October 12, 2000; "Hammurabi Division (Armored) [History]," www.globalsecurity.org (accessed March 3, 2006); Frank Gardner, "Saddam Threatens Israel," BBC News, October 4, 2000.

3. See "Suicide and Other Bombing Attacks in Israel Since the Declaration of Principles (September 1993)," Fact Sheet, Israel Ministry of Foreign Affairs, www.mfa.gov.il (accessed March 2, 2006).

4. Arutz 2 [Israeli media], "Netanyahu: Barak's concessions will destroy the country," July 24, 2000.

5. "Sharon Wins Landslide Victory," CNN, February 7, 2001.

6. Ibid.

7. Benjamin Netanyahu, *Fighting Terrorism; How Democracies Can Defeat the International Terrorist Network* (New York: Farrar, Straus & Giroux, 1995), 96. Note: The publisher rereleased the book in late 2001, with a new foreword by the author, following the terrorist attacks on the World Trade Center and the Pentagon.

8. Ibid., 126.

9. Ibid., 125.

10. Netanyahu's book was updated in 2000 and retitled *A Durable Peace: Israel and Its Place among the Nations.*

11. Benjamin Netanyahu, *A Durable Peace: Israel and Its Place among the Nations* (New York: Warner, 1993 and 2000), 135.

12. Ibid., 136.

13. See Judith S. Yaphe, statement to the National Commission on Terrorist Attacks upon the United States (commonly known as the 9/11 Commission), July 9, 2003. Yaphe served for twenty years as a CIA analyst, specializing in the Middle East. She now works with the National Defense University in Washington, DC.

CHAPTER 4: THE THIRD LENS

1. Cited by Steven Komarow and Tom Squitieri, "NORAD Had Drills of Jets As Weapons," *USA Today*, April 18, 2004.

2. Condoleezza Rice, testimony before the 9/11 Commission, May 19, 2004, transcript by CNN.

3. Richard Armitage, testimony before the 9/11 Commission, March 24, 2004, transcript by CNN.

4. See Peter Jennings, *America Strikes Back*, ABC News Special, transcript, September 21, 2001.

5. Tom Kean, et al., *Final Report of the National Commission on Terrorist Attacks upon the United States*, Executive Summary, "General Findings," 7, www.9-11commission.gov/report/911Report_Exec.htm (accessed February 27, 2006).

6. Nick B. Williams Jr. and Daniel Williams, "Iraq Threatens Israel with Use of Nerve Gas," *Los Angeles Times*, April 3, 1990.

7. Jill Smolowe, "Sword of the Arabs," *Time* magazine, June 11, 1990.

8. Andrew McEwen, "Experts Believe Iraq Will Stop Short of Invasion," *Times* (London), July 26, 1990.

9. Michael Wines, "U.S. Says Bush Was Surprised by the Iraqi Strike," *New York Times*, August 5, 1990.

10. Ibid.

11. Rowan Scarborough, "CIA, Defense Saw Different Aims in Buildup," *Washington Times*, August 3, 1990.

12. The points that follow are from Brian Shellum, *A Chronology of Defense Intelligence in the*

Gulf War: A Research Aid for Analysts, Defense Intelligence Agency, July 1997. See the National Security Archive, George Washington University, www.gwu.edu/~nsarchiv/ (accessed on March 1, 2006).

13. Gershom Gorenberg, *The End of Days: Fundamentalism and the Struggle for the Temple Mount* (New York: Free Press, 2000, updated in 2002), 1–4, 223.

14. Bill Moyers, speech accepting the Global Environmental Citizen Award, Harvard University Center for Health and the Global Environment, New York City, December 1, 2004.

15. Kevin Phillips, *American Theocracy: The Peril and Politics of Radical Religion, Oil, and Borrowed Money in the 21st Century* (New York: Viking, 2006), 252–255 and vii, respectively.

16. Survey for Joel C. Rosenberg, "American Attitudes toward Bible Prophecy," National Omnibus Survey, conducted by McLaughlin & Associates on February 13, 2006, of 1,000 likely voters. Margin of error +/- 3%. See appendix for more survey results.

CHAPTER 5: ISRAEL DISCOVERS MASSIVE RESERVES OF OIL, GAS

1. Tim LaHaye, *The Coming Peace in the Middle East* (Grand Rapids, Mich.: Zondervan, 1984), 105.

2. Cited in "Moses' Oily Blessing," *The Economist,* June 18, 2005.

3. William A. Orme Jr., "Gas Deposits off Israel and Gaza Opening Vision of Joint Ventures," *New York Times,* September 15, 2000.

4. William A. Orme Jr., "Arafat Hails Big Gas Find off the Coast of Gaza Strip," *New York Times,* September 28, 2000.

5. Ross Dunn, "Israeli Geologist Drills for Oil Based on Biblical Guidance," VOA/Israel Faxx, November 20, 2002.

6. "Oil Traces Found East of Kfar Sava," *Haaretz,* September 12, 2003.

7. Associated Press, "Israeli Oil Company Claims Oil Find Valued at US $6 Billion," May 4, 2004. Luskin told reporters that he believed "about 20 percent [of the reserves] are commercially exploitable," though he cautioned that much more testing had to be done and said "the company would need to raise between US $20 million and US $50 million to develop the find." See also Amiram Cohen, "Givot Olam Drills Afresh at Kfar Sava," *Haaretz,* November 23, 2004, which notes, "Based on rock properties of the Meged 4 site, Givot Olam calculated that each square kilometer of the oil structure contains approximately 5 million barrels of oil, which translates into a total of 980 million barrels of oil at the site."

8. "Moses' Oily Blessing," *The Economist,* June 18, 2005.

9. Tovia Luskin, personal interview with author, March 22, 2006.

10. Spillman's son, Steve, recently updated the book. See James R. Spillman and Steven M. Spillman, *Breaking the Treasure Code: The Hunt for Israel's Oil* (Medford, Oregon: True Potential Publishing, 2005; original copyright 1981), 3–4.

11. The abbreviation "G_d" is included in Zion Oil's mission statement as a gesture of respect to Orthodox Jews, who traditionally do not write the name of God.

12. Spillman, 2005 ed., 134–35.

13. Philip Mandelker, personal interview with the author, November 14, 2005. Among the other companies that recently have been pursuing oil and/or gas exploration (some with a biblical perspective, but not all): Avner Oil Exploration, based in Israel; BG (formerly British Gas), based in Great Britain; Delek Group, based in Israel; Ginko Oil Exploration Ltd. (which estimated in 2004 that there were some 20 billion barrels of oil in the Dead Sea basin), based in Israel; Isramco, based in Texas; Ness Energy Inc., based in Texas; Lapidoth Israel Oil Prospectors, based in Israel; Modii Energy, based in Israel; and Sdot Neft, based in Israel.

14. Shlomy Golovinski, "Israel, the Home of the Millionaire," *Haaretz*, June 15, 2005.
15. Amy Teibel, "Buffet Pays $4B For Stake In Israeli Firm," Associated Press, May 9, 2006.
16. See "Investing in Israel" and "Venture Capital in Israel," Updates, Israeli Ministry of Industry, Trade and Labor, www.moit.gov.il (accessed March 15, 2006).
17. Ibid.
18. The Israel Center dinner was held on June 27, 2005. See www.icsep.org.il for details (accessed on March 15, 2006).

CHAPTER 6: TREATIES AND TRUCES LEAVE ISRAELIS MORE SECURE THAN EVER BEFORE

1. Joel C. Rosenberg, "For Real?" *National Review Online*, February 9, 2005.
2. Total attacks in 2001: 7,634. Total attacks in 2005: 2,365. Suicide bombings specifically have dropped from a peak of 60 in 2002 to 7 in 2005. See "Palestinian Terrorism in 2005," Intelligence and Terrorism Information Center, Center for Special Studies (Israel), December 31, 2005, 17; www.intelligence.org.il (accessed March 16, 2006).
3. Major General Yaakov Amidror, personal interview with author, June 8, 2005.
4. Joel C. Rosenberg, "Pakistan Moves toward Ties with Israel after Gaza Pullout," joelrosenberg.blogspot.com, weblog, September 10, 2005.
5. Arieh O'Sullivan, "Halutz: Sanctions Won't Deter Iran," *Jerusalem Post*, November 21, 2005.
6. Ted Koppel, conversation with author, February 23, 2004. For more on my conversation with Koppel about *The Passion of the Christ*, see Joel C. Rosenberg, "Koppel Tackles *The Passion*," *National Review*, February 24, 2004.
7. The other Palestinian participants in the *Nightline* broadcast from Jerusalem were Hanan Ashrawi and Dr. Haidar Abdel Shafi.
8. Shimon Peres, personal interview with author, November 16, 2005.
9. Saeb Erekat, personal interview with author, November 16, 2005.
10. Dean Yates, "Olmert Sees Final Israeli Borders by 2010," Reuters, March 9, 2006. See also BBC News, "Olmert Vows to Set Final Borders," February 13, 2006. For Mofaz quote, see Yaakov Katz, "Mofaz Presents Israel's Final Borders," *Jerusalem Post*, March 21, 2006. See also Associated Press, "Israel Offers Outline to Divide Jerusalem," May 4, 2006.
11. Yates, "Olmert Sees Final Israeli Borders by 2010," Reuters, March 9, 2006.
12. Akiva Eldar, "Abu Mazen to Israel: 'Let's Discuss the End of the Conflict,'" *Haaretz*, March 24, 2006.
13. Khaled Abu Toameh, "Arafat Enraged at Being Called 'Incompetent' by PA Minister," *Jerusalem Post*, September 12, 2003.
14. General Nasser Youssef, interview with the author at an American Enterprise Institute event on June 6, 2006.
15. Abdul Salam al-Majali, interview with the author at an American Enterprise Institute event on June 6, 2006. For more, see Dan Diker and Pinchas Inbari, "Are There Really Signs of a Jordanian-Palestinian Reengagement?" Jerusalem Issue Brief, vol. 5, no. 1, Jerusalem Center for Public Affairs, July 19, 2005.

CHAPTER 7: A CZAR RISES IN RUSSIA, RAISING FEARS OF A NEW COLD WAR

1. Voltaire, *The Portable Voltaire* (paperback), ed. Ben Ray Redman (New York: Viking Penguin, 1977), 101.
2. Ibid.
3. Flavius Josephus, *Josephus: The Complete Works*, trans. William Whiston (Nashville: Nelson, 1998), 41, citing *Antiquities*, Book One, chapters 5 and 6.
4. See article, "Scythian," *The Encyclopedia Britannica*, online edition, www.britannica.com (accessed March 17, 2006).

5. William Gesenius, *Gesenius' Hebrew-Chaldee Lexicon to the Old Testament* (Boston, [n.d.]), quoted in Tim LaHaye, *The Coming Peace in the Middle East* (Grand Rapids: Zondervan, 1984), 123.

6. Arno C. Gaebelein, *The Prophet Ezekiel: An Exposition* (Neptune, New Jersey: Loizeaux Brothers, 1918), 258, cited from the 1972 edition.

7. J. Dwight Pentecost, *Things to Come: A Study in Biblical Eschatology* (Grand Rapids: Zondervan, 1958), 328.

8. Among the Bible scholars: C. I. Scofield, editor of the *Scofield Reference Bible,* wrote in 1909: "That the primary reference is to the Northern (European) powers headed by Russia, all agree. . . . The reference to Meshech and Tubal (Moscow and Tobolsk) is a clear mark of identification." Dr. Charles Ryrie, editor of the *Ryrie Study Bible,* wrote in the 1995 edition: "Magog was identified by Josephus as the land of the Scythians, the region North and Northeast of the Black Sea and East of the Caspian Sea (now occupied by three members of the Commonwealth of Independent States: Russia, the Ukraine, and Kazakhstan)." Dr. John Walvoord, the late Chancellor of Dallas Theological Seminary and widely considered one of the leading prophecy experts of the twentieth century, wrote in 1990 in *Every Prophecy of the Bible*: "If Ezekiel 38–39 is studied carefully, it reveals a future invasion of the land of Israel by the armies of Russia. . . . In the quarter of a century since World War II Russia has risen to be one of the great military powers of the modern world. To a far greater extent than ever before Russia has become a prominent nation, especially in its influence on the Middle East. The possibility of Russia attacking Israel is a modern concern of the United States and other nations." Dr. Tim LaHaye, arguably the world's preeminent prophecy expert, and coauthor (with Jerry Jenkins) of the phenomenally successful Left Behind series (over 62 million copies sold), wrote in 1984 in *The Coming Peace in the Middle East*: "Magog is an ancient name for the nation now known as Russia. . . . The name 'Moscow' derives from the tribal name 'Meschech,' and 'Tobolsk,' the name of the principal state, from 'Tubal.' The noun 'Gog' is from the original tribal name 'Magog,' which gradually became 'Rash,' then 'Russ,' and today is known as 'Russia.'" Hal Lindsey, author of the nonfiction best seller *Late Great Planet Earth* (over 15 million copies sold), wrote in 1970: "For centuries, long before the current events could have influenced the interpreter's ideas, men have recognized that Ezekiel's prophecy about the northern commander [Gog] referred to Russia." Lindsey cited Dr. John Cumming, who wrote in 1864, "The king of the North I conceive to be the autocrat of Russia . . . that Russia occupies a place, and a very momentous place, in the prophetic word has been admitted by almost all expositors." Lindsey also cited Bishop Lowth of England, who wrote in 1710, "Rosh, taken as a proper name, in Ezekiel signifies the inhabitants of Scythia, from whom the modern Russians derive their name."

9. See biography of Josh McDowell, Josh McDowell Ministries, www.josh.org (accessed March 18, 2006).

10. Joel C. Rosenberg, "Dispatch from Moscow: Putin and Terror," joelrosenberg.blogspot.com, weblog, September 1, 2004.

11. Peter Baker, "Putin Moves to Centralize Authority: Plan Would Restrict Elections in Russia," *Washington Post*, September 14, 2004.

12. Ibid.

13. Ibid.

14. Tom Parfitt, "Putin's Reforms Are Undemocratic Says Governor," *Daily Telegraph*, September 19, 2004.

15. Mikhail Gorbachev, op-ed, "Mikhail Gorbachev on Putin's Reforms: 'A Step Back from Democracy,'" *Moscow News*, September 16, 2004.

16. Quoted by Parfitt, "Putin's Reforms."

17. Voice of America News, "Russia's Upper House Passes Bill Tightening Putin's Grip on Regions," December 8, 2004.

18. Jackson Diehl, "Putin's Unchallenged Imperialism," *Washington Post*, October 25, 2004.

19. Ibid.

20. See Peter Biles, "Ukraine Crisis Exposes Putin's Plans," BBC News, December 1, 2004; Associated Press, "Putin Opposes Ukraine Runoff," December 2, 2004; BBC News, "Yushchenko Wins Ukraine Election," December 27, 2004.

21. Joel C. Rosenberg, "A New Czar Rises in Russia," joelrosenberg.blogspot.com, weblog, December 3, 2004.

22. Reuters, "Russian Premier Vows to Rebuild Military Might," October 28, 1999, noted in David Johnson's Russia List, #3592, Center for Defense Information, www.cdi.org.

23. BBC News, "Putin: Russia Must Be Great Again," January 11, 2000.

24. Associated Press, "Russia Planning Maneuvers of Its Nuclear Forces Next Month," January 30, 2004.

25. "Putin Urges Enhancement of Russian Army's Combat Capability," *China People's Daily*, February 23, 2004.

26. See "Defense Spending to Be Raised 40% in 2005," www.Gateway2Russia.com, August 12, 2004; BBC News, "Russia Plans Defence Budget Boost," August 13, 2004.

27. Associated Press, "Cold War Missile Test-Fired from Russia," December 22, 2004.

28. BBC News, "Putin Address to Nation: Excerpts," April 25, 2005; BBC News, "Putin Deplores Collapse of USSR," April 25, 2005; Associated Press, "Putin: Soviet Collapse a 'Genuine Tragedy,'" April 25, 2005.

29. Vladimir Putin, *First Person: An Astonishingly Frank Self-Portrait By Russia's President,* with Nataliya Gevorkyan, Natalya Timokova, and Andrei Kolesnikov, trans. Catherine A. Fitzpatrick (New York: Public Affairs, 2000).

30. On May 1, 2000, for example, Putin delivered a speech in which he said: "Some have even suggested more radical measures than those contained in the submitted draft laws, going so far as suggesting that governors should be appointed by the Russian president. But I still think that the heads of the regions of the federation must be elected by the people. This procedure has become established, it has become part of our democratic system," Peter Baker and Susan Glasser, *Kremlin Rising: Vladimir Putin's Russia and the End of the Revolution* (New York: Scribner, 2005), 371.

31. Putin was born October 7, 1952, in Leningrad, Russia (now called St. Petersburg).

32. Olena Horodetska, "Lukashenko win in Belarus sets US, Russia at odds," Reuters, March 20, 2006.

33. "Support for Third Term for Putin Growing," Gazeta.ru, March 16, 2006, cited in Johnson's Russia List, 2006-#66, Center for Defense Information, www.cdi.org, March 17, 2006.

34. "When Putin was taken off the list of contenders in a July [2005] Yury Levada Analytical Center study, Zyuganov and Zhirinovsky were tied for first place," though each had only 10 percent support. See Mario Canseco, *Angus Reid Global Scan*, September 9, 2005; cited in Johnson's Russia List, #9241, Center for Defense Information, www.cdi.org, September 11, 2005.

35. RIA Novosti, "Sucessor should be responsible decision-maker—President Putin," June 16, 2006, cited by David Johnson, Johnson's Russia List, 2006-#139, Center for Defense Information, June 16, 2006.

36. See Andrei P. Tsygankov, "Why Russians 'Love' Stalin," cited in Johnson's Russia List, 2006-#66, March 17, 2006. M. Tsygankov is an associate professor of international relations and political science at San Francisco State University and program chair of the International Studies Association.

CHAPTER 8: KREMLIN JOINS "AXIS OF EVIL," FORMS MILITARY ALLIANCE WITH IRAN

1. Vice President Dick Cheney, address to the 2006 Vilnius Conference, May 4, 2006, www.whitehouse.gov.
2. See Ariel Cohen and James A. Phillips, "Countering Russian-Iranian Military Cooperation," *Heritage Backgrounder* #1425, The Heritage Foundation, April 5, 2001.
3. UPI, "Russia, Iran Renew Ties," March 13, 2001.
4. See Cohen and Phillips, "Countering Russian-Iranian Military Cooperation."
5. Aljazeera, "Putin: Iran Will Not Seek Nuclear Arms," February 18, 2005.
6. Agence France-Presse, "Putin Opposes Iranian Nuclear Bomb," April 28, 2005.
7. President Ali Khamenei, address to Iran's nuclear scientific community (speech, Tehran, January 1987), quoted in Kenneth R. Timmerman, *Countdown to Crisis: The Coming Nuclear Showdown with Iran* (New York: Crown Forum, 2005), 42.
8. Timmerman, *Countdown to Crisis*, 66.
9. Iran Press Service, "Rafsanjani Says Muslims Should Use Nuclear Weapon against Israel," December 14, 2001, www.iran-press-service.com.
10. "Iranian President at Tehran Conference," Special Dispatch Series, No. 1013, Middle East Media Research Institute, October 28, 2005.
11. Stefan Smith, "Move Israel to Europe, Ahmadinejad Suggests," Agence France-Presse, December 9, 2005.
12. Mossad official, personal interview with author, given on condition of anonymity. Name and date of interview withheld at interviewee's request.
13. Donald H. Rumsfeld and others, "Executive Summary," *The Report of the Commission to Assess the Ballistic Missile Threat to the United States*, July 15, 1998. Available online at www.fas.org/irp/threat/bm-threat.htm.
14. UPI, "Lockheed Continues Study of Ship-Launched Threat," November 9, 2005, cited on www.missilethreat.com, (accessed on March 30, 2006).
15. David Albright, "Iran Hid Nuclear Plans for Nearly Two Decades," interview on FOX News, April 24, 2005.
16. Kenneth M. Pollack, *The Persian Puzzle: The Conflict between Iran and America* (New York: Random, 2004), 362. For more on Iran's clandestine nuclear research, read 361–74.
17. Viktor Mikhailov (director of the Strategic Stability Institute of Russia's Ministry of Atomic Energy), "Iran Can Create Nuclear Bomb," interview with RIA Novosti, March 10, 2006.
18. Dore Gold, personal interview with author, November 14, 2005.
19. Putin has made increasing arms sales a top priority. In 1990, the Soviet Union sold some $16 billion worth of weaponry, military equipment, and spare parts worldwide. After the collapse of the USSR, sales plummeted to under $4 billion a year through 2000. In February 2006, however, Moscow's top arms sales official said, "The figure for Russia's [arms] exports in 2005 was [the] highest for the past few years. The final figure is $6.126 billion." See BBC News, "Russian Arms Exports at 10-Year High," February 7, 2001; RIA Novosti, "Russian 2005 Arms Exports Hit Record $6.1 Billion," February 9, 2006.
20. Yuri Shtern, (member of Knesset), personal interview with author, November 13, 2005.
21. Natan Sharansky, interview with author, February 2005. For abridged version of the interview, see Joel C. Rosenberg, "Free Societies vs. Fear Societies," *World* magazine, February 26, 2005. For full version, see Joel C. Rosenberg, "Russia, Iran & the Future in the Middle East," www.leftbehind.com, posted March 8, 2005.
22. "Within the United States Armed Forces, the Secretary of Defense is often referred to

as SecDef. The SecDef and the President of the United States together constitute the National Command Authority (NCA), which has sole authority to launch strategic nuclear weapons. All nuclear weapons are governed by the two-man rule, even at the highest levels in government. Both individuals must concur before a strategic nuclear strike may be ordered" ("United States Secretary of Defense," www.answers.com, accessed March 23, 2006).

23. Caspar Weinberger, personal interview with author, February 23, 2006.

24. Most Americans do not realize, for example, that Putin has already survived at least three assassination attempts (February 2000, August 2000, and October 2001), and a radical Islamic Chechen terrorist group known as the Brigades of Islambuli has reportedly put a $20 million bounty on Putin's head. See "$20 Million For Vladimir Putin," *Pravda.com*, September 10, 2004 (accessed March 16, 2006). Also, fears of a revolution in Russia have been rising in recent years. As I wrote in a 2005 article, "When I was in Moscow for ten days last September doing research for [*The Ezekiel Option*], I met with top Russian officials and political analysts, senior officials at the U.S. Embassy, and a number of journalists, including the *New York Times* bureau chief. The unanimous consensus was that a coup wasn't necessary to create a Russian dictator, because Russia already has a rising dictator— Vladimir Putin. Nevertheless, the coup remains in the novel. So it is with particular interest that I've been watching the recent political upheavals in the former Soviet republics of Ukraine, Georgia and Kyrgyzstan, and their reverberations in Moscow. Putin, once thought to be invulnerable, is now the subject of growing controversy and dissatisfaction." See Joel C. Rosenberg, "Revolution Brewing in Russia?" joelrosenberg.blogspot.com, weblog, March 31, 2005; also see "Whither Uzbekistan? Another Fmr. Soviet Republic on the Brink," joelrosenberg.blogspot.com, weblog, May 24, 2005.

25. See Amos Harel, "Ex-Military Intelligence Chief Ze'evi Warns of Impending World Jihad 'Tsunami,'" *Haaretz*, May 15, 2006; Daniel Pipes, "The Mystical Menace of Mahmoud Ahmadinejad," *New York Sun*, January 10, 2006; Charles Krauthammer, "In Iran, Arming for Armageddon," *Washington Post*, December 16, 2005.

26. Amir Taheri, "The Frightening Truth of Why Iran Wants a Bomb," *Sunday Telegraph*, April 16, 2006.

27. Hossein Bostani, "Ahmadinejad in Touch with 12th Imam," www.roozonline.com (popular Iranian dissident Weblog), March 15, 2006.

28. Ayatollah Ibrahim Amini, *Al-Imam al-Mahdi, The Just Leader of Humanity*, trans. Dr. Abdulaziz Sachedina (Qum, Iran: Ahul Bayt Digital Islamic Library Project, electronic online version), al-islam.org/mahdi/nontl/Toc.htm (accessed April 15, 2006).

29. Ibid.

30. Nearly all religious Muslims, both Sunnis and Shiites, share a view of the end times that involves wars and the coming of a Messiah who will ultimately bring peace and justice to the world. According to Ayatollah Baqir al-Sadr and Ayatollah Murtada Mutahhari, authors of *The Awaited Savior*, "the idea of the final victory of the forces of righteousness, peace and justice over those of evil, oppression and tyranny, of the world-wide spread of the Islamic faith, the complete and all-round establishment of high human values, the formation of a utopian and an ideal society and lastly the accomplishment of this ideal at the hands of a holy and eminent personality called, according to the Islamic traditions, Mahdi is a belief which, of course with variations in details, is shared by all the Muslim sects and schools of thought." See al-islam.org/awaited/index.htm (accessed April 20, 2006).

CHAPTER 9: MOSCOW EXTENDS MILITARY ALLIANCE
TO INCLUDE ARAB, ISLAMIC WORLD

1. Sun Tzu, *The Art of War, Special Edition*, trans. Lionel Giles (Editorial Benei Noaj, 2005), 65 ("XIII, The Use of Spies").
2. Captured Iraqi Document, CMPC-2003-001950, Foreign Military Studies Office, Joint Reserve Intelligence Center, fmso.leavenworth.army.mil/recent.htm, see http://70.69.163.24 (accessed March 23, 2006). See also ABC News, "Did Russian Ambassador Give Saddam the U.S. War Plan?" March 23, 2006; and Will Dunham, "Russia Gave Iraq Intelligence: Pentagon Report," Reuters, March 24, 2006.
3. Captured Iraqi Document, CMPC-2004-001117, Foreign Military Studies Office, Joint Reserve Intelligence Center, fmso.leavenworth.army.mil/recent.htm, see http://70.69.163.24 (accessed March 23, 2006). See also Captured Iraqi Document, "Letter From Ministry of Foreign Affairs to Office of the President Regarding Russian Intel," April 2, 2003, quoted in an unclassified version of a U.S. Joint Forces Command report; Kevin M. Woods, and others., *Iraqi Perspectives Project: A View of Operation Iraqi Freedom from Saddam's Senior Leadership*, Joint Center for Operational Analysis, Joint Forces Command (JFCOM), March 2006, www.jfcom.mil/newslink/storyarchive/2006/ipp.pdf (accessed March 24, 2006).
4. The New American Standard Bible translates Cush as "Ethiopia," as do the King James Version, the New King James Version, and the New Living Translation.
5. Flavius Josephus, *The Antiquities of the Jews*, trans. William Whiston, Book One, Chapter 6, Paragraph 2 in *Josephus: The Complete Works* (Nashville: Nelson, 1998), 42.
6. Tim LaHaye identified Cush as Ethiopia and other "African nations" in *The Coming Peace in the Middle East* (Grand Rapids, Mich.: Zondervan, 1984), 135. Hal Lindsey and C. C. Carlson identified Cush as Ethiopia and other "African nations" in *The Late, Great Planet Earth* (Grand Rapids, Mich.: Zondervan, 1970), 68. Mark Hitchcock identified Cush as "the land just south of Egypt on the Nile," which he notes includes Ethiopia and Sudan, in *The Coming Islamic Invasion of Israel* (Sisters, Ore.: Multonomah, 2002), 55–56. Charles Ryrie identified Cush as "Ethiopia" and "northern Sudan" in the *Ryrie Study Bible* (Chicago: Moody, 1995), 1323. J. Dwight Pentecost identifies Cush as Ethiopia and "a region south of Egypt" in *Things to Come: A Study in Biblical Eschatology* (Grand Rapids, Mich.: Academie, 1958), 329, though he also cites a source who suggests Cush could refer to people of Babylonia or "a land and people in northern Arabia." It should be noted that Babylonia and Mesopotamia are never mentioned directly by Ezekiel, though they certainly could have been if they were to be involved in this attack against Israel. Ezekiel was, after all, writing the prophecy in Babylon at the time.
7. Josephus, *Complete Works*, 42.
8. LaHaye, Lindsey, Hitchcock, Ryrie, and Pentecost all agree that Put is Libya. LaHaye and Lindsey believe that modern-day Algeria and Tunisia are likely included, though they include Morocco as well. Pentecost cites a source that suggests Put could be "adjacent to Persia or Iran" instead of North Africa.
9. Josephus, *Complete Works*, 42.
10. Voltaire, *The Portable Voltaire* (paperback), ed. Ben Ray Redman (New York: Viking Penguin, 1977), 101.
11. Arno Clemens Gaebelein, *The Prophet Ezekiel* (New York: Publication Office "Our Hope," 1917), 259. On page 135 of *Coming Peace*, Tim LaHaye identifies "Gomer and its hordes" as "involving either just East Germany and the Soviet satellite countries of Eastern Europe, or all of Germany and the Eastern European satellites." On page 87 of the 1999 nonfiction book *Are We Living in the End Times?* (Wheaton: Tyndale, 1999), LaHaye and coauthor Jerry Jenkins say Gomer is "thought to be Turkey." On page 69

of *Late, Great Planet Earth*, Hal Lindsey cites Gesenius who "speaks of part of Gomer's 'hordes' as being Ashkenaz . . . 'the proper name of a region and a nation in northern Asia [minor], sprung from the Cimmerians who are the ancient people of Gomer. The modern Jews understand it to be Germany, and call that country by this Hebrew name.'" Charles Ryrie identifies Gomer as "probably the eastern part of Turkey and the Ukraine" on page 1323 of his study Bible. Mark Hitchcock sides with the Turkey theory (page 59 of *Islamic Invasion*), and J. Dwight Pentecost concludes on page 330 of *Things to Come* that "there seems to be evidence to support the view that [Gomer] refers to modern Germany."

12. Josephus, *Complete Works*, 42.

13. See "Phrygia" on www.wikipedia.org; "Origins of the Armenian People," www.armenianheritage.com/peorigin.htm (accessed March 23, 2006); and Todd B. Krause and Jonathan Slocum, "Classical Armenian Online," Linguistics Research Center, University of Texas at Austin, www.utexas.edu/cola/depts/lrc/eieol/armol-0.html (accessed March 23, 2006).

14. On page 35 of *Coming Peace*, LaHaye identifies Togarmah and its hordes as "Armenia, which may well involve Turkey and other nations or peoples remaining from the Turkish Empire." On page 70 of *Late, Great*, Lindsey identifies Beth-togarmah as Armenia and "the Turkoman tribes of Central Asia," including "modern Southern Russia." On page 1323 of his study Bible, Ryrie identifies Beth-togarmah as "the part of Turkey near the Syrian border." On page 59 of *Islamic Invasion*, Hitchcock identifies Beth-togarmah as "southern Turkey." On page 330 of *Things to Come*, Pentecost says Beth-togarmah is "generally identified as Turkey or Armenia, although it is extended by some to include Central Asia," and cites several sources reaffirming this conclusion.

15. LaHaye does not identify Sheba and Dedan specifically in either *Coming Peace* or *The End Times Controversy*, ed. Tim LaHaye and Thomas Ice (Eugene, Ore.: Harvest, 2003).

16. "Arafat Hopscotches from Tehran to Moscow," CNN, August 10, 2000; "Putin Tells Arafat That Russia Backs Palestinian Independence," CNN, August 11, 2000.

17. "Khatami Visit Heralds New Iran-Russia Ties," *China People's Daily*, March 13, 2001; Brenda Shaffer, "Khatami in Moscow Boosts Russian-Iranian Arms Cooperation," *Policy Watch* #522, Washington Institute for Near East Policy, March 5, 2001.

18. See "Ethiopian Premier Visits Moscow," *China People's Daily*, December 4, 2001; "Russia Agrees To Sell Arms To Ethiopia," *Russian Reform Monitor*, December 3, 2001; BBC News, "Russia Writes Off Ethiopian Debt," May 30, 2001; "Russia To Develop Gas Fields In Ethiopia," *Pravda*, September 2, 2002.

19. See "Saudi crown prince in Russia today in the first visit of its kind," *ArabicNews.com*, September 2, 2003; and "Saudi-Russian Oil and Gas Agreement; Abdullah: A Historical Day in the Relations Record," *ArabicNews.com*, September 3, 2003. See also Dr. Ariel Cohen, "Saudi-Russian Rapprochement: U.S. Should Beware," Web Memo #336, The Heritage Foundation, September 12, 2003.

20. Russian president Vladimir Putin, Tenth Summit of Heads of State and Government of the Organization of the Islamic Conference (speech, Ministry of Foreign Affairs of the Russian Federation, Information and Press Department, Putrajaya, Malaysia, October 16, 2003). See also Agence France-Presse, "Putin's Call to Join OIC Helps Improve Russian Relations with Muslim World," January 2, 2004. See also "OIC Grants Observer Status to Russia," *Daily Times* (Pakistan), July 1, 2005.

21. Agence France-Presse, "Putin Plans to Visit Iran," October 6, 2004.

22. Steve Gutterman, "Putin First Russian Chief to Visit Turkey," Associated Press, December 5, 2004.

23. See "Putin OKs Russian Troops for Sudan," CBC News (Canadian), February 3, 2005;

"Oil-Rich Sudan Buys Arms from China, Russia, Iran, Belarus," *WorldTribune.com*, November 23, 2004; "Russia Sells Missiles to Sudan, Syria, Libya," *WorldNetDaily.com*, September 18, 2002.

24. "Putin Makes Landmark Visit to Egypt," *Aljazeera.com*, April 26, 2005; Associated Press, "Putin Pushes 'Road Map' in Historic Visit to Egypt," April 27, 2005.

25. See "President Putin to Visit Middle East Despite Arms Delivery Scandal with Israel and Syria," *Pravda*, March 24, 2005; ABC News, "Putin Makes Historic Visit to Israel," April 27, 2005; BBC News, "Putin Plays Down Israel Arms Fear," April 28, 2005; Molly Moore, "Putin Calls Arms Aid No Threat to Israel," *Washington Post*, April 30, 2005. See also Joel C. Rosenberg, "Putin's Historic Trip to Israel," www.leftbehind.com, May 3, 2005.

26. Aljazeera, "Putin Invites Hamas to Moscow," February 9, 2006; "Russia May Sell Arms to Hamas," *The Australian*, February 18, 2006; "Russia to Consider Selling Helicopters to PA," *www.YnetNews.com* (Israel), February 16, 2006. See also Joel C. Rosenberg, "Putin Says Hamas Not a Terrorist Organization," joelrosenberg.blogspot.com, weblog, February 2, 2006.

27. Khaled Mash'al declared: "America will be defeated in Iraq. Wherever the [Islamic] nation is targeted, its enemies will be defeated, Allah willing. The nation of Muhammad is gaining victory in Palestine. The nation of Muhammad is gaining victory in Iraq, and it will be victorious in all Arab and Muslim lands. . . . These fools will be defeated, the wheel of time will turn, and times of victory and glory will be upon our nation, and the West will be full of remorse, when it is too late. . . . We say to this West, which does not act reasonably, and does not learn its lessons: By Allah, you will be defeated. Israel will be defeated, and so will whoever supported or supports it. . . . I say to the [European countries]: Hurry up and apologize to our nation, because if you do not, you will regret it." See Joel C. Rosenberg, "Hamas Threatens America, Putin Invites Them to Moscow," joelrosenberg.blogspot.com, weblog, February 9, 2006, citing the Middle East Media Research Institute, www.memri.org.

28. See Agence France-Presse, "Putin to Press Algeria to Buy Arms," March 10, 2006; RIA Novosti, "Rosoboronexport Strikes $7.5 Billion Deal with Algeria," March 10, 2006; "Russia Strikes $7.5 Billion Arms Deal with Algeria," *MosNews.com*, March 10, 2006.

29. Interfax News Agency, "Dialogue with Muslim World among Russia's Priorities—Putin," March 27, 2006.

CHAPTER 10: GLOBAL TENSIONS SOAR AS RUSSIA TARGETS ISRAEL

1. Agence France-Presse, "Russia Would Never Harm Israel: Olmert," March 2, 2006.

2. "Acting PM Olmert Speaks with Russian President Putin," Office of the Israeli Prime Minister, March 5, 2006, www.pmo.gov.il/PMOEng/Communication/ Spokesman/2006/03/spokeputin050306.htm (accessed March 28, 2006).

3. Ariel Cohen, "Zhirinovsky in His Own Words: Excerpts from *The Final Thrust South*," trans. Cohen and Melana Zyla, The Heritage Foundation, February 4, 1994.

4. Kevin Fedarko, "Rising Czar?" *Time* magazine, July 11, 1994.

5. Cohen, "Zhirinovsky in His Own Words."

6. *CIA World Fact Handbook*, www.cia.gov (accessed March 29, 2006).

7. Alexei Mitrofanov, personal interview with author, September 1, 2004.

8. "Begin Describes Soviet Arms Cache," *Washington Post*, July 7, 1982.

9. Caspar W. Weinberger, interview with author, February 23, 2006.

10. "Message from Brezhnev to Nixon," October 24, 1973, U.S. State Department. See The

National Security Archive, George Washington University, www.gwu.edu/~nsarchiv/ (accessed on March 1, 2006).

11. Some may characterize Brezhnev's threat not as a Soviet plan to attack Israel but as a bluff. But Kissinger said: "I did not see it as a bluff, but it made no difference. We could not run the risk that [it was not]. We had no choice except to call the bluff." "The October War and U.S. Policy," William Burr, ed., The National Security Archive, October 7, 2003. Dr. Burr is a senior analyst of nuclear history with the National Security Archive at George Washington University, www.gwu.edu/~nsarchiv/ (accessed on March 1, 2006).

12. "Message from Nixon to Brezhnev."

13. Transcript of "Secretary's Staff Meeting: Tuesday, October 23, 1973—4:35pm," classified as "Secret/NODIS." The National Security Archive, George Washington University, www.gwu.edu/~nsarchiv/ (accessed on March 1, 2006).

14. Michael B. Oren, Six Days of War (New York: Oxford University Press, 2002), 123.

15. Oren, 25.

16. Oren, 149.

17. Ibid.

18. "Message from Eshkol to Johnson," telegram from the U.S. Embassy in Israel to the State Department, classified at the time as "Secret," June 5, 1967, Johnson Library, National Security File, NSC Histories, Middle East Crisis, vol. 3; Published by The National Security Archive, George Washington University, www.gwu.edu/~nsarchiv/ (accessed on February 22, 2006).

19. Oren, 29, 27.

20. Oren, 57, 65.

21. "President's Daily Brief," June 9, 1967, then classified "Top Secret," Johnson Library, National Security File, NSC Histories, Middle East Crisis, vol. 6, Appendix A. Published by the U.S. State Department, Foreign Relations, 1964-1968, Volume XIX, Arab-Israeli Crisis and War, 1967, www.state.gov/r/pa/ho/frus/johnsonlb/xix/28059.htm (accessed on March 29, 2006).

22. "Message from Kosygin to Johnson," June 10, 1967, National Security File, NSC Histories, container 19 volume 7, LBJ Presidential Library, quoted in Isabella Ginor, "The Russians Were Coming: The Soviet Military Threat in the 1967 Six-Day War," Middle East Review of International Affairs (MERIA) 4, no. 4 (December 2000): 48. See also Isabella Ginor, "How the Six Day War Almost Led to Armageddon," The Guardian (London), June 10, 2000.

23. Statement to the Knesset by Prime Minister Eshkol, June 12, 1967, Israel Ministry of Foreign Affairs, www.mfa.gov.il (accessed on March 29, 2006).

24. Richard Helms, "Memorandum for the Record," including oral history from CIA Director Richard Helms, prepared in Washington, October 22, 1968. Source: Johnson Library, National Security File, NSC Histories, Middle East Crisis, vol. 7, Appendix G. Top Secret. Published by the U.S. State Department, Foreign Relations, 1964–1968, Volume XIX, Arab-Israeli Crisis and War, 1967, www.state.gov/r/pa/ho/frus/johnsonlb/xix/28059.htm, (accessed on March 29, 2006).

25. Ibid., 54.

26. Ginor, "How the Six Day War."

27. Nikita S. Kruschev, Vremya. Ludi. Vlast., memoirs in four volumes (Moscow: MN, 1999), volume 3, 435; vol. 4, 460; cited by Ginor in "The Russians Were Coming," 45.

28. Yuri V. Nastenko, "Aviatsiya v Egypte," in Grif "Sekrentno" Sniat (Moscow: Committee of Veterans of Military Actions in Egypt, 1998), quoted in Ginor, "The Russians Were Coming."

29. Ginor, "The Russians Were Coming," 49.

30. Isabella Ginor, "The Cold War's Longest Cover-Up: How and Why the USSR Instigated the 1967 War," *Middle East Review of International Affairs*, 7, no. 3 (September 2003): 46, 57.
31. Among them are Professor Robert O. Freedman of Baltimore Hebrew University and Professor Galia Golan of Hebrew University, both of whom have written extensively on Soviet policy in the Middle East. I spoke by phone with Professor Freedman, who dismissed Ginor's findings. I also spoke by phone with Ginor, who lives in Israel. She stands by her reporting. She notes that she has carefully documented her findings, has spoken directly to most of the people she cites, and even quotes those who disagree with her, including then–Soviet ambassador to Washington Anatoly F. Dobrynin. She chose not to be quoted directly for this book, but approved of my quoting extensively from her articles.

CHAPTER 11: NEW WAR ERUPTS IN MIDDLE EAST AS EARTHQUAKES, PANDEMICS HIT EUROPE, AFRICA, ASIA

1. Paul Johnson, "The Necessity of Christianity," *Truth Journal*, Volume 1, 1985, see www.leaderu.com/truth/1truth08.html (accessed May 24, 2006).
2. Adolf Hitler, *Mein Kampf*, quoted in William L. Shirer, *The Rise and Fall of the Third Reich: A History of Nazi Germany* (New York: Simon & Schuster, 1959), 26.
3. Arnold Beichman, "How Stalin, the 'Breaker of Nations,' Hated, Murdered Jews," *Washington Times*, August 16, 2003. Beichman was reviewing Arno Lustiger's book, *Stalin and the Jews: The Red Book; The Tragedy of the Jews*, published by Enigma Books.
4. Aljazeera, "Ahmadinejad: Wipe Israel off map," October 26, 2005.
5. Arnaud de Borchgrave, "Later Than We Think," *Washington Times*, February 6, 2006. See also Charles Krauthammer, "Today Tehran, Tomorrow the World," *Time* magazine, March 26, 2006; and Anton La Guardia, "'Divine Mission' Driving Iran's New Leader," *London Telegraph*, January 14, 2006.
6. ABC News, "An exclusive interview with Osama bin Laden," TK, 1998; cited by Gershom Gorenberg, *The End of Days* (New York: Free Press, 2000, updated in 2002), v–vi.
7. "Bird Flu Could Take 142m Lives," CNN, February 16, 2006.
8. Warwick McKibbin, *Global Macroeconomic Consequences of Pandemic Influenza*, Lowry Institute for International Policy, February 2006, 57.
9. Charles Ryrie, *Ryrie Study Bible* (Chicago: Moody, 1995), 1326.
10. Russian pastor, interview with author, given on condition of anonymity, September 2004.

CHAPTER 12: IRAQ EMERGES FROM CHAOS AS REGION'S WEALTHIEST COUNTRY

1. "Democrats Broaden Criticism of Administration on Iraq," *CNN.com*, July 15, 2003.
2. Robert C. Byrd, Remarks on the Senate Floor, January 25, 2005, byrd.senate.gov (accessed October 13, 2005).
3. John Kerry, speech at New York University (September 20, 2004).
4. Kevin Whitelaw, "Sen. Chuck Hagel Criticizes President Bush's Performance on Iraq," *U.S. News & World Report*, June 20, 2005.
5. "Hagel: Iraq War Has Destabilized Mideast, Resembles Vietnam," *CNN.com*, August 21, 2005.
6. Ibid.
7. Georges Sada (Iraqi General), interview with author, March 30, 2006.
8. *Measuring Stability and Security in Iraq*, February 2006, report to Congress in accordance with the Department of Defense Appropriations Act 2006 (Section 9010), U.S. Defense Department, www.defenselink.mil/home/features/Iraq_Reports/docs/2006-02-

Report.pdf.

9. Ali Abdul Ameer Allawi (Iraq's minister of finance), interview with author, April 26, 2006.

10. Dr. Sinan Al-Shabibi (governor of Iraq's Central Bank), interview with author, April 26, 2006.

11. "Iraq's Economy Nearly Doubled—Report," April 9, 2006, www.portaliraq.com.

12. "Infrastructure: Visa Accepts International Card Payments In Iraq," June 2, 2003, www.portaliraq.com.

13. "FedEx Express Launches Service in Iraq," press release, August 11, 2003, www.fedex.com/us/about/news/pressreleases/archives/pressrelease232234786.html?link=4 (accessed April 15, 2006).

14. Reuters, "Coca-Cola in Iraqi Joint Venture Talks," November 19, 2003, noted on www.portaliraq.com. See also Rory Carroll, "Cola Wars As Coke Moves on Baghdad," *The Guardian* (London), July 5, 2005.

15. Kamel al-Gailani, "Iraq: Open for Business," *Wall Street Journal*, December 29, 2003.

16. See "Operation Iraqi Freedom: Three Year Anniversary, Project Fact Sheet," March 23, 2006, U.S. Defense Department.

17. *Measuring Stability and Security in Iraq*, 13.

18. Allawi, interview with author.

19. See "Operation Iraqi Freedom: Three Year Anniversary, Project Fact Sheet," U.S. Defense Department, March 23, 2006.

20. Lawrence Kumins, "Iraq Oil: Reserves, Production and Potential Revenues," Congressional Research Service, April 13, 2005, 1, 5.

21. North American oil executive, interview with author, given on condition of anonymity, April 2005.

22. Kevin Phillips, *American Theocracy* (New York: Viking, 2006), 261. See also 253.

23. John F. Burns, "New Babylon Is Stalled by a Modern Upheaval," *New York Times*, October 11, 1990.

24. Charles H. Dyer, *The Rise of Babylon* (Chicago: Moody, revised 2003 version of the original 1991 edition), 14.

25. Jeffrey Gettleman, "Babylon Awaits an Iraq without Fighting," *New York Times*, April 18, 2006.

26. Ali Abdul Ameer Allawi (Iraqi finance minister), interview with the author, April 26, 2006.

CHAPTER 13: JEWS BUILD THIRD TEMPLE IN JERUSALEM

1. See Isaiah 2:2; Micah 4:1; Daniel 9:27; Matthew 24:15; 2 Thessalonians 2:3-4; and Revelation 11, among many other verses in both the Old and New Testaments that concern a future Temple.

2. See "Another Outrageous Claim by Arafat: Ancient Jewish Temple Was in Nablus, Not Jerusalem," press release, Zionist Organization of America, May 21, 2002, www.zoa.org; see also Daniel Pipes, "More on the Muslim Claim to Jerusalem," May 2002, www.danielpipes.org.

3. For more on the threats to the Temple Mount, see Gershom Gorenberg, *The End of Days: Fundamentalism and the Struggle for the Temple Mount* (New York: Free Press, 2000, updated in 2002).

4. In many Hebrew writings, the name of God is omitted or abbreviated, according to the Orthodox Jewish custom of not writing down the name of God.

5. Gershon Salomon, "Long-Term Objectives, Short-Term Objectives,"

www.templemountfaithful.org (accessed April 4, 2006). Last phrase regarding the Messiah comes from Salomon's "Vision of Redemption" on the same Web site.

6. Gershon Salomon, "The Voice of the Temple Mount," newsletter, Spring 1998, www.templemountfaithful.org (accessed April 4, 2006).

7. See "The Temple Mount Faithful Will Go up to the Temple Mount on Tisha B'Av," www.templemountfaithful.org/Events/tishabav5761.htm, July 29, 2001. See also "Court Won't Let Temple Mount Group Lay 'Cornerstone' of Third Temple," *Haaretz*, October 16, 2005.

8. Gershon Salomon, "An Open Letter about the Critical Situation on the Temple Mount and Its Godly Endtime Solution," April 3, 2003, www.templemountfaithful.org (accessed April 4, 2006).

9. Yisrael Ariel (Rabbi), writings, www.templeinstitute.org.

10. "About the Temple Institute," www.templeinstitute.org (accessed April 4, 2006).

11. "Sanhedrin Launched in Tiberias," Arutz Sheva/Israel National News, January 20, 2005.

12. "Reestablished Sanhedrin Convenes to Discuss Temple," Arutz Sheva/Israel National News, February 9, 2005. See also Hal Lindsey, "Revived Sanhedrin Discusses Temple," *WorldNetDaily.com*, February 17, 2005.

13. Gershon Gorenberg, *The End of Days*, 13.

14. Ibid., 10.

15. For more on this subject, I would highly recommend two books by Randall Price, an evangelical Christian scholar of the ancient Temples and their treasures. One is *The Temple and Bible Prophecy: A Definitive Look at Its Past, Present and Future*, published in 2005 by Harvest House. The other is *Secrets of the Dead Sea Scrolls*, published in 1996 by Harvest House. Both were invaluable tools as I wrote *The Copper Scroll*.

16. Yisrael Ariel (Rabbi) and others, "Where Is the Ark of the Covenant?" www.templeinstitute.org/ark_of_the_covenant.htm (accessed on April 4, 2006).

17. Glenn Frankel, "Brooklyn Rabbi a Power in Israel," *Washington Post*, November 23, 1988.

18. Charles Fenyvesi, "Awaiting the Messiah," *U.S. News & World Report*, June 27, 1994.

19. "Today: The Goal," www.chabad.org/therebbe/timeline.asp?AID=62188 (accessed April 4, 2006).

20. Yisrael Ariel, "Which Comes First, the Messiah or the Temple?" www.templeinstitute.org (accessed April 4, 2006).

21. Ian MacKinnon, "Old Shack Will Give Madonna Front-Row Seat for Arrival of Her Messiah," *Times* (London), March 4, 2006.

22. Martin Buber, *Gog and Magog: A Novel*, paperback ed., trans. Ludwig Lewisohn (Syracuse: Syracuse University Press, 1999), 284. The book was originally published in German in 1981 by Atheneum.

23. Elie Wiesel, *Souls on Fire*, paperback ed. (1972; repr., New York: Touchstone, 1993), 206–7.

24. Elie Wiesel, *Elie Wiesel: Conversations*, ed. Robert Franciosi (Jackson: University Press of Mississippi, 2002), 138.

25. Figures based on interviews with messianic Jewish leaders in Israel and the U.S.

26. Ibid.

27. Patrick Johnstone and others, *Operation World* (Waynesboro: Authentic Media, 2001), 362. *Operation World* was a winner of the Gold Medallion Book Award and is researched and produced by WEC International. See www.gmi.org/ow/.

CHAPTER 14: MUSLIMS TURN TO CHRIST IN RECORD NUMBERS

1. Charles M. Sennott, *The Body and the Blood: The Middle East's Vanishing Christians and the Possibility for Peace* (New York: Public Affairs, 2001), prologue.

2. Sennott, *The Body and the Blood,* endorsements on the 2003 paperback edition.

3. Jonathan Mann and Gerald Kessel, "Christians Leaving Middle East," CNN, April 21, 1992.

4. Roger Hardy, "Christians Quit Christ's Birthplace," BBC News, December 21, 2001.

5. Bob Edwards and Sylvia Poggioli, coverage of the Pope's visit to Syria, *Morning Edition,* National Public Radio, May 7, 2001.

6. Jonathan Adelman and Agota Kuperman, "Christian Eclipse in Shadow of Radical Islam," op-ed, *Rocky Mountain News/Denver Post,* December 22, 2001.

7. William Dalrymple, "William Dalrymple on how the Christians of the East became an endangered species," *The Guardian* (London), October 30, 2001.

8. Salim Mansur, "A Christian Exodus?" *Toronto Sun,* December 23, 2004.

9. Samuel P. Huntington, *The Clash of Civilizations and the Remaking of World Order,* 1998 paperback ed. (New York: Simon & Schuster, 1996), 65. Quoted by Philip Jenkins, *The Next Christendom: The Coming of Global Christianity* (New York: Oxford University Press, 2002), 5.

10. Gayle Young, "Fast-Growing Islam Winning Converts in Western World," CNN, April 14, 1997.

11. Ray Suarez, "Observing Islam," *The NewsHour with Jim Lehrer,* PBS, November 16, 1997.

12. For example, see www.islamicity.com/Mosque/aboutislam.htm, www.allaahuakbar.net/womens/islam.htm#Listen, www.riseofislam.com/western_world_02b.html.

13. Dan Woodling, "Cairo's Extraordinary Garbage Dump Priest and His Cave Cathedral," Assist News Service, www.assistnews.net/strategic/s0000020.htm (accessed April 5, 2006). See also the church's Web site, www.saman-church.org/English.htm (accessed April 5, 2006).

14. Egyptian Bible Society leaders, interview with author given on condition of anonymity, January 23, 2006.

15. The *Morocco Times* ran an article on March 12, 2005, entitled "Why Are Moroccans Converting to Christianity?" The *Times* published a story on January 24, 2006, entitled "Evangelical Missionaries Back in the Limelight." Other Moroccan publications that have run similar stories include *Attajdid, Le Journal Hebdomadaire, Le Matin,* and *La Gazette Du Maroc.* The U.S. State Department's *International Religious Freedom Report 2005* included this item on Morocco: "The generally amicable relationship among religions in society contributed to religious freedom; however, converts to Christianity generally face social ostracism. From January until the May concert of contemporary Christian music, there was an ongoing societal debate on the influence of evangelical Christianity in the country. In January, the French language weekly *Le Journal* reported that an Istiqlal (Nationalist Party) party member, Jilali Abouali, challenged the minister of Islamic affairs in Parliament about allowing Christian evangelical missionaries into the country. In April, an Islamist Arabic-daily newspaper, *Attajdid,* carried an editorial by Habib Choubani, a member of parliament representing the Islamist Party for Justice and Development (PJD), charging that evangelicals were invading and that the Government, by permitting the concert, was undermining the country's 'spiritual security.' In spite of considerable criticism, the Government allowed the May concert to take place and no negative incidents occurred." See www.state.gov/g/drl/rls/irf/2005/51606.htm.

16. Ahmed Kostas (senior advisor to the Moroccan king), interview with author, November 28, 2005.

17. Dr. Ahmed Abaddi, interview with author, April 24, 2006.

18. Arab pastor, interview with author, given on condition of anonymity. Name of interviewee and date of interview withheld.

19. "Algeria bans Muslims from learning about Christianity," *ArabicNews.com,* March 21, 2006.

20. Sudanese evangelical leader, interview with author, given on condition of anonymity. Name of interviewee and date of interview withheld.

21. Stan Guthrie, "Hope amid the Ruins: Anglican Bishop Sees Massive Church Growth," *Christianity Today*, January 2004.

22. Sheikh Salman Al-Odeh, "Christian Missionaries Sweeping the Islamic World," transcript, Lesson 66, Monday 12th of Safar, 1413 Hijra (1993), from www.islamworld.net/tanseer. htm (accessed February 3, 2006). Al-Odeh was apparently citing the 1982 edition of the *World Christian Encyclopedia*. The updated figures in the 2001 edition found that the number of Christians in Africa had jumped from 9.9 million in 1900 to 360 million in 2000, still an enormous growth and a significant degree of it from Muslim converts. See David B. Barrett and others, *World Christian Encyclopedia* (New York: Oxford University Press, 2001), 5.

23. Sheikh Ahmad Al Qataani, interview on Aljazeera, transcript, December 12, 2000. Transcript available from Ali Sina, Iranian dissident, on his Web site, www.faithfreedom. org/oped/sina31103.htm (accessed February 3, 2006).

24. "More Christians Arrested in Wake of 'Apostasy' Case," Open Doors USA Web site, www.opendoorsusa.org/Display.asp?Page=AfghanArrests (accessed on April 3, 2006). See also www.compassdirect.org.

25. Afghan evangelical Christian leader, interview with author, given on condition of anonymity. Name of interviewee and date of interview withheld.

26. Georges Sada (Iraqi general), interview with author, May 22, 2006.

27. Iraqi pastor, interview with author, given on condition of anonymity. Name of interviewee and date of interview withheld.

28. Iraqi evangelical leader, interview with author, given on condition of anonymity. Name of interviewee and date of interview withheld.

29. Iraqi pastor from Baghdad, interview with author, given on condition of anonymity. Name of interviewee and date of interview withheld.

30. Cited by Julian Lukins, "Behind the Black Veil," *Charisma*, June 2004.

31. Patrick Johnstone and others, *Operation World* (Waynesboro: Authentic Media, 2001), 353.

32. Iranian evangelical leader, interview with author, given on condition of anonymity. Name of interviewee and date of interview withheld.

33. Ramin Mostaghim, "Ruling Shiites Influence Eroded by Other Faiths," Inter Press Service, May 5, 2004.

34. Compass Direct news service, "Government Officials Admit Christianity 'Out of Control,'" October 7, 2004.

35. Compass Direct, "Iranian Convert Stabbed to Death," November 28, 2005; see also *World Watch List 2006*, Open Doors, www.opendoorsuk.org/downloads/wwl_downloads/WorldWatchList.pdf (accessed April 3, 2006).

36. Compass Direct, "Iranian Convert." See also Nina Shea, "The Real War on Christmas: Being a Christian Can Be Deadly," *National Review*, December 19, 2005. Shea cited Rev. Keith Roderick, an Episcopal priest representing Christian Solidarity International. The Voice of the Martyrs news agency also reported Ahmadinejad's quote.

37. Iranian pastor, interview with author, given on condition of anonymity. Name of interviewee and date of interview withheld.

38. Based on interviews with Iranian pastors and Christians who have been inside Iran in recent years.

39. Iranian pastor, interview with author, given on condition of anonymity. Name of interviewee and date of interview withheld.

40. Brother Andrew kept his full name secret during his years of work behind the Iron Curtain and has revealed it to only a few people since.

41. Brother Andrew, interview with the author, October 2004.

CHAPTER 15: TRACKING THE TREMORS

1. Brian Williams, "Now It Can Be Told: Notes on the Eve of Destruction," weblog entry, September 5, 2005, www.msnbc.msn.com/id/9216831/#050905.
2. Ibid.
3. Brian Williams, "The weatherman nobody heard—Robert Ricks predicted Katrina's wrath; why didn't more people listen?" *NBC Nightly News,* September 15, 2005.
4. Associated Press, "Iran Leader: Israel Will Be Eliminated," April 14, 2006.
5. Mortimer B. Zuckerman, "Moscow's Mad Gamble," *U.S. News & World Report,* January 30, 2006.
6. Georges Sada, *Saddam's Secrets* (Brentwood, Tenn.:Integrity Publishers, 2006), 148.
7. *The Four Spiritual Laws* is an executive summary of the New Testament's plan of salvation. It was written in 1965 by Bill Bright, the founder of Campus Crusade for Christ. It has become so popular as a clear and simple presentation of this Good News or "gospel" that more than 1.5 billion copies are now in print around the world. It can be read in its entirety at www.greatcom.org/laws/.

AFTERWORD

1. "Rice sees bombs and birth pangs," *Aljazeera.net,* July 29, 2006.
2. This leader or "prince" is often referred to by Christians as the "Antichrist." For the record, I have no idea who the Antichrist is or will be. Moreover, I strongly discourage speculation along these lines. It is not productive in any way, shape, or form for followers of Jesus Christ—especially pastors, Bible teachers, seminary professors, or other Christian leaders—to speculate about what current or emerging world leader may be the Antichrist. Indeed, it is deeply counterproductive. It invites scorn and ridicule on the teaching of prophecy just at a time in history when both Christians and non-Christians need and increasingly want to hear sane, rational, thoughtful voices about the intersection of Bible prophecy and current events. Personally, based in part on 2 Thessalonians chapter 2, I believe the Bible teaches that the Antichrist's identity will not be revealed until after the Rapture. This is another reason not to guess before the Rapture happens. For a brief definition of the Rapture, please see *Epicenter* p. 251.
3. "Q&A: Rome Conference on Lebanon," *CNN.com,* June 26, 2006.
4. "Transcript of Rome News Conference," *CNN.com,* June 26, 2006.
5. Haro Chakmakjian, "Russian Troops Make First Mideast Foray in Lebanon for Centuries," Agence France-Presse, September 27, 2006.
6. Suzan Fraser, "Turkey Agrees to Send Troops to Lebanon," Associated Press, September 5, 2006.
7. Werner Sonne, "German Troops to the Middle East?" *Jerusalem Post,* August 1, 2006.
8. Ibid.
9. For more background, see Ulf Gartzke, "Germany Goes to the Middle East," *The Weekly Standard,* August 22, 2006. See also Ulf Gartzke, "German Cabinet Reviews Maritime Mission in Lebanon," *The Weekly Standard* blog, August 2, 2007.
10. U.N. Security Council Press Release SC/8181, September 9, 2004.
11. U.N. Security Council Press Release SC/8808, August 11, 2006.
12. Associated Press, "UN report: Israel Says Hezbollah's Arsenal Includes 30,000 Rockets," March 4, 2008.
13. Associated Press, "Israel: Hezbollah Used Russian Missiles," August 18, 2006.
14. Associated Press, "Peres: Moscow Asked Syria to Explain Why Hezbollah Had Russian Missiles," September 6, 2006.
15. Christiane Amanpour, "Czar Putin," CNN, November 30, 2007.

16. Anna Politkovskaya, *Putin's Russia: Life in a Failing Democracy* (New York: Metropolitan Books, 2004), 242.

17. See Joel C. Rosenberg, "Sharp Critic of Putin Murdered," joelrosenberg.blogspot.com, weblog, October 8, 2006.

18. Bob Simon, "Who Killed Alexander Litvinenko?" *60 Minutes*, January 7, 2007.

19. "Litvinenko's Death Marks a New Kind of Chernobyl—It Threatens Us All," *Daily Mail*, November 30, 2006. See also Joel C. Rosenberg, "Assassination Raises Critical Question: Who Is Vladimir Putin?" joelrosenberg.blogspot.com, weblog, November 28, 2006.

20. Associated Press, "UK: Radioactive Isotope Killed Ex-KGB," November 25, 2006.

21. Christian Lowe, "Russia Rejects UK's Litvinenko Extradition Request," Reuters, July 5, 2007.

22. Adi Ignatius, "A Tsar Is Born," *Time*, December 4, 2007.

23. "Supporters Want Putin to Stay in Power," *USA Today*, December 5, 2007.

24. *Bloomberg.com*, October 1, 2007.

25. Clifford J. Levy, "Medvedev, Putin's Chosen Heir, Speaks, and the Plot Thickens in Russia," *International Herald Tribune*, December 11, 2007.

26. Putin quotes cited by Dr. Ariel Cohen, "Russia's Presidential Elections: Management Reshuffle for 'Russia Inc.'?" Heritage Foundation WebMemo #1825, February 25, 2008.

27. Cited by the BBC, February 10, 2007.

28. Associated Press, "Report: Russia, Iran Helped Syria Bolster Arsenal," based on reporting from *Haaretz*, February 22, 2007.

29. Associated Press, "Russian Died Reporting on Arms Sales to Iran, Syria," March 7, 2007. Excerpt: "Ivan Safronov, a military affairs writer for the daily *Kommersant*, died Friday after plunging from a stairwell window between the fourth and fifth stories. *Kommersant* reported Tuesday that Safronov had told his editors he was working on a story about Russian plans to sell weapons to Iran and Syria via Belarus. The deals, if concluded, could upset the balance of power in the Middle East and strain Russia's relations with Israel and the United States, which strongly objected to earlier Russian weapons sales to the two countries. *Kommersant* reported that Safronov, 51, had recently told colleagues he was warned he would face a criminal investigation for possibly releasing state secrets if he reported allegations that Russia had struck a deal to supply Iskander missiles to Syria."

30. Associated Press, "Putin Threatens Pullout from Arms Pact; Putin Calls for Moratorium on Russian Participation in Soviet-Era Arms Control Treaty," April 26, 2007.

31. Andy McSmith, "Russia Refuses to Extradite Man Accused of Murdering Litvinenko," *The (U.K.) Independent*, May 23, 2007.

32. Demetri Sevastopulo, "Putin Threatens to Target Missiles at Europe," *Financial Times*, June 4, 2007.

33. Associated Press, "Newspaper: Russia Starts Delivery of Advanced Fighter Jets to Syria," based on reports from the Russian business journal *Kommersant*, June 19, 2007.

34. Associated Press, "Russia successfully tests new sea-based missile," June 28, 2007.

35. "Putin's Arctic Invasion: Russia Lays Claim to the North Pole—and All Its Gas, Oil, and Diamonds," *Daily Mail*, June 30, 2007.

36. Yaakov Katz and Herb Keinon, "Reports: Iran to Buy Jets from Russia," *Jerusalem Post*, July 30, 2007.

37. Associated Press, "Putin Suspends Russia's Participation in Conventional Forces in Europe Treaty," July 14, 2007.

38. Ynet News, "Russia Navy to Operate from Syria," August 6, 2007.

39. "Russia, China Host Ahmadinejad at Anti-U.S. Security Summit," *Bloomberg.com*, August 16, 2007. For more on the Shanghai Cooperation Council—an alliance of countries with

a combined population of 1.5 billion people possessing three-fifths of the landmass of Eurasia—see the organization's Web site, www.sectsco.org.

40. "Memorandum of Understanding between SCO Secretariat and CSTO Secretariat," www.sectsco.org, October 5, 2007 (accessed March 24, 2008).

41. RIA Novosti, "Use of force in Iran would threaten Central Asia—CSTO," March 1, 2007.

42. See Associated Press, "Putin Expected to Visit Belarus to Discuss Plans for Closer Union," December 6, 2007; RIA Novosti, "Kremlin Denies Putin Will Head Russia-Belarus Union," December 7, 2007. See also, "Will Putin Swallow Belarus?" *Jane's*, September 4, 2002; Associated Press, "Putin Urges Belarus on Union," September 4, 2002.

43. "Russia Delivers Nuclear Fuel to Iran," CNN, December 17, 2007.

44. "Iran Announces Purchase of Missiles from Russia," *Jerusalem Post*, December 26, 2007.

45. Peter Finn, "Putin Threatens Ukraine on NATO," *Washington Post*, February 13, 2008.

46. Agence France-Presse, "Russia Scraps Libya's Debts as Putin Visits Tripoli," April 17, 2008.

47. Associated Press, "In Iran, Putin warns U.S.," October 16, 2007.

48. "Press Conference with the President," White House transcript, October 17, 2007.

49. See Charles Krauthammer, "In Iran, Arming For Armageddon," *Washington Post*, December 16, 2005; Daniel Pipes, "The Mystical Menace of Mahmoud Ahmadinejad," *New York Post*, January 10, 2006. For a fuller and more detailed treatment of this topic, see Yossi Melman and Meir Javedanfar, *The Nuclear Sphinx of Tehran: Mahmoud Ahmadinejad and the State of Iran*, (New York: Carroll & Graf, 2007).

50. Y. Mansharof and A. Savyon, "Escalation in the Positions of Iranian President Mahmoud Ahmadinejad—A Special Report," MEMRI Inquiry and Analysis Series #389, www.memri.org, September 17, 2007.

51. Ibid.

52. "President Ahmadinejad Delivers Remarks at Columbia University," transcript published by the *Washington Post*, September 24, 2007.

53. For more, see Joel C. Rosenberg, "Iran Sobered Us Up on New Year's: A Message of Nuclear Proportions," *National Review Online*, January 3, 2007.

54. Mark Mazzetti, "U.S. Report Says Iran Halted Nuclear Weapons Program in 2003," *International Herald Tribune*, December 3, 2007.

55. Ibid.

56. See interview with Senator Shelby transcript from the *PBS NewsHour*, June 3, 1998. See also "CIA Caught off Guard on India Nuclear Test," *CNNInterctive.com*, www.cnn.com/WORLD/asiapcf/9805/12/india.cia/index.html (accessed March 24, 2008); and "U.S. Intelligence and the Indian Bomb: Documents Show U.S. Intelligence Failed to Warn of India's Nuclear Tests Despite Tracking Nuclear Weapons Potential Since 1950s," National Security Archive Electronic Briefing Book No. 187, George Washington University, available online at: www.gwu.edu/~nsarchiv/NSAEBB/NSAEBB187/index.htm (accessed March 24, 2008).

57. For examples, see Amb. John Bolton, "The Flaws in the Iran Report," *Washington Post*, December 6, 2007; and Gerald M. Steinberg, "Decoding the U.S. National Intelligence Estimate on Iran's Nuclear Weapons Program," Jerusalem Center for Public Affairs, www.jcpa.org, December 5, 2007.

58. "Good and Bad News about Iran," *New York Times* editorial, December 5, 2007.

59. "'High Confidence' Games: The CIA's Flip-Flop on Iran Is Hardly Reassuring," *Wall Street Journal* editorial, December 5, 2007.

60. "Intelligence on Iran," *Washington Post* editorial, December 5, 2007.

61. Agence France-Presse, "Israel PM Warns Iran Can Develop Nuclear Bomb by 2010," December 11, 2007.

62. Charles Hurt, "Bush: Beware Iran 'Nuclear Holocaust,'" *New York Post*, August 29, 2007.
63. Sen. John McCain, transcript, NBC's *Meet the Press*, April 2, 2006.
64. Ines Ehrlich, "Modern Day Gog and Magog: Similarities between Ezekiel's Prophecies, Today's Mideast Reality Uncanny," Ynet News, December 10, 2006.
65. Glenn Beck, "Honest Questions about the End of Days," transcript, *Glenn Beck Show*, March 30, 2007.
66. "Israel Warns World War III May be Biblical War of Gog and Magog," Arutz Sheva, October 18, 2007.

APPENDIX 1: FREQUENTLY ASKED QUESTIONS

1. "Gallup Polls on American Sympathy toward Israel and the Arabs/Palestinians," *Jewish Virtual Library*, www.jewishvirtuallibrary.org/jsource/US-Israel/gallup.html (accessed April 20, 2006).
2. "Reliable Ally Polls," based on Harris data, *Jewish Virtual Library*, www.jewishvirtuallibrary.org/jsource/US-Israel/poally.html (accessed April 20, 2006).
3. Joel C. Rosenberg, "A Vicious, Anti-Semitic Film," *National Review Online*, February 25, 2004; and Reuters, "U.S. Envoy: Anti-Semitism in Europe Nearly as Bad as in 1930s," February 13, 2004.
4. Robin Shepherd, "In Europe, an Unhealthy Fixation on Israel," *Washington Post*, January 30, 2005.
5. *The Rapture* is a term used by evangelical Christians. It refers to a moment in the last days when true followers of Jesus Christ will be suddenly snatched up to heaven and thus disappear from the earth, as described in 1 Thessalonians 4:16-17. It is followed by seven years of terrible judgments known as the Tribulation, the battle of Armageddon, and then the second coming of Christ to reign on earth for one thousand years.
6. For descriptions of Israel as figs and fig trees, see Jeremiah 24; Hosea 9:10; and Micah 4:1-4.
7. See Gore Vidal, *United States: Essays, 1952-1992* (New York: Broadway Books), 1993, 1001–2, drawing upon an August 1985 article written by Senator James Mills for *San Diego Magazine*.
8. Edmund Morris, *Dutch: A Memoir of Ronald Reagan* (New York: Random, 1999), 835.
9. Ibid., 632–33.
10. Michael Reagan, phone conversation with author, June 24, 2005.
11. See "Al Qaeda's Poison Gas; The foiled attack in Jordan might have killed thousands," *Wall Street Journal* editorial, April 29, 2004; Gethin Chamberlain, "How Al Qaeda plotted to kill 80,000 in Jordan," *The Scotsman*, April 29, 2004.
12. Author interview with General Sada, May 22, 2006.
13. See "Hotel Blasts Kill Dozens in Jordan," *CNN.com*, November 9, 2005; "Jordan Confirms Al-Qaeda behind Hotel Blasts," *CNN.com*, November 12, 2005; Nibras Kazimi, "The Islamist Threat to Jordan," *Jerusalem Issue Brief*, vol. 5, no. 25, Jerusalem Center for Public Affairs, May 25, 2006.
14. Bernard Lewis, responding to a question from the author at an American Enterprise Institute event, June 6, 2006.

APPENDIX 3: AMERICAN CHRISTIAN ATTITUDES TOWARD ISRAEL AND EPICENTER ISSUES

1. This national survey was conducted among 1,000 Christian likely voters between March 16-18, 2008, by McLaughlin & Associates. All interviews were conducted by professional interviewers via telephone. Respondent selection was at random The accuracy of the sample of 1,000 Christian likely voters is within +/- 3.1% at a 95% confidence interval. The survey was paid for by November Communications, Inc., the message strategy

company I founded in 2000. The results to nonpartisan questions (that is, questions not pertaining to specifically identified candidates, such as John McCain, Hillary Clinton, and Barack Obama) were then made available for use by the Joshua Fund, in keeping with the fund's nonprofit, nonpartisan status. Any comments made or implied by me in this book or in public of a partisan nature—or perceived to be partisan—were and are made in my capacity as a private citizen, not in connection to the Joshua Fund.

2. "Defining Evangelicalism," Institute for the Study of American Evangelicals, Wheaton College, statistics reported online at http://www.wheaton.edu/isae/defining_evangelicalism.html (accessed March 31, 2008).

3. UPI, "Roman Catholics Total 64 million in U.S.," June 25, 2007.

ACKNOWLEDGMENTS

I am exceedingly grateful for the assistance of so many over the years, more than I could possibly properly acknowledge here. Yet some deserve special thanks with regards to making this book happen.

Among them: my amazing wife, Lynn; our four wonderful sons; Len and Mary Rosenberg; June Meyers; Edward and Kailea Hunt; Tim and Carolyn Lugbill; Steve and Barb Klemke; Jim and Sharon Supp; Dan and Susan Rebeiz; Wendy and Colin Ligon; Todd and Amy Adkins; Amy Knapp; Cindy Shiblie; John Black; Fred and Sue Schwein; Bill and Lani Shelton; and our "Connections" family.

The friends and colleagues throughout the Middle East, North Africa and Russia that we have been honored to know cannot be thanked enough. We are grateful to have been welcomed into their hearts and homes. The life of our family has been deeply and forever blessed by walking with them on this journey.

Special thanks, too, to Mark Taylor, Ron Beers, Becky Nesbitt, Jan Stob, Jeremy Taylor, Cheryl Kerwin, Andrea Martin, Beverly Rykerd, and the entire Tyndale team; Peter Robbio and the Creative Response Concepts team; Wes Yoder and the Ambassador Agency team; and my agent, Scott Miller, at Trident Media Group.

Whatever is interesting and helpful in this book is truly a result of their help. Any errors of fact or judgment are mine and mine alone.

JOEL C. ROSENBERG

Joel C. Rosenberg is the founder of the Joshua Fund and the *New York Times* best-selling author of *The Last Jihad*, *The Last Days*, *The Ezekiel Option*, *The Copper Scroll*, *Dead Heat*, and *Epicenter*, with more than 1.5 million copies in print. As a communications strategist, he has worked with some of the world's most influential leaders in business, politics, and media, including Steve Forbes, Rush Limbaugh, and former Israeli prime minister Benjamin Netanyahu. As a novelist, he has been interviewed on hundreds of radio and TV programs, including ABC's *Nightline*, *CNN Headline News*, FOX News Channel, The History Channel, MSNBC, *The Rush Limbaugh Show*, and *The Sean Hannity Show*. He has been profiled by the *New York Times*, the *Washington Times*, *World* magazine, and the *Jerusalem Post*. He has addressed audiences all over the world, including Russia, Israel, Iraq, Jordan, Egypt, Turkey, and Belgium, and has spoken at the White House, the Pentagon, and the U.S. Capitol.

The first page of his first novel—*The Last Jihad*—puts readers inside the cockpit of a hijacked jet, coming in on a kamikaze attack into an American city, which leads to a war with Saddam Hussein over weapons of mass destruction. Yet it was written before 9/11 and published before the actual war with Iraq. *The Last Jihad* spent eleven weeks on the *New*

York Times hardcover fiction best-seller list, reaching as high as #7. It raced up the *USA Today* and *Publishers Weekly* best-seller lists, hit #4 on the *Wall Street Journal* list, and hit #1 on Amazon.com.

His second thriller—*The Last Days*—opens with the death of Yasser Arafat and a U.S. diplomatic convoy ambushed in Gaza. Two weeks before *The Last Days* was published in hardcover, a U.S. diplomatic convoy was ambushed in Gaza. Thirteen months later, Yasser Arafat was dead. *The Last Days* spent four weeks on the *New York Times* hardcover fiction best-seller list, hit #5 on the *Denver Post* list, and hit #8 on the *Dallas Morning News* list. Both books have been optioned by a Hollywood producer.

The Ezekiel Option centers on a dictator rising in Russia who forms a military alliance with the leaders of Iran as they feverishly pursue nuclear weapons and threaten to wipe Israel off the face of the earth. On the very day it was published in June 2005, Iran elected a new leader who vowed to accelerate the country's nuclear program and later threatened to "wipe Israel off the map." Six months after it was published, Moscow signed a $1 billion arms deal with Tehran. *The Ezekiel Option* spent four weeks on the *New York Times* hardcover fiction bestseller list and five months on the Christian Bookseller Association bestseller list, reaching as high as #4. It won the 2006 Christian Book Award for fiction.

In *The Copper Scroll*, an ancient scroll describes unimaginable treasures worth untold billions buried in the hills east of Jerusalem and under the Holy City itself—treasures that could come from the Second Temple and whose discovery could lead to the building of the Third Temple and a war of biblical proportions. One month after it was released, *Biblical Archaeology Review* published a story describing the real-life, intensified hunt for the treasures of the actual Copper Scroll. *The Copper Scroll* spent four weeks on the *New York Times* hardcover fiction best-seller list, two weeks on the *Wall Street Journal* best-seller list, two weeks on the *Publishers Weekly* hardcover fiction list, and several months on the CBA best-seller list. It won the 2007 Logos Bookstores Best Fiction Award.

In *Dead Heat*, America is in the midst of a heated presidential election when the Secret Service learns of a catastrophic terrorist plot to assassinate one of the candidates. U.S. forces attempt to stop the terrorists before millions lose their lives, but events threaten to spin out of control. *Dead Heat* debuted at #4 on the *New York Times* hardcover best-seller list. It also became a *USA Today, Wall Street Journal, Publishers Weekly,* and CBA hardcover best seller.

www.joelrosenberg.com
www.joshuafund.net

May 27, 2008

TO: Pastors, Business Leaders, Political Leaders,
     and Interested Parties
FROM: Joel C. Rosenberg, Founder of the Joshua Fund
SUBJECT: Launching "Operation Epicenter"

The prospects of a devastating new military confrontation in the Middle East are real and growing. How will we as evangelical Christians respond? Will we help those in harm's way? Will we do what we can to care for the real and practical needs of millions of innocent people caught in the cross fire? What's more, will we do so with unconditional love and unwavering support, the kind of generous, gracious love Jesus modeled for us in the Scriptures? Or will we turn a blind eye and a deaf ear?

Israeli political, military, and intelligence leaders tell me they believe Iran, Syria, Hezbollah, and Hamas are preparing for all-out war against the Jewish state. U.S. intelligence officials tell me they fear a catastrophic new conflict in the epicenter may not be far off. No one can be certain when hostilities will begin. But the warning signs are everywhere.

And let's be clear: the stakes could not be higher.

Iranian president Mahmoud Ahmadinejad has, of course, vowed to "wipe Israel off the map" and says Israel's destruction will happen "soon." If Iranian leaders are able to acquire nuclear warheads, and are able to match those warheads with the high-speed ballistic missiles they already have, they could do in about six minutes what it took Adolf Hitler six years to do—kill six million Jews.

Meanwhile, Israeli intelligence estimates that Iran and Syria have completely rearmed Hezbollah with more than 30,000 rockets and missiles, all aimed at the Jewish state. What's more, Moscow is selling billions of dollars worth of missiles, fighter jets, and other high-tech armaments to Iran and Syria. North Korea is also working closely with Iran on its long-range ballistic missile program.

Then, of course, there is Iraq. Some important progress has been made in that vital epicenter country. But should the American government precipitously withdraw U.S. military forces from Iraq before Iraqi security forces are fully prepared to make and keep order, many experts fear Sunni and Shiite radicals inside Iraq could be emboldened, leading to a full-blown civil war.

At the same time, death and destruction continue to plague the people of Sudan, who have been suffering genocide in recent years. We also must keep our eye on Lebanon, Jordan, and Egypt, where radical Islamic jihadists are trying to destabilize those governments. The possibility of coups or civil war is particularly acute in Lebanon and Jordan.

THE BIBLICAL COMMAND TO BE READY

The Scriptures command followers of Jesus Christ to love their neighbors and their enemies, bless the poor and needy, and care for victims of war and terrorism, and to do so with unconditional love—that is, with no strings attached. (See Deuteronomy 15:7-11, Leviticus 19:18, Proverbs 25:21-22, Isaiah 58:6-12, Matthew 5:42-44, Matthew 14:16-21, Matthew 15:32-39, Matthew 25:31-46, Luke 4:18-19, Romans 15:25-27, Galatians 2:7-10.)

Severe poverty is rampant in the Arab world. But even in Israel, nearly a quarter of the Israeli population—more than 1.5 million people—lives on less than $800 a month for a family of four. One in five Israelis live on less than $500 a month. When the next war hits, the needs will even be greater.

It is critically important that we be prepared to care for *all* the people of the region, regardless of race, religion, color, or creed. The Bible says God loves the whole world and cares for all who suffer, Jews and Gentiles alike (John 3:16). The ministry of Jesus was certainly to the children of Israel. But in Matthew 15:21, where was Jesus? He was in southern Lebanon, in the "district of Tyre and Sidon." Matthew 4:24-25 says the news about Jesus "spread throughout all Syria" and "large crowds followed Him from Galilee and the Decapolis and Jerusalem and Judea and from beyond the Jordan" (NASB). In Acts chapter 2, the followers of Jesus sought to bless everyone they could find. The text says that they reached out to "Medes and Elamites" (Kurds and Iranians), "residents of Mesopotamia" (Iraqis), "Egypt and the districts of Libya," and "both Jews . . . and Arabs." This is our mandate too.

The Joshua Fund, therefore, is committed to building a global alliance of evangelical Christians ready, willing, and able to bless Israel and her neighbors in the name of Jesus, according to Genesis 12:1-3. We also believe we must move quickly, because war is coming, and the clock is ticking.

THE OPERATION EPICENTER APPROACH

Operation Epicenter is a Joshua Fund initiative to provide at least $120 million worth of humanitarian relief supplies to the epicenter over the next few years to care for those in need today, as well as to pre-position supplies ahead of future wars.

Here is a quick overview of our goals and objectives:

OPERATION EPICENTER STRATEGIES
The Joshua Fund seeks to build a global alliance of evangelical Christians that will:

- Bless the poor and needy in Israel and the Muslim world
- Bless victims of war and terrorism in Israel and the Muslim world
- Pre-position humanitarian relief supplies ahead of coming wars
- Work closely with local and national political leaders to bless those in need

- Distribute aid through local believers, congregations, and ministries when possible, as well as through local officials and in cooperation with other aid organizations
- Communicate the urgent needs of the epicenter to believers around the world
- Build a global movement of believers praying for the people of the epicenter
- Assist in the restoration of Israel and reconciliation between Jews and Muslims

OPERATION EPICENTER PROJECTS

Over the next few years, the Joshua Fund and our allies seek to:

- Bless Israel with at least $100 million in humanitarian relief
- Bless Israel's neighbors with at least $20 million in humanitarian relief
- Invest in projects to expand "pipeline capacity" in the epicenter, enabling local ministries to better receive and distribute humanitarian relief supplies and helping them acquire warehouse space, trucks, forklifts, etc.
- Hold Epicenter Conferences around the world to help evangelical Christians understand God's love for the people of the Middle East, understand the threats facing the people of the region, and learn how they can bless Israel and her neighbors in real and practical ways, showing unconditional love and unwavering support
- Recruit at least 100,000 people around the world to pray faithfully for the people of the epicenter

THE JOSHUA FUND'S ACCOMPLISHMENTS TO DATE:

Over the past few years, the Joshua Fund and our allies have—by God's grace—been able to:

- Provide much-needed relief to 3,500 needy residents (including some 700 seniors) of Kiryat Shmona, an Israeli town on the northern border with Lebanon that was hit by more than 1,000 rockets during the Second Lebanon War. These residents—all of whom live below the poverty level—received Hannukah gifts for their children, clothes, diapers, kitchen supplies, warm comforters for the winter, and other essentials.

- Provide blankets, heaters, clothing, kitchen supplies, toys, school supplies, and other relief for hundreds of needy residents of Sderot, an Israeli town on the southern border with Gaza that has been hit by thousands of rockets, mortars, and missiles since the Israeli military withdrawal from Gaza in the summer of 2005.
- Provide vans to local officials and relief organizations in Israel to help them transport volunteers and relief supplies.
- Finance the purchase of hundreds of tons of food in Israel, some of which is provided to the poor and needy in Jerusalem, some of which is provided to those in need in northern Israel, and some of which is being stockpiled for use in the next war.
- Finance the purchase of much-needed medical equipment and supplies for the Barzilai Medical Center, the only hospital available to the 500,000 Israelis living on the border with Gaza.
- Stock bomb shelters in northern Israel with food, water, and other essential supplies in preparation for the next war.
- Provide financial assistance to organizations in Israel that care for needy Holocaust survivors, new immigrants and refugees, homeless men and women, and victims of terrorist attacks.
- Provide thousands of new backpacks and school supplies to Israeli schoolchildren who live below the poverty level.
- Provide relief packages through trusted evangelical Christian ministry partners for some 6,000 Arab families in Lebanon devastated by the Second Lebanon War. These care packages included nonperishable food items such as

beans, rice, pasta, canned meat, processed cheese, oil, and powdered milk. In addition, each package contains basic supplies such as soap, candles, matches, and aspirin, along with a *JESUS* film DVD in Arabic.

- Provide financial assistance to trusted evangelical Christian ministries that distribute food, clothing, Arabic Bibles, and other essential relief supplies to Palestinian Arabs in the West Bank and Gaza.
- Finance the establishment of evangelical Christian radio ministries in the West Bank and Iraq.
- Finance shipments of humanitarian relief supplies into Iraq and Sudan, working closely with trusted evangelical Christian ministries.
- Hold the inaugural Epicenter Conference in Jerusalem in April 2008, attended by some 2,000 Christian leaders from all over the world and webcast to thousands more. (See www.epicenter08.com.)
- Speak at pastors' conferences, retreats, and other assemblies throughout the epicenter—in Israel, Iraq, Jordan, Egypt, Turkey, and elsewhere—to encourage local Christian leaders, pray with them, and find ways to stand with them and support the vital work of building and strengthening the church of Jesus Christ in the lands of its birth.
- Sign up more than 50,000 subscribers to "Flash Traffic" to receive geopolitical updates from the epicenter, Joshua Fund project updates, and urgent prayer requests.
- Educate more than 30 million people about the work of the Joshua Fund and the threats to Israel and her neighbors through hundreds of radio, television, and print interviews.

This is just a snapshot of what we are doing, but I hope it gives you a sense of where our hearts are and how we are investing the resources you and others are investing in us. There is much more to be done, of course. The good news is that we have been deeply encouraged by the number of Israeli and Arab leaders who have sought the help of the Joshua Fund and by the enthusiastic and generous response of evangelical Christian pastors, businessmen and women, and lay leaders around the world.

One example: When we completed our first project in Kiryat Shmona—in close cooperation with our Jewish and Christian allies in Israel—we had the privilege of meeting with the mayor, a former Israeli defense minister, and other local and national officials to better understand the situation Israelis face in the north. That night, I was asked to address an audience of some 350 Israelis to explain why evangelical Christians want to bless Israel. After a few minutes of speaking by translation, I concluded by saying, "You will soon forget who I am, what organization I represent, and what I've said here tonight. That's fine. But if you happen to remember one thing, I hope it is this: The followers of Sheikh Nasrallah and Hezbollah hate you and want to destroy you. But the followers of Jesus love you and will stand with you." The audience erupted with applause. Many Israelis came up to us afterward to thank us for caring for them in their time of need.

This is the Operation Epicenter approach—by building strategic alliances between evangelical Christians, Jewish leaders, Arab leaders, local pastors, and local officials in every country in which we work, we believe that together we can leverage limited amounts of financial resources in order to bless the maximum amount of people.

HOW YOU CAN HELP

Interested in joining the Operation Epicenter movement? There are lots of ways to help. Consider this list of 60 ways to bless Israel and her neighbors in the name of Jesus.

1. Stock one bomb shelter in northern Israel with food, water, a first aid kit, other emergency supplies, and a secure storage locker. There are currently more than 5,000 bomb shelters that need to be stocked with supplies before the next war. Each bomb shelter costs approximately $5,500 to stock (though prices have been

going up due to the rising cost of food and gas and other transportation costs).

2. Provide one ton of food to care for needy families in northern Israel who were hit by 4,000 rockets and missiles during the 2006 war with Hezbollah. These families are still recovering from that war. Many live on less than $500 a month. And food prices are rising in Israel, as they are around the globe. Every month, therefore, the Joshua Fund pays for about 10 tons of food to be purchased by one of our allies in Israel and distributed to the needy in the north as well as stockpiled for the next war. Cost: $2,500 per ton.

3. Help purchase desperately needed medical equipment such as respirators, ventilators, operating room lamps, mobile X-ray machines, and the like for underfunded regional hospitals in Israel. At the request of hospital administrators, the Joshua Fund has adopted the Barzilai Medical Center in the southern Israeli city of Ashkelon to help them raise funds for such equipment. Barzilai is the only hospital and trauma center serving the 500,000 Israelis living near the Gaza border and facing a nearly constant barrage of rockets, missiles, and mortars. They are doing heroic work, but they do need our help. Some of this equipment is very costly, averaging $20,000 to $80,000 each. A donation of $5,000 would help significantly toward meeting these vital needs.

4. Help provide food baskets to needy families in Jerusalem on Jewish holidays. Working with our local allies, the Joshua Fund recently helped finance the distribution of 680 food baskets to needy Israeli families for Passover.

5. Provide food, blankets, wheelchairs, and other assistance to Holocaust victims in Israel, many of whom tragically live at or below the poverty level, even within the Jewish state.

6. Help care for the homeless, finance soup kitchens, and care for Sudanese refugees in Israel.

7. Help provide backpacks and new school supplies for needy children in Israel.

8. Help provide backpacks and new school supplies for needy children in the West Bank, Gaza, Iraq, and other epicenter nations.

9. Help provide blankets and heaters for the elderly in Israel during the cold winter months, since many do not have—or cannot afford—central heating, and help provide fans during the summer months, since many do not have—or cannot afford—central air conditioning.

10. Help finance the purchase of vans for Israeli organizations that distribute humanitarian aid so they can get supplies to the people who need them most in a more efficient manner. The Joshua Fund is involved in all these areas of relief work—caring for Holocaust victims, the homeless, refugees, and others—and we would be honored to get you involved in funding critically important projects such as these.

11. Track daily news coverage of Israel and the epicenter through the *Jerusalem Post*, Ynetnews.com, and Haaretz.com.

12. Track the latest statements and interviews by radical Islamic fanatics—translated into English—at the Web site of the Middle East Media Research Institute (MEMRI).

13. Track the latest developments in the Middle East through the "Daily Alert" e-mails published by the Jerusalem Center for Public Affairs. Go to www.jcpa.org for more details.

14. Become a faithful prayer partner for Israel and her neighbors. The Joshua Fund is looking for 100,000 partners to sign up for free "Flash Traffic" e-mail alerts that include analysis and commentary on events and trends in Israel and the epicenter, Joshua Fund project updates, and prayer requests. More than 52,000 people from all over the world have joined already.

15. Take your family on a tour of Israel.

16. Join us on a future Joshua Fund "Prayer & Vision Trip" to Israel.

17. Take Hebrew classes for the summer at your local Jewish community center.

18. Make friends with a local rabbi, find ways to bless his synagogue, and discuss ways to bless Israel together.

19. Learn more about the Israeli economy and business opportunities through the Federation of Israeli Chambers of Commerce.
20. Consider investing in Israeli companies listed on the New York Stock Exchange with the help of knowlegeable, qualified financial advisors.
21. Consider investing in Israeli high-tech companies listed on NASDAQ with the help of knowledgeable, qualified financial advisors.
22. Carve out 30 minutes a day to study the Bible, focusing on God's love and plan for the Jewish people and the nation of Israel.
23. Carve out 15 minutes a day to pray for peace in Jerusalem (Psalm 122:6).
24. Learn more about efforts by Israeli and international politicians to divide Jerusalem—and why this would be such a disaster—by visiting the Web site of Natan Sharansky's organization, OneJerusalem.org.
25. Sign the One Jerusalem petition to keep Jerusalem the eternal, undivided capital of the Jewish state.
26. Pray daily for peace on Israel's southern border with Gaza.
27. Pray daily for peace on Israel's northern borders with Lebanon and Syria.
28. Pray daily for regime change to come soon in Iran, bringing a moderate, pro-Western, democratic government that will abandon President Ahmadinejad's nuclear ambitions and live at peace with Israel and her neighbors.
29. Pray daily for wisdom for Israeli, American, and NATO leaders to know how to prevent Iran from developing nuclear weapons.
30. Pray for the Lord to raise up leaders like "the men of Issachar, who understood the times and knew what Israel should do" (I Chronicles 12:32, NIV).
31. Pray that a truly just, fair, and compassionate peace treaty could be forged soon between Israel and Lebanon.
32. Pray that a truly just, fair, and compassionate peace treaty could be forged soon between Israel and Syria.

33. Pray for new leaders to emerge in the West Bank and Gaza who truly oppose violence against Israel, have the courage and ability to hunt down and imprison Palestinian terrorists, are dedicated to preventing Iran and al-Qaeda from seizing effective control of these disputed territories, and will work tirelessly to stop the incitement of children against the Jewish people in the Palestinian schools and refugee camps.

34. Pray that a truly just, fair and compassionate peace treaty could be forged soon between Israel and the Palestinians, one that would give the Palestinians true autonomy in the West Bank and Gaza to run their own lives, lead their own government, and have full human rights, civil rights, freedom of religion, and freedom of the press, without threatening Israel.

35. Pray that U.S., European, and UN leaders would stop pressuring Israel to make unwise concessions in the peace process.

36. Pray that the UN would start fully enforcing the Security Resolutions that ended the Second Lebanon War in 2006, notably by disarming Hezbollah and other militias in the region.

37. Pray that followers of Jesus in the land of Israel would draw even closer to the Lord who loves them and gave himself for them, have courage to love their neighbors and their enemies, be a light in the land, be a true blessing to all those in Israel, and "preach good news to the poor" as instructed by the Hebrew prophet Isaiah (in chapter 61) and exemplified by Jesus in the Gospels.

38. Pray that the followers of Jesus in the West Bank and Gaza would also draw close to the Lord who loves them, have courage in the face of opposition, be able to love their neighbors and their enemies, be a light in the land, and be willing and able to preach the Good News to all who would listen.

39. Pray for all the people of the epicenter to find true hope, peace, forgiveness, and reconciliation through faith in Jesus the Messiah, and pray that Jewish and Arab followers of Jesus in the Holy Land would be wonderful models of true reconciliation, would become dear friends with each other and worship the Lord and pray together in the unity the Scriptures command.

40. Pray for evangelical Christians around the world to LEARN more about God's plan and purpose for the people of the epicenter.
41. Pray for evangelical Christians around the world to PRAY knowledgeably and consistently for the people of Israel and the epicenter.
42. Pray for evangelical Christians around the world to GIVE generously and cheerfully to organizations that bless Israel.
43. Pray for evangelical Christians around the world to GO visit Israel and bring many with them, both as tourists and as prayer allies for the Jewish and Palestinian people of the region.
44. Visit the Holocaust Museum in Washington, DC.
45. Learn about Jewish holidays such as Passover, Purim, and Hanukkah and celebrate them with friends and family.
46. Read *A History of the Jews* by renowned historian Paul Johnson.
47. Teach a Bible study or Sunday School class about the history of the Jewish people, including Scriptures such as Genesis 12:1-3, in which God says He will bless those who bless Israel and curse those who curse Israel.
48. Read *From Beirut to Jerusalem* by *New York Times* correspondent and columnist Thomas L. Friedman, one of my all-time favorite books about the Arab-Israeli conflict.
49. Learn more about how important evangelical Christians were to the establishment and development of the modern State of Israel by reading *Standing With Israel: Why Christians Support the Jewish State* by David Brog.
50. Read *Two Nations Under God: Why Should America Care About Israel and the Middle East*, an excellent primer written by my friend Tom Doyle.
51. Learn more about God's plan and purpose for Israel and her neighbors, and how Bible prophecy is being fulfilled even as we speak, by reading *Epicenter: Why the Current Rumblings in the Middle East Will Change Your Future.*
52. Host a book club discussion about Israel—or host a small group Bible study in your home about the future of the Jewish state—using the *Epicenter Study Guide.*

53. Consider showing the *Epicenter* documentary film on DVD at your church or to your book club, home fellowship group, or small group Bible study.

54. Organize and run a Joshua Fund event at your church, school, synagogue, or club to raise funds to bless the poor and needy in Israel and Israeli victims of war and terrorism. All kinds of events are possible, including banquets, car washes, bake sales, golf tournaments, silent auctions, Bible memorization contests, and candy sales, just to name a few.

55. Ask your pastor to host a day of prayer for Israel at your church once a year.

56. Call into a local talk radio show and defend Israel and the Jewish people when you hear anti-Israel or anti-Semitic comments.

57. Attend a future Epicenter Conference and track with the latest developments in Israel and the Middle East.

58. Invite speakers to your churches and conferences to talk about how to bless Israel and her neighbors and to share what God is doing in the Middle East today.

59. Contact the Joshua Fund, request a copy of the new *Operation Epicenter* DVD, and watch it with family and friends—even show it to your small group Bible study, home fellowship group, or your entire congregation.

60. Sign up to make a monthly contribution of $25, $50, or $100 to the Joshua Fund to support these and other Operation Epicenter relief projects on a regular basis. The Joshua Fund is an official 501©3 nonprofit organization under the codes of the Internal Revenue Service and all U.S. donations are tax-deductible. You can make secure donations online at www.joshuafund.net, or send your check payable to "The Joshua Fund" to:

The Joshua Fund
18950 Base Camp Road
Monument, Colorado 80132-8009
(888)792-4544

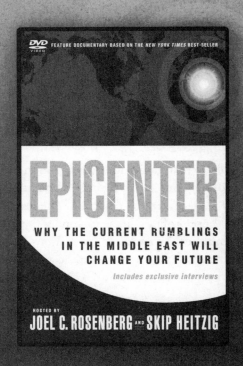

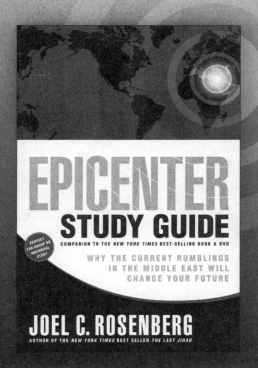